LAW AND THE WEALTH OF NATIONS

LAW AND
THE WEALTH
OF NATIONS

Finance, Prosperity, and Democracy

Tamara Lothian

Columbia University Press
New York

Columbia University Press
Publishers Since 1893
New York   Chichester, West Sussex
cup.columbia.edu
Copyright © 2017 Columbia University Press
All rights reserved
Library of Congress Cataloging-in-Publication Data
Names: Lothian, Tamara, 1958–2016, author.
Title: Law and the wealth of nations : finance, prosperity, and democracy /
Tamara Lothian.
Description: New York : Columbia University Press, [2017] | Includes
bibliographical references and index.
Identifiers: LCCN 2017004660 (print) | LCCN 2017022377 (ebook) | ISBN
9780231545839 (electronic) | ISBN 9780231174664 (cloth : alk. paper)
Subjects: LCSH: Finance—United States. | Financial crises—United States. |
Financial institutions—Law and legislation—United States. | Capital
market—Law and legislation—United States. | Monetary policy—United
States. | Democracy—Economic aspects—United States.
Classification: LCC HG181 (ebook) | LCC HG181 .L68 2017 (print) |
DDC 332.0973—dc23
LC record available at https://lccn.loc.gov/2017004660

Columbia University Press books are printed on permanent and durable
acid-free paper.
Printed in the United States of America

Contents

CHAPTER FIVE
Economic Progress and Structural Vision
197

APPENDIX
Crisis, Slump, Superstition, and Recovery:
Thinking and Acting Beyond Vulgar Keynesianism
(with Roberto Mangabeira Unger)
337

A Note Regarding the Circumstance in Which This Book Is Published

ON JUNE 8, 2016, Tamara Lothian died. She left at her death, among many other unpublished writings, the nearly finished manuscripts of two books dealing with finance and its reorganization in the context of broader ideas about democratizing the market economy and deepening democracy. The present work, *Law and the Wealth of Nations: Finance, Prosperity, and Democracy*, is to be followed by a shorter book, *Finance and Democracy in America*.

It fell to me to prepare for publication these two books by my friend and wife. As both texts were all but complete, my part in their preparation for the press has been slight. Only in a few places have I felt the need to adjust the words on the page to the motivating thought, to add a missing reference, or to render more fully a compressed line of reasoning.

Tamara Lothian was born in Chicago on February 28, 1958. She studied economics and law. From the outset, however, her overriding interests were philosophical and political. Her thinking combined a visionary impulse with mastery of technical detail in the areas that she addressed. She believed that intellectual ambition, political hope, and spiritual ardor would come to little if they failed to reckon with the parts of social and economic life that have proved most resistant to criticism and reform.

After an early career in finance, in which she dealt mainly with emerging economies, she turned to teaching and writing and to the pursuit of her central concern: the constraints that established social and economic regimes impose on the development of our powers and the expression of our humanity. She came increasingly to bring this concern home to the study of her country, the United States. In the years preceding her death at the age of fifty-eight, she and I had begun to work out the argument and the early drafts of a work provisionally titled *Growth, Crisis, and Inequality: Economics as Social Theory.*

Roberto Mangabeira Unger
March 2017

Introduction

We are accustomed to view finance as a constraint on the feasibility of progressive alternatives to the established regime of economic life: alternatives that would set economic growth on an inclusive social base. Finance, so it seems, crushes dreams.

By the same token, we have learned to see finance as a threat to democracy. By its effects, it undermines economic and social reform. By its influence, it corrupts democratic government. To control finance—to put it in its place, to prevent it from running roughshod over the interests of ordinary men and women—has long been a major concern of all who seek a better chance for the many. They have often failed to understand that the best way to tame finance is to make it more useful.

Finance—reimagined and reshaped—can serve production and innovation more effectively than it now does. It can also become a friend to democracy, a front line in the effort to democratize the market economy, and a powerful instrument in the hands of the enemies of disempowerment, dispossession, and inequality. That it can be made more useful to the real economy and be reconciled with democracy is a central thesis of this book. It is a goal, however, that we cannot achieve without changing how we think: not just about finance but also about economics and politics.

This book has three objectives. Its first aim is to reconsider the actual and possible roles of finance in a market economy under democracy. Its second purpose is to use the discussion of finance as a wedge into an exploration of the alternative futures and institutional forms of the market economy. We cannot organize socially inclusive economic growth without reforming the institutional arrangements of the market order, including the arrangements governing finance and its relation to the real economy. It is not enough to regulate the market or to diminish its inequalities after the fact by progressive taxation and redistributive social spending. For the sake of both growth and inclusion, we must innovate in the institutions and laws shaping the market economy, the better to broaden access to resources, opportunities, and capabilities. The third goal of this book is to exemplify an approach to legal analysis and political economy that enables them to fulfill their vocation as the twin disciplines of the institutional imagination. The realization of our most fundamental interests and ideals requires structural change, informed by structural vision. Such change must almost always be gradual and fragmentary, reshaping the formative arrangements and assumptions of a society, piece by piece and step by step. Pursued over time, with the help of ideas corrected in the light of experience, it can nevertheless be far-reaching and even revolutionary.

In another, shorter work to be published after this one, *Finance and Democracy in America*, I retake the themes of this book in the context of the history and prospects of the United States.

BEYOND THE IDEA THAT THE MARKET ECONOMY HAS A SINGLE NATURAL FORM

More than two centuries of ideological conflict have been dominated by a simple contrast between the market and the state. According to this view—we might call it the "hydraulic model"—the axis of ideological dispute runs along the relative assignment of responsibilities to either the market or the state: more market, less state; more state, less market; or some compromise between market and state. The compromise has gone under names such as the "regulated market economy" (in the United States) or the "social market economy" (in Europe).

The crucial premise of this way of thinking is that the market economy has, within a small range of variation, a single natural or necessary form. This form is expressed in institutional arrangements defined by law. Accepting this premise narrows our thinking to whether to extend or restrict the room allowed to market transactions and whether to strengthen or weaken the effort to moderate, through progressive taxation and redistributive social spending, the inequalities generated in the market.

A literature about "varieties of capitalism" focuses on differences among the economic institutions of contemporary market economies.[1] It compares the forms taken by the market order under different variants of European social democracy and contrasts them to American arrangements. However, little in this literature challenges the idea that all versions of the market economy share a stable legal and institutional core. This core includes private property, freedom of contract, wage labor, a restricted stock of legal forms of business organization, and a sharp separation between the market and the state.

The influence of this idea helps account for the deployment of the term "capitalism" by Karl Marx and others to designate a system, all of whose parts supposedly stand or fall together. Nothing in this conception contradicts the economist's commonplace belief that a market is a market, property is property, and a contract is a contract. One hundred fifty years of legal analysis should have banished these beliefs. They nevertheless survive, as if barely touched by the discoveries that should have discredited them.

A major ambition of this book is to challenge the assumption that the market economy has a single natural and necessary form, within a tight margin of variation, and to replace it with another idea: that the relatively modest range of institutional distinction that now exists or has existed in the arrangements of a market economy amounts to a token of a much wider range of possible variation. Our most powerful economic and social interests are at stake in the development of such innovations in the market economy. On them depends our prospects of creating conditions that would make it possible to accelerate economic growth and broaden its social base by disseminating throughout much of the economy the practices of the new, knowledge-intensive forms of production. On them turns as well our best chance to moderate the extremes of economic inequality and exclusion. History has shown that compensatory redistribution by tax and transfer (progressive taxation and social entitlements) can have only a limited effect on access to income and wealth in society. The potential impact of corrective redistribution pales in comparison to the effects of institutional innovations—beginning with reforms in the organization of the market economy. Such innovations shape the primary distribution of advantage and opportunity.

So what seems to be a merely theoretical idea—that a market economy can be organized in different ways, with far-reaching consequences for society—is pregnant with practical implications. We need not look far to see and recognize these implications. They are all around us—for example, in the present and past of the United States.

BEYOND THE SHARED PREMISE OF THE TWO MAJOR TRADITIONS OF PROGRESSIVE REFORM IN AMERICAN HISTORY

For much of American history, there have been two major traditions of progressive reform. One of these traditions, which began in the Jeffersonian ideals of the late eighteenth and early nineteenth centuries and continued through the agrarian populism of the late nineteenth century, emphasizes the defense of the small, independent proprietor or businessman against those who would lord over him by accumulating wealth as well as the political influence that wealth can bring. The doctrine of property-owning democracy, later explored by social scientists such as Barrington Moore Jr. as well as by political philosophers such as John Rawls, represents the closest that we have to a theory of this reform tradition.[2]

The other major tradition of progressive reform in America, most closely associated with the two Roosevelts—the progressivism of the early twentieth century and the New Deal of the mid–twentieth century—accepts the control of the "commanding heights" of the economy by big business. It wants the federal government to put big business in its place, especially through strong regulation. It expects regulation to diminish the discrepancy between what is profitable for business and what is useful to society,

A shared premise of these two reform traditions has been the same assumption that I earlier singled out for critical comment: the naturalization of the inherited and established form of the market economy, also known as capitalism. According to this assumption, we cannot reinvent and reshape the capitalist regime; we can only humanize or improve it. One way to do so is to protect small business and small-scale property against the encroachments of what the progressives called "malefactors of great wealth." Another approach is to accept the leading role of big business under the restraints of strong national regulation. Yet another, more common route is to combine these two responses.

Whatever the choice, we continue to assume that the market order has an intrinsic constitution, open to only modest variation. That constitution includes the familiar forms of the law of property, contract, and corporate organization as well as the legal boundary between private initiative and public policy. Against the background of an unchanged and unchallenged private order, we balance the competing goals of equity and efficiency.

Yet these beliefs have not always provided the country with its sense of direction. In the early, formative history of the independent republic, we find signs of a different direction. It combined the mobilization of national resources for development with the democratization of opportunities in particular sectors of the economy.

A first set of initiatives opened up the country, built its infrastructure, and enlisted public finance and governmental power in the service of national development. The government acted as a partner to private enterprise: a coterie of politicians, entrepreneurs, bureaucrats, profiteers, and adventurers worked together to get the job the done, for their own benefit as well as for the benefit of the country. This was the project that Hamilton put at the center of national politics. It continued to guide America and its leaders long after his death, until the eve of the Civil War.

A second set of initiatives worked bottom up, although it required federal as well as state legislation and policy. It democratized the market economy in particular sectors, especially agriculture and finance. Democratizing the market required bold and imaginative institutional innovation in the arrangements defining the market order, not just regulating economic activity or using redistributive taxation and social spending to attenuate economic inequalities.

Democratizing the market happened in agriculture on the basis of what in today's vocabulary we would call decentralized strategic coordination between national and local governments and the family farmer, providing everything from title to land to access to best practice and technology as well as protection from the combination of climate risk and price risk that always besets family-scale agriculture. And it included support for what in a contemporary idiom we would call cooperative competition among the family farmers: they competed against one another even as they pooled labor and resources. It happened in finance through the dissolution of the Second Bank of the United States (in Jackson's presidency), followed by the creation of the most decentralized system of credit at the local producer's disposal that the world had ever seen.

These early-nineteenth-century initiatives in agriculture and finance did what has remained unimagined in the discourse of the two dominant traditions of progressive reform: they innovated in the institutional arrangements defining the market economy, and they amended the constitution of the market order.

In the discourse of American politics our two major reform traditions of progressive reform, and their opponents, have spoken with the loudest voice. However, they have not exercised the biggest influence on the development of the country. That merit goes to the combination of mobilization from above and democratization from below to which I have just alluded—a practice not a doctrine, never comprehensively theorized. This combination is a formula to relearn and practice in spades in every department of national life, throughout the world as well as in the United States. I explore its American expressions and its American future in the companion to this book, *Finance and Democracy in America*.

Call this practice, central to the making of the country, the "double movement." The double movement has helped build both American democracy and the American economy. Whenever it has weakened, the result has been to open a space for the marriage of high finance and big business. Its further weakening has led to the outright financialization of the economy (financial hypertrophy in place of financial deepening, as later defined and discussed in this book).

The double movement has recurred at different moments in American history. It exercised decisive influence in the formative period of the republic with Hamilton and Jefferson; in the time of Lincoln and the aftermath of the Civil War; in the Progressive and Populist movements and the administration of the first Roosevelt; and in the New Deal.

The two major enemies of the double movement have been the faltering of democracy and the illusions of thought. The protodemocratic liberalism enshrined in the constitutional arrangements of the country creates a permanent vulnerability: a formidable obstacle to political rule by the people, falsely justified in the name of individual freedom. Ways of thinking that naturalize the established forms of both democracy and the market—in particular the belief that a market economy has a single natural and necessary institutional content—have completed the work of protodemocratic liberalism. They continue to be entrenched in the two most important institutional disciplines: economics and law.

The infirmities of democracy have joined the mystifications of thought to disrupt the double movement. Whenever they have weakened it, the result has been to substitute corporate power for democratic power and to allow the marriage of big business and high finance to set the course of the country. In that marriage, high finance has held the upper hand—first at the end of the nineteenth century and again at the end of the twentieth. Now even more than then, finance has come to absorb an increasing portion of gains in the economy and of talent in the society, to the detriment of the productive potential of the economy and against the interests of ordinary Americans and American democracy.

At the same time, all pretense that corporations exercise a power delegated from government to serve a public purpose is long gone. The freeing of the corporations from any semblance of public duty, often mistaken for an empty genuflection to social responsibility, has as its counterpart the empowerment of finance. It is not finance narrowly construed as banking or even as the business and interests of bank-holding companies that has come to play this exorbitant role. It is finance let loose and placed in command of vast amounts of liquid cash: cash represented notionally in the securities markets, cash accumulated by the most profitable corporations, cash paid to the elite that deals with other people's money. Advanced manufacturing has become all but indistinguishable from the invention of ideas—the materialization of a conceptual activity. The actual making of material objects is farmed out to poorer and less-financialized economies.

The marriage of big business to high finance under the eyes of a weakened democracy has in a sense been replaced by the marriage of high finance to itself, a phenomenon that I earlier described under the label *financial hypertrophy*. No wonder some economists, mistaking a perversion of economic life for its natural state, have proposed to the think of the entire economy as a bank and to view all economic activity as a flow of funds.

The outright financialization of the American economy represents a momentous inflection in the history of American democracy: the extreme, American version of a phenomenon common to the advanced economies today. The themes of this book speak to this circumstance: finance against democracy; finance reconciled to democracy and made more useful to production rather than allowed to serve itself, to the detriment of both production and democracy; theory as insight into transformative opportunity rather than as retrospective rationalization of established arrangements.

FINANCE, PRODUCTION, AND DEMOCRACY

The conception animating my argument comes to life in the details of its explanations and proposals: in a view of the relation of finance to the real economy and to democracy. I place at the foreground of my argument in this book the part of economic activity that has traditionally been seen as the least open to progressive innovation and the least friendly to popular interests and democratic ideals: finance—the inner sanctum of a "capitalist system" that is understood to be unforgiving of dreamy aspirations. If the imagination of progressive alternatives makes sense in this most hostile terrain, it can make sense in every aspect of economic life.

In our thinking about finance, there is a counterpart to the thesis that the market economy has a single natural and necessary institutional form. According to this application of the general idea, if something has gone wrong in the workings of finance, the mishap must result from a localized failure of competition in the capital markets (such as oligopoly or asymmetrical information) or from a localized defect in the regulatory response to the localized market flaw. It cannot occur because something is wrong with the overall arrangements governing the relation of finance to the real economy. There can be no systemic or structural problem, according to this widely shared premise, nor can there be systemic or structural alternatives compatible with the wide decentralization of initiative that any market economy requires.

Yet that there are such problems and such alternatives is what I claim in this book. I argue for this idea on several levels: as a way of thinking about finance and production (in the context of a more general way of thinking about market economies and their alternative futures), as an alternative to the narrowed horizons of present-day reformism, and as a way to ensure that finance becomes useful to us as a good servant rather than continuing to threaten us as a bad master.

Different ways of organizing finance can either tighten or loosen the relation of finance to the real economy. They can either enlist finance more effectively in the service of production or allow it to serve itself under the pretext of funding consumers and producers. The existence and the significance of such differences may seem intuitively apparent to the layman. The established way of thinking, however, with its single-minded focus on localized market and regulatory failures, has no place for them.

Financial deepening—institutionalized tightening of the link between finance and the real economy—enables us better to tap the underutilized productive potential of finance: under current arrangements, production remains largely self-financed on the basis of the retained and reinvested earnings of private firms.[3] Reimagined and reformed, finance can prevent or moderate the destructive effect of financial volatility on economic growth and employment. It can help broaden economic opportunity to produce as well as to consume and especially to participate in the advanced, knowledge-intensive practice of production. This practice remains confined to insular vanguards from which the vast majority of the labor force remains excluded even in the richest countries of the world. We have no chance of advancing such aims so long as we continue to think of finance and democracy as inevitable antagonists. Relatively recent events should remind us of how important it is to get these matters right.

In 2007–2009, the United States underwent a financial crisis that then spread through much of the developed world. The response to the crisis—addressed in three of the five chapters of this book—revealed the practical significance of the way of thinking about the role of finance that I criticize and seek to replace. Of the four major reform programs proposed in the aftermath of the crisis—the reassertion of the New

Deal wall between proprietary trading and federally insured banking; the creation in the federal government of stronger authority to close down or turn around failing financial organizations; the imposition of higher standards of capital adequacy; and the enhancement of protection for the consumers of financial services—none gestured toward the institutional innovations that might have made finance more useful to socially inclusive economic growth. None made use of the truths studied here: that every approach to the regulation of finance can represent a first step toward its reconstruction and that the most compelling criterion by which to choose among regulatory strategies is to assess the merits of the alternative programs that each such strategy prefigures.

IDEAS THAT PLAY A MAJOR ROLE IN THE ARGUMENT OF THIS BOOK

The proximate subject matter of this book is finance—what it does and fails to do in contemporary economies and what it might do if we were to reshape the arrangements that organize it and govern its relation to the real economy. The study of finance can help us imagine a broader agenda of practical progressive reform. Finance and its relation to production form only one aspect of the organization of the economy, an aspect that we commonly associate with dream-destroying constraint rather than, as we also can and should, with transformative opportunity.

The ulterior topic of the book is the institutional redesign of the market economy: a project that cannot advance beyond its initial steps without success in loosening the political limits to economic reform. My argument goes from the alternative futures of finance to the democratizing of the market and from the democratizing of the market to the deepening of democracy.

To address finance in this spirit, we need to appreciate its reality and recent evolution in detail, as this book does. However, we also require ideas that can help guide us in understanding what finance might become in the light of what it has been. Such ideas must suggest a way of thinking that can do justice to their subject matter only by relating insight into present practices and institutions to imagination of their alternative possible forms. Technical detail must somehow be married to transformative vision.

Here, the instrument of this marriage is the unifying role that a small number of ideas plays in this book. Some of these conceptions are distinctive to finance; others relate to the market economy or more generally to how we think about structural change in history. By "structural change," I mean change in the institutional arrangements and ideological assumptions defining the options open to us as individuals or as collective agents in our ordinary activities.

Here is an incomplete, open-ended, and exemplary list of such propositions. I state them as a set of theses. The first five theses have to do with a practice of explanation; they do not apply exclusively to finance or even to economic organization. The last three bear on the direction of my proposals for the reform of finance and of the relation of finance to the real economy as well as more generally for the remaking of the market economy and its reconciliation with democracy.

1. *The thesis of alternative market regimes. The market economy can take radically different institutional forms. Existing and past variations of the market economy represent a subset of a wider array of accessible alternatives.* The single greatest influence on thinking about finance and its promise for prosperity and democracy has been the belief that within a narrow and even diminishing range of variation, a market economy has a relatively predetermined institutional form. This regime finds expression in the law of private property and contract. It is embodied as well in the public-law arrangements ensuring that economic agents can make their own decisions about how to spend their resources and what to do with their time.

The abstract idea of a market economy as an organized anarchy allowing a multitude of firms and individuals to act on their own initiative and bargain on their own account is associated in practice with a conception of institutional convergence. According to this conception, the institutional arrangements and the private law of a successful market economy must resemble those that we see established in the richest countries today. Legal theorists may read the history of legal thought over the past 150 years as demonstrating the legal and institutional indeterminacy of the market idea. The practical economist and the policy maker, however, continue to believe that a market is a market, private property is private property, and contract is contract. They have long been joined in this belief by Marxists, who think that "capitalism" possesses, as every "mode of production" does, a set legal and economic content—its intrinsic legal architecture.

To be sure, there exists a literature about "varieties of capitalism" professing to describe and to explain the existing, relatively narrow range of institutional variations—for example, in the reach of the regulatory and redistributive powers of the state or the extent to which social entitlements are universal and portable or the toleration of a division in the labor force between relatively privileged and legally protected workers and a mass of marginalized outsiders confined to precarious employment, with minimal legal protection and collective representation, or the degree to which the market in corporate control exposes controlling shareholders and the managers that they appoint to challenge and ouster.

Such variations, however, rarely penetrate the elements of private law; they suggest no room for choice in the basic terms on which firms and individuals can gain access to productive resources and opportunities, including the resources and opportunities that may be either afforded or denied by the capital markets. Nor do they exemplify innovations in public law that might engage government, acting through legislation, in the development of new market regimes in particular parts of the economy, such as finance, rather than in a preferential allocation of public resources.

I write here in opposition to this naturalization of economic arrangements. My working assumption is that the existing variations of the market economy represent a subset of a much wider range of accessible alternatives: innovations in the institutional arrangements of the market economy that we can build with the institutional and ideological materials that our historical circumstance has given us. Instead of defending this idea in the abstract, as a proposition in social and economic theory, I illustrate its value in reckoning with a particular domain: finance. For this purpose, finance has an advantage: it has often been seen as the hard edge of constraint on the aspirations of reformers. If we can find room for reinvention in this seemingly most recalcitrant part of the market economy, we can hope to find it elsewhere or even everywhere.

2. *The thesis of the institutional variability of the relation of finance to the real economy. We can change the relation of finance to the real economy, the better to enlist finance in the service of production.* A market economy can be organized in ways that either tighten or loosen the relation of finance to the real economy. Financial services can increase in scale and prominence; they can absorb more talent and time; they can generate more profit, even as their usefulness to the producers of goods and services diminishes. The

production system can finance itself, notably by relying on the retained and reinvested earnings of private firms. Instead of serving production, finance can serve itself, taking the transactions of the real economy less as the object of its work than as a pretext for financial trading. Such trading may then generate the lion's share of financial profits.

This thesis contradicts the dominant view in policy discourse as well as in economics that a competitive capital market automatically allocates resources to their most efficient uses. According to this view, a failure adequately to enlist savings in the service of production can occur only if there is a localized market failure or an omission in the regulatory response to such a discrete market flaw.

Both "neoclassical" and Keynesian thinking have contributed to excluding a conception that plays a central role in this book: the productive potential of the surplus over current consumption that we call savings may be underutilized not because of a localized market or regulatory failure but because of the way in which the institutional arrangements of the market order shape the relation of finance to the real economy. Thus, this second thesis amounts to a special case, or corollary, of the first thesis.

A view of the real worlds of production and finance in an economy such as that of the United States today informs the thesis of institutional variability in the relation of finance to the real economy. From this picture and from other facts about finance and production in contemporary economies, three enigmas result. A major aim of the part of my argument that addresses finance is to elucidate these enigmas.

From the perspective of the role of finance in production, there are three distinct worlds in the American economic order, as in other contemporary market economies.

The first world of production and finance is that of large and medium-size firms rich in capital and technology. They finance their activities largely on the basis of retained earnings, During the period of high economic growth from 1950 to 1975, retained earnings accounted for around 90 percent of capital spending, a more precise proxy for the funding of productive activity. Reliance on retained earnings has remained higher than 80 percent ever since. Many of the most successful firms now hold vast pools of liquid capital.

Businesses in this first world of production and finance do engage the capital and securities markets (which from here on I call "external or autonomous finance": external because it is outside the firm and autonomous because it is not embedded within the firm). However, they are at least as likely to access these markets to share in the trading gains of external finance, to reap benefits for their managers, or to diminish their vulnerability to takeovers by buying back their own stock to fund an expansion of output or to enhance productivity. They habitually go to the capital markets as financiers rather than as producers.

The second world of production and finance is that of small business. In the United States, as in every advanced economy in the world, the dominant presence in the economy and the chief source of jobs and activity remain a mass of relatively backward small firms, with modest stores of capital and technology and limited reliance on external finance. Everywhere the chief mainstays of small business have been self-exploitation (working for long hours at low pay) and family savings. In the United States, small firms often borrow money from the country's unparalleled network of local banks, a legacy of the first half of the nineteenth century, when self-exploitation and family savings fail to suffice. That such borrowing plays a restricted role in the financing of small business is suggested by its limited significance for the lenders. The sum of consumer, credit-card, and mortgage lending greatly exceeds commercial lending in the loan portfolios of the decisive majority of local banks as well as of the national retail banks in the United States.

The third world of production and finance is that of innovative start-ups, especially those seeking to find a place in knowledge-intensive, high-technology production. These are the firms that propose to create new assets in new ways. Here at last external finance plays a central role, especially in the form of venture capital. Venture capital (and the financial activities closest to it) is the form of finance that most directly carries out what is widely regarded as the central responsibility of finance in a market economy: channeling part of the surplus over current consumption to the funding of productive activity in the real economy. A strategic part of that responsibility is to finance the creation of new assets, especially when they are created in new ways. Yet in every advanced economy, venture capital, expansively defined, amounts to a minute part of financial activity. In the United States, which hosts 80 percent of all venture capital activity in the world, venture capital accounts for less than 0.4 percent of gross domestic product (GDP).

Against the background of this picture of the three worlds of finance and production, we confront three enigmas. In each instance, the theoretical conundrum reveals a practical problem requiring practical solutions.

The shared element among them is innovation in the institutional arrangements of the market economy.

The first enigma concerns the superfluity or marginality of much financial activity to production in the real economy. If to a large extent the production system finances itself—on the basis of retained and reinvested earnings in large or medium-size mature firms and of self-exploitation and family savings in retrograde small business—what is the social purpose and justification of the tremendous accumulation of capital in the banks and stock markets? Their contribution to the productive agenda of society is for the most part modest, episodic, and oblique. Much of the productive potential of savings seems to lie dormant and sterile in the capital markets, dissipated in trading and speculation unrelated to production—the expansion of output or the improvement of productivity.

The practical solution to this theoretical conundrum is to innovate in the arrangements governing finance and shaping its relation to the real economy. It is to prefer rules and policies that discourage or prohibit financial activity making no plausible contribution to the expansion of either supply or demand or to the improvement productivity. It is also to multiply initiatives that channel savings to established and potential production. Such formative institutional variation is more than a programmatic conjecture or proposal; it is a historical fact. Institutional arrangements expressed as law have been decisive in determining what finance does or fails to do for production.

Theories of corporate finance lend a semblance of naturalness and rationality to the relative disconnection between production and external finance. For example, the most influential such view—the "pecking order theory of corporate finance"—holds that internal finance will normally be preferred to external finance and that within external finance debt will be preferred to equity.[4] The less-preferred ways of funding production are said to impose greater costs of asymmetrical information on lenders or investors and derivatively on the firm itself.

Yet students of corporate finance have observed that for "entrepreneurial firms" (especially in what I have labeled the third world of finance and production), the pecking order may be regularly inverted: equity is preferred to debt and debt to internal financing. A measure of economic progress is that an increasing percentage of businesses act as such "entrepreneurial firms," inverting, as a result, the ranking of sources of finance. Moreover, asymmetries of information between insiders and outsiders are shaped by the rules of the market: to contain such asymmetries, if not to annul them, has long been a major aim of the securities laws, even in the absence of efforts more effectively to enlist finance in the service of production.

Another influential idea in the theory of corporate finance serves further to refine the meaning of the first enigma. According to the Modigliani–Miller theorem, in an efficient market a firm's value is unaffected by how it is financed.[5] Some might read this theorem to suggest that the relative weight of the internal and external financing of production is unimportant. The first enigma, however, poses a question different from the one that Modigliani and Miller answered: not "How does finance influence the creation of value *in* the firm?" but "How does finance influence the creation of value *by* the economy?" The subject matter of the first enigma is the relation of finance to economic growth, especially through the creation of new assets, rather than to the value of the firm, as measured by the securities markets. Moreover, we would commit a "fallacy of composition" if we were to treat the economy for this purpose as simply a collection of firms and its ability to create value (especially in new assets, made in new ways) as a straightforward extension of the process by which firms enhance their value and find the enhancement confirmed over time by their market capitalization.

Within the restrictive assumptions of the theorem, all sources of finance may be equivalent. Nevertheless, an overwhelming reliance on retained earnings, by contrast to the mobilization of external finance, implies the existence of an economic regime organized for the benefit of incumbents and to the detriment of innovators and disruptors. This implication gives cause for concern if, as turns out to be the case, the most radical and fertile innovations are capital intensive rather than capital sparing. These innovations require capital to produce new goods and services in new ways. They do not spare capital by finding more efficient ways to continue making familiar products for established markets. The third enigma bears on the relation of finance to this contrast between incumbency and innovation.

The second enigma has to do with an asymmetry of a different order. Under current arrangements, finance may be largely indifferent to the real economy in good times. It nonetheless has the power to destroy in bad times: financial crisis harms activity in that economy.

No legal or institutional innovation can suppress the instability of finance and avoid the occurrence of financial crisis. The ineradicable instability of finance arises from two basic sources. Its first cause is the capital markets' dependence on a regime of law, policy, and institutions that finance cannot control, no matter how great its political influence may be. Its second cause is that liquid capital, the resource with which finance works, is, by virtue of the ease with which we can deploy it, the part of our material lives that most readily bears the imprint of elation and despondency, greed and fear. It also registers the ways in which these passions color our views of the future. It was on this susceptibility of the allocation of liquid capital to our humors and illusions that Keynes and his disciples, working within the psychological tradition of English political economy, chiefly fixed when they set out to account for the havoc that the disposition of money balances can wreak on economic activity.

I argue that we can nevertheless diminish the dangers of finance through the same measures by which we can increase its usefulness to production in the real economy. Its relative disengagement from production strengthens its destructive potency.

The third enigma returns to the first from another angle. Why does the activity of financing the creation of new assets in new ways represent such a small part of financial activity under present arrangements? How can it cease to be so insignificant? Many will answer that in the advanced economies there is no lack of capital available for gainful investment in innovative production. There is instead, they will protest, a scarcity of such investment opportunities: venture capitalists go begging for entrepreneurs and projects offering a prospect of return proportional to the risk of investing in young, innovative enterprise.

We can redress this scarcity of investment opportunities only by disseminating throughout the economy the most advanced practices of production and by meeting the educational and social requirements of such a dissemination. Finance can make a distinct and important contribution to an economy-wide, socially inclusive enhancement of productivity. It can do so, however, only as part of a larger project. I call this project the "democratization of the market economy."

3. *The thesis of structure, not system. The institutional and ideological regime of a society shapes its routine activities, including its economic life. Such structures are not indivisible systems, conforming to a coherent logic and incapable of piecemeal transformation.* The way of thinking that I put to work and exemplify, rather than theorize, in this book is one that shares with many strands of classical European social theory, including

Marxism, a belief in the primacy of structural vision and structural reform. In every society, there are arrangements and assumptions that are normally left unchanged and even unchallenged but that shape its routines of exchange, power, and discourse. This framework is its structure.

A structure always has two sides: the side of the institutions and practices and the side of the representations or beliefs that make sense of them. These two sides are intimately and internally related. The institutions and practices are not like natural phenomena that we can grasp without regard to ideas held by the people who live with them and act through them. They draw their life from beliefs: less beliefs as disembodied doctrines than beliefs incarnate in practical arrangements as well as in the economic, political, and cultural routines that such arrangements mold.

The organization of finance and of its relation to the real economy is only one of many parts of a social and economic regime. Whether we want to or not, we cannot address any significant feature of economic or political activity without making assumptions about the existence, constitution, and significance of such regimes and about the way these regimes get made and revised.

The understanding of structure is or should be the chief object of explanatory ambition in all branches of social and historical study, including economics and law. Innovation in structure is the main goal and test of transformative politics.

The same traditions of social theory that have most emphasized the priority of structural insight, such as Marxism, have taught us to think of structure as system: capitalism in Marx's theory, for example. The system's parts are inseparable. We cannot pick and choose among them. Either we manage the system, allowing only such modest reforms as are compatible with its preservation, or we replace it with another equally indivisible system. The system has its built-in institutional content, susceptible to variation only at the margin. It may even represent a moment or a stage in a foreordained succession of such systems, governed by laws of historical change.

I am a structuralist if by structuralist we mean someone who places structure at the center of her thinking. But I do not approach structure in the spirit of the structuralist tradition to which I have just alluded. The real structures of history are indeed powerful in their influence and resistant to challenge and change. They do not, however, function as systems. They are ramshackle constructions made from the elements lying at hand. They are neither the source nor the product of laws of historical change. We make them, albeit under constraint.

Such structures often reflect elites' effort to absorb innovations useful to the prosperity and power of the state and its masters while minimizing disturbance to dominant interests and entrenched preconceptions: the path of least resistance. The path of least resistance is never the only path: the aim of a properly progressive politics is to find alternatives to it. The development of such alternatives requires guidance from structural insight. In the present situation of the social sciences and of economic and legal analysis, such help remains hard to get.

It is in this spirit, at once structuralist and skeptical of the most influential approaches to structure and structural change, that I address in this book the problems of finance. I exemplify another view and argue for it on the basis of the insights that it makes possible rather than presenting it as abstract social theory.

A consequence of this method is to emphasize, with respect to problems of financial and economic reform, what the major tradition of structural theorizing—and of the left-leaning politics that it has informed—denies: the attractions and feasibility of reforms that are structural but nevertheless piecemeal. Instead of replacing one system by another, such reforms take initial steps by which to move in a certain direction in a particular circumstance. One such direction takes initiatives meant to give practical content to widely proposed goals of socially inclusive growth, to enhance our agency—our individual and collective power to act and to innovate—and to breathe new life and meaning into the progressive cause. There is no place better in which to test such a program than the field widely believed to be most hostile to it: the harsh realities of capital and its relation to political power.

4. *The thesis of the need for a revised practice of legal and economic analysis informed by institutional imagination. The prevailing modes of social science and of legal and economic analysis are deficient in structural vision: they either disregard or misrepresent the structural element in social and economic life. We can begin to correct this deficiency without waiting for a comprehensive social theory to guide us.* To embrace a structural approach in the spirit of the preceding propositions, we need help from a style of legal and economic analysis that has nowhere been fully developed, although it is already practiced in fragmentary form.

It is in law that the institutional arrangements of society appear at the level of detail enabling us to recognize them as structures rather than as systems in just the sense that my fourth thesis describes. In law, we have the opportunity to explore and to reimagine the tangible institutional content of both the economic and the political regime. The institutions and practices that make up such regimes fail to fit together in the way that both Marxists and conservative economic and political theorists suppose they do. They are full of contradictions. This contradictory material—the real stuff of institutional history—supplies us with materials with which to define the initial moves in contrasting directions of institutional change. Structure as system is programmatically sterile. Structure as a revised practice of legal analysis allows us to define it supplies the programmatic imagination with its most substantial and fertile subject matter.

To tap this potential, however, we must not reduce law to what judges and other legal professionals practice. Nor must we allow ourselves to be distracted by a style of legal analysis representing the law as an idealized system. We must turn legal analysis into something that it has yet to become: a study of the compromises and contradictions in the present institutional regime of society, as they are expressed in law, and an exploration of the institutional alternatives that we can build from these points of departure. The imagination of institutional possibility has as its counterpart a revision of the way in which we understand our interests and ideals; every understanding of ideals and interests relies on assumptions about how they are or can be realized in practice. Much of *Law and the Wealth of Nations* amounts to an illustration of this method at work, both as a way of explaining and as a way of proposing.

Law, however, is not enough. We require as well help from the other master discipline of the institutional imagination: economics. To secure that help, we must deal with economics in the spirit in which I argue we should approach law. There, too, what chiefly prevails since the Marginalist turn of the late nineteenth century—a model-building science of trade-offs and constraints—is both indispensable and insufficient. To accomplish an intellectual program like the one to which this book points, we must redress, less in theory than in practice, two of the major defects of the central tradition in the economics of the past 130 years.

One of these flaws is a deficiency of institutional imagination: in particular, imagination of alternative ways to organize the decentralized initiative by relatively autonomous economic agents—including their decentralized access to capital—that forms part of the core meaning of the idea of a market economy. Here legal thought can perform a vital role by its negative but immensely important discovery of a market's institutional indeterminacy. Contrary to what Hayek and many others supposed, we cannot infer a detailed legal regime of contract, property, and business organizations from the abstract idea of coordination and exchange among free and equal economic agents.

Another failing of this central tradition in economics is its lack of a proper view of production and thus as well of the relation of production to finance. Unlike the pre-Marginalist economics of either Adam Smith or Karl Marx, the economics resulting from the Marginalist turn was and has ever since remained a theory of competitive, market-based exchange. It has viewed production as a shadowy extension of exchange under the lens of relative prices. Rather than treating the organization of production as a subject in its own right, Marginalist economics approaches the problems of production from the angle of its characteristic concern with the role of relative prices in shaping market transactions and individual incentives.

Marginalism found encouragement for this reduction in an attribute of contemporary market economies that came to be considered natural and legitimate only in the late nineteenth century—the same moment of the Marginalist revolution in economics. Wage labor began only then to be accepted as the predominant and in most circumstances the unavoidable mode of free labor. It was accepted to the detriment of self-employment and cooperation, which liberals and socialists alike had up to the middle of the nineteenth century viewed as a superior variant of the work of free men and women.

It forms no part of my purpose to debate in this book the rights and wrongs of established economics. However, I cannot execute the task on which I set out here without at least suggesting how we might begin to redress these defects in an explanatory and programmatic practice. I revisit these methodological tenets, almost always implicitly rather than explicitly, in the first four chapters of this book and draw out the significance of their revision for the reimagination and reconstruction of the market economy and of the role that finance plays within it.

The three remaining theses concern the programmatic horizon of my argument. They place my proposals about finance in the broader context of two overlapping sets of ideas: ideas about the strategies of economic development that can give practical content to the aim of socially inclusive economic growth and ideas about institutional innovation in the arrangements of the market economy, including the arrangements that we recognize to be most basic and therefore (in the predominant spirit of seeing structure as system) view as least susceptible to change—the regimes of contract and property as well as the relations between governments and firms. These larger ideas, implicit in the discussion of finance in chapters 1 and 2, become explicit in the comparison of the recent development paths of the Unites States and Latin America in chapter 4 and in my interpretation of exemplary episodes of economic and financial history in chapter 5.

5. *The high-savings requirement thesis. A high level of domestic saving, both private and public, has strategic importance. It enables countries to resist the interests and preconceptions of the domestic and international capital markets in the design of their development strategies.* A high level of domestic saving allows national economies and governments to innovate and to rebel. In particular, it permits them to rebel against interests and preconceptions held dear in the capital markets, both domestic and international. By the same token, it makes it possible for them to say no to the advice of the Bretton Woods organizations as well as to the prescriptions urged on them by global economic experts.

The gist of the next two theses is that successful economic growth in both richer and poorer countries is likely to require what I call a progressive approach to the supply side and consequently institutional and legal innovation in the arrangements, even the most basic arrangements, of the market economy and those shaping the way in which and the extent to which finance serves or fails to serve the real economy. Such innovation will regularly contradict the interests and beliefs prominent in high finance—at home and especially in the world at large. Governments and countries that undertake them must not be on their knees, needing to placate the masters of capital or the convenience and opinions of those with the ability to deploy capital.

In the medium and long term, money goes to where it can find the greatest chance for gain, regardless of deference to the pieties and doctrines of the moment. (China, prodigal in insults to economic and financial orthodoxy, has long been the favored destination of foreign direct investment. The lure of profit, if sustained over time, ends up trumping any offense to doctrinal rectitude.) In the short term, however, homage to the reigning orthodoxies (about public finance or the labor laws, for example) ordinarily serves as a proxy for the real thing: the chance to make money. The mobilization of national resources—a concerted, organized, and even forced raising of the level of national saving—enables a country and its government to resist such pressure and avoid such vulnerability.

Keynes's influence and the practical policies that his followers around the world drew from his teachings have confused what is at issue. It may be true in theory that the level of saving is more a consequence than a cause of economic growth. This economic truth, however, fails to take account of the strategic imperative on which I have just remarked: the use of a shield of heightened national saving in enabling a rebellious strategy of national growth.

As we acknowledge this strategic imperative, we must also pay heed to another, yet more familiar element in Keynes's message: saving may be dangerous to prosperity if it is hoarded rather than put to productive use because the economy may rebalance at a persistently low or lower level of employment. To reckon properly with this other truth, however, we must enlarge the conception of hoarding to include what I describe in this book as financial hypertrophy without financial deepening.[6] The greater the reliance on domestic saving as a strategic requirement of strong initiatives of national development, the more important it becomes to create rules and institutions that enlist finance in the service of production rather than allow it to serve itself—a major theme of this book.

Rules and policies that implement this twofold task—raising the level of saving and preventing the dissipation of its productive potential in trading tenuously related, if at all, to the expansion of output and the enhancement of productivity—may override the justifications for countercyclical management of the economy through easy money and budget deficits. It may be more important to ensure the potential for national divergence from the growth path favored by orthodox opinion and financial interest. However, the reason to sacrifice countercyclical economic policy in such a circumstance is opposite to the reason that is ordinarily invoked. The point is not to win financial confidence. The point is not to depend on financial confidence. Such independence exacts a cost.

As progressives and leftists have retreated from faith in governmental control of the economy, they have embraced the vulgar Keynesianism criticized in the appendix to this book. The alternative to vulgar Keynesianism is the position that I label "structural" or "structure not system." It is not "structuralist" in the sense of the old development economics, with its characteristic emphasis on the importance of moving workers from less-productive sectors (especially agriculture) to more-productive ones (notably manufacturing). That emphasis has lost validity as the distinctions among sectors have weakened and vanguards embodying the most advanced practice of productive have appeared in almost every sector. It is structuralist by virtue of its focus on the institutional arrangements and ideological assumptions defining an economic and political regime.

6. *The institutionalist thesis. We cannot achieve the goal of socially inclusive economic growth, on the basis of energized democracy, unless we pursue an agenda of institutional reconstruction, changing the established institutional forms of the market and of democracy. Finance is a promising and even indispensable domain in which to begin defining such an agenda.* The heart of development is the broadening of economic and educational opportunities and capabilities in a setting in which no privileged class can bend the state and the law exclusively or decisively to its own interests. National development requires the mobilization of physical, financial, and human resources. But in what form, by what agents, and to what ends?

The market economy and democracy provide two ways of answering these questions. However, every particular way of organizing a market economy or a democracy is flawed. To recognize and to seize the advantages of economic and political pluralism without mistaking any of its forms for a perfect and definitive vessel is the task of those who fight for a subset of what I have just called strong projects of national development. This subset is marked by a commitment to a socially inclusive ideal of agency: making everyone more capable of taking initiative both as an individual and as part of a group through cooperative action. Decentralization of economic initiative is the heart of a market economy. Openness to the engagement of the people in defining the terms of their life together is central to democracy. Both of these achievements have to do with the strengthening of our power to take control of the social world in which we live. For democrats and progressives, the enhancement of agency is not acceptable as an ideal until its beneficiary becomes, in principle, everyone.

If the socially inclusive enhancement of agency is the progressive goal, the progressive method or practice is piecemeal but cumulative change in the economic and political arrangements of society. The view that I have labeled "structure not system" supports and informs such change. The educational empowerment of the individual—in youth and throughout life—complements the democratization of the market and the deepening of democracy.

Chapters 1 and 2 of this book address an aspect of democratizing the market: the reorganization of finance and the reshaping of its relation to production. Chapter 3 explores the institutional content of a democratized market economy. Chapter 4 steps back to discuss the democratization of the market through a comparison of the American and Latin American experiences and prospects. Chapter 5 explores the character of the intellectual instruments, especially in law and in economics, that we need in such an endeavor.

7. The supply-side thesis. Socially inclusive economic growth and the democratization of the market economy require a progressive approach to the supply side of the economy. They cannot be accomplished solely by policies designed to support demand, combined with progressive taxation and redistributive social programs.

The proposals that I make in this book embody a progressive approach to the supply side of the economy. In contemporary debates about economic policy, progressives in developing countries as well as in the richest societies have often been content to focus on the demand side—that is, the fiscal and monetary policies that can sustain aggregate demand. The intellectual support for this orientation is the vulgar Keynesianism that they came to embrace as they lost faith in governmental direction of the economy.

A clear and extreme instance is the United States in the early twenty-first century. In and out of political office, contemporary American progressives have often invoked as elements of a growth strategy a combination of educational reform, investment in infrastructure, advance toward low-carbon forms of production, and programs intended to offset the social costs of structural change in the American economy. Little, however, has come of such talk even when the talkers have been in national office. The real growth strategy of the United States, insofar as the country has one, has been easy money: a policy of enduringly low interest rates implemented in the hope that, in the absence of a more substantial program, cheap money will spur economic growth. The architect of this residual strategy—the strategy that survives when all other strategies remain talk—has been the Federal Reserve rather either the president or Congress.

In much of the world, including the most advanced economies, discussion of the supply-side bases of economic growth has been largely abandoned to conservative economists and right-wing political forces. The central premise of the conventional approach to supply-side constraints has been the naturalization of the market economy's established legal and institutional form. The adoption of ideas and policies intended to reform the relation of finance to the real economy relates to the supply side as well as to the demand side of the economy: it is finance as instrument or obstacle to the productive agenda of society that mainly interests me here. Chapters 1 and 2 detail a view of the opportunities for reimagination and reform in what can be only one component of such a project. Chapters 3 and 4 develop this agenda in more comprehensive form and in comparative and historical context. Chapter 5 makes explicit the way of thinking implicit in these arguments and illustrates its use in the interpretation and criticism of historical experience.

There is a difference, rich in consequence, between the levels of transformative ambition required by the popularization of demand, on the one hand, and by the democratization of supply, on the other—that is to say, of access to the resources, opportunities, and capabilities of production. To democratize demand, it may suffice to reallocate money from one use to another or entitlements from one set of beneficiaries to other groups. To democratize supply, structural change—innovation in the institutional arrangements defining the market economy and shaping the primary distribution of economic advantage—is vital. A progressive approach to the supply side requires the methods and practices associated with the notion of structure not system.

By the same token, the direction of reform for which I argue in this book stands in contrast to the two sets of growth strategies that now enjoy wide influence among developing countries, especially among middle-income economies, including the largest.

One such approach, which has prevailed in South America in recent decades, is the effort to base economic growth on the twin foundations of mass consumption, supported by a rise in the income of the working class, and the production and export of commodities—agriculture, ranching, and mining, encouraged by high commodity prices in the world economy. A simplified and extreme but nevertheless common instance is the expropriation of part of the earnings of agrarian exporters by a tax on their exports and the use of this tax to subsidize the consumption of the urban population. It is an orientation that works when commodity prices are booming but that fails when they fall.

When it fails, governments may seek to prolong the life of the compromised strategy by heavy-handed use of fiscal, trade, and capital-account deficits. The efficacy of the expedients of vulgar Keynesianism is soon exhausted because they do nothing to address the supply-side constraints on economic growth. Their foreseeable outcome is to aggravate the consequences of the failure of the consumption and commodity-based growth strategy in the resource-rich, populous, and very unequal societies whose governments follow this road. Electoral reversal soon follows economic slump.

Such an orientation focuses on the demand side of the economy, un-committed to the creation of new comparative advantage and heedless of the imperative of institutional innovation. The qualification is that some demand-oriented policies such as conditional cash-transfer pro-grams, typically tying entitlements to education, may cross the divide between the demand side and the supply side and involve in their design a measure of legal and institutional innovation. This model of develop-ment leaves economic progress hostage to the riches of nature rather than supported by the enhancement of our powers, although advanced prac-tice in agriculture and natural-resource extraction increasingly embodies science and technology. No wonder that in its approach to finance this model veers between surrendering to the demands of foreign or domestic financial confidence and confronting these demands. What it cannot do, for lack of institutional imagination as well as of political will, is to change what finance does and how it works.

Another influential contemporary approach to development combines three elements. A first element is "state capitalism," often against the back-ground of authoritarian government. A second element consists in adopt-ing a variant of the market economy that is both relatively unregulated and relatively unqualified by progressive taxation and redistributive social spending. A third element is a form of export-led growth in which manu-facturing continues to play a major role. Advanced, knowledge-intensive production figures in this development strategy not just in one sector (high-technology industry) but in all sectors, including precision agricul-ture and knowledge-intensive services combined with knowledge-inten-sive manufacturing. However, such vanguards employ only a small part of the labor force and remain relatively disconnected from the other parts of the economy to which they sell their products.

The star instance of such a growth path has been China, preceded by the Northeast Asian "tiger" economies and accompanied by other more recently developing economies in Southeast Asia. One of this path's pre-conditions has been the effective control of the state by an elite claiming to serve both the national interest and the popular interest. Another pre-condition has been the pursuit and persistence of major trade and capital surpluses in the relation of the national economy to some of its major trading partners. Nowhere have such imbalances been more striking or more important than in the relation between the Chinese and the American economies, especially in the years leading up to the financial and economic crisis of 2007–2009 as well as in its aftermath. For economies on both sides of the imbalances, the ability to sustain capital and trade surpluses and deficits has served as a way of evading the imperative of structural change.

For the United States, trade and capital deficits (most strikingly manifest in the relation of the American economy to the Chinese) served as a way of continuing to grow on the basis of debt and credit-fueled consumption. It has been growth continued in the absence of a national project that is both production oriented and socially inclusive. The impulse of radical innovation has remained quarantined within relatively insular productive vanguards, reliant on formidable accumulation of cognitive, social, and financial capital. The vanguards of knowledge-rich production assign parts of the implementation of their plans to less-advanced firms spread around the world. Credit, debt, and the residual growth strategy of easy money practiced by the central bank have allowed the country to avoid confronting a fundamental weakness: it has ceased to make enough goods and services that the rest of the world wants.

For China, on the other side of the imbalances, the ability to exploit trade and capital surpluses has meant a way of avoiding the work of deepening its internal market so that production for export can complement domestic consumption rather than substitute for it. Contrary to what is often implied, the achievement of this goal is no mere technical problem to be solved by a change of policy and a reassignment of resources. It requires major, conflict-ridden redistribution among classes, sectors, and regions. There is no ready-made formula for its accomplishment; the path must be opened up by local experiment and national debate. Such an alternative demands a new political life for the Chinese people.

Here, too, the potential of finance to be useful to both growth and democracy remains disregarded and diminished. Instead of serving as a bridge to an inclusive productivism in the United States, finance has largely been allowed to revel in a proliferation of products and services often only tenuously related to the production system's capital needs. Established firms largely finance themselves with their own stores of liquid capital while the production-oriented work of venture capital remains dwarfed by financial trading weakly linked to production and innovation in the real economy. Similarly in China, finance has turned into a source of expedients with which to fund and reconcile the otherwise contradictory elements of the established economic regime: state-owned enterprises in search of subsidized credit, private firms in quest of opportunities for the gainful placement of extra cash, and households.

In both the United States and China, the center of gravity of financial activity has shifted away from banks, bank-holding companies, and other designated and accountable financial organizations to a vast world of "shadow banking": banking by nonbanks under nonbank rules or no rules at all. Finance as an activity has increasingly been divorced from finance as what a recognized and regulated cast of recognized financial organizations do. The diffusion of finance beyond the range of its traditional agents has not served socially inclusive economic growth or tightened the link between finance and production. It has instead mainly given an advantage those who, in the shadows or in the light, exercise effective control over large pools of capital in economies as different as the American and the Chinese.

A central claim of this book is that the resulting circumstance is neither desirable nor inevitable. We can best understand it as a series of accommodations to the path of least resistance in the area of finance: the way of managing new national and global financial practices that least disturbs the most powerful interests and the most entrenched preconceptions. It is also, however, connected to a failure that is at once political and intellectual. I write in the spirit of one who disputes both the necessity and legitimacy of this result. We already have at hand the intellectual instruments and the institutional materials with which to begin marking out movement in another direction.

PLAN OF THIS BOOK

Chapter 1 considers the financial and economic crisis of 2007–2009 as well as the regulatory and legislative response to it as a lesson in the dangers of finance and in the failings of the ideas that have shaped and continue to shape the regulation of financial activity. It begins to plot an alternative trajectory. Chapter 2 places the argument about financial reform in a longer historical context and gives it a broader programmatic horizon. It shows how we can move from the regulation to the reordering of finance and of its relation to the real economy in the interest of an effort to democratize the market. Chapter 3 explores the institutional conditions of socially inclusive economic growth: the higher use of financial deepening. Chapter 4 reconsiders these problems and opportunities chiefly from the standpoint of the travails of our sister republics in Latin America in the period between the Second World War and the financial and economic crisis of 2007–2009. It compares the course followed by Latin America to the development experiences of the United States and Northeast Asia in the same historical circumstance. By placing the argument about finance in comparative historical context, this chapter shows how the discussion of finance opens up a larger inquiry into the alternative forms of the market economy. We cannot advance toward the most widely professed policy goal in the world today—socially inclusive economic growth—without innovating in the economic institutions of contemporary societies. A vital part of such innovation is to reshape finance and its relation to the real economy. Chapter 5 articulates and develops the way of thinking about law, finance, and markets that the explanations and proposals of this book exemplify. In this mode of thought, legal analysis and political economy come together as disciplines of institutional imagination. Institutional imagination—even about economic constraints that we have often mistaken for immutable laws—is my method and my hope.

The argument of this book moves from a narrower focus on the troubles and reform of finance to a broader exploration of what a market economy can and should become under democracy. Finance stands, by synecdoche, as a part for the whole. As the argument broadens, it also—I hope—deepens. The proposals to reorganize finance and to redefine its role in the economy turn into a search for the institutional basis on which we can best achieve socially inclusive economic growth and reconcile markets with democracies. What our stake in markets has in common with our stake in democracies is an interest in the enhancement of agency—the powers of creative initiative vested in ordinary men and women. We enhance agency by freeing ourselves from superstition about society and by developing practices and institutions hospitable to a decentralized experimentalism and open to the lessons of experience.

Throughout the book, a programmatic intention motivates my explanatory conjectures: I explain to the end of proposing. But my proposals of an alternative direction are not confined to any one part of this work and are not separated from its interpretations of economic and financial history. They are present in each of the five chapters, sometimes expressed in universalizing and abstract form, as in chapter 3 (about the institutional content of a democratized market economy), but more often developed in particular national settings, especially the contemporary United States, as well as in the realm of the adjacent possible—what we can and should do next, as in the other chapters.

Yet this alternative direction is always the same direction that I here explore and defend, whether at points closer to our present arrangements and preconceptions or at points more remote from them. As a consequence, there is no one part of this text to which the reader can turn to find the blueprint of an alternative regime of financial and economic organization. I propose no blueprint because I seek instead a pathway, defined as a succession of steps. In the marking of such a pathway, everything depends on the interplay between our choice of direction and our selection of next moves.

This book exemplifies a way of thinking, at once explanatory and programmatic, about structural change in economies and societies. However, it does not present this way of thinking as a theoretical system. Rather, it develops it cumulatively and in context, especially by discussing in chapters 4 and 5 a wide range of exemplary episodes in economic and financial history. Along the way, it suggests and embodies a view of the practice of legal and economic analysis needed to do such work. I call this practice "fragmentary theory."

The chief concerns of fragmentary theory are the understanding of structure and of structural change as well as the imagination of structural alternatives. A society's institutional and ideological regime is never a system that changes all at once or not at all. Change that matters, structural change or radical reform, is almost always piecemeal. In the fifth and final chapter of this book, I address the marriage of fragmentary theory to radical reform.

CHAPTER ONE

The Past and Future of American Finance Seen Through the Lens of Crisis

THE FINANCIAL CRISIS of 2007–2009 and the subsequent economic slump provided an opportunity to reform finance in the service of both production and democracy. The opportunity for reform has largely been wasted, but the opportunity for insight has not yet. Insight today can inform reconstruction tomorrow. It cannot do so unless we trade in some bad American exceptionalism for some good American experimentalism.

Finance and its reform now lie at the center of American and world attention. Yet the debate that has taken place about the reform of finance, at home as well as abroad, has been extraordinarily narrow. I argue here that its central defect has been to remain within the limits of attempts to regulate finance rather than to reshape it.

A central thesis of my argument in this chapter is that regulation is not enough. The problems revealed by the present crisis can be adequately addressed only by initiatives designed to reorganize the relation of finance to the real economy. These initiatives should in turn be understood as the front line of an institutional reorganization of the market economy in the service of three goals that enjoy great authority in the world today: growth with social inclusion; innovation in the forms of finance capable of promoting savings, investment, and production in the real economy; and an increase in the capacity of countries in every region of the world to participate actively rather than passively in global markets.

My argument here forms part of a developing body of work that explores these matters from a number of complementary perspectives but always with the same purpose in mind: to develop a way of thinking that helps us enlist existing institutional variations in the imagination and development of new institutional alternatives. I begin with a simple typology. It both refines and develops an analytic approach that is explored in greater detail later in this book as well in other work I have done, and it suggests a programmatic orientation.

The typology contrasts three programs for the reform of finance: the New Deal reforms, the current deal, and a better deal. In passing from the first to the second, I consider the nature and the implications of the partial hollowing out of the New Deal reforms that preceded and help explain the present crisis.

My aim is not to supply a historical narrative. It is to summarize, in the form of this compressed typology, a toolbox of analytic categories (i.e., the categories described later and exhibited in table 1.1 at the end of this chapter). I believe these categories to be indispensable to an argument capable of moving beyond the boundaries of the established debate about finance and its reform.

At the heart of my argument stand three ideas. The first idea is programmatic, the second critical, and the third methodological. All three have to do with the role of institutional arrangements.

The programmatic idea is that there is a pathway of piecemeal and cumulative reform that would enable us to channel more effectively the long-term savings of society into long-term productive investment rather than into speculative financial transactions that contribute little or nothing to the enhancement of productivity and the expansion of output.

The critical and historical idea is that the needed innovations cannot be accommodated within the two major traditions of progressive reform seen in American history: the defense of small-scale property and business against large-scale property and business and the acceptance of big business combined with a commitment to use the powers of strong national government to regulate big business. Finance has served as a testing ground for both traditions and has highlighted their failures.

The methodological idea is that the concepts and categories required both to understand and to reshape established institutional arrangements exist in the form of legally defined institutional detail. They are inevitably informed by conceptions of law as well as by ideas about the role of finance in our democracy and in a market economy. Legal analysis matters; it has an indispensable—and misunderstood—role to play. It represents a starting point for the disciplinary approach we need to understand opportunities for and constraints in transforming finance and other areas of social practice in the world today.

The disadvantage of the extreme concision I have opted for here is that the ideas remain incompletely developed; they do not yet amount to fully worked-out arguments. The advantage of this approach, however, is that it will help us recognize how much more has happened and can be made to happen than the now dominant ideas about financial reform acknowledge. There can be no significant reform until we develop a way of thinking that loosens the hold of a series of restrictive assumptions about finance and its reform that we have long come to accept. A first step in this direction is to understand the historical background of this stronghold.

FINANCIAL REFORM IN THE UNITED STATES AND THE CONTEMPORARY GLOBAL DEBATE ON ALTERNATIVES TO THE WASHINGTON CONSENSUS

One of the premises of my argument is that the contemporary worldwide debate about the adequacy of established institutional arrangements, including arrangements for organizing finance and shaping its relation to the real economy, apply to the United States just as much as they do to any other country. Before the onset of the financial and economic crisis of 2007–2009, there was already widespread debate about the thesis of convergence to a single set of supposedly best economic institutions and practices—the set described by the so-called Washington Consensus and in particular by the "second-generation" Washington Consensus reforms.

The orthodox position in this debate defended the necessity and desirability of institutional convergence.[1] Critics and progressives of many stripes disputed the case for such convergence.[2] They have argued that circumstantial and cumulative innovations in the institutional arrangements organizing a market economy are both possible and necessary. A frequently voiced claim among them is that a market economy cannot be made more inclusive—and afford more access to more markets for more people—without being institutionally reordered.[3]

The worldwide financial and economic crisis of 2007–2009 gave new life to this dispute. It also brought into focus those institutional arrangements that govern finance and its relation to the production system.

Both before and after the crisis, a persistent but largely unexamined premise among American policy makers and academics has been that the United States is not a proper subject for this debate. Although American economic, political, and academic authorities have often been in the forefront of the effort to press Washington Consensus–style reforms on developing countries, it has frequently been remarked that the United States itself has traditionally been loath to follow its own advice. It has been hard to see the American experience from either the vantage point of the institutional orthodoxy or the perspective of its critics. In the specific area of financial institutions, the old American exceptionalism has joined hands with particular circumstances that seem to afford the United States an exemption from the trials and tribulations central to the global debate. Prominent among these circumstances is the American stranglehold on what remains the world's reserve currency.

A working assumption of this chapter's argument is that we have good theoretical and practical reason to regard the United States, for the purpose of the issues I here address, as a normal country. The need to address pressing questions of financial reform and reorganization provides one more motive (if many others did not exist) to sacrifice American exceptionalism to American experimentalism.

PLAN OF THE ARGUMENT

I now develop the contrast among three projects of reform in the area of finance in the wake of the financial crisis. I contrast the New Deal, the current deal, and a better deal with regard to five dimensions of change: reforming the basic institutional framework of finance; extending the institutional framework through intermediate organizations; preventing and managing crisis; putting finance at the service of the real economy; and placing finance in its broader setting (meaning everything that has to do with the relation of finance to the broader, established model of economic organization and growth). I present these contrasts against the background of a comparative analysis of the historical origins of our present experience. The point of the reference to this background is to encourage and guide us in the search for usable institutional innovations.

A BIRD'S-EYE VIEW OF THE WORK OF THE NEW DEAL IN THE AREA OF FINANCIAL REFORM

Two approaches to progressive financial reform have been available in the United States since the founding of the republic. They are the direct application to finance of the two American traditions of progress reform discussed in the introduction. The approach pits the little against the big, exemplified in the nineteenth-century struggles over the national bank and the development of a nationwide system of local banks.[4] The second approach accepts large-scale, national banking and securities markets but wants to subject them to strong regulation by the federal government.[5]

We can best understand the New Deal financial reforms as an example of the second, classic regulatory approach. They represent an effort not to cut banking down to size, either in local or global markets, but to hold finance accountable in the interest of greater economic security for those who use financial—and especially banking—services. The New Deal reforms in the area of finance sought to promote these goals by limiting risk, insuring deposits, and promoting transparency and fair dealing between financial markets or financial intermediaries and the constituencies that they are supposed to serve.[6]

Three main concerns animated the New Deal reforms in the area of finance. The first concern was the enhancement of safeguards for the individual against insecurity, in particular against the effects of major instability in the level of economic activity. The second aim was the curbing of the speculative excesses of finance, particularly with regard to other people's money (i.e., the use of individual savings to fuel financial speculation). The third ambition was the popularization of consumption, in particular housing.

In the advancement of these goals, the reformers were inventive in creating a new set of agents, policies, and arrangements. I address the main New Deal policies and arrangements in the first row in table 1.1 at the end of this chapter.

1. Reforming the Institutional Setting of Finance

The New Deal financial reforms are best known for limiting risk and imposing regulation in the core areas of the financial system. The signature New Deal reform separated commercial and investment banking and created federally sponsored deposit insurance. In this framework, banks were supposed to collect and preserve the value of insured deposits. They were not supposed to engage in risky financial speculation, especially with other people's money. Broker-dealers, investment trusts, and other regulated nonbank financial institutions were placed under separate regulatory regimes and subject to monitoring and supervision by independent regulatory agencies.[7]

2. Extending the Institutional Framework of Finance: Quasi-governmental Organizations

A second key set of reforms dealt with the creation of a series of quasi- or paragovernmental organizations.

Among the many quasi-governmental organizations established at the time, none would prove as important as the series of mortgage agencies and auxiliary institutions designed to create a nationwide mortgage market. A key innovation in this area consisted in the creation of a government-sponsored secondary mortgage market. In the context of the current crisis, the idea of targeted-credit and government-sponsored financial organizations is often dismissed out of hand. But the skepticism that dominates the contemporary debate is most appropriately addressed to the present framework of financial markets and arrangements rather than to the original New Deal legal and institutional reforms.

Three different sets of institutional innovations would further this part of the New Deal agenda. A first set included the creation of public banks and investment funds designed to facilitate the restructuring of outstanding mortgage obligations. A second set involved the creation of a series of intermediate organizations, including the Federal National Mortgage Association (Fannie Mae) and the Federal Home Loan Banking System. Together, these institutions would provide the institutional framework for the secondary mortgage market.

Two main ideas motivated the establishment of these organizations. One idea was to create a structure parallel to but outside government that would coordinate economic activity and to that extent displace the market. A second idea was to use the powers of government to create a new market or new markets that would be open to more people on more terms.[8]

These two ideas were in tension. The second conception was in fact more innovative than the first. The trouble was that the innovative market arrangements envisioned by the second idea were realized only within an enclave: the housing and mortgage market. That enclave and the idea for which it stood would first be isolated and later (with the resurgence of primitive financial ideology) undermined.

3. Preventing and Managing Crises

A third key set of institutional innovations would serve to strengthen and extend the existing framework for monetary policy and financial regulation. The New Deal banking reforms included provisions for the reorganization of the central bank (creating a new Board of Governors of the Federal Reserve and centralizing power over monetary policy in that board). They also resulted in the creation of the Federal Depository Insurance Corporation (FDIC), which was set up to administer the new system of deposit insurance and to supervise and stabilize the banking system. It enjoyed the authority to forestall imminent bank insolvencies under the aegis of a new, special-resolution regime.[9]

4. Putting Finance at the Service of the Real Economy

In each of these three different areas, the New Deal reforms gave tangible expression to an idea about finance that seems radical to us today. Then, as now, the reigning orthodoxy assumed that the relation between savings and productive investment took care of itself automatically through the normal working of the financial market and the forces of supply and demand.[10] The New Deal reforms rejected this idea. Their public justification defied it directly. Already in his first inaugural speech Roosevelt promised to drive money changers from the temple. His first-term administration pursued reforms designed to curb speculation, promote fair dealing, and develop the nationwide system of local banks. These banks would channel savings to local communities and promote access to certain forms of consumption vital to economic security and independence (e.g., home ownership).[11]

5. From Regulation to Reorganization

The New Deal's approach to finance culminated in a new system of financial regulation. The system was designed to fulfill two key functions. In the sector of housing and mortgage finance, New Deal financial regulation would help to establish uniform guidelines for the underwriting of residential mortgages and their sale to the secondary market. In the area of thrifts and other depository institutions, newly enacted financial legislation would create the institutional framework for the mobilization of local savings and the channeling of those savings into new forms of commercial and consumer finance.

6. General Observations

Each of the policies and arrangements described in the preceding pages may be viewed from two perspectives. According to the conventional view, we should understand the New Deal reforms as an effort to respond to a series of localized market failures: for example, as a result of oligopoly or asymmetrical information. According to this view, regulation can compensate for these market failures, imposing restraints on their beneficiaries and affording protection to the victims, unless and until they can be overcome. Viewed in light of this perspective, the history of the New Deal reforms is a story of more or less successful regulatory response to market failure.[12]

But there is also a second perspective from which to view the New Deal agenda. According to this second perspective, the New Deal reforms should be understood not merely as an effort to regulate financial markets but also as an attempt to reorganize financial markets in the service of three connected interests: (1) economic security for the individual and home owner (manifest, above all, in the New Deal's social security and mortgage-market programs); (2) financial stability; and (3) tightening of the link between finance and the real economy.[13]

From the standpoint of this second perspective, the New Deal reforms succeeded in some respects but failed in others. They were most successful when they sought to innovate in the institutional organization of the market economy in the service of greater security against certain forms of economic risk (e.g., bank failures) and greater access to certain forms of consumption vital to economic security and independence (e.g., home ownership).

They were less successful in two other areas that have become of paramount importance today. The first of these suppressed interests was the more effective mobilization of long-term savings for long-term productive investment. The second important omission was the failure to pursue innovations in institutional arrangements and public policy capable of broadening access to economic opportunity.

Neither limitation was insurmountable. Indeed, the very logic of mass consumption would eventually imply the need for something more—greater growth with social inclusion as the commanding theme of a reform project. Democratizing the economy on the demand side might have helped set the stage for the more ambitious institutional innovations required to democratize the economy on the supply side.

Such movements, however, failed to take place. Instead, a series of developments in the postwar period derailed the New Deal reforms (see the discussion in the following section). Together with changes in the global economy (including the buildup of trade imbalances and the recycling of reserves from surplus to deficit countries), the reversal of the New Deal reforms opened the way for the return of financial instability and economic insecurity, culminating in the financial crisis of 2007–2009.

A SUMMARY ACCOUNT OF THE CURRENT DEAL

Consider next the transformation of the New Deal framework of finance and its effect on the financial crisis of 2007–2009. I divide this discussion into two parts. The first part describes the specific series of steps involved in the reversal of the New Deal agenda in the closing decades of the twentieth century.[14] The second part describes the U.S.

government's response to the financial crisis—both the emergency initiatives undertaken beginning in the fall of 2008 and the regulatory response to the crisis. At each of these two moments, an inadequate understanding of how finance works under current arrangements and of how we might make it work under alternative arrangements exercised a fateful influence.

Reversal of the New Deal Agenda and the Financial Crisis of 2007–2009

Beginning in 1970s, four convergent trends contributed to the reversal of the New Deal agenda. Two of these trends were structural: they involved a change in the institutional framework of finance. Together, these four developments hollowed out the New Deal agenda.[15] They weakened the connection of finance to the real economy and by so doing paradoxically increased the threat that the former could present to the latter.

1. Weakening of Restrictions on Finance and the Rise of Shadow Banking

The legal framework for the regulation of finance was progressively eviscerated from the 1970s on. This hollowing out took place in two waves.

The first wave was the emergence of financial institutions free from the New Deal restrictions, such as money-market mutual funds, lightly regulated finance companies, and a burgeoning commercial paper market.[16]

The second wave consisted in the rationalization of the system that arose from the emergence of relatively unregulated banks alongside the regulated financial organizations. The rationalization took the form of what was to become the leading regulatory approach to finance in the second half of the twentieth century: regulatory dualism. This approach distinguished between a thinly regulated and a thickly regulated sector of finance.[17]

Examples of the thinly regulated sector under the umbrella of regulatory dualism include (*a*) a new generation of nonbank financial intermediaries (i.e., conduits, special-purpose vehicles, hedge funds, and private-equity firms); (*b*) private-label securitization, increasingly concentrated in complex structured credit and derivative transactions (i.e., collateralized debt obligations and credit default swaps based on pooling and tranching of actual and synthetic exposures); and (*c*) the development of new money and funding markets outside the traditional banking sector (i.e., wholesale certificates of deposit; federal funds; triparty repo; auction-rate securities; and asset-backed commercial paper).

The chief justification of regulatory dualism was an argument about the appropriate and inappropriate contexts for paternalism in financial regulation. Unlike the thickly regulated sector, the thinly regulated sector is populated by financial professionals and high-net-worth individuals who can take care of themselves. The argument from paternalism disregarded a reality that was to play a role in causing the crisis of 2007–2009: financial products and services prohibited in the thickly regulated sector could be repackaged under a different label and practiced in the thinly regulated sector. Regulatory dualism represented a standing invitation to ingenuity at the service of subterfuge.

To the argument from paternalism was added the conviction that trouble in the thinly regulated sector could pose no threat to the essential functions of the thickly regulated one and especially to the soundness of banks or bank-holding companies and the continuity of their payments. Events were to prove otherwise. Nevertheless, to this day, long after the crisis of 2007–2009, regulatory dualism has yet to be unequivocally and comprehensively repudiated as the dominant approach to the regulation of financial activity.

In the years leading up to the financial crisis, excessive risk taking took place on a massive scale, especially in the thinly regulated sector. Regulatory dualism provided the context and the occasion for this massive risk taking by creating the conditions for regulatory arbitrage and the wholesale circumvention of rules.[18]

For students and observers of the financial crisis, the arrangements described earlier are by now easily recognizable. The conventional view interprets these trends as the spontaneous response to increased complexity and sophistication.[19] However, the more closely we observe the actual trajectory of reform, the more clearly we are able to see that what appears at first to be "spontaneous financial innovation" is often, in fact, a product of political choice embodied in law (and conceived against a backdrop of ideas available at the time but subject to an ongoing process of criticism and transformation).[20] Consider, for example, the rise of shadow banking described in the preceding paragraphs. According to the conventional view, both the breakdown of the New Deal framework of financial regulation and the rise of shadow banking from the 1970s on were inevitable, given developments in the U.S. and world economies. With the breakdown of the original Bretton Woods regime and the increasing scale, complexity, and turbulence that came to characterize local and global markets, the effort to subsidize and support local banks by limiting rates and restricting competition was bound to fail.

It would be wrong to conclude from these facts alone that the deterioration of traditional banking was inevitable or that the rise of shadow banking represented the outcome of spontaneous financial innovation, driven by irresistible practical needs. Without government sponsorship and support, neither change would have occurred. For example, the government (in this instance, the Securities and Exchange Commission) collaborated with industry in the development of new savings vehicles outside traditional banking.[21] It allowed, through a process of regulatory forbearance, nonbank financial institutions to form and compete with the banks.[22] Moreover, the regulators encouraged the banks to provide lender-of-last-resort protection to the entire shadow-banking sector (e.g., through the provision of off-balance-sheet letters of credit and other forms of backstop liquidity facilities), thus facilitating simultaneously the rise of one and the fall of the other (together with the hollowing out of the New Deal financial agenda).[23]

Three points emerge from even the most cursory review of these developments. The first point to note is that they represented the relatively accidental outcome of compromises struck under the shadow of the powerful interests of high finance and of a way of thinking deficient in institutional imagination. Neither the relaxation of the New Deal regulatory regime nor the post–New Deal reforms can be plausibly represented as inferences, implications, or requirements of the abstract conception of a market-oriented financial system.

Second, neither the programmatic response as a whole nor the detailed legal and institutional arrangements that it informed amounted to a coherent system. The emerging framework of American finance and financial regulation contained no single doctrine or principle of reform. In each domain of financial policy and regulation, it was easy to imagine a series of alternative small-scale legal and institutional reforms, departing in varying measure from established policies and arrangements.[24]

Third, although these arrangements formed no coherent system, they were decisive in shaping the structure and development of U.S. finance in the decades following the Second World War. We see this effect in the development of the shadow-banking sector. Many of the financial innovations described earlier are unintelligible apart from the specific legal and institutional arrangements adopted in the postwar period.[25]

2. Reorganization of the Federally Sponsored Regime of Mortgage Finance: Government-Sponsored Enterprises and Other Quasi-governmental Organizations

The reorganization of the mortgage market provided an opportunity for the development of shadow banking.[26] Like the development of shadow banking, the transformation of the mortgage market occurred in two stages. The first stage consisted in the restructuring of the federally sponsored mortgage agencies and the introduction of securitization for government-sponsored enterprise (GSE) mortgage pools.[27] The second stage involved the development of "private-label securitization"—that is, a parallel system for the origination, pooling, and securitization of residential mortgages that failed to meet the standards established in the GSE segment of the market (thus, the name "subprime-mortgage market").[28]

Recent critics of securitization have focused on the many different market imperfections and regulatory deficiencies allegedly inherent in securitization. Thus, a series of claims are repeatedly made: for example, that securitization is intrinsically fragile due to problems of moral hazard or asymmetric information or conflict of interest and regulatory capture by privately organized ratings agencies, which provide analysis at program sponsors' behest.[29]

Many of these claims are undoubtedly valid. They nevertheless fail to take into account the very different experiences of securitization in the two different historical situations and the very great influence of radically contrasting legal and institutional practices and arrangements.[30]

There was no reason why the new markets in credit-risk transfer had to develop in this manner. After all, the banks responsible for the vast majority of these trades were legally permitted to participate in the securitization and derivatives markets as part of their ordinary banking activities. Yet the emerging legal and regulatory regime created both the opportunity and the incentives to develop these markets in the shadow-banking sector. Only over time would the country come to realize the consequences of this shift and the effect it would have throughout the financial system.[31]

3. Decline of Traditional Bank-Based Financial Intermediation

Two main consequences flowed from these developments. The first was the decline in traditional, bank-based financial intermediation. From the 1980s on, the business model of the leading U.S. commercial banks would change. Buffeted by the tendencies described earlier (e.g., mortgage securitization, loss of deposits to money-market mutual funds, loss of the primary corporate customer base to the commercial paper market), U.S. banks would increasingly adopt their European competitors' business model: increasing emphasis on proprietary trading and position taking in derivatives and securities markets; origination and securitization of mortgages and other standardized financial assets; and the provision of liquidity and risk-management tools to players in the shadow market.[32]

4. Increasing Importance of Capital Markets in the Intermediation of Credit and in Financial-Market Activity More Generally in the United States

The counterpart to the decline of traditional, bank-based financial intermediation was an increase in the role of capital markets in the intermediation of credit and in financial-market activity more generally in the United States. As the new markets and arrangements took hold, the capital markets would become the leading sector of finance, outpacing and displacing the banks that once served as the heart of the mortgage market.[33]

5. General Observations

For theorists of comparative finance, this move from "banking" to "capital markets" has often been seen as part of a natural evolutionary tendency, in which institutions (or firms, in the sense of the theory of the firm in economics) are increasingly replaced by ever more perfect markets.[34] As a descriptive matter, it was certainly true that many of the traditional loans and financial instruments formerly originated and held by banks would—in the United States—be transferred to the money and capital markets. However, the idea that markets were replacing banks and through this replacement contributing to a process of socially optimal risk diffusion was wrong in several respects.

First, there is no reason to believe that the new forms of finance were more rather than less conducive to more economic growth and improved productivity than the ones they replaced. The financial deepening associated with the trends described earlier should not be understood as the sign of a more efficient allocation of resources to opportunities in the real economy. Instead, the pull of savings into profit-making opportunities provided by speculative financial transactions has been increasingly unrelated to real economic activity.[35]

Second, it is commonly understood that proprietary trading and other forms of capital market activity are inherently risky. In the context of the new shadow market, however, the riskiness of speculative trading increased in several respects. Speculative trading in the shadow market existed beyond the "safety and soundness" provisions provided in the official banking sector.[36] As many have pointed out, the funding for the financial trading activities relied on short-term borrowing in wholesale markets. Moreover, the trading was increasingly fueled by an enormous expansion in credit (i.e., leverage) made available to the financial sector.[37]

Two further features of the institutional setting aggravated systemic risk. For one thing, the entire system of shadow banking was ultimately backstopped by the official banking sector.[38] For another thing, the official banking sector (i.e., the traditional, insured depository institutions, including commercial banks) was entirely dependent on governmental guarantees, whether in the form of explicit, lender-of-last-resort facilities or by the existence of an implicit guarantee, provided on the grounds of "too big to fail."[39]

These misunderstandings and indirections helped create the conditions for the crisis of 2007–2009. If the schematic account presented in the previous pages is correct, we cannot adequately understand the causes of this crisis or its implications for reform today in the language of spontaneous adjustments to market forces. The explanation of the crisis must instead allow a prominent place to the four tendencies described earlier. Together they resulted in a hollowing out of the

New Deal framework of arrangements for the governance of finance, all in the service increasingly of speculative finance disconnected from the agenda of production in the economy.

The U.S. Government's Response to the Financial Crisis of 2007–2009: The Current Deal

In these circumstances, there at least two ways of responding to a financial crisis such as the one that the United States and other rich North Atlantic countries underwent at the end of the first decade of the twenty-first century. One approach recognizes no institutional alternatives in the organization of a market regime or in the way of governing the relation of finance to the real economy. All it recognizes are localized failures of competition (including failures of equal access to information) in the capital markets and localized failures in the regulatory response to these localized market failures. Consequently, it sees financial crisis only as an interruption of economic growth.

The champions of this first approach want to get back to business as usual by redressing what they believe to be the localized flaws in competition and regulation. These flaws accentuate, according to this view, the inherent instability of finance: the ease with which liquid capital, by virtue of its very liquidity, suffers the effect of waves of euphoria and despondency, greed and fear. The point is to contain the effects of this inherent instability by improving both competition and regulation.[40]

At the hour of crisis, the concerns of this approach were the rescue or turnaround of failed or failing financial firms, the disposal of their "toxic assets," the re-regulation of finance, and the adoption of expansionary monetary and fiscal policy. This approach fails to recognize in crisis an opportunity for institutional reconstruction because it lacks the imagination of institutional alternatives.

We can think of the second, alternative approach as beginning where the New Deal stopped. It would preserve and extend the emphasis on structural reform, innovate in arrangements designed to mobilize long-term saving for long-term productive investment, and develop practices and institutions useful to the enhancement of the productive capabilities of the nation rather than to the interests of high finance. I call this approach "institutional reconstruction."[41]

The effort to imagine and create new financial markets would inevitably prove contentious and provoke political and economic opposition as well as ideological debate. Yet only by confronting the inherent difficulties and risks of economic and financial experimentation can the country have any chance to mark out a different path, using crisis to deepen the connection of finance to production and to broaden access to productive resources and opportunities.

In response to the crisis of 2007–2009, the U.S. government followed the rescue-and-regulation approach, as did its European and Japanese counterparts. It wasted the transformative opportunity presented by the crisis, treating it a shadow that it desired to see pass rather than as a provocation to do by different means what Americans had done in the early nineteenth century, when they used the creation of a network of local banks and the extinction of the national bank to enlist finance more effectively in the service of production and to democratize economic opportunity.

Under the heading "Current Deal," table 1.1 summarizes the way that the government responded to the crisis. The response had five parts.

1. Bailout: Minor Innovations Undertaken to Avoid Major Ones

The government acted to rescue a number of large failing financial organizations, after having allowed one (Lehman Brothers) to fail. The federal government executed these bailouts without acquiring a decisive stake within the leading financial institutions or forcing a fundamental change in the way they do business. At the same time, small banks were allowed to fail. Moreover, the administration did little to enhance the capabilities of the nationwide network of small local banks even though these banks represent the country's most distinctive asset in the organization of finance.[42]

Defenders of the government's program of financial rescue and regulation have argued that these initiatives, however distasteful, were required by the extraordinary conditions that existed at the time and that the only goals of public intervention were stabilization and restoration of the self-regulating market system. However, it is not true that the government enjoyed no margin to develop alternatives or that it acted under intractable constraint.

In fact, its policy was in many respects a bold and surprising response to the crisis, albeit bereft of any interest in alternatives designed to make finance more useful to production or to democratize economic opportunity. The problem was not that the government had no room for maneuver but that it used what room it had to rescue some of the country's largest financial firms with little discussion or debate beforehand about the terms of the rescue package or about whether other segments of the financial sector might be more deserving of financial support.

Many creative policy tools were deployed in this effort. These tools included capital injections, debt buybacks, subsidies, and loan guaranties provided by the Treasury, the Federal Reserve, and the FDIC.[43]

2. GSEs and Other Intermediate Organizations

During the crisis, the government's handling of the GSEs created by the New Deal resembled in many ways its treatment of the banking sector. The GSEs were placed into receivership in September 2008, without, however, undergoing any fundamental reversal of the post–New Deal developments that had rendered them—together with the entire secondary mortgage market—subservient to speculative finance.

The administration took the same approach in the area of housing and foreclosure. It launched a number of antiforeclosure initiatives in an effort to keep people in their homes, without, however, calling into question the prevailing arrangements in the mortgage market. It took no initiative that would do for home owners anything comparable to what it had done for big banks in the generosity of rescue.[44]

In the wake of the financial crisis, the housing GSEs became again a subject of heated debate. In this debate, public officials as well as academic experts staked out many different positions. Some insisted on the total elimination or liquidation of government-sponsored financial institutions, whether in the area of housing or in any other area. At least some in the administration recognized the worth of quasi-governmental organizations in the context of the financial crisis.[45] Yet without a more vibrant discourse about alternative institutional possibilities, an effort to preserve and promote the GSEs as agents of financial deepening and democratization could gain no influence.

3. Preventing and Managing Crisis

Among all the initiatives undertaken by the government in the wake of the financial breakdown, none was as bold or imaginative as the Federal Reserve's efforts to arrest the crisis. Acting under the aegis of its new program of "quantitative easing," the Fed innovated and acted on a heroic scale to prevent the collapse of money and credit.[46]

Yet when all is said and done, there is a problem even here. In the design and development of these many programs—especially the program of quantitative easing—the government (and, more specifically, the central bank) acted as boldly and as imaginatively as any U.S. government has in the past thirty years with regard to the governance of finance. Yet that same boldness and ingenuity could have been put to other uses, with a better chance to support socially inclusive growth and to deepen the linkage of finance to the real economy.

The fundamental problem with the policy of maintaining a low interest rate is that in the years after the crisis it became increasingly what it could not be: a surrogate for a strategy of economic growth. It was useful as a preliminary to such a strategy. The most effective way to diminish the vulnerability of the economy to future financial crisis would be to deepen and democratize finance. A major thesis of this book is that democratizing finance—making it part of a strategy of socially inclusive economic growth—can begin in deepening finance—tightening its links to the real economy rather than allowing it to use the real economy's transactions as a pretext for successive layers of financial trading and speculation (as discussed later in this chapter).

An additional flaw of the easy-money policy is that the Federal Reserve tried to make money cheap without paying adequate attention to the supply of credit. The central bank was so determined to keep interest rates low that it did what it could to make long-term rates low as well in the hope that they would help lower short-term rates. The flattening of the yield curve—that is to say, of the relation between long-term rates and short-term rates—undermined the supply of credit in an economy in which both firms and households were attempting to deleverage and restore their balance sheets. The result was that several years after the crisis the aggregate level of credit in the economy remained lower than what it had been at the lowest point of earlier recessions.

4. Putting Finance at the Service of the Real Economy

Almost nothing was done or even conceived to move forward along the spectrum from the re-regulation of finance to the reshaping of the relation between finance and the real economy. The few apparent exceptions confirm the rule.

Help for small business—the most important part of the economy with regard to jobs, output, and potential—was modest.[47] Above all, such help was designed solely with a view to the recovery of economic activity as part of the fiscal stimulus. No thought was given to ways in which pre-Fordist forms of production can, with governmental support, be brought closer to the front line of post-Fordist forms of flexible and innovative production. Such an effort would require a fundamental reinvention of industrial policy, not as a practice of "picking winners" but rather as a practice of propagating successful local experiments and, above of all, of opening up access to credit, technology, knowledge, and advanced practice.[48]

The country's most important financial asset—its unparalleled network of local banks, an inheritance of the nineteenth century—has largely been abandoned, despite occasional and modest gestures to narrow interests, while the government chose to focus its attention and its favors on a handful of gigantic financial firms. The discourse of "systemic risk" encouraged the administration in this perverse selectivity.

The short-sightedness of this policy was astonishing when we consider the importance of the country's local and regional banks to the larger project of economic recovery and revitalization. It is widely recognized that the United States confronts today two simultaneous tasks in economic and industrial reconstruction. The first task is to accelerate and broaden the movement beyond traditional forms of mass production. The second task is to move from a world of undercapitalized rearguard small and medium-size businesses to a world of frontline innovators. Yet no such passage is possible without the experimental reconstruction of our system of finance, including that part of the financial system that has largely been abandoned in recent years. Third-party funding of enterprise and innovation remains woefully inadequate in the country as a whole. Enhancing the capabilities of the nation's community and regional banks, whether alone or in partnership with public and private venture-capital funds, provides a point of departure for the more general reorientation we need to foster throughout the financial system.[49]

5. From Regulation to Reorganization: Regulation as an Alternative to Reorganization

Consider, finally, the fifth and final element of the analytical framework developed here: the government's approach to financial regulation and the view of the alternative futures of finance that is revealed by its regulatory strategy. Among all the many policies launched by the U.S. government in response to the financial crisis, it is here in the domain of financial regulatory reform that the government's orientation became explicit. Four main projects composed the U.S. approach to financial regulation.[50]

The first project (embodied in the Volcker proposals) was to reestablish a limited version of the New Deal–era separation of financial organizations that do proprietary trading from financial firms that take governmentally insured deposits.

The second project was to create an enhanced supervisory and resolution authority (that is to say, authority to liquidate failed or failing financial institutions) applicable to all financial institutions, not just to bank-holding companies. The point was to put fires out, even before they start. However, I argue here that the most reliable safeguard against these financial fires would be financial deepening, in particular through the enhancement of the capabilities of the resources of local banks. No interest was taken in such an enhancement.

The third project was to establish more stringent requirements of capital adequacy, more restrictive limitations on leverage, and a renewed appreciation for liquidity management. This project was inspired by concerns of the international financial technocracy, as represented by, among other organizations, the Bank of International Settlements in Basel. We might call it the "Basel agenda."

The fourth project was to protect consumers of financial services. Its signal achievement was the Consumer Financial Protection Agency Act of 2009.

These four projects, taken together, fell short of the challenge and the opportunity presented by the crisis of 2007–2009. They did not take up the tasks of institutional innovation that I have explored up to now in this chapter. They failed to repudiate regulatory dualism and to replace it by a unified regulation of finance. They did not progress in the work of tightening the link between finance and the real economy so that more of the long-term saving of society could be channeled into long-term productive investment and less of it squandered in financial trading unrelated to the expansion of output or the improvement of productivity. They never began to design and implement institutional innovations useful to the organization of socially inclusive economic growth. They neglected that larger work in a circumstance in which the United States could no longer rely on its earlier dominance in industry and finance to maintain a leading position in global markets.

6. General Observations

Notice how extraordinarily limited the approach taken by the government in the wake of the crisis of 2007–2009 was. The administration defended its policy as the contemporary equivalent of the New Deal financial reforms. Many of the policies and arrangements pursued by the United States and other countries indeed resembled, in scale and scope, governmental initiatives of the 1930s.

However, the response of the U.S. government to the crisis pales in comparison to the way in which the New Deal responded to the Great Depression, even when we take into account the larger scale of the slump of the 1930s and the immense flaws and limitations of Roosevelt's program for financial and economic reform. In each major policy area, the government's recent approach was less a return to the New Deal agenda than a step backward into the earlier world of pre-Keynesian finance.

The basic ideas animating this step backward are easy to state: Markets are self-correcting when they work properly, without restraints on competition. It is the responsibility of regulation to correct localized market failures. Talk of structural flaws and alternatives is empty or misguided and in any case unrealistic and dangerous. Once governments and central banks work in concert to correct the excesses of finance and to compensate for failures of competition and asymmetries of information, the capital markets will return to equilibrium, automatic adjustment, and self-regulation.

These ideas are mistaken on the view for which I argue in this book. Their main function, however, was not to guide policy. It was to exorcise any consideration of institutional alternatives. The initiatives pursued by the government bore little or no relation to such alternatives and were inadequate, but not for the same reasons or in the same way.

The exorcizing ideas fail to explain or describe the governmental response to the initial crisis (i.e., the package of emergency measures introduced beginning in the summer of 2007 and continuing through the fall of 2008). They also fail to make sense of the administration's subsequent efforts to develop a new regulatory framework, allegedly calculated to instill market discipline through what came to be called macroprudential regulation.

Nor did the banks (especially the largest financial houses) and the capital markets generally respond according to plan in the period following the rescue-and-regulate operation. Little new lending took place as a result of governmental largesse. Similarly, little reorientation of financial markets occurred as a result of the efforts by central bankers, governmental officials, and taxpayers to bail out a financial order that remained largely disconnected from the production system it was meant to serve.[51]

As the government prepared and eventually passed its program of financial regulatory reform, the view began to circulate among policy makers and practitioners that the crisis was over and that the capital markets had returned to normal. Yet the continuing shortage of enterprise credit and the general weakness in employment and growth continued to trouble the authorities. The gap between the government's vision of financial regulation and the structural change required to implement a program of structural reform began to become clear in the process of implementing the new legislation.

For example, the Wall Street Reform and Consumer Protection Act of 2010 (otherwise known as the Dodd–Frank Act) created the Financial Stability Oversight Council (FSOC) to design and implement measures for the prevention of systemic risk. But whether the supervisory powers entrusted to the FSOC would be enough to prevent the next great financial panic remained an open question. The same was true of the new resolution regime designed to bring market discipline to shadow banking. There were too many unknown variables to create confidence in the procedures adopted, however excellent their execution. [52]

For the government, elaboration of the measures required to create an effective "macroprudential" framework could be safely entrusted to administrative rule making. However, the choices made in the rule-making process were no more or less consequential than the ones that had served to inspire the initial project of regulatory reform. There was no evidence that the government's regulatory approach and its non-structural reform agendas had made finance either less likely to cause harm to the real economy in bad times or more useful to production.

To be sure, any change in the institutional setting of finance, especially in the context of crisis, would lead in the short term to even more trouble in financial markets. The consequence of refusing to accept heightened conflict and controversy was to leave unchanged the arrangements under which finance had become at once bloated, unmoored from the real economy, and all the more dangerous to real economic activity because less engaged in the financing of production and innovation.

There was no single path forward. Each strategy of development and project of reform required governmental initiative and collective choice. To use crisis as an occasion for structural change has a price. The price is more—not less—disruption in the short term: the dismantlement of ideas and arrangements that have dominated debate and practice in the United States and other countries for the past several decades.

A RUDIMENTARY PROPOSAL OF A BETTER DEAL

I now sketch an alternative direction for reform. The goal of this alternative is not to return to the New Deal agenda. It is to address the work that the New Deal left undone and even unformulated. To do so, however, we cannot remain within the intellectual limits of the "first conversation"—about localized market failures. We need to undertake the second conversation—about the institutional reorganization of the arrangements governing the relation between finance and the real economy. The tools we require lie largely in the area of law and legal thought.

Two main premises underlie the approach. The first premise is descriptive: under present arrangements, finance has turned in upon itself. Giving credit to producers and consumers has been secondary to financial trading by and among highly leveraged financial institutions. It is to this circumstance that I apply the label *financial hypertrophy* in contrast to *financial deepening*: finance has become bloated in the proportion of talent and profit that it absorbs even as its service to the funding of production has diminished.

The second premise is programmatic: we have no reason to accept the circumstance that I have described. This circumstance wastes the potential of finance to contribute to economic growth. It reinforces the tendencies that make such growth in the United States and in other advanced contemporary economies less rather than more inclusive. It sets finance in a direction that turns it into a threat to democracy: a concentration of money detached from production but anxious to influence the exercise of political power. Institutional arrangements made this finance what it is. Institutional innovations can change.

Outline of a Better Deal: A Proposal for the Reorganization of Finance and Its Relation to the Real Economy

1. Reorganization of the Banking System: Creating a System of Entrepreneurial Finance Rooted in Community and Regional Banking

A historical strength of the U.S. financial system has been its unrivaled network of local banks. Local banking helped promote development in the nineteenth and twentieth centuries by putting savings at the disposal of producers as well as consumers in every region and every state.[53]

The network of local banks is commonly criticized as incompatible with requirements of scale and sophistication. According to this view, the United States needs to follow the path of "universal" large-scale banks. This prejudice is groundless.[54] With the right institutional innovations, the network of local and regional banks can be revived. It can be made useful to the cause of socially inclusive economic growth by gaining access to the instruments, ideas, and opportunities created in the vanguard of financial practice and required today to participate actively in the opportunities offered by innovative forms of production in both national and global markets. The aim is to combine decentralization, flexibility, and proximity to the local producer with scale and sophistication.

Consider three forms of finance capable of achieving scale and sophistication. The first is public venture capital: the extension of long-term investment in new and emergent businesses, whether in vanguard or rearguard sectors of production. The second is finance as an instrument for the turnaround and restructuring of troubled firms or firms whose potential remains suppressed. The third is the development and application of new risk-management tools, including derivatives and structured credits.

As part of this initiative, the government would work with local banks through new GSEs. It would help these banks develop new forms of venture capital, enterprise restructuring, and risk management, broadly conceived.

That such an enhancement of the nation's local-bank legacy holds promise is suggested by many historical experiences. State-level governments encouraged the development of local banks and the development of the physical infrastructure of the country by awarding corporate charters, organizing local securities markets, and raising capital on international markets to fund railroads and canals.[55] In the early twentieth century, government collaborated with farmers and manufacturers to stabilize and expand production through the creation of novel financial practices and vehicles: for example, installment loans and agricultural cooperatives.[56]

In our own day, the forms of finance required to expand opportunity and innovation in different regions of the national economy are likely to be very different. The challenge of economic organization and development today is less a matter of gaining access (although this part of the financial package remains important) than of enjoying the conditions to master practices and opportunities at the frontiers of finance and production. In this process, collaboration and strategic coordination between outsiders (i.e., local producers and banks) and insiders (firms and financial institutions in the vanguard of finance) are likely to be crucial. The purpose of the GSEs (considered at greater length later in this chapter) is to create the social context in which new practices and arrangements can flourish beyond their established domain(s).

Such an initiative would retake the enduring achievement of finance-related innovations in the two periods of greatest innovation in U.S. history. American economic development and organization in the first half of the nineteenth century could not have achieved its uniquely decentralized form without the prior and simultaneous development of a national monetary and financial system by the federal government. It was a regime that made possible the flow of money, credit, and banking from one end of the country to the other.[57]

The rise of big business and mass-production industry at the end of the nineteenth century occurred in tandem with the rise of the large New York merchant banks. These banks used instruments of private law—notably trusts—to organize large-scale business. The marriage of high finance and big business was in turn disciplined and shaped by the development of a legal and regulatory framework that began with the regulation of interstate commerce and with the antitrust laws.

We are accustomed to think of this framework as a check on big business and on its partnership with high finance in the spirit of the second American tradition of progressive reform: the tradition exemplified by the progressivism of the early twentieth century and the policies of the first President Roosevelt. It operated, however, as much more than a check. It was an enabler. It established ground rules without which American finance could not perform its organizing role in this historical moment. Without those ground rules, the organization of industries and railroads by the banks through the trust device would have degenerated into a free-for-all: a contest in which the weakening of competition by oligopoly, the subordination of political power to the moneyed interests, and the further strengthening of the bankers' hand would have threatened economic growth. It would have put American democracy yet further under the shadow of finance capital. It might also have weakened the contribution that the big banks did make to the real economy, despite industrial and financial concentration.[58] What was only a counterfactual possibility at the end of the nineteenth century became a dangerous reality at the end of the twentieth.

I discussed earlier how New Deal innovations in the regulation of finance and in the organization of the mortgage market promoted financial deepening while enlisting finance in a limited but real democratization of economic opportunity. Today the task is to reinvent and generalize what the New Deal did for American finance in the relatively narrow areas in which it took action. Such a reinvention and generalization would place advanced techniques of capital allocation and risk management at the disposal of small and medium-size businesses across the country. It would develop the financial element in the program of disseminating and supporting knowledge-intensive experimentalist production in socially inclusive form. In the absence of such a project, the most advanced contemporary practice of production remains confined to relatively insular productive vanguards that exclude the vast majority of the labor force. The consequences are a magnification of the forces aggravating inequality and the diminishment of the country's chance to retake high-productivity economic growth.

2. Reinvention of the GSEs

In this task of tapping into the opportunity-broadening and capability-enhancing potential of local banks, new forms of strategic coordination between government and firms may play a crucial part. They should be market creating rather than market suppressing. They should be pluralistic, participatory, and experimental.[59]

The purpose of strategic coordination is to create the context for socially inclusive growth and reform, with finance at the very center. The idea would be to create both the agents and the instruments of "financial best practice," capable of reconciling the twin goals of localism with scale and sophistication.

Two main premises underlie this part of the proposal.

The first premise is that, contrary to the common view, these problems cannot be solved spontaneously by delegating the tasks to existing capital markets. They require a new cast of financial agents. The purpose of this premise is to imagine who these agents might be, what tasks they might perform, and under which specific policies and arrangements.

The second premise is that the government can—and should—act as a catalyst in the design and development of these agents. The reason why is very simple: only the government has the capacity, authority, and resources needed to help spearhead the development of the new intermediate organizations.

A reinvented GSE (as described more fully in chapter 2) would serve as the vehicle for the new form of decentralized strategic coordination. The purpose of the GSE would be to enhance the capabilities and the access of the network of local banks. It would do so in one way by creating a context for the pooling and diffusion of risk from many small or medium-size firms. It would do so in another way by facilitating the formation of syndicates of banks and facilitating the syndicates' access to sophisticated forms of finance and risk management. It would do so in yet a third way by participating either directly or indirectly in the design and development of new forms of finance or new forms of collaboration between local firms, financial institutions, and agents from the world of high finance.

Consider an example that is useful because it is simple, in the domain not of industry but of agriculture, especially relatively small or family-scale agriculture, which faces a combination of physical risk (climate volatility) and economic risk (price volatility). When family-scale agriculture lacks the means to face this superimposition of risks, it typically stumbles. The traditional devices for facing this combination of risks have been price supports (outright agricultural subsidies), guaranteed purchases of output, and countercyclical food stockpiles, managed by the government.

These devices have been replaced, both in the United States and in other countries, by financial engineering: financial products and services that enable the farmer to hedge risks. This was the original motivation behind the development of commodity futures and future exchanges. It represents the legitimate use of financial derivatives, which, perverted in their application, have formed part of the immediate background of the present crisis.[60] The problem is that such sophisticated services and products are often readily accessible only to the largest producers—for example, multinational firms and commodity producers.

The task of adapting such financial products and services to the needs and capabilities of a broader range of firms is one that is likely to be accomplished in an American setting by local banks, supported as well as monitored by government entities or by entities designed and developed with the help of quasi-governmental organizations: bodies intermediate between the state and the firms such as the government-sponsored organizations created by the New Deal. The more we ensure that local banks are professionally staffed and subject to market discipline, the more likely it is that they will be able to perform this role effectively.

3. Preventing and Managing Crisis: Beyond Regulatory Dualism

The preliminary aims of reform are to separate proprietary trading from governmentally insured deposit taking; to establish in the federal government stronger authority both to supervise and to liquidate financial firms; to impose stronger restraints on leverage and more demanding standards of capital adequacy; and to protect consumers more effectively through the work of an agency designed for this purpose. These defining aims of the reform project now before us are useful and even indispensable. However, they are also insufficient, even in the pursuit of the narrow goal of preventing a major financial crisis and of mitigating its effects when it occurs. These initiatives must be supplemented by three other sets of innovations.

The first set of innovations involves the decisive repudiation of regulatory dualism, the approach to the regulation of finance that has emerged, with increasing clarity, in the United States and elsewhere in the past several decades. The contrast between a thinly regulated sector and a thickly regulated sector has enabled large-scale subversion and circumvention of the regulation of finance, even as the rules themselves have been eviscerated.[61]

The second series of measures would be a set of regulatory and tax changes designed to discourage the uncoupling of finance from the underlying transactions of the real economy. The subprime-mortgage crisis provides an example of what is at stake, of what must be avoided, and of what is needed. As the subprime-mortgage market expanded exponentially, it became increasingly clear that the market had turned into an instrument of the financial system rather than of the households, firms, and communities that the market is supposed to serve. The layering of complex derivative securities on top of the underlying pool of (dubious) assets only made matters worse. Yet neither the monetary nor the regulatory authorities had the appropriate tools—practical or conceptual—to curb the growth of credit (beyond the banking system) or the resulting asset boom.[62]

It is easy to imagine any number of practical solutions to the problem of "overinvestment" described here. To begin with, the government could have imposed a series of outright prohibitions of financial instruments permissible in the mortgage market. Teaser loans, with interest-rate resets above a certain level, provided an easy target. So do loans with inadequate up-front collateral and nonamortizing principle repayments.

The third series of initiatives would consist of regulatory and tax changes designed to encourage the connection between finance and the real economy. Once again it is important to emphasize that the problem is not speculative trading per se but the separation of speculative trading from the real economy. An example of the latter is the development of collateralized debt obligations (CDOs), designed to enable side bets on already existing pools of derivatives and securities. Examples of the former include commodity futures and other risk-management tools, traded on public exchanges by producers and trading companies involved in the real business of commodity production and exchange.

Speculative trading is useful and legitimate insofar as it helps to generate information and organize entrepreneurial risk taking. It should, however, be discouraged by the tax laws or prohibited by the securities regulations when it makes no plausible contribution to the real economy—that is, to the expansion of output or the enhancement of production, Once again, the evil to avoid or to redress is the unmooring of finance from the real economy. We misdirect the argument when we mistake it for a blanket condemnation of speculative finance and disregard what should be the true target of concern: the substitution of financial hypertrophy for financial deepening.

4. Putting Finance at the Service of the Real Economy: From the Regulation of Finance to the Reorganization of Its Relation to the Agenda of Production

The central assumption of my argument is that, contrary to much conventional thinking, the relation between finance and the real economy or between saving and the funding of production is not a constant, much less tautological identity. It is a variable: it is susceptible to institutional variation in light of the institutional arrangements that govern the relation of finance to the real economy. Such arrangements may either tighten or loosen the link between them. The looser the link, the greater the dangers that the accumulated saving of society will be squandered in speculative financial transactions, unrelated to the requirements of production and consumption, and that the excesses of speculation will help ignite periodic financial crisis.

Three different series of initiatives would be most useful here. A first initiative involves doing the work of venture capital far more broadly and deeply than it is now done. That might require new institutional vehicles, such as GSEs designed to work with local banks. Such an initiative might also include targeted credit and credit enhancements as parts of a broader effort to support economic and financial recovery in the regions most battered by the recent (or future) crisis. It might rely as well on a publicly sponsored venture-capital fund. Such a fund would complement the halting attempts that both the Treasury and the Federal Reserve have made to restore short-term funding mechanisms for the benefit of small and medium-size businesses.

A second initiative consists in a modified practice of restructuring. Restructuring in the narrow sense arises today in the context of discussions over expanding the government's "resolution authority." Restructuring may also be defined in a second and larger sense as turnaround of nonfinancial firms in the real economy. Finance has a vital role to play in the organization of turnaround—one of the most important contributions that finance can make to the real economy. Turnaround for both financial and nonfinancial firms should be designed in ways that meet both a substantive and a procedural test.

The substantive test is to take account of a firm's past or potential contribution to productive activity in the real economy. For financial firms, the emphasis has been on systemic connections to other financial organizations. It is a criterion to be viewed and used with caution when the whole financial system has a tenuous, oblique, or episodic connection to production. It should be qualified by the judgment of use to real economic activity: the denser a financial firm's engagement with funding of production or consumption, the more reason (other things being equal) to try to save the firm and turn it around.

The procedural test in making such a judgment is to rely on the tacit knowledge of those who have close acquaintance with the operation of the business in question or with the context in which it operates: individual and corporate clients, managers of other firms in the sector, local communities, local governments, experts, as well as the staff of the failing firm itself. A centralized bureaucracy in the Treasury Department, acting alone, is likely to overstate the significance of the systemic connections ("too big to fail") and to understate the importance of function or of the lack of it in the real economy.

The existing arrangements of resolution, bailout, and bankruptcy fail these substantive and procedural tests. To the concern with minimizing both taxpayer cost and moral hazard, we should add the focus on engagement with the real economy. And to the institutional apparatus of bankruptcy courts and governmental authorities charged with the responsibility of resolution and liquidation, we should add consultative boards possessing tacit knowledge of economic reality and potential.

The laws should be revised to give such boards an official role as consultants to both the bankruptcy judges and the resolution officials.

Although the immediate topic of concern here is the failure of financial firms, the same regime would in principle apply as well to the failure of nonfinancial firms. Concern for actual or potential function in the real economy should be decisive in the former instance as well as in the latter. In both, the stakeholders in the sector of the economy and in the part of the country where their lives and fortunes may be touched by a firm's failure should gain a voice and a role in the work of restructuring.

A third set of initiatives involves the adaptation and extension of the sophisticated risk-management tools developed by contemporary finance—such as varieties of financial hedging—to smaller firms in local or regional economies in the country. These tools would need to be redesigned for this purpose. They might well have to be pooled, as mortgages were in the secondary mortgage market, to achieve greater efficiency and cost reduction through economies of scale.

Such innovations would further exploit the ingenuity and inventiveness of high finance in the interests of emerging production. It would combine the emphasis on accountability and security characteristic of the New Deal financial reforms with the focus on experimental decentralization and localism—placing finance at the service of the local producer—characteristic of the reforms of the Jacksonian and post-Jacksonian periods in U.S. history.

5. The Reform of Finance as Part of the Organization of Socially Inclusive Economic Growth

Finance, I argue throughout this book, has become a bad master rather than the good servant that it can be. The New Deal reformers understood that they could not achieve their goal of ensuring economic security as a basis for broader economic opportunity without reforming finance. Security through financial reform came with deposit insurance and then with home ownership made possible by the reorganization of the mortgage market. The New Dealers' reform of finance bore the mark of the limitations of their general project (discussed in chapter 5). However, they recognized what their successors in politics and in thought have failed to appreciate: that regulation and redistribution are no substitute for structural change, understood as innovation in the

TABLE 1.1

Three Projects for the Reorganization of Finance and Its Relation to the Real Economy (Especially in the Context of Crisis): New Deal, Current Deal, Better Deal

	Basic Institutional Framework	Extending the Institutional Framework: quasi-governmental organizations	Preventing and Managing Crisis	Putting Finance at the Service of the Real Economy	Finance in Its Broader Setting
New Deal	Strict separation between commercial and investment banking; utility banks; disclosure regime; state polices boundary conditions (domestic and global markets)	Creation of public banks and investment funds; secondary mortgage market; GSEs; Federal Housing Administration; provision of liquidity and insurance facilities for mortgage and banking system	Registered Financial Corporations, Home Owners' Loan Corporation, expansion of government emergency powers; strengthening of Federal Reserve (new instruments of monetary policy and lender of last resort); new regulatory regime and depository insurance (FDIC and special bank resolution regime)	Use of federal agencies and GSEs to create new financial markets; use of tax, legal, regulatory tools to improve functioning of private credit markets	Experiments in new forms of government-business relations, followed by acceptance of established form of the market economy, with greater economic security for the individual
Reversal of New Deal agenda	Relaxation of restrictions on finance; rise of shadow banking;	Privatization of GSEs and secondary mortgage market (securitization);	Resolution Trust Corporation and regulatory forbearance (savings-and-loan crisis);	Reorganization of GSEs; deregulation of the banking system; creation of	Emergence of shadow banking, institutionalized and generalized through

	creation of links between formal and shadow banking as well as between local and global markets	delegation of power to rating agencies, industry groups, international banks, and broker-dealers via emphasis on internal risk management	consolidation and extension of regulatory framework; extension of lender of last resort to shadow banking	new channels connecting official banks to shadow-banking sector	regulatory dualism; move from institutions to markets
Current deal	Bailout of big banks and systemically important nonbanks; little banks allowed to fail	Reorganization and capitalization of GSEs; creation of new special-purpose funding and liquidity facilities through the Fed and the FDIC	Bailouts, nationalizations, debt buybacks and guarantees; swap lines, new liquidity facilities, expansion of the liquidity/illiquidity ratio, and access to the discount window	Creation of funding and liquidity facilities by the Treasury, the Fed, and the FDIC; Term Asset-Backed Securities Loan Facility; targeted credit through GSEs	Regulation as an alternative to reorganization
Better deal	Rejection of regulatory dualism; reorganization of big banks, little banks, and nonbanks and their relation to the real economy	Public–private partnerships, agents of restructuring and innovation, linking the global and the local, the big and the little, sophisticated and local finance	Reintroduction of limits on financial speculation; breakup of big banks without a purpose; temporary and contingent controls on capital; restructuring as experimental reinvention	Reinvention of GSEs as agents of strategic coordination and decentralized access to venture capital; tools of risk management; experimental restructuring; participation in global markets	Regulation as a first step toward reorganization; finance reconnected with the real economy and made subservient to the institutional agenda of socially inclusive growth

legal and institutional framework of the market. It falls to us to take up that task again and bring it to a different end.

The techniques that I have discussed in this section—the reinvention of venture capital in public or quasi-governmental as well as private firms (but with managerial independence and market competition), enterprise turnaround and restructuring, the development and application of new risk-management tools—can contribute to financial deepening. They can help enlist finance more effectively in the service of production and economic innovation. These goals define the minimalist justification of the approach and the reforms I have outlined here.

The maximalist justification is that the approach and reforms can form part of a larger project of organizing socially inclusive economic growth: the objective most widely professed by governments and reformers in the world today. A driving and defining commitment of that project is the distribution of opportunity and capability within the real economy. The United States can no longer rely on its earlier preeminence in manufacturing and finance to sustain its place in the world economy. To enhance productivity and accelerate economic growth on a broad base across sectors, regions, and classes, it must disseminate the practices of advanced, knowledge-intensive production widely throughout the economy, extending access to capital as well as to advanced technology and practice.

In chapters 3, 4, and 5, I sketch the elements of such a program. Its working assumption is what the major traditions of progressive reform in American history deny: that we can do more than use compensatory redistribution through progressive taxation and social entitlements to diminish the inequalities generated by the market as it is now organized. We can reimagine and remake the market economy.

CHAPTER TWO

The Past and Future of Financial Reform

From Regulation to Reorganization

ONCE WE SEE our narrow present debates about finance and democracy in broader historical context, we can begin to define a better direction: one that holds the promise of turning finance into a friend of both production and democracy. It is never enough to regulate finance. Every way of regulating finance presages a way of reorganizing it. Only when regulation turns into reorganization can we begin to solve the problems and seize the opportunities identified earlier in this book. The development of the argument provides an opportunity to exemplify a style of legal analysis marshaling the institutional variations expressed in law to inform the design of alternative institutional arrangements.[1]

This chapter addresses the present American debate about the regulation of finance as an opportunity to rethink the role of finance in our democracy and in our economy from the vantage point of lawyers' ideas and lawyers' skills. Its central idea is that the regulation of finance is best understood and practiced as an initial step toward the reorganization of the institutional arrangements, defined in law, that govern the relation of finance to the real economy. The reorganization should—and can—be motivated by two overriding goals: tightening the link of finance to the productive agenda of society and broadening access not just to credit but also to economic opportunity more generally. Although much of what I have to say presupposes or implies the theses set out in the introduction, my argument in this chapter is inspired largely by engagement with the detailed materials of law and the distinctive methods of legal analysis.

I advance in three steps:

1. Offering a view of the larger intellectual and practical issues at stake
2. Discussing the contemporary debate about financial regulation as well as the resulting legal enactments from the highly selective—but I hope revealing—standpoint of the conception and agenda outlined
3. Working out the implications of this conception and this analysis for the regulation of finance, understood as an initial step toward the reorganization of finance and the reshaping of its relation to the real economy

PART 1: ELEMENTS OF A CONCEPTION

The Problem

Finance matters, above all, because it represents the economic surplus used to build the future.[2]

Under present arrangements, finance falls far short of its potential in carrying out this task. There has been an enormous increase in financial activity in recent years. Yet little of this financial activity has contributed to the process of long-term savings, investment, and growth. In advanced and developing countries, the vast bulk of productive investment still comes from firms' retained earnings. Retained earnings are calculated to have amounted to around 90 percent of capital spending. By 2000, gross-equity issues by nonfinancial firms increased four times from their previous peak in the 1980s. Their increase since then, however, appears to have had only a relatively modest effect on the overwhelmingly predominant role that retained and reinvested earnings perform in the funding of production. In all contemporary economies, production is financed mainly within the production itself through the reinvestment of previous gains.

This relatively straightforward observation suggests a disquieting question, best asked with the same artless simplicity: What is the point of all that liquid capital in banks and stock markets and of the myriad forms of financial trading if indeed all this liquid capital and the financial activity around it have relatively so little to do with financing the economy's productive agenda? The elucidation of this enigma represents a major concern of my argument about finance in this chapter and throughout this book.

The theoretical conundrum has a practical and programmatic resolution. I deal with the enigma by arguing that the degree to which finance serves the real economy and its productive activities rather than serving itself is not a constant, natural, or necessary feature of economic life. It is a consequence of institutions and practices that we have the power to change.

Although this view may seem almost self-evident to the nonspecialist, it contradicts ideas that continue to exercise immense and damaging influence on policy as well as on theory. What it chiefly and ultimately contradicts is the belief that there are no systemic alternative ways of organizing a market economy, including capital markets. Insofar as they are closer, they allocate resources to their most efficient uses. Insofar as they are less close, they require a regulatory counterweight to their competitive flaws. On this view, there are only variations in a single direction or on a continuous spectrum, not institutional alternatives that take the organization of markets in general and of capital markets in particular in different directions, with distinct consequences for the organization of both production and exchange as well as for the distribution of economic advantage.

In the real worlds of finance and production, traditional banks and securities markets continue to play an important role in the channeling of savings to firms and households. But the bulk of this external finance has had little or nothing to do with funding of resources for investment in production, whether long term or short term. For a while, at least, it was possible to believe that this vast increase in financial activity helped to create the conditions for growth and increasing prosperity.

Yet the financial crisis of 2007–2009 revealed that few if any of the new-mode markets functioned according to plan. Financial innovations led to concentration rather than to diffusion of risk and often damaged the economic development that they were claimed to support. Turmoil in the capital markets ended up damaging activity in the real economy by mechanisms that I later discuss and helped fuel asset booms and busts.

THE CONTEXT OF THE ARGUMENT IN THE HISTORY OF PRACTICAL POLITICAL ECONOMY

Two main views informed the intellectual and policy response to the crisis. According to the dominant, neoclassical view, trouble in finance results from localized failures of market competition (including asymmetries of information) as well as from failures in the localized regulatory response to such localized market imperfections. By repairing these specific market and regulatory failures, this view goes, we can make private returns converge to social returns. According to this idea, no systemic problem in the organization of finance and of its relation to the real economy ever existed. There was only an ill-advised and long-standing relaxation of regulatory vigilance. The loss of regulatory attention was most harmful and troubling with respect to new markets in financial derivatives and to the shadow-banking sector that proliferated alongside the standard, regulated banks.

According to the second, "Keynes–Minsky" view, financial markets and markets in general are vulnerable to cycles of euphoria and despondency.[3] There is a permanent danger that their oscillations may amplify rather than attenuate the instability of the real economy.[4] In this respect, the Keynes–Minsky position continued and exaggerated the psychological, anti-institutional bias of Anglo-American political economy. The task of regulation, according to this conception, is to provide buffers and counterweights to dangerous disturbances of the financial markets. Regulation seeks to attenuate cycles that we cannot hope fully to suppress or avoid because they are rooted in the bearing of certain psychological impulses on the workings of any market economy.

Here I develop and defend a position differing from both of these views and based on two propositions.

1. The first proposition is that the relation of finance to the real economy can and should be reshaped.
2. The second proposition is that the regulation of finance can and should be a first step toward reorganization of finance and the institutional structure of the financial system.[5]

To appreciate the nature and significance of this alternative view—and of the way it differs from the prevailing view and the prescription that view implies—consider its implications for the debate about regulation. According to the standard, neoclassical approach to regulatory policy in general and to regulation of finance in particular, the aim of regulation is simply to redress the effects of localized market imperfections, the better to make private returns converge to social returns to economic activity.

According to the Keynes–Minsky view, the problem is less one of localized market imperfections and constraints than one of the inherent tendency of the money economy to amplify cycles of despondency and euphoria. On this view, the role of the state is to build buffers and safeguards against the inherent instability of modern, market-oriented financial systems and the economies they are meant to serve.

Excluded from these ways of thinking about finance and its regulation is the idea that there can be alternative ways of organizing the role of finance in the real economy. The severity and course of financial crises are always shaped by their institutional settings. We should not think of this setting as given or as fully determined by any abstract institutional conception, such as the idea of the regulated market economy or the idea of a free and competitive capital market. The arrangements governing the relation between finance and the real economy can take radically different directions. In some of these directions, the arrangements loosen the link between finance and the real economy. In other directions, the arrangements tighten this relation.

The present arrangements governing the relation of finance and the real economy produce a result that is only apparently paradoxical. Finance remains relatively indifferent to the real economy in good times: the vast amount of capital assembled in all the capital markets in all the major economies of the world bears an oblique relation to the financing of productive activity. Yet major disturbances do arise within finance. They arise all the more readily because the ties of finance to the real economy remain so loose. When they do occur, they can wreak havoc, as we have recently seen.

John Maynard Keynes's idea of multiple equilibria in the economy—some of them compatible with massive unemployment—was central to his doctrine. At the same time, he took an interest in the content and effect of institutional arrangements in particular areas of the market economy, including the stock market. Remarkably, however, neither he nor his successors connected the general concept of multiple equilibria at higher and lower levels of activity and employment with the institutional concerns exemplified by his discussion of the stock market in chapter 12 of *General Theory of Employment, Interest, and Money*. He failed to turn his localized interest in institutions and institutional alternatives, expressed in that book, into a general basis for thinking about multiple equilibria in the economy. As a result, Keynes's heresy has little to say about the distinctive character of American arrangements or about the contribution of these arrangements to the boom–bust cycle of debt-fueled asset speculation and collapse that would characterize the financial crisis of 2007–2009.

KEY CONCEPTS AND DISTINCTIONS

Conceptual distinctions first presented in the introduction are crucial to the argument of this chapter and this book. Before proceeding further, I restate and develop them.

Finance may be internal or external. It is internal when it remains embedded within a firm whose principal business is not finance—typically by reliance on retained and reinvested earnings. It is external or autonomous when it is conducted outside such firms. When I use the term *finance* without qualifying it, I have external finance in mind: a part of the economy peopled—under the aegis of what I describe and criticize as regulatory dualism, the dominant approach to the regulation of finance—by both thickly and thinly regulated financial organizations.

External finance is more than a function. It is a world and a culture with a characteristic stock of types of business and financial professionals: asset managers and hedge funds, private-equity firms and venture capitalists, financial traders and speculators, the contemporary equivalents of the nineteenth-century merchant banks, as well as large and small commercial banks closely regulated by the state.

Crucial to my argument are the concepts *financial deepening* and *financial hypertrophy*. By *financial deepening*, I mean increasing engagement of external finance with the real economy, manifest in the contribution it makes to the expansion of output and the improvement of productivity: to production as well as consumption, to supply as well as demand. The idea of financial deepening makes sense only in the context of a view, like the one I develop and defend here, that affirms the historical occurrence and future possibility of alternative market regimes and, as part of that variation, of alternatives ways of organizing finance and relating it to the real economy.

This assumption may seem all but self-evident to many. Moreover, it represents in many ways a straightforward implication of the discovery by mid-nineteenth-century legal thought of the legal and institutional indeterminacy of the abstract idea of a market economy: the market economy lacks a single natural and necessary form. Nevertheless, this assumption contradicts, as I earlier remarked, views deeply entrenched in the main tradition of economics since the Marginalist turn in the late nineteenth century. In fact, the national-accounting categories worked out by some of Keynes's followers in the aftermath of the Second World War, with their characteristic equivalence of aggregate saving and aggregate investment and their implicit dismissal of any distinction between productive and unproductive investment, make it hard even to pose the question to which the ideas presented here offer an answer.

By *financial hypertrophy*, I mean the expansion of the finance industry (external finance) as a proportion of profits in the economy (today around 30 percent) and as a magnet for talent without a corresponding engagement by finance with the growth of output and the enhancement of productivity in the work of nonfinancial firms. Financial hypertrophy is the expansion of finance without financial deepening. It is thus closely related to the idea of financialization.[6]

By using a different word—*financial hypertrophy* rather than *financialization*—I intend to emphasize a connotation not captured by the standard use of the term *financialization*: function diminishes as size increases. (When I use the word *financialization*, I use it to encompass this emphasis.) The seemingly paradoxical reality to which the term *financial hypertrophy* calls attention—at least paradoxical to any believer in the canonical view of the purpose of finance as the mobilization of the accumulated surplus over current and past consumption to build the economic future—is that bloated finance does less for the real economy even as it does more for itself. It not only contributes less to real economic activity but also threatens real economic activity more once financial trouble breaks out.

Financialization in the American and other advanced economies in the late twentieth century was powerfully assisted by two forces. The first force was the dominant approach to the regulation of finance, regulatory dualism, which, with its distinction between thickly and thinly regulated finance, allowed the emergence of a vast shadow-banking system in the penumbra of the accredited financial organizations. The second force was the encouragement of indebtedness, primarily by households and secondarily by nonfinancial firms.

A pressing task in this historical period was to reconcile a regressive distribution of income and wealth, which had worsened inequality in all dimensions over several decades, with the development of a market in mass-consumption goods. The solution was to substitute the reality of a fake credit democracy for the ideal of a property-owning democracy. The central bank's easy-money policies and the accumulation of vast current-account deficits (especially in trade with China) provided the vital enabling conditions.

I explore the broader political economy of financial hypertrophy in chapter 5 as well as in the appendix to this book. The argument in the remainder of this chapter focuses more narrowly on the institutional genealogy and the legal architecture of financialization. This deliberate narrowing of focus has a practical purpose: to develop, in the light of past and present law, a toolbox of instruments with which to understand, challenge, and replace the compromises and abdications from which financialization resulted and on which it continues to depend.

The relation of these concepts to the idea of capital must be probed as well, though. There are three elements in the notion of capital. Capital consists of man-made things. We can use these man-made things to produce other man-made things or to extract resources from nature. We can sell man-made things for money, productive of other man-made things, or use them to command an income stream. Once converted into money, capital becomes liquid capital, which is the resource with which finance, whether internal or external, deals.

Because of the ease with which we can deploy disembedded or liquid capital, our disposition of money balances readily suffers the influence of our humors and illusions. Their instability becomes one of the sources of the intrinsic instability of finance, aggravated by its decoupling from the production system. (The other fundamental source of the instability of finance is its subjection to a regime of law, policies, and institutions over whose evolution it never enjoys a monopoly of influence.)

Unlike finance, capital is not a world apart or a set of activities and people. It is just an accumulation of things. It is dumb and voiceless. Hence, the questions of who should command its deployment and how they should command it become central to both political economy and politics. When we say that the market or the state or some combination of both should command it, we leave out almost everything that is interesting about this question: Which market and which state?

The introduction of the concept of capital serves to allude to another set of fundamental problems touching on the concerns of this book. One of the underlying constraints on economic growth, together with our power to transform or mobilize nature through science and technology and our ability to innovate in the way we cooperate, is the relation of the stock of capital to opportunities for gainful investment. The interest rate—the cost of capital—can serve as a rough proxy for this ratio. It performs this role less fully, however, to the extent that central banks and national governments use the interest rate to serve other goals—the aims to which they habitually devote monetary and fiscal policy.

If there is any constant in economic life deserving to be considered lawlike (by analogy to the laws of nature), it is the constraint of diminishing returns to capital. There are ultimately only two ways in which we can lift this constraint. The first, episodic way is through technological and organization innovation in the context of institutional innovation, resulting in an improvement of productivity. The second, more definitive way is through the emergence of a form of production that is no longer subject to the constraint of diminishing returns: that form has the potential to relax or even to reverse the constraint.

We have reason to hope that such a form of production has now appeared. In knowledge-intensive production, whether undertaken in the setting of what we recognize as high-technology industry or not, the more we materialize our ideas in products and services, the easier it may become to materialize more of them and the faster we may be able to go in doing so. We even have machine tools, such as the three-dimensional printer, that allow us to move more rapidly back and forth between conception and execution. We cannot fully achieve the potential of this transformation so long as the most advanced practice of production remains quarantined in relatively isolated pockets of each national economy: the scope of social and economic life over which a style of production ranges and the radicalness with which we seize on its potential are closely connected.

Later in this book, I ask under what conditions we can develop this potential and what role finance, reimagined and reformed, can play in developing it.

PLAN OF THE ARGUMENT: ITS SIGNIFICANCE FOR THE REGULATION AND REORGANIZATION OF FINANCE

In the remainder of this chapter, I develop my argument at two levels. At one level—national and historical—I present a schematic view of the genealogy of the crisis of 2007–2009 in its American setting. A central idea in my account is that the hollowing out of the New Deal arrangements in the closing decades of the twentieth century, to the benefit of speculative finance and of the interests associated with it, produced a regime that was neither the social-democratic framework of the mid–twentieth century nor a coherent alternative to it. It was a hodgepodge created by a circumstantial evisceration of the New Deal regime. Here I continue and develop the argument of chapter 1.

At a second level—analytic and programmatic—I use the national and historical discussion as a point of departure for the outline of a more general way of thinking about the role of law and legal thought in generating or suppressing institutional alternatives, not just in finance but also for economic and social organization more generally. A key idea in this part of the chapter is that the variations and contradictions of established arrangements supply practical and conceptual materials for the construction of institutional alternatives. To seize this constructive potential is the most important vocation of legal analysis and comparative law today. I conclude the chapter by exploring the programmatic uses of a revised practice of legal analysis in the debate about the reformation of finance. The same revised practice plays a central role in my broader argument in chapters 3, 4, and 5 about the institutional architecture of a democratized market economy.

An understanding of financial crisis and of alternative ways of organizing finance must begin in the recognition of the dependence of finance on an institutional setting beyond its control and even beyond its field of vision. That dependence represents both a threat and an opportunity. It is a threat because it represents one of the two major sources of perennial instability in finance. It is an opportunity because the institutional framework of finance, as of every aspect of the market economy, is established outside the market in politics and thought and is expressed in law. As a result, politics, informed by thought and resulting in law, can change that framework.

Consider, as an example, the following list of institutional factors that played a decisive role both in the buildup of systemic risk and in the relative weakness of the U.S. government's response to the crisis of 2007–2009.

1. The transformation of the laws and institutions of finance in the United States and other countries. The present framework is a hodgepodge rather than a system, resulting from the hollowing out of the New Deal financial reforms, especially in the areas of banking and the mortgage market.
2. Attempts to use popularization of credit as a functional surrogate for redistribution of wealth and income.
3. Anarchy in international monetary arrangements after the collapse of Bretton Woods in August 1971.
4. Fads and fashions in the policies of central banks.[7]

It is now widely recognized that these policies and arrangements may themselves have been major sources of instability. To blame them forms part of the stock and trade of conventional narratives of the financial crisis. But in the view informing most mainstream economic and policy analysis, these features are trivialized and reduced to failures of regulatory vigilance, when in fact no amount of regulatory vigilance would ever suffice to deal with these vast sources of instability. What can alter the situation over time is a change in the balance between hypertrophy and deepening. Financial deepening works to limit financial instability. Financial hypertrophy tends to aggravate it.

Three different sets of institutional arrangements bear on finance: (*a*) the arrangements governing the actual organization of the financial system; (*b*) the arrangements governing the relation between finance and the real economy; and (*c*) the broader institutional setting of the market economy within which financial markets operate.

Consider the following example. Suppose that an economy depends for aggregate demand on a market for mass consumption. Suppose, further, that established institutional arrangements fail to ensure broad access to economic and educational opportunity while at the same time favoring a regressive redistribution of income, wealth, and advantage (as has, in fact, occurred). Under these conditions, it is likely that there will be an attempt to use the expansion of credit to support a market in mass-consumption goods in the absence of a progressive redistribution of wealth and income.

The most effective way to redistribute economic advantage is not compensatory redistribution by tax and transfer; it is a redistribution of primary (before-tax) income and wealth, achieved through an organized broadening of educational and economic opportunity.

The expansion of credit may be achieved through a policy of monetary easing in the domestic economy or through dependence on foreign capital or through an overvaluation of the housing stock, which can then serve as collateral for credit expansion. At some point, the combination of these methods will generate a crisis troubling finance.

It would be wrong to interpret this sequence of events as simply the outcome of inadequate financial regulation. The sequence results from the broader institutional structure of the predominant political economy. Institutions matter at each of these three levels.[8]

Three programmatic consequences follow from these considerations. Together they begin to define an approach to the regulation and reorganization of finance. They suggest ways both to deepen finance and to democratize it: to enlist it more effectively in the service of production while making it more useful to the organization of socially inclusive economic growth. A species of growth deserving special attention is growth based on the economy-wide dissemination of the most advanced practice of production, which continues to be confined to the insular vanguards of the knowledge economy and advanced manufacturing with its retinue of associated services. The economy-wide diffusion of the most advanced productive practices, associated with these vanguards, directly associates economic growth with empowerment and inclusion. It does more than diminish inequality by influencing the primary distribution of economic advantage; it enhances the agency—the powers of initiative and creation—of all whom it benefits.

The first implication of this reasoning is that any adequate response to a financial crisis like the crisis of 2007–2009 must include two elements: one preliminary, the other fundamental. The preliminary element is the repudiation of regulatory dualism: the distinction between a thinly and thickly regulated part of finance. The fundamental element is the conception and implementation of initiatives that would favor financial deepening over financial hypertrophy, making finance more useful to production, especially to the creation of new assets in new ways and thus to the enhancement of productivity. Such initiatives must ultimately be institutional and legal innovations in the arrangements governing finance and shaping its relation to the real economy.

The second implication is that the need to counteract, manage, and avert instability creates a permanent opportunity to turn regulation into reorganization: reordering finance and its relation to the real economy in the service of financial deepening. This opportunity is always present. Under conditions of crisis, this opportunity for transformation increases in the realms of politics and finance thanks to the loosening in the hold of financial interests as well as to the state's direct participation in bailing out and supporting the banks and the financial system.

The third implication has to do with the role of law and legal analysis and in particular with the uses of comparative legal study. Alternative sets of institutional arrangements, in finance as in any other aspect of the market economy, exist only as law—law not simply as rules but as the detailed dialectic between institutional arrangements and the ideological conceptions informing them. From this idea, there results a view of the task of legal analysis and the role of comparative legal study, which I here seek to illustrate.

A major task of legal analysis is to reveal the range of hidden, existing institutional variation, delineated in the detailed institutional arrangements defined as law, far more tangible than abstractions, such as the idea of a regulated market economy. What characteristically happens in each branch of law is that certain dominant solutions are surrounded by a periphery of contrasting approaches or by often rejected but not wholly suppressed pathways of legal evolution. For example, a body of contract law organized around the idea of a fully articulated arm's-length bargain—a bilateral, executory promise in the language of Anglo-American law—may coexist with rules and doctrines appealing to relational contracts. Such contracts organize a relation between parties. They are incomplete or not fully bargained out. And no single performance exhausts them; the maintenance of the relation and of its open-ended benefits is the overriding goal. In the history of law, as in other aspects of our historical experience, vestiges can serve as prophecies. The multitude of small variations and contradictors can serve as points of departure for more fundamental changes. The peripheral can become central.

From here I go on to a detailed analysis and criticism of contemporary arrangements and debates, for that is where we can find the materials of critique and reconstruction: in the realm of historically specific legal and institutional detail in which diversity is disclosed and constructed, for better or worse.

PART 2: THE HISTORICAL CONTEXT OF OUR PRESENT PREDICAMENT—AN ELEMENTARY INSTITUTIONAL GENEALOGY

Aim and Scope of This Institutional Genealogy

In this part, I look back to salient features of the history from which the present debate over financial regulatory reform has emerged. My purpose is not to provide a historical narrative, however schematic. It is to select from the historical background to our present predicament a number of aspects that are directly pertinent to the analytic and programmatic claims standing at the center of my argument. I preface this exercise with a summary statement of what I see as the chief lessons of this historical experience for insight and reform today.

When the financial crisis broke in 2007, the institutional setting in which finance operated had degenerated into a ramshackle construction. (A similar evolution or involution took place in many of the other rich industrial democracies.) The New Deal arrangements for the governance of finance had been partly but not completely bent and gutted. They had been hollowed out, unevenly and discontinuously, in response to an alliance of powerful interests and ideas.

The interests were chiefly those of high finance. The more high finance succeeded in getting its way, the larger it grew and the weaker its links to the system of production became. It gained a degree of influence over government that led one mainstream economist to describe this influence as a coup d'état.

The interests of high finance could not have made so powerful a dent on the New Deal regime for the governance of finance had they not been able to count on the support of prestigious economic ideas. Rational-expectations doctrine, the efficient-market hypothesis, and real business-cycle theory represented extreme but influential examples of an approach to theory and policy that derided the efficacy of many forms of financial regulation, including the forms to which the New Deal had given prominence, and that attacked the case for the quasi-governmental entities—the GSEs—that the New Deal had crafted.

We cannot understand the influence exercised by these putatively "free-market" ideas unless we appreciate what they shared in common with the two major theoretical traditions in modern economics: the neoclassical and the Keynesian. What they shared was the conviction that problems arise from localized market failures and from localized failures in the regulatory response to such localized market failures. The basic assumption is that there are no systemic alternatives—that is, no alternative sets of institutional arrangements, detailed in law—for shaping the service that finance can render to production and, more generally, no alternative ways of organizing a market economy in institutional detail. I develop my argument from a perspective contradicting this key and almost universally shared assumption, although I contradict it here in a way that remains fragmentary and half-explicit and goes only as far as my thesis and topic require.

The outcome of this loose but powerful alliance between financial interests and economic ideas was not, however, the total overthrow of the New Deal system in finance. It was its partial evisceration and its juxtaposition with policies, practices, and institutions that ran in a direction opposite to the New Dealers' goals. What resulted was not the replacement of one system by another; it was a gingerbread construction, a crazy quilt of compromise and concession.

There was nevertheless a method in this madness. The doctrinal and institutional disharmonies that ensued from this bricolage enabled finance to grow in a fashion that weakened its links to production and to society's productive agenda rather than strengthened them. In the analytic categories central to this piece, financial hypertrophy came to prevail over financial deepening. Each of the points I single out for attention in the next few pages represents a part of the road to the triumph of the former over the latter.

If the foreground theme of this institutional genealogy is the partial hollowing out of the New Deal framework as a major source of our present predicament, the background theme is the interpretation of the goals and nature of that framework. This concern is of more than antiquarian interest. We cannot and should not seek simply to repeat or to reinstate the work of the Rooseveltian reformers (or of their European counterparts). We must nevertheless learn from what they achieved as well as from what they failed to accomplish.

The New Deal, it has often been remarked, went through an evolution: it began as one project or array of projects and ended as another. We must understand this shift in order to appreciate its financial reforms. The early New Deal was characterized by bold albeit often half-baked institutional experiments in the reshaping of the market economy. Some of these experiments looked in the direction of corporatism or managed competition, pinning their hopes on new forms of coordination between governments and firms. Others used public works—such as the Hoover Dam under the Tennessee Valley Authority—to find new ways to broaden economic opportunity. They amounted to projects of social, not just physical, engineering.

Almost all of these experiments were struck down, politically or constitutionally, before they had a chance either to succeed or to fail on their own merits. After their repudiation, the New Deal came to settle on a narrower focus of economic security and mass consumption. That was the orientation that became "normalized" after the Second World War.

The transformation of the New Deal agenda was not completed, however, before the astonishing and misunderstood interlude of the war economy. Under the provocation of a life-and-death threat to the country, the forced, large-scale mobilization of resources was combined with institutional experiments even bolder and certainly more sustained than those that had been tried out half-heartedly in the early New Deal. However, the resulting innovations remained quarantined, as if pertinent only to the special circumstances of a nation at war.

Two features of this evolution deserve emphasis if we are to understand correctly both the nature and the limits of what the New Deal achieved in the domain of the governance of finance.

The New Dealers' concern with economic insecurity resulted in the new system of federal deposit insurance and in the crystalline distinction (later to be attacked by the perpetrators of the hollowing out of the New Deal) between governmentally insured deposit taking and proprietary trading in the finance industry. The individual's savings were not to be placed at risk—at least not at uninsured risk—by bankers' bets.

The combination of a commitment to economic security with a commitment to the popularization of consumption opportunities prompted the New Dealers to go further in the reorganization of the housing market than in their reform of any other aspect of the American economy. Finance was mobilized in the service of a chance for the working family to own a family home. One of the few institutional New Deal innovations to survive—the public–private GSEs (Fannie Mae first among them)—survived as an instrument of this policy, until much later diverted to the service of speculative finance.

Two limitations of this achievement stand out. The first limitation is that at no point did the New Deal advance toward institutional innovations designed to make finance more serviceable to production and to ensure the ascendancy of financial deepening over financial hypertrophy. The second limitation is that where the New Deal reforms went deepest—in the housing market and in the redesign of its legal-institutional framework—they did so only narrowly. The sector-specific character of the legal and institutional arrangements made them appear to be and to be in fact exceptions rather than instances of a broader institutional logic, thus depriving them of practical and doctrinal supports and rendering them susceptible to reversal or perversion.

The purpose of this commentary on the background theme of the nature and limits of the New Deal program in finance is to make clear at the outset that this institutional genealogy should not be read as a lament over a lost paradise. The New Deal framework fails to provide a model for today. It was not good enough then, and it is certainly not good enough now. However, we cannot grasp our opportunities of insight and of reform without understanding both the New Deal's accomplishments and its failures. The brief programmatic argument in the third part of this chapter proposes, in the light of this experience, a path beyond what the New Deal accomplished in finance, not back to what it achieved, and argues that having taken a step back, we can and should now take two steps forward.

With these observations in mind, I now turn to my highly selective institutional genealogy: the analysis of certain changes that weakened the New Deal framework and thus sacrificed financial deepening to financial hypertrophy

How We Got Here: A Simplified Institutional Genealogy

Beginning in the 1970s, the legal framework for the regulation of finance was progressively eviscerated. At the same time, increasing inequality in income and wealth would lead policy makers to rely on monetary ease and credit expansion as a surrogate for a strategy of socially inclusive growth and redistribution.

Neither of these tendencies was insuperable. They formed no part of a systemic assault—or systemic alternative—to the social-democratic settlement of the postwar era. The effect was substantial nonetheless. Financial deepening had in effect been sacrificed to financial hypertrophy.

Four key developments would contribute to this result.

Privatization of the GSEs and the Secondary Mortgage Market

A first development was the hijacking of the mortgage market and its New Deal institutions and arrangements by speculative, private finance. This development took place in two steps. The first step consisted in the restructuring of the federally sponsored mortgage agencies and the introduction of securitization for mortgage pools backed by GSEs.[9]

A second step involved the development of "private-label securitization"—that is, a parallel system for the origination, pooling, and securitization of residential mortgages that failed to meet the standards established in the GSE segment of the market (thus, the name "subprime-mortgage market").[10]

It is commonplace today to treat the outcome of this process as the natural and necessary counterpart to increasing complexity and sophistication. But this interpretation is clearly wrong. Even the slightest scratching of the historical record is enough to suggest the complex and contradictory process involved in the move from state-sponsored securitization to the highly speculative and at times even fraudulent process of private-label securitization—which would be applied to great effect in the development of the subprime-mortgage market.

The movement to privatize securitization fatally weakened the New Deal regime in the very sector—the housing market—in which it had advanced furthest in the attempt to combine its devotion to economic security for the individual with its interest in the expansion of his opportunities to consume. The GSEs were eventually transformed into instruments of speculative finance as the secondary, asset-based mortgage market turned into the largest free-floating pool of resources on which the bankers could draw to keep doubling their bets and expanding the market for profitable (and unprofitable) trading opportunities.

Hollowing Out of the New Deal Reforms and the Rise of Shadow Banking

A corollary to the privatization of securitization was the rise of shadow banking. This point is often overlooked, but it is of the utmost importance. In the U.S. setting, the hollowing out of the New Deal arrangements in the area of mortgage finance would provide the context and occasion for the vast expansion of shadow banking. Shadow banking would, in turn, provide a stimulus for the hypertrophy of finance in the area of housing and mortgage finance.

There were two major developments. The first was the emergence of new money and funding markets beyond the traditional banking system. Examples include money-market mutual funds; triparty repurchase agreements (repos), and asset-backed commercial paper.

The second development was the proliferation of nonbank financial intermediaries, free from the New Deal regulatory restrictions but nonetheless supported in many ways by monetary and regulatory authorities. In the U.S. setting, finance companies, conduits, and special-purpose vehicles would come to define the new "shadow-banking" system. But they were not alone. Together with leading broker-dealers and investment banks, the new intermediaries in the shadow-banking system would come to dominate U.S. credit markets.[11]

The shadow banks' assumption of many traditional banking functions illustrates two connected themes. The first, relatively more superficial theme is the damage done by the main strategy for the regulation of finance in the second half of the twentieth century: regulatory dualism, with its contrast between a thickly regulated sector and a thinly regulated sector of finance. Regulatory dualism was advanced on the ground that the high-net-worth individuals and financial professionals who populated what was to be the thinly regulated sector did not require a heavy-handed paternalism. However, the practical result was to make it possible to repackage—and to implement under different form—in the thinly regulated sector everything prohibited in the thickly regulated sector. The shadow-banking system served this purpose.

The second theme is the sacrifice of financial deepening to financial hypertrophy: size without productive function. The central point of shadow banking was always to expand the opportunity to profit from financial trades. It was never to enhance the funding of productive activity.

Imagine a legal test—simple in conception although difficult in application—that would forbid or burden (with regulatory restraints and tax burdens) all financial transactions not plausibly useful to the expansion of GDP or to the enhancement of productivity in the economy. Under such a test, the vast majority of the transactions in which the shadow-banking system has specialized would be outlawed or discouraged.

Creation of Institutional Links Connecting Shadow Banking to the Traditional Banking System

Neither the hollowing out of the New Deal framework nor the rise of shadow banking would have created the conditions for the crisis of 2007–2009. The amplification of the crisis from a breakdown in the tiny subprime-mortgage market to the breakdown in global markets was made possible by the rationalization and extension of a generalized system of regulatory dualism from the 1970s on.

We can understand this part of the historical trajectory as a succession of three steps:

1. Elimination of regulatory restrictions on bank activities and affiliations
2. Creation of new legal and institutional vehicles designed to facilitate the extension of credit from the traditional to the shadow-banking sector
3. Rationalization and integration of the new shadow-banking sector into a generalized system of regulatory dualism

The last extraordinary development exemplifies the dependence of finance on its institutional setting. It is commonplace to consider the rise and fall of the New Deal reforms as a natural and necessary process that responds to changing circumstance and the imperatives of objective, economic constraint.

Nothing could be further from the truth. The liberalization of the rules governing bank activities and affiliations as well as the creation of a new legal vehicle—the complex, multipurpose bank-holding company—to rationalize and integrate commercial banking into the new system of market-oriented financial activity would create the conditions for an unrivaled shift in the balance between financial deepening and financial hypertrophy.

It would be wrong to treat these developments as the natural unfolding of a higher logic or rationality. At each step along the way, both in the design and in the defense of the emerging pattern of finance, government took the lead.

As the functional separation broke down, monetary and regulatory authorities crafted new forms of monetary and fiscal policy—to strengthen and support the financial sector, which would increasingly be seen as an entity in itself rather than as the servant of society or the public interest. The process culminated in the repeal of the Banking Act of 1933 (Glass–Steagall Act) and the passing of the Financial Services Modernization Act (Graham–Leach–Bliley Act) in 1999, which sanctioned the connection and through the device of the new bank-holding company charter provided a formal way to integrate and cross-subsidize all financial activities.

The point is simple and telling. The extraordinary scope and scale of the worldwide financial crisis was not—as so many have argued—the natural result of globalization or financial innovation in the banking sector. Nor are we able to understand the content and course of the crisis merely by reference to the inherent tendencies of modern financial markets. In the closing decades of the twentieth century, the U.S. government undertook a series of bold initiatives to construct the emerging order in local and global markets.

It is difficult to underestimate the contribution of this set of policies and arrangements to the phenomenon of leverage, instability, and speculative risk taking within the U.S. banking system. Just as the crisis of 2007–2009 was primarily a first-world banking crisis, so the standardization and integration of the shadow and formal banking systems would create a series of amplification or transmission devices for speculative risk taking and leverage in the U.S. and global banking system.[12]

Increasing Reliance on Foreign Portfolio Capital to Finance Trade Deficits and to Fuel Credit-Driven, Household Consumption

To understand the developments cited in the previous three elements of this simplified genealogy, it is necessary to place the elements in a broader context.[13] The most important aspect of this context is that the United States failed to establish a viable strategy of broad-based, socially inclusive economic growth. It stopped producing enough of the goods and services that the rest of the world wanted.

Rather than confront this problem, however, the United States tried to make up the shortfall through a debt-driven expansion of consumption, made possible by foreign money (the foreign-capital inflows as the inverse to the ballooning trade deficit) and accommodating monetary policy (including the creation of paper money).

These tactics were like throwing kerosene on the flame. The hypertrophic financial system, already increasingly decoupled from the real economy by the hollowing out of the New Deal arrangements, now found almost unlimited opportunities in a circumstance of massive consumption-oriented liquidity and diminished regulatory vigilance.

The diminished regulatory vigilance helps explain the immediate triggers of the crisis. However, it is a mistake to suppose that the triggers had a causal efficacy independent of these deeper background factors.

Many have argued that the crisis had localized and shallow causes: for example, failures of judgment and regulation in the repurchase agreement markets for certain classes of asset-backed securities. The fact that the sudden and massive expansion of trading in such securities was almost exactly paralleled by a similar expansion in the oldest and most conventional forms of finance (such as commercial paper) shows that these explanations are false.

The key to understanding the crisis lies in the interaction between reliance on expansionary monetary policy, debt and credit at home, and trade and capital deficits with our chief trading partners (especially China), as surrogates for a better strategy of economic growth, on the one hand, and the institutional changes (described in the previous three subsections of the genealogy) that took the country toward financial hypertrophy rather than financial deepening, on the other hand.

The interpretation of the genealogy of the crisis that I have just stated contrasts with many familiar and influential understandings of its causes in several ways. The conventional view has resulted in a conception of the genealogy of the crisis that combines two elements: (*a*) a very general element, such as the view that financial crises are simply part of the natural scheme of things or a permanent and recurring feature of a modern, market-oriented economy; and (*b*) a very concrete element, such as the view that each crisis has a set of relatively accidental and narrowly focused triggers. For example, an analyst might emphasize the sudden shift in perceptions of risk spurred by the decline in the housing market in 2007 or the failure of Lehman Brothers in September 2008 or any other market or regulatory failures revealed in hindsight by the collapse of financial markets in the United States and around the world.

By contrast, on the account sketched here, the key factors leading up to the crisis were neither just accidental triggers nor elements in a recurrent pattern of financial crisis and reform. Instead, the center of gravity was at an intermediate level, emphasizing the decisive influence of institutional arrangements that may either tighten or loosen the link between savings and productive investment. And it is at this intermediate level that law is decisive because the arrangements are products of law.

The argument may be formulated in different terms. On the view presented here, the nature and significance of the crisis cannot be understood merely by appealing to the supposed regularities inherent in an abstract conception of the market economy or financial system. Instead, policies and arrangements of the kind summarized in the previous brief list become pivotal at each stage in the analysis: both in the diagnosis of the structural and institutional factors leading up to the financial crisis and in the design and development of an appropriate project of reform.

This account of the institutional and legal elements in the origins of the crisis of 2007–2009 directs our attention to the interplay between a momentous legal-institutional transformation and a doomed effort to use debt-driven consumption and easy money as a substitute for a productivist strategy, or a trajectory of broad-based economic growth. I speak to the content of this missing strategy in part 3 of this chapter.

The Structure and Limits of the Present Debate

The inconclusive hollowing out of the New Deal regime helps account for the shape and limits of the contemporary debate about the reform of financial regulation. The most striking feature of this debate is its emptiness of structural imagination: the lack of understanding of the institutional genealogy of the present ramshackle set of arrangements is wedded to a failure of insight into institutional alternatives. Fragmentary reforms proposed in the course of this debate can nevertheless serve as material for the development of alternatives if only we could understand both the actual and the possible under the lens of a view more penetrating than the one offered by ruling ideas.

The Four Main Reform Agendas

Both in the United States and elsewhere, the debate about financial regulatory reform has been dominated by four agendas. Neither separately nor together do they amount to an alternative capable of addressing the problems discussed in this chapter.

The New Deal Agenda

The first agenda is the New Deal agenda. Its characteristic concern is to insulate the core banking and payments system from the excesses of speculative finance. To this end, it advocates structural and institutional precautions, such as the division between insured deposit taking and proprietary trading, tools prominent in the American and European response to the Depression of the 1930s.

The New Technocratic Agenda

The second agenda is a New Technocratic agenda. Sponsored by the high governmental officials in finance and treasury departments or ministries, its guiding concerns are the strengthening of supervisory and resolution authority—meaning authority to take over, close down, or turn around failing financial institutions, especially when their instability threatens the stability of the financial system as a whole. The perspective is very clear. It views the crisis as a threat rather than as a harbinger of things to come. Once the threat is contained, everything else can presumably go back to the way it was in the good old days, presumably before the conflagration.

The Basel Agenda

The third agenda can be called the "Basel agenda." Its source is the intellectual and bureaucratic elite of international high finance, as represented in the Bank for International Settlements in Basel. The chief concern of this third agenda is to contain the risks of financial instability through capital adequacy and other requirements designed to limit risk taking in individual banks and in the financial sector as a whole.

The Consumer-Protection Agenda

The fourth agenda, the only one with overtly popular concerns, is a consumer-protection agenda. Through a combination of paternalism and mandated transparency, it seeks to better protect the public against the abuses of the finance industry. In the United States, the favored instrument would become the Consumer Protection Agency, one of the hallmarks of the Dodd–Frank reforms.

Together, these four initiatives represent a variety of concerns and perspectives. Yet from the standpoint of my argument here, the most important point to note is that they share the lack of a structural agenda. None of the different agendas succeeds in addressing—much less solving—the twin structural problems that are central to the genealogy of the financial crisis.

Little or nothing was done to tighten the links between finance and the real economy in general or in the area of production and innovation in particular. Nor was there an effort to connect the debate about financial regulation to an exploration of policies and arrangements required to support a broadening of economic and educational opportunity.

It may well be said in defense of these reform programs, with their poverty of structural content, that they had goals different from those of the alternatives that I propose here. Their, intent, it may be objected, was to discipline finance and to prevent it from continuing to do or from doing once again the harm that it had just done to the livelihood and welfare of millions of people. But, as I argued earlier in this chapter, neither of these tasks can be separated from the effort to deal with larger structural concerns.

Two objections are commonly made to any alternatives raised in response to the argument on behalf of structural reform. The first objection is that the government simply had no room for maneuver: the effects of the crisis and the bankers' lobby made more consequential reform impossible. Yet the administration was not passive. It took bold and unprecedented actions both in the period immediately following the crisis and in the period leading up to the Dodd–Frank reforms. Indeed, as many have pointed out, the crisis created an opportunity for the government to act in ways unthinkable before the crisis.

The second and deeper common objection is that no structural alternatives exist. Even if the government had an open hand, there was simply nothing more to be done. No alternative strategy of development or project of reform could or would have improved on the basic framework of the market economy and financial system as developed in the United States and other North Atlantic countries at the close of the twentieth century.[14]

The appeal of this position is obvious. Our lack of faith in institutional alternatives seems to be confirmed by both contemporary and historical experience. The message of skepticism is nevertheless misguided. To recognize its inadequacy, it suffices to look again at the reform projects that were offered as responses to the crisis. Their proponents underestimate the margin of maneuver that they enjoyed despite the array of interests aligned against reform.

This margin of maneuver had three components:

1. The disharmonies evident in the four reform agendas, the plurality of reform agendas, and the many different ways in which each of the four agendas could have been developed.
2. The ramshackle character of the present institutional arrangements. The hollowing out of the New Deal reforms was incomplete. Moreover, it failed to create a coherent and developed alternative to the New Deal settlement. As a result, the reforms and re-regulations could have taken many turns, even apart from any broader ideological or political agenda.

3. The—as yet voiceless—opposing interests and aspirations, reflected throughout the debate about reform as well as throughout the crisis and response itself.

An opportunity for reconstruction persists today, even as the crisis recedes into the past. The variety of contradictory interests, aspirations, and views at stake, together with the lack of any settled interpretation or approach creates an opening for new ideas as well as arrangements. New ideas and approaches, once accepted, can have a large effect. They can inform a cumulative trajectory of legal and institutional reform capable of making good on this underutilized room for maneuver.

The Dodd–Frank Act of 2010 as an Illustration of the Nature and Limitations of the Contemporary Debate and of the Squandering of Transformative Potential

The Dodd–Frank reforms provide a perfect illustration both of the nature and limitations of the contemporary debate and of the possibility of using practical reforms, inspired by inadequate ideas, for another, better purpose. The central theme of the new legislation would be that the arrangements are essentially sound. But the very act of legislation would belie this idea and provide an opening for transformation.[15]

The Basic Structure and Orientation of the Dodd–Frank Program of Financial Regulatory Reform

Consider first the basic structure of the Dodd–Frank reforms. The main focus fell on too-big-to-fail institutions. The key premise was that some organizations had been allowed to become so large that they could take the government hostage. There was here no vision of alternative ways of organizing finance and shaping its relation to the real economy. The fear was not just that some institutions controlled, directly or indirectly, a large amount of capital but also that they occupied a strategic position in the capital markets and therefore in the whole economy. Such firms were regarded as nodal points in a dense network of interconnections, as if they were large stars organizing the gravitational field around them. The search for culprits took place on the basis of these assumptions. To the suspect classes of financial transactions there was added a suspect class of financial organization that required a heightened level of scrutiny.

Four sets of institutional arrangements and legal provisions lay at the heart of the new reforms.

1. A classification of financial organization subject to heightened scrutiny.

   The Dodd–Frank Act identified and drew a ring around systemically important financial institutions—the largest and most "interconnected" financial intermediaries. Such banks were singled out for heightened scrutiny and supervision. Increased capital and liquidity requirements were to be the chief tools for heightened regulatory vigilance and control.

2. A new apparatus of supervision and resolution, especially in relation to the risks assumed by these organizations.

   The act created a new apparatus for supervising and monitoring systemically important financial institutions (SIFIs). Two new institutional vehicles anchor the new regime. The first is the Financial Stability Oversight Council (FSOC), an assembly of regulators charged with three main tasks: monitoring and identifying systemically important financial institutions; ensuring the development of appropriate micro- and macroprudential policies and arrangements; and deciding, in the latter instance, whether to subject a SIFI to the new Orderly Liquidation Authority (OLA). The OLA is the second main institutional innovation established by the Dodd–Frank reforms. Although scholars disagree on both the merits and the feasibility of the new special-resolution regime, the OLA has been designed as an alternative to the perceived inadequacies of the traditional instruments of bankruptcy and bailout, especially as those instruments were deployed in recent years.

3. A prohibition of certain kinds of trading in the spirit of the New Deal agenda.

   The third pillar of the new regime was the reinstatement of a series of restrictions on proprietary trading and position taking by commercial banks and bank-holding companies. Commercial banks and bank-holding companies were subject to enhanced restrictions on proprietary trading, position making, and other forms of heightened risk taking. Speculative investments in hedge funds and equity funds were to be subject to only light regulation in the spirit of the long-standing practice of regulatory dualism. These prohibitions express the view that "socially useful" banking should return to an earlier paradigm in which banking was first and foremost an instrument for the extension of consumer and commercial credit rather than an agent of high-stakes gambling, or the placing of bets in financial trading. Little was thought, said, or done about the relation of the capital markets to the production system.

4. A demand for heightened transparency and scrutiny, to be achieved mainly through an exchange for derivatives under government supervision.

The fourth main pillar of the Dodd–Frank regime involves the regulation of derivatives trading. Intended as a belated defense to the runaway market in over-the-counter derivative transactions, the new rules required that the vast majority of derivatives be listed and cleared on a public exchange. The idea was not new. After all, the Commodities Exchange Act of 1936 had established a similar principle at the time of the New Deal reforms. But in the context of recent practice, this regulation amounted to a striking change in direction.

Consequences and Lessons of the Dodd–Frank Reforms

At their best, these reforms represented a strike against what I call the hypertrophy of finance.

However, even as these reforms resisted financial hypertrophy, they failed to advance financial deepening. Little or nothing has been done to tighten the link between savings and productive investment or between finance and the real economy or to promote an expansion of credit to productive sectors or to limit the size or scale of risk taking in finance outside the commercial banks. There was not even an outright repudiation of regulatory dualism.

Similarly, there was no attempt to propose and implement an agenda of socially inclusive production: one that would signal a way to increase productivity through the economy-wide diffusion of the advanced, knowledge-intensive experimental production, which remained confined largely to insular productive vanguards (e.g., Silicon Valley). Such a diffusion would depend on initiatives designed to fulfill the educational and social conditions of the most advanced practice of production. Among these conditions are a style of both technical and general education according priority to generic capabilities of analysis and innovation rather than to job-specific and machine-specific skills. Among them as well are the institutional and legal innovations (making use, for example, of relational contract and disaggregated property rights) conducive to cooperative competition among and within firms and supportive of a higher level of trust and discretion allowed to all who share in the process of production.

In such an alternative, finance has a role to play. Financial deepening—that is, the tightening of the links between finance and the real economy—is the threshold requirement for the changes that would prepare finance to contribute to such an alternative.

A government that rejects institutional innovation and even institutional debate and that insists on focusing only on the regulation of finance has an institutional project despite itself. There is only a relative distinction between regulation and reorganization: every regulatory strategy makes institutional assumptions and has institutional consequences. A regulatory strategy intended to preserve a set of institutional arrangements may nevertheless turn out be a first step in the reshaping of the relation of finance to the real economy.

Thus, the Dodd–Frank regulatory reforms, chiefly conceived as an attempt to preserve rather than revise the existing institutional organization of the financial system and its relation to the real economy, could have been enlisted in the service of a program of more consequential change, as I argue next. This argument is of more than historical and counterfactual interest. The Dodd–Frank reforms were characteristic of the contemporary approach to the regulation of finance in their commitment to heightened regulatory dualism; in their lack of attention to the central problem of the relation of finance to the real economy in genera and to production in particular; in their failure to pursue institutional alternatives; and even in their continuing acceptance of regulatory dualism, despite their commitment to the application of more stringent regulatory standards to the traditional sector of finance. My argument about the Dodd–Frank reforms is in fact an argument about this entire tradition, which has not stopped with Dodd–Frank; it is likely to have many sequels and equivalents until we awaken to the need for a more fundamental change.

Such change, along the lines I argue here, may seem radical in its advanced stages and forms. It can, indeed it must, be fragmentary and gradual in its development. It is only a prejudice, which we inherit both from Marxism (and other social theories of the nineteenth century) and from classical legal thought (with its conception of types of economic and political regimes, each possessing in-built institutional architecture), that radical transformation must be total and sudden but change that happens in steps and in pieces—as almost all real change does—cannot be fundamental.

Take, for example, the separation of proprietary trading from government-insured depositary institutions. Both the Volcker Rule and the Lincoln Amendment imposed restrictions on finance, but they did and do nothing to increase financial deepening. But if these measures were accompanied by institutions designed to channel to local banks the whole apparatus of modern, financial engineering, then this purely negative restriction would have turned out to be an element in a broader project of reconstruction to achieve financial deepening.

The same principle applies to the two main institutional innovations of the Dodd–Frank regime: the new FSOC and the new OLA. The narrow mandate to mitigate the risk of collapse of a large and highly connected financial institution could in the course of time be broadened into the more transformative mandate of discouraging—or outlawing—financial activities of little use to the growth of output and the enhancement of productivity as well as of encouraging the financial activities that are useful to this endeavor.

Consider, finally, the new special-resolution regime placed at the center of the campaign to prevent any particular financial organization from threatening the stability of the economy and financial system. This lesser mandate can gradually be expanded into a broader task. What is now understood as a device for the orderly liquidation of a failing institution, or even for the socialization by government of private losses, can over time become an instrument for reshaping these organizations and redirecting them to the work of inventing new forms of finance and financial organization that are useful to enterprise.

Each piece of the Dodd–Frank reforms, although conceived as part of an attempt to restore the existing system, could have been (or may yet be) reinterpreted and redirected to reorganize finance and reshape its relation to the real economy. The reinterpretation and redeployment of the halting measures that always and everywhere form the staple of politics and policy to more transformative uses requires the imagination of institutional alternatives. Such alternatives must ultimately translate into legal detail. The dialectic of structural vision and legal analysis is central to both economic progress and democratic politics. It is one of the means by which we rescue the idea of structural change from a fantasy that continues to confound us: the false belief that we must choose between a reformism of modest reach and ambition—committed to regulate and redistribute without reorganizing—and a revolutionary substitution of one regime for another, a substitution so inaccessible and dangerous that its terrors serve as an excuse for resignation.

PART 3: ANOTHER DIRECTION FOR AMERICAN FINANCE

I now develop the programmatic implications of my treatment of the regulatory and legislative response to the crisis of 2007–2009: an alternative direction for the arrangements governing the organization of finance and its relation to the real economy.[16]

Two main principles guide the approach. The first is the belief that the process of financial regulatory reform can and should serve as the front line in the effort to reshape the institutional organization of the financial system in the service of the democratic reorganization of finance. The second is the belief that the recently enacted Dodd–Frank reforms—or more generally the regulatory and reform tradition that they exemplify—can serve as a point of departure for innovations that both deepen and democratize finance.

I organize this programmatic discussion around six complementary themes. Each marks an axis of change.

1. Repudiating regulatory dualism
2. Restricting financial activities unrelated to the expansion of output or the enhancement of productivity
3. Transforming local banks and financial institutions
4. Reinventing and multiplying the GSEs
5. Popularizing and democratizing financial services
6. Reinventing and popularizing venture capital

Each of these sets of legal-institutional innovations responded to the problems presented by the events of 2007–2009 or by similar financial crises that may occur in the future. It did so in ways that contribute to the advancement of two overriding goals. The first aim is to make finance more useful to the expansion of output and the improvement of productivity in the real economy while diminishing the likelihood of major financial instability that is damaging to real economic activity. The second objective is to reshape finance so that it can play a role within a program of socially mobilize finance in the service of the most widely professed social and economic goal in the world today: the promotion of socially inclusive economic growth.

These proposals are addressed in the first instance to the United States today. They nevertheless apply with adjustments to a broad range of contemporary advanced and middle-income economies given these economies' analogous structural problems and the restricted stock of economic institutions and practices now on offer in the world.

The six sets of proposed legal and institutional innovations that I sketch in the following pages fall into three pairs. The first pair addresses the enabling conditions for movement in the direction that I defend. The second pair regards the legal and institutional vehicles or agents of the change. The third pair reflects the concern with access and inclusion: the range of beneficiaries.

1. Repudiating Regulatory Dualism

The dominant strategy for the regulation of finance over the past half-century has been regulatory dualism. Although formulated most clearly and forcefully in the United States, regulatory dualism has long been the dominant approach to the regulation of finance throughout the world.

The distinction between a thickly regulated sector and a thinly regulated sector of finance traditionally rests, as I have observed, on an argument from the appropriate and inappropriate conditions of paternalism. The standard justification of the distinction is that the high-net-worth individuals and financial professionals populating the thinly regulated sector are supposed to require less monitoring, as if such monitoring were not needed to defend the rest of the population from them rather than to defend them against themselves.

To the argument from the conditions of paternalism is added an argument from the requirements of efficiency. To impose on all financial activity the same regulatory standard would, according to this view, be to compromise both allocational and dynamic efficiency. It would do so in a context in which flexibility and the financial innovations it makes possible count for much and the risks of financial speculation are borne by those who are best able to understand and bear them. Moreover, in the thinly regulated sector public resources are not committed, as they are in the situation of governmentally insured deposits in deposit-taking financial institutions.

The chief objection to regulatory dualism is that it represents a standing invitation to circumvention. The transactions prohibited in the thinly regulated sector can be repackaged and offered under different labels. That is not a hypothetical danger; it formed a significant element in the run-up to the recent crisis.

There is an additional objection, briefly invoked in an earlier passage of this text. Finance operates in a broader institutional setting from which destabilizing forces of great power may arise at any moment. These forces cannot be controlled by finance and to some extent may not even be visible or intelligible to financiers. Instability is not simply endogenous to finance; it is also exogenous to it.

The repudiation of regulatory dualism would be followed by the imposition of a single, uniform level of regulatory severity throughout the whole range of financial activities and organizations. The imposition of regulatory uniformity is not all itself a solution to any problem other than the specific problem of massive circumvention created by regulatory dualism. It is a necessary but not sufficient condition of an alternative faithful to the interests and ideals that I take here as paramount.

2. Discouraging or Prohibiting Transactions That Do Not Benefit the Real Economy and Increase Risks to Real Economic Activity

A major premise of my argument has been that the institutional arrangements governing the relation of finance to the real economy can either tighten or loosen the link between the former and the latter. Neoclassical economics supposes that insofar as there are no market failures, capital will be allocated by a market to its most efficient uses. The fundamental institutional and legal content of a market economy is, according to that point of view, not in doubt. To the extent that there are market failures, they are to be redressed by similarly targeted exercises of regulatory vigilance.

A simple and incontestable observation already begins to create trouble for this view. The whole panoply of organizations that channel long-term saving into long-term productive investment—the different kinds of banks, capital markets, stock markets, and, more generally, financial and nonfinancial firms that exist in contemporary economies—are inventions developed in politics and thought and confirmed by the law. An institutional invention such as the remarkable network of local banks that the United States developed in the nineteenth century may make finance more useful to society's productive agenda. Contrary to many of the dominant ideas, the link between finance and production is far from being an analytical tautology; it is to a large extent a function of the institutions that organize finance and that shape its place in the economy.

A corollary of this thesis is that we should and can distinguish between desirable and undesirable forms of financial speculation. What makes finance speculative is the making of judgments or bets on an uncertain future, particularly on the unquantifiable uncertainties that we cannot hope to reduce to quantifiable probabilities. Speculative finance performs a valuable role in generating information and in organizing the allocation of risk.

It is not financial speculation in itself that represents a danger to be averted; it is the disassociation of speculation from service to the real economy. The evil to be avoided arises when the transactions of the real economy become mere pretexts for the self-referential activities of finance itself. If such a diversion or perversion is repeated on a large scale and in many different theaters of economic activity, the result is a situation in which finance, relatively indifferent to the real economy in good times, becomes a threat to the maintenance of the level of real economic activity once major financial instability breaks out.

The practical significance of this problem is not limited to the effects of financial instability on the real economy. Its broader dimension is the squandering, under present arrangements, of the productive potential of saving. Under those arrangements, production is largely self-financed on the basis of private firms' retained and reinvested earnings. The vast capital held in the banks and invested in the stock markets has, I have argued, an episodic or oblique relation to the funding of production.

To make finance more useful and less dangerous to the production system requires a series of institutional innovations. I discuss some of them in other parts of this book. They should and can be complemented by initiatives designed to discourage and in some instances to prohibit financial activity yielding no significant advantage to the real economy, on either its demand side or its supply side.

The advantage may be to consumption, for example, in the form of consumer credit. Or it may be in the expansion of output and the improvement of productivity. An especially important role of finance, one that under present arrangements occupies a subordinate and even minor place in the totality of financial activities, is the creation of new assets in new ways.

An economist inattentive to the systemic consequences of present institutions may respond that, absent specific market failures or failures in the regulatory response to them, a financial activity that makes no such contribution to real economic activity cannot be sustained over time. Unhappily, however, it can be, given the enormous potential under established arrangements for finance to develop a parasitic relation to the real economy and the consequent divergence, in the area of finance, between private and social returns.

Consider the homely but revealing example of futures contracts. They were pioneered in commodities markets, in which they make an indisputable contribution to liquidity. Many keen observers have remarked, however, that their extension to securities markets is devoid of any such justification. In securities markets, futures contracts amount to gambles that do nothing to enhance liquidity.

The analysis of reasons to bring particular families of financial transactions under the aegis of this negative presumption lies beyond the scope of the present programmatic argument. Such a presumption depends on far-reaching empirical study, which should be one of the responsibilities of research organizations assisting the executive and legislative branches of government.

To the extent, however, that we conclude that financial transactions, such as future contracts outside the setting of commodities markets, make no colorable contribution to the expansion of GDP or to the increase of productivity, we should either discourage such transactions (by tax and regulatory means) or, in the most egregious and dangerous instances, forbid them outright.

3. Enhancing the Capabilities of Local Banks

I now pass from the preliminaries or conditions to the agents or vehicles of an alternative direction.

A major resource of American democracy is its unrivaled network of local banks. The struggle over national banks in early American history culminated in the disbanding of the Second Bank of the United States during the presidency of Andrew Jackson in the 1830s. The outcome was the most decentralized system of finance at the service of the local producer and consumer that had ever existed in the history of the world up to that time. This broad-based network of local banks is a powerful tool that can be mobilized in the service of an effort to ensure that financial deepening triumphs over financial hypertrophy. The most important area for this enhancement is not credit for consumption (including housing), with regard to which the local financial institutions have always been prominent agents. It is the financing of small business and its development: credit for production.

There has long been a striking disparity between the sophistication and diversity of the capabilities deployed by the major national banks in the design of their services and the relative primitiveness of the skills, products, and services offered by the local banks. The capabilities of the local banks would need to be dramatically enhanced. As examples further ahead in this programmatic argument suggest (the democratization of options and hedges for agriculture), it is not enough to transpose mechanically the transactions designed for large, multinational enterprises to the environment of a local economy and of small and medium-size businesses. It is necessary to reinvent those transactions and to make the skills that they require stronger and more adaptable.

4. Establishing New GSEs: Agents for a Redesigned Industrial Policy

Such a transfer of skills from the commanding heights of national and international finance to local financial organizations cannot take place spontaneously. It requires initiatives and agents.

This task represents one spur among many to the creation of new GSEs, giving that New Deal invention a broader remit well outside the narrow albeit important area of the mortgage market. Such quasi-governmental organizations might be designed to include representatives of private industry, especially small business, as well as of the federal, state, and local governments.

One of these organizations' responsibilities would be to enhance the capabilities of local banks. This work should best be seen as a fragment of a novel conception of industrial policy. I use the term *industrial policy* as a term of art, describing collaboration between governments and firms in all sectors of the economy, including financial services, not just industry.

Understood in this way, industrial policy would have as its main addressees small and medium-size firms, which in the United States, as in every economy in the world, generate the major part of output and support the vast majority of jobs. In its guiding concerns, it would seek to expand access not just to credit but also to advanced practices and technologies rather than dogmatically to advance or subsidize certain sectors ("picking winners"). What would above all distinguish industrial policy in its subsequent and future developments would be a horizon of institutional innovation marked by two sets of advances.

On the vertical axis of relations between governments and firms, this policy would seek a form of coordination between governments and firms that is decentralized, pluralistic, participatory, and experimental. Thus, it would diverge from the Northeast Asian model of unitary trade and industrial policy, imposed top down by the state's bureaucratic apparatus. It would also differ, however, from the traditional American model that reduces the dealings between government and business to the arm's-length regulation of the latter by the former.

On the horizontal axis of relations among firms, industrial policy would favor the development of regimes of cooperative competition, such as those that have come to characterize some of the more successful subnational economies within the European Union as well as certain high-tech economies within the United States. Groups of small and medium-size firms would cooperate with one another, pooling certain financial, technological, or cognitive resources at the same time that they compete against one another. Through cooperation, they would achieve economies of scale and scope.

Finance is not simply an important requirement for the development of such an alternative form of industrial policy. The relations between finance and local economies are also a propitious terrain for the advancement of this institutional innovation. The broader goal is to enlist finance in the effort to afford more people access to more markets in more ways, thus democratizing the market economy rather than only regulating it.

5. The Democratizing Reinvention of Financial Products and Services

I now turn to a final pair of institutional and legal innovations intended to serve, in the realm of finance, the twin interests of making finance more useful and less dangerous to the real economy and enlisting finance in the effort to democratize rather than just to regulate the market economy.

To this end, a broad array of financial products and services would have to reinvented. As with the enhancement of local banks' financial capabilities, the simple transposition of the established products and services as well as of the skills and practices that sustain them to a less-advanced environment would not be enough. These skills and practices would need to be broadened and the products and services redesigned. Once again, a coordinated combination of governmental and private initiatives would be vital to secure this result.

Consider an agricultural example. We are accustomed to think of agriculture as an isolated exception within the economic order, requiring idiosyncratic policies. In the perspective of history, however, agriculture has often been a front line: a sector in which new forms of economic organization emerge before spreading to other sectors of the economy.

Family-scale agriculture, a historical strength of the United States, can be mechanized and capitalized to the point that any clear distinction between it and entrepreneurial agriculture is effaced. Beneath the largest scale of agribusiness, agriculture always faces the combination of physical and economic risk: climate volatility and price volatility. All over the world, the traditional antidotes to the threat presented by the combination of physical and economic risk—food stockpiles, price supports, and insurance (whether of crops or of income)—are giving way to new financial products for risk management—options and hedges—and to the financial services associated with them.

The problem is that such products and services are not normally accessible to even the entrepreneurial family famer. They would have to be redesigned to become accessible. And, once again, given costs of scale, a combination of private and governmental initiatives as well as new institutional agents—possibly in the form of a governmentally sponsored enterprise—may be needed to secure the result.

You may well suppose that such innovation will come too late to rescue the family farmer in the United States: if he has not grown his farm into a larger-scale agribusiness, he has vanished. Nevertheless, take the agricultural example as a small and simple paradigm of a democratizing reinvention of financial products and services that can and should take place over a broad range of financial activity.

6. Deepening the Venture-Capital Function

If there is one financial activity that most directly and fully embodies the idea of financial deepening as I have described it here, it is venture capital: the mobilization of capital not only to invest in emerging, innovative enterprise but also to bring together the capital, the practices, the technologies, and the people needed to make it a success. If financial deepening had advanced more than it in fact has in contemporary market economies, venture capital would be a central activity of the capital markets. Where it is absent, its functions would be performed in other ways and by agents other than self-described venture capitalists.

In fact, venture capital is minuscule as a proportion of financial activity, by any standard, even in the United States, the country in which it is by far most established in absolute terms, outreached only by Israel in relative terms. (The American economy accounts for 80 percent of venture-capital activity within the Organization for Economic Cooperation and Development.) In most advanced contemporary economies, venture capital has been calculated to amount to less than 0.05 percent of GDP. In the two countries in which it is most developed, Israel and the United States, it represents 0.38 and 0.028 percent, respectively. It should become a major financial activity, exercised through a wide array of private and public agents. It can and should serve as one of the instrumentalities of the alternative style of industrial policy I previously sketched.

In the absence of such a rapid expansion of private venture capital, a task for government would be to mimic in market form what venture capital does. Here is an example among many of how such an initiative might be pursued.

A major part of saving in the United States, as in all the rich industrial democracies, lies in the accumulated pension moneys: not just the private pension funds to which employers and employees contribute but also the public, defined-benefit systems such as Social Security. Without any privatization of these public pension systems, part of this vast store of capital might be placed under independent, competitive, and professional management in diversified portfolios of venture-capital-style investment. In this way, the dormant productive potential of saving could begin to be put to more effective use. The benefits for the pensioners as well as for the country could then be easily compared to the results of other forms of private and public investment.

Such an initiative would not represent a displacement of the market by the state. In the vital area of finance in a country that has assigned to finance a major if not a leading role, it would be an example of the use of the powers of government to democratize the market economy and to bind finance more closely to the real economy.

———————

In this chapter, I have developed an argument about the past, present, and future of American finance, seen from the limited by revealing vantage point of the crisis of 2007–2009 and the continuing effort to respond to its consequences. More important to this argument than the particular explanatory, critical, and programmatic ideas that I have put forward is the way of thinking about law and finance that these ideas are intended to exemplify.

I conclude by emphasizing three aspects of this way of thinking. One aspect is an approach to the legal and institutional setting of public policy as well as of finance. It is common today to insist that we no longer believe in the existence of "systems." Yet we remain inclined to imagine that the established institutional regime and the ideological assumptions informing it are a system with a logic all its own. According to our ideological and theoretical orientations, we may call this system "capitalism" or the "regulated market economy" or any other number of names reassuring to the cryptosystematizer.

A society's institutional and ideological settlement—its formative institutional arrangements and ideological assumptions—is not a system in any recognizable sense of the term, and it has no systemic logic. It is instead what in the introduction to this book I call "structure not system." It exerts pervasive influence on the routines of social, economic, and political life. It evades challenge and resists change, depending on the extent to which it is organized to entrench itself rather than to permit and even facilitate its revision. However, even at its most entrenched, it is not a system. It conforms to no logic that can be expounded in general ideas. Its parts did not spring into existence together, nor do they represent an indissoluble package that must be changed all at once or not at all. It is a ramshackle construction and is no less ramshackle for being fateful to the experiences of the societies and the lives of the individuals that it helps shape.

The New Deal framework for the organization of finance and of its relation to the real economy formed part of such a structure not system. What the New Dealers built has been gutted for a long time—relentlessly but evenly and inconclusively. What was never a system in the first place has been left in ruins rather than being replaced by another construction—even a ramshackle one.

The New Deal arrangements have been hollowed out or selectively destroyed and replaced to serve the interests of autonomous, hypertrophic finance as well as to suit the prejudices of the doctrines with which those interests have been allied. The hollowing out has not been succeeded by another scheme or another coherent logic. It has instead been followed by a gingerbread construction, a series of ad hoc compromises among conflicting interests and ideas. In this chapter, I have explored by example the demands that a structure not system places on the practice of explanation, criticism, and proposal.

A second aspect of the way of thinking exemplified here is that it takes there to be an intimate relation between two goals that we often value but only rarely connect. The first goal is financial deepening: the organization of finance so that it in fact does or does better what it is supposed to do—support the expansion of output and the enhancement of productivity in the real economy. The second goal is the democratization of finance: the reorganization of the market economy so that it affords more people more access to more markets in more ways and turns the broadening of opportunity and inclusion into a driving force of economic growth.

Many of the New Dealers, Louis Brandeis and William O. Douglas first among them, intuitively grasped the connection between these two

TABLE 2.1
The Institutional Context of Finance: Comparative Variations and Their Consequences

	Internal organization of national finance	Finance and the real economy	Finance in its institutional setting	Consequences: internal institutional dynamic
United States today	Short-term portfolio flows intermediated through the shadow-banking system	Decoupling of finance from the real economy; government intervenes to stabilize and support the existing financial system	Dependent on massive inflows of foreign-portfolio capital	Credit boom–asset bubble; debt deflation on systemic basis
United States in the 1930s and the early postwar period	Ample domestic savings intermediated through regulated banks, GSEs, and newly created institutional investors	Household savings channeled to government and nonfinancial enterprises	Relatively high domestic savings, institutional impediments to speculative trading by leveraged intermediaries	Virtuous cycle of domestic savings, investment, growth; active engagement in global markets
Mexico and Argentina in the 1980s and 1990s	Foreign-portfolio inflows intermediated through domestic banking system	Decoupling of finance from the real economy; increased internal and external liquidity fuels asset inflation and debt-fueled consumption	Dependent on massive inflows of foreign portfolio capital, increasingly based on the U.S. dollar	Credit boom–asset bubble; debt deflation on systemic basis
Brazil, Russia, India, China (BRIC countries) today	Foreign and domestic funding intermediated via strategically coordinated banking system; capital controls and surplus reserves	State-owned banks and development agencies channel funding to firms and sectors deemed "strategically" important	Relative autarky: high level of domestic savings fuels domestic spending and investment; capital controls limit exposure to global shocks	Virtuous cycle of domestic savings, investment, and growth; active participation in global markets
A better alternative	Rejection of credit dualism; decentralization of domestic banking system to broaden access and opportunity; institutional diversification and experimentation	Use of public–private partnerships to deepen domestic markets and to accelerate innovation in the forms and uses of finance	Active participation in global markets; restrictive treatment of short-term portfolio capital; accommodating treatments of investment in production	Finance subservient to the creation of new forms of production and new forms of finance

goals, although they lacked both the analytic apparatus and the institutional program that could do it justice. It has been my purpose to resurrect their aspiration but to establish it on another basis in a new historical circumstance.

A third aspect of the way of thinking that this book embodies is the identification in law and legal thought an extraordinary storehouse of materials for the institutional imagination. By understanding the genealogy of our present institutional settlement, by recognizing the hidden variations and contradictions that this nonsystem contains, and by enlisting some of them as material for the development of institutional alternatives, we can rediscover and reaffirm our power to transform the arrangements of the economy and society from the bottom up and from the inside out.

Economics may take a long time to become again what it once was: a discipline of the institutional imagination. Legal thought can become such a discipline right now. As an object of this work of insight and reform, finance, so widely feared for its manifest harms and so little understood for its potential benefits, offers a good place to begin.

CHAPTER THREE

The Democratized Market Economy

Chapters 1 and 2 of this book considered closely the problems of American finance as presented by the crisis of 2007–2009. They discussed legal and institutional innovations that might better draw finance into the service of production rather than allowing it to serve chiefly itself. It was a view through the microscope. This chapter takes a look through the telescope, placing those reform ideas and proposals in the setting of a larger endeavor: the organization of socially inclusive growth on the basis of a democratized market economy—goals widely advocated but little detailed and enacted in the world.

Chapter 4 trades one telescope for another, locating the argument about finance in a comparative-historical context rather than in a programmatic one: it compares some aspects of American, Latin American, and Northeast Asian development in the second half of the twentieth century. It explores the institutional commitments and innovations that have advanced or inhibited the deepening of finance and the democratization of the market economy. It concludes by giving greater detail, informed by the comparative-historical argument, to the institutional proposals advanced in this brief chapter.

In chapter 5, I make explicit the way of thinking that this book seeks to develop and exemplify: its central ideas, its method, and their implications for legal and economic analysis. From beginning to end, my interest is in structural vision and structural change.

THE BROADER PROGRAMMATIC SETTING OF THE REFORM OF FINANCE

Reforms of finance like those for which I have argued may be driven by practical concerns: the prevention or mitigation of financial crisis and the better use of the potential of finance to serve production and innovation. However, to see the reform of finance only from this perspective is to diminish its significance. The reshaping of finance and of its relation to the real economy is important as well because it forms an indispensable part of the effort to give practical substance to the most widely professed political-economic goal in our time: the organization of socially inclusive economic growth.

Indeed, unless we perceive and manage the reform of finance as a contribution to socially inclusive economic growth, it is unlikely to prevail against the interests and preconceptions that are ranged against it. It can draw clarity and power from its connection to a larger purpose: the aim of giving more people the opportunity and the capability to become agents as well as beneficiaries of economic growth.

Experience has shown that no one who is committed to placing economic growth on a broad social base can afford to disregard finance. Left unreformed, finance imposes a formidable obstacle to the pursuit of socially inclusive growth. Finance may help defeat that pursuit by the threat or the reality of capital flight, by recurrent financial volatility and crisis, as well as by the effect of such crisis on the level of economic activity. Moreover, high finance regularly wields enormous political influence.

The relation of my financial proposals and ideas to a larger program of socially inclusive economic growth is, however, neither accidental nor merely instrumental. Financial deepening—the tightening of the relation of finance to the real economy and the enhancement of finance's service to production and innovation—can begin to advance without the democratization of finance—the broadening of the base of economic agents who as both producers and consumers can make use of external finance (finance not internalized in the firm). However, we cannot hope to go far in deepening finance unless we also begin to democratize it.

In the absence of such a democratization, financial deepening will spell greater engagement with the real economy as this economy is now organized in highly hierarchical and segmented form. That form includes divisions among the worlds of large capital-rich firms, capital-starved small businesses, and a small periphery of innovative, knowledge-rich start-ups. Such innovative start-ups are more likely than the participants in the other two worlds to use finance in the way it is supposed to be used but rarely is.

The democratization of finance can in turn begin to advance without any larger reshaping of the economic order. It can move forward thanks to a succession of small measures. It cannot, however, continue to advance without structural change in the economy.

By structural change, I do not mean simply change in the relation among sectors of production (the sense of the term structural change in twentieth-century development economics). I mean change in the institutional and legal arrangements of the economy. Such arrangements influence who can do what with which resources. They powerfully shape the division of the economy into different domains, not just different sectors of production, such as the three worlds of sophisticated big business; traditional, relatively backward small business; and innovative, emergent enterprise. Each of these realms of economic life affords opportunities and imposes limits in its own manner, empowering and disempowering economic agents at the same time. Each of them uses and fails to use finance in distinct ways.

Consider, as an example, the daunting problem of the relation of the productive vanguard to the rest of the economy. Today this vanguard is what I have described as knowledge-intensive, experimentalist production. We associate it most readily with high-tech industry. But in an economy in which the distinctions among sectors wane, this vanguard appears in every sector: in agriculture and services as well as in industry. Will it remain the province of an entrepreneurial and technological elite? Or will the most advanced practice of production be widely disseminated within the economy so that many can share in its development and its wealth as well as enjoy its products and platforms? Socially inclusive economic growth must mean, among other things, a form of economic growth based on the widest propagation of the most advanced productive practice. Inclusive growth must be able to count on an inclusive vanguardism.

Such a dissemination cannot happen spontaneously. Today's most advanced practice of production, unlike the mechanized manufacturing and mass production of earlier periods, has demanding cognitive and moral as well as narrowly economic requirements. Fulfillment of these requirements depends on a broad range of institutional, educational, and cultural changes. For such changes to come about, the organization and role of finance must also shift.

It follows from this reasoning that financial deepening, the democratization of finance, and the institutional reshaping of the market economy are neither the same tasks nor tasks unrelated to each other. They are overlapping, internally connected projects.

There is, however, a weakness in this logic that this brief chapter addresses. The goal of organizing socially inclusive growth may be almost universally entertained. It is, however, also almost always left empty of institutional content. The prestige of this ideal cannot conceal the relatively meager results that have been achieved by policies crafted in its name.

My thesis is that the commitment to socially inclusive economic growth can be effective only if it is achieved through a change in the organization of the market economy. A major part of such change must be institutional innovation, expressed as law.

What this thesis chiefly contradicts is the belief that economic growth can be made more inclusive by combining the present organization of the market economy with progressive taxation and redistributive social programs. Such initiatives are designed to attenuate the inequalities generated in the market rather than to reshape the market itself. Instead of influencing the primary distribution of economic advantage—the one resulting from the operation of the market economy as this economy is now organized—they seek to create, through compensatory and retrospective measures, a secondary distribution of economic advantage.

The lesson of historical experience, however, is that compensatory and retrospective redistribution has limited effect on the class structure of society and on the assignment of economic advantage. The basic reason for its relative inefficacy is that it has to become massive to achieve a significant equalizing outcome. Long before it has reached this threshold of scale (it never does), it would start to disrupt incentives to save, invest, and employ, thus harming economic growth.

This problem is captured in the familiar rhetoric of a tension between equity and efficiency. The idea of such a tension presupposes the maintenance of the market economy's present institutional form. Compensatory and retrospective redistribution has been most effective when it has been ancillary to institutional changes that broaden economic and educational opportunity and empowerment. It has been least effective when it has been used to substitute for them. That is the lesson to be inferred from the history of Scandinavian social democracy, so widely admired throughout the world.

We can generalize this lesson. On the one hand, the greatest achievement of European social democracy in the twentieth century was a high level of public investment in people—in their physical integrity and their capabilities. On the other hand, the defining compromise of historical social democracy was a retreat by the Left and the labor movement from any attempt to reshape substantially the institutional arrangements of power and production. In return for this retreat, the state was allowed to expand its power to regulate and redistribute. The market order was to be left in place but humanized. The predominant impulse of institutionally conservative social democracy became pietistic rather than transformative.

The price of this deal has now become too high. The social-democratic settlement prevents us from reckoning with structural problems central to the future of society and to the accomplishment of socially inclusive economic growth. Among those problems are the disconnection of finance from the real economy and the confinement of the most advanced practice of production to relatively insular vanguards that exclude the vast majority of the labor force. This confinement causes an injury at once to economic growth (because it squanders the talents of the majority) and to an ideal of inclusion. The ideal has two sides: agency and equality. It seeks to contain inequality by enhancing agency and to ignite and accelerate economic growth by enabling more people to share in making economic growth happen. It requires institutional innovation on the supply side of the economy, not just an attenuation of inequalities on the demand side of the economy through progressive taxation and social entitlements.

In marking this contrast, we must guard against a misunderstanding. A progressive alternative to institutionally conservative social democracy need not and should not be expressed as an institutional blueprint. It should instead mark a direction of cumulative institutional change: a succession of steps rather than a system of parts. We can explore any such direction at points close to present reality and in particular areas of economic and social life, as I have done in the first two chapters of this book, or at points remote from present arrangements and pertinent to the economy and the polity broadly, as I do in this chapter.

The reader may be taken aback by the contrast between the character of the argument in the previous chapters and my argument in this one: in those chapters addressed to a particular context—the United States of the early twenty-first century—and engaged with a distinct area of economic life—finance and its reform; in this chapter ranging more widely over the organization of markets and democracies and turned to a more distant future. These two approaches are complementary. I described them in the opening paragraphs of this chapter as views through the microscope and the telescope. They are fixed on the same direction.

The advantage of exploring a direction close by in the realm of the proximate possible is to benefit from the discipline imposed on the programmatic imagination by tangible realities and constraints. The advantage of exploring the direction farther ahead and farther afield is to gain clarity in articulating the interests and ideals from which a trajectory of institutional change gains energy and authority.

What we say when we look through the microscope may seem to be merely "reformist" temporizing, as if structural change were not always taking place in steps and working with the fragmentary materials supplied by our historical circumstance. What we say when we look through the telescope may appear to be a visionary and voluntarist discourse without purchase on social and economic reality, as if even the most modest reforms fail to imply a choice of route and a conception of the interests and ideals supporting it. We must look through both the microscope and the telescope, using the view through one to correct the view through the other.

There is no contradiction in adopting both views, only a departure from intellectual and political convention. The impression of a clash between moderate and radical proposals results from thinking of programmatic ideas as blueprints rather than as pathways. We can chart a pathway close to its beginnings and or map out where it takes us. We develop our view of the next steps and our idea of the direction in the light of each approach, revising each as we advance in practice and thought.

The complementarity of the view through the microscope and the view through the telescope provides no excuse for wishful thinking. An understanding of structural change and structural constraints must inform the imagination of institutional alternatives if a programmatic argument is not to degenerate into a dream. A dream may bear all too clearly the marks of a past from which it wants itself to be free but does not know how to be. In the final two chapters of this book, I propose elements of such an understanding and develop that understanding through the elucidation of some turning points in the history of finance and production. In this way, I hope to fill in the space between the view through the microscope and the view through the telescope.

The remainder of this chapter explores three connected agendas of institutional innovation: democratizing the market economy, deepening democracy, and empowering the individual through the assignment of basic endowments to everyone as well as through change in the character and setting of education. Of these three agendas, the first—the democratized market economy—is the one most closely connected to the concerns of this book. For this reason, it holds the foreground of my discussion here. A democratized market economy, however, can flourish only against the background of a deepened democracy. Moreover, it requires as its protagonist an empowered worker and citizen. I conclude the chapter by relating the first agenda to the other two.

DEMOCRATIZING THE MARKET ECONOMY

A major premise of my argument about finance is that the market economy lacks a single natural and necessary form. That there are many ways of organizing a market economy is one of the chief insights achieved by legal thought over the past 150 years. Jurists discovered, often at cross purposes to their predispositions, that ideas such as contract and property can be realized in very different kinds of economic arrangements, with consequences for the organization of production and exchange as well for the distribution of economic advantage. They found that the choices to be made at each level down in concreteness, in the design of each aspect of the market economy, involve contests among interests and among visions. Such contests cannot legitimately be settled by referring back to abstract notions of contract, property, and the market, as if these notions had predetermined content.

One such dimension of variance in the institutional organization of a market system is the way in which it relates finance to the real economy. The concepts of financial deepening and financial hypertrophy, defined and discussed earlier in this book, help explore this range of variation.

We are accustomed to think that there are two major ways in which law and politics can engage a market economy under democracy: by regulating it or by attenuating inequalities of income and wealth. They may attenuate such inequalities through retrospective redistribution by means of progressive taxation and social spending. There is, however, a third activity that we can undertake with respect to markets: we can change them by reshaping the institutions that make them what they are and that mold the primary distribution of economic advantage— the distribution existing before any attempt at correction of what the market has wrought. The reforms in American history to which I referred under the label *democratizing from below*—the reconstruction of agricultural and financial markets in the period before the Civil War—supply examples.

This third class of activities—the class of market-changing initiatives—is more fundamental than the other two classes—regulation and retrospective or secondary redistribution. It is more fundamental than regulation because by definition it changes what regulation takes for granted. In fact, regulatory policy must always contend with the consequences of the plurality of market-shaping arrangements even when it fails to acknowledge that plurality. Every regulatory strategy represents a possible point of departure for a distinctive reorganization of the market economy, as I earlier showed with respect to the regulation of finance.

The third class of activities is also more fundamental than corrective redistribution because it powerfully influences the primary distribution of advantage—economic power and opportunity as well as wealth and income. Retrospective redistribution—historical experience demonstrates—can rarely do more than marginally modify the effects of the primary distribution of advantage, a fact than many of the most influential contemporary theories of distributive justice fail to take into account.

A market-changing reform counts as democratizing when it results in a broadening of access to effective economic agency—that is, to the resources and opportunities of productive activity. Reforms addressed to this goal are very likely to diminish inequality of income and wealth over time for one simple reason: they spread the opportunity to engage in gainful activity. They are especially likely to do so when access is gained to advanced forms of production.

Agency or empowerment lies at the heart of the democratic ideal and accounts for much of its power. Representative democracy in its conventional contemporary forms is associated with a characteristic repertory of arrangements that sustain self-government, political pluralism, and rotation in power as well as temper a devotion to popular self-rule with a commitment to safeguarding political and social minorities and to protecting the individual against oppression. But this familiar stock of institutional ideas and arrangements is only one variant among many of a devotion to the democratic ideal of agency: our power to rule ourselves, as individuals and as a people, and to set through such self-rule the terms of social life. A problem arises when the marriage of this ideal to the contingent and flawed institutional arrangements of contemporary polities and economies is left unchallenged and even unremarked.

These comments require elucidation. One way of organizing a market economy may differ from another in the extent to which it broadens or narrows the life chances of ordinary men and women for such agency. Political institutions represent an important part of this variation, but they do not tell the whole story.

Take, for example, the role of regimes of production and labor in giving shape to the experience of agency. In Adam Smith's pin factory or Henry Ford's assembly line, the worker worked as if he were a machine—indeed, as if he were one of the old-style machines (such as the metal-cutting lathe) that he operated. Agency may be enhanced, however, when the worker works as the opposite of a machine, nonformulaically—indeed, as the master of the instruments and process of production and as a collaborator with other similarly situated individuals. The combination of the machine and the worker as antimachine then becomes more powerful than either of them alone. Work then becomes more productive and more human.

Similarly, the experience of agency—as heightened self-consciousness and effective action—will be enhanced or diminished according to the legal regime of the employment relation. In the nineteenth century, liberals and socialists alike—including, for example, Abraham Lincoln—believed wage labor to be an inferior form of free labor, tainted by traits of serfdom and slavery. No free man, Lincoln said in his address to the Wisconsin Agricultural Society in 1859, would settle for it unless weakened by "a dependent nature which prefers it, or improvidence, folly, or singular misfortune."

The higher forms of free labor were, according to this view, self-employment and cooperation. Once combined, they could reconcile enhanced economic freedom with the pitiless imperative of economies of scale. Yet later in the nineteenth century and in the course of the twentieth, wage labor began to be naturalized as the default form of free labor. What had earlier been seen as an unacceptable diminishment of personal freedom came to be viewed as inescapable.

Today, however, this nineteenth-century dream gains new pertinence. The emerging practices of production, sometimes dubbed "post-Fordist" or the "knowledge economy," and the reorganization of production on a worldwide basis as a decentralized network of contractual arrangements establish a new putting-out system. They encourage us to revive that nineteenth-century dream. To give it practical consequence under the new circumstances would be to strike a powerful blow in favor of an ideal of greater agency for ordinary people.

An especially important dimension of democratizing the market economy is broadening access to the most advanced practice of production. The most advanced practice is not necessarily in the short term the most efficient form of production, though it tends to become the most efficient as its potential is realized. It has the greatest fecundity: the facility to serve as a starting point for further organizational and technological innovations. Nor is it any longer confined to a single sector of production like mechanized manufacturing, the most advanced practice of an earlier era, was; it can develop as a vanguard in all sectors: agriculture and services as well as industry. Today we can best understand it as the practice that most clearly and fully expresses the power of the imagination in the cooperative arrangements of production: the side of the mind that can detach function from structure, combine everything with everything else, and transgress its own methods and assumptions.

The embodiment of our imaginative powers in the arrangements of production is closely related to the enhancement of agency. It means that no predetermined scheme of social division and hierarchy must be allowed to restrict how we can work together to produce goods and services. It implies as well that prerogative and power must be subordinated to unrealized opportunities of invention, innovation, and production.

The more we realize and radicalize this ideal in our material life, the less we will be willing to confine it to any limited part of economic life. The more we deepen and disseminate its practical expressions, the greater becomes the element of discretion or creative freedom in our productive activity.

Consider two moments of modern economic history and the role of the most advanced practice of production in each of them. In the aftermath of the Industrial Revolution, the most advanced practice was mechanized manufacturing. Every part of the economy, including agriculture, was soon transformed on the model of mechanized manufacturing. Mass production, sometimes called Fordist mass production—the production of standardized goods and commodities by means of relatively rigid machines and production processes, semiskilled labor, and highly specialized and hierarchical work relations—was to be the apogee of mechanized manufacturing. Under this regime, discretion at work was reserved to the managers and supervisors. The worker worked as if he were one of the machines that he operated. And the employment relation consisted in the buying and selling of labor under the terms of the wage contract, the prevalence of which Karl Marx singled out as the most characteristic feature of the supposedly recurrent and indivisible regime that he called capitalism.

Now compare this circumstance to the most advanced areas of production today. They can no longer be identified by a sector, such as high technology. The distinctions among sectors have faded as advanced manufacturing takes on the character of crystallized services and the most advanced practice of production appears as a relatively insular vanguard in every part of the economy—in agriculture, for example, as precision agriculture.

This most advanced productive practice is sometimes labeled post-Fordist production or the knowledge economy or the new economy. Its arrangements bear a closer relation to the imaginative side of the mind than mechanized manufacturing ever did. Their superficial attributes are the use of technologies and practices that make it possible to destandardize or customize production and to involve workers as well as mangers in continuous innovation. Their deeper characteristics are the attenuation of contrasts between conception and execution, the combination of cooperation and competition in the same domains of activity (cooperative competition), and the turning of production into a practice of permanent innovation.

In principle, this paradigm of production should be susceptible to even more rapid diffusion than was mechanized manufacturing in its heyday. Yet the opposite has happened. Although many of the products and platforms created by the high-tech firms most commonly associated with the knowledge economy (e.g., computers and other information-related gadgets) are widely used, the new advanced productive practice, unlike its nineteenth-century predecessor, has remained confined largely to advanced parts of each national economy.

The productive vanguards of the knowledge economy are strongly linked to one another around the world. However, they remain weakly linked to other, relatively more backward parts of the production system at home. The model that they present fails to be emulated on a large scale, notwithstanding the efforts of national and local governments to support their reproduction.

We must seek the reason for this reversal of circumstance outside economics in the social and cultural requirements of this new paradigm of production: access to technical education focused on higher-order and flexible capabilities; a density of forms of association within and outside the workplace; a heightening of trust and discretion at work against the background of such social capital; and political-legal arrangements facilitating the collaboration between governmental initiative and private enterprise in ways that resist cronyism and collusion.

What, then, are the distinctive traits of a democratized market economy, understood as a direction and a regulative ideal rather than as a blueprint or a system? If a program such as this one marks a direction rather than describing a blueprint, we must be able to represent it at points remote from existing arrangements or close to them. In most of this book, I address the direction close to them, in the realm of the proximate possible. But here, exceptionally, in the hope of stating a conception of the regulative ideal at stake in democratizing the market, I suggest a view of this direction many steps into the future.

First, a democratized market economy extends access to the resources and opportunities of production (as the reform tradition committed to defending small business against big business and the doctrine of property-owning democracy wanted) without equating this goal with a single-minded commitment to traditional family business. It must find ways to reconcile, through legal and institutional innovation, economic decentralization with economies of scale rather than to accept (as the reform tradition that sought rescue in the regulation of big business did) economic concentration as the inevitable price of such economies of scale.

Second, a democratized market economy broadens the gateways of access to advanced manufacturing and its counterparts in services and agriculture (the creative, knowledge-based economy), supplying their social and educational conditions whenever they are missing.

Third, to the end of achieving these two goals, it insists on innovating in the legal arrangements of the market economy and in the terms on which people have access to capital and technology. That means allowing alternative regimes of contract and private and social property to coexist experimentally within the same market economy.

It also means refusing to accept a choice between the two models of government–business relations that are now available in the world: the American model of arm's-length regulation of business by government and the Northeast Asian model of unitary industrial and trade policy imposed top down by a governmental bureaucracy. The democratized market economy must allow the government to act in partnership with business, especially small and medium-size firms, in ways that are pluralistic, participatory, and experimental to the end of facilitating the economy-wide diffusion of the most advanced practices of production. For the same reason, it must allow and encourage cooperative competition among such firms, which would continue to compete against one another while pooling some financial, technological, or commercial resources.

Fourth, through such innovations in its legal regime, the democratized market economy begins to deprive wage labor of the appearance of naturalness and necessity implicit in the present understanding of free labor. It creates facilities for the combination of the two higher forms of free labor—self-employment and cooperation—seizing the opportunities opened up by the decline and replacement of mass production.

Fifth, it secures to all, independently of the jobs that they hold, a universal core of capability-enhancing endowments: a basic patrimony or social inheritance (of which a guaranteed minimum income is a particular variant) and a set of universal social and economic rights. It must understand and implement this conception in ways that prevent it from depending on the preservation of the unified property right as the tradition of thinking about property-owning democracy was all too willing to allow.

Sixth, it seizes on the immense transformative opportunity presented by change in the practices of production. It does not allow the new productive vanguardism to remain isolated within advanced parts of the production system, weakly linked to the rest of the national economy. It insists on promoting advanced production outside the established vanguard as the surest way both to enhance economic agency and to diminish inequality in the primary distribution of economic advantage.

Will finance be friend or enemy to this agenda of liberation? The generally accepted view is that we can at best hope to contain its restrictive and prejudicial effect. A major contention of this work is that, better understood and properly reformed, finance can play a major role in the development of such a progressive alternative to the present organization of the market economy.

DEEPENING DEMOCRACY

Deepening democracy is the second transformative project that helps form the larger programmatic setting of this argument.

The conception of democracy to which I appeal is one that gives a central role to mastery of the structure of society—to its basic institutional arrangements and ideological assumptions. Such assumptions and arrangements shape the routines of social life. They fall as the dead hand of the past on the living—unless and until they are mastered by a practice of democratic politics equipped to master them.

The two parts of the traditional view of democracy—the part about popular self-government and the part about minority and individual rights—add up to a view of collective self-determination. On that view, collective self-determination thrives only in the presence of safeguards for group difference and individual autonomy. The structure of society must, on this view, be chosen even though the arrangements of society may not for the most part be actively contested at any given time.

Yet if this received view of democracy is to make sense, social and economic arrangements must never lie beyond the reach of collective deliberation and change. They must be susceptible to revision, with such (constitutional) restraints as may be designed to prevent ephemeral majorities from eroding the base of continuing pluralism. Prominent among such restraints are protections for the individual against governmental or private oppression.

It requires, however, only a moment's reflection to note how far all present and past democracies fall below this standard. In fact, the democracies that we know reach only episodically and marginally into the received structure of society. They exceed their transformative modesty only when crisis, usually in the form of economic ruin or armed conflict among states, forces their hand.

For much of the history of modern politics and political thought, it was understood that politics is consequential only when it has structural ambitions, even if its aim is to defend established arrangements and assumptions against some threat to their continuance. Like the nineteenth-century liberals and socialists and unlike their late-twentieth-century neoliberal or social-democratic successors, we have reason to take the structure of society as the true object of transformative engagement in politics. However, unlike them, we can no longer confidently embrace a dogmatic institutional formula for the progress of society and the achievement of its material and moral interests. How, then, can we entertain structural ambitions without succumbing to structural dogmatism?

The answer lies in developing the element of collective discovery and construction in democracy: the sense in which democracy can represent an organized process of collective learning and inspiration. Instead of committing ourselves to a definitive blueprint, we can organize a practice for finding the way. This view exploits the affinity between science and democracy and has found expression in the ideas of American philosophers such as John Dewey.

This approach can be reconciled with the traditional view of democracy as majority rule qualified by individual and group rights. It places that view, however, in a different light. It sees the arrangements of democracy as a method for the continuing invention of the best way to realize our recognized interests and professed ideals, if only by revising the practices and institutions with which we habitually associate them.

This understanding of democracy has practical consequences; it is more than a different way of talking. Its most direct and important implication is that all our institutions, especially our political institutions, should help encourage a broad social experimentalism. They should also lend themselves to ongoing challenge and revision. What this means for the direction in which democracy can and should be deepened I shall soon consider, but only after first relating this conception of democracy to the American constitutional tradition.

The constitutional arrangements of the United States embody a protodemocratic liberalism. Many students of American institutions have drawn attention to their undemocratic aspects. They have resisted the temptation to see these undemocratic elements as the inevitable price of a proper regard to the safeguarding of individual rights and political and social pluralism.

These critics have traditionally focused on those aspects of the U.S. Constitution that represent vestiges of the limits to universal suffrage in the early republic. Among such vestiges are the Electoral College and the aspects of bicameralism and federalism that distort the political representation of the people in the name of allegedly countervailing considerations.

Such criticisms, however, fail to go to the heart of what makes the constitutional arrangements of the United States and the beliefs supporting them less than democratic. A major element in this deficit of democracy concerns the misunderstood relation between two sets of constitutional ideas and institutions. One set of arrangements in the American constitutional design is organized around a liberal principle of the fragmentation of power. Many centers of political initiative coexist. Another set of arrangements is centered on the conservative principle of slowing down politics. Its chief expression is the Madisonian scheme of checks and balances in the design of the separation of powers. The effect of this conservative principle is to perpetuate impasse in the form of divided government. The facility for impasse and the lack of constitutional devices to overcome it whenever the presidency and both houses of Congress are not in the same party's control—or even whenever the same current of opinion is not held within one party— virtually condemn all plans for structural reform. At least, they condemn those plans when they cannot count on the favoring circumstance of economic crisis or war.

A characteristic tenet of American constitutional thinking is that these two principles—the liberal and the conservative—are naturally and necessarily connected: the liberal principle presupposes the conservative one. In fact, however, they are connected by design rather than by practical or rational necessity. An underlying aim of their intentional connection is to inhibit the transformation of the social and economic order through political activity. The constitutional entrenchment of this inhibition makes sense if private freedom is thought to have a natural form that, once established, must be protected against perversion. The exemplary form of perversion, according to this way of thinking, is one group's attempt to gain political power for the purpose of serving its own interests to the detriment of other groups' interests.

Justified in the name of securing society against such perversion, the association of the liberal and the conservative principles produces the opposite effect. It allows the moneyed classes and the corporations to secure their interests in a private order that is naturalized (rather than being seen as the accidental political construction that it is) and relatively barred against political challenge. In such a circumstance, economic theories that take present arrangements to be the natural expression of a free-enterprise system may seem plausible. Influential economic doctrines work together with constitutional arrangements and ideas to support and enact this naturalization of the economic regime. It then requires a major crisis, such as the Depression and the world war of the mid–twentieth century, to override the deliberate inhibition on the transformative potential of democratic politics.

The combination of the liberal and the conservative principles in constitutional design is not the sole source of the deficit of democracy in America. There are at least two other major sources.

A second source is a combination of beliefs, practices, and institutions that impede or discourage the mass of ordinary men and women from participating more fully in political life. The rules governing the use of money in politics, the ability to buy and sell access to the means of mass communication, the amorphous, unprogrammatic character of political parties, the optional character of the vote (despite the existence of other mandatory public duties in American practice), and, most fundamentally, the limitation of political life to a cadre of professional politicians and their associates and to momentary electoral episodes—all these factors combine to keep society at a low political temperature.

A close connection exists between the level of popular engagement in the politics of a democracy and the structural content of its political life. A politics rich in structural content is generally a hot politics: one that sustains a high level of political participation. A cold politics—one that keeps the people at a low level of engagement—is likely to be thin in its openness to structural alternatives.

A characteristic tenet of conservative political science makes the commitment to a low level of popular engagement seem inevitable. It claims that an inverse relation exists between political mobilization and political institutionalization. (See, for example, Samuel Huntington.[1]) An institutional politics is, according to this view, necessarily cold, keeping political society at a low level of engagement. By contrast, a hot politics is necessarily anti- or extrainstitutional. What this tenet disregards is what comparative historical experience has amply demonstrated: political institutions differ in the extent to which they either suppress or encourage organized popular participation in political life. (Similarly, I argue throughout this book that market institutions differ in the extent to which they either tighten or loosen the relation of finance to the real economy.)

A third source of the democratic deficit in the United States is a failure to tap more fully the experimentalist potential of federalism and more generally of the relation between democratic experimentalism conducted top down by the federal government and the democratic experimentalism conducted bottom up by the states and municipalities. There is an unresolved contradiction between the official doctrine and the institutional framework of American federalism. The doctrine is experimentalist: the states have long been described as "laboratories of experimentation." However, the institutional framework, with its rigid allocation of powers among the levels of the federal system and its consequent antipathy to cooperative federalism, works against experimentalism in the enactment of federalism. This failure becomes more significant when we are determined to associate democracy with experimentalism and to achieve structural change without succumbing to structural dogmatism.

The failure is not limited to federal systems like the American. It extends as well to unitary states (e.g., the United Kingdom and France) in the way that they understand and organize the relation between initiative by central government and devolution to local authorities. In both unitary and federal regimes, a mistaken premise helps justify and sustain a flawed practice. The premise is the existence of a hydraulic or inverse relation between central power and decentralized initiative. Power built by the center is taken away from the periphery. Power won below must be taken away from central government above.

No such necessary inverse relation exists. The federal government and the lower levels of the federation—states, municipalities, and other bodies—may do more at the same time. Similarly, in a unitary state, strong central initiative may advance together with radical devolution. In fact, it may be easier to combine strong central initiative with radical devolution in a unitary state than to reform federalism, given the constitutional and ideological obstacles to the reform of federal systems. Under federal and unitary regimes alike, national and local initiative may reinforce rather than restrain each other: what is added to one is not necessarily subtracted from the other.

Such a combination, so vital to the progress of democratic experimentalism and to the pursuit of structural change without fixed blueprints, is more than a philosophical speculation. It is, according to my earlier argument, one of the most important lessons of American history. In the early formative period of the republic, the national government's mobilization of national resources for development was combined with democratizing institutional innovation down below, especially in agriculture and finance. It was a duo that built both American democracy and the U.S. economy. Whenever this beneficial combination weakened, the result was to open a space for the marriage of high finance and big business. It has further been weakened to the outright financialization of the economy (financial hypertrophy in place of financial deepening).

Among its many lessons, this feature of American experience suggests a reinterpretation and a reconstruction of federalism in United States. The redress of the democratic deficit in the country requires that activism by the federal government go hand in hand with a substantial expansion of decentralized initiative at the local—state and municipal—level. Much can be accomplished by a simple change of attitude and practice without legal or constitutional change. But for the movement to continue, both the laws and the Constitution may need to be amended. (In the United States, the preferred way of amending the Constitution is to reinterpret it. However, this technique is more readily applied to the understanding of rights such as equal protection and due process than to the design of the government.)

The institutional requirements for deepening democracy in America follow directly from the preceding discussion of the democratic deficit in the country. I next outline a direction of institutional change with the United States in mind. But these proposals apply generally to democracies around the world, with adjustments required by context—for example, according to the differences between federal and unitary states or among presidential, semipresidential, and parliamentary forms of government. The stock of institutional options available throughout the world in this area as in others is now both very limited and relatively inelastic. Moreover, the structural problems of contemporary societies and economies are similar, despite all differences in history, culture, and economic development. Institutional innovation must be rooted in a place as well as in a moment. The ideas informing it can nevertheless speak across a wide range of countries given the analogies, in structural problems as well as in possible structural responses to them, that now bind contemporary societies together.

Three sets of institutional innovations are required to remedy the deficit in the United States and other contemporary democracies. They form no take-it-or-leave-it system. We may develop some before we have advanced others. Yet they reinforce one another by their presence and restrain one another by their absence.

A first set of innovations would heighten the level of organized popular engagement in political life. Such initiatives would include those that provide for the public finance of political activity and limit or prohibit private funding. These innovations would extend to organized social movements as well as political parties free access to the means of mass communication as a condition of the revocable licenses under which media firms do their business. They would make liberal use of comprehensive programmatic plebiscites and referendums as opposed to single-issue consultations of the electorate. And they would seize the potential of contemporary technologies to involve citizens in the business of local and national government while adopting electoral rules hospitable to a diversification of representation and voice.

A second set of innovations would reaffirm the liberal principle of the fragmentation of power in the organization of government while repudiating the conservative principle of the slowing down of politics. A pure parliamentary regime may appear to dispose of the problem of divided government, but it does so at the risk of concentrating power in the political class. It may be better to maintain the presidency but equip it with instruments for the rapid overcoming of deadlock between the executive and the legislative branches. One such means is to resort to comprehensive programmatic plebiscites and referendums, pitting one set of institutional and policy changes against another, as distinguished from single-issue consultations of the electorate. Another such means is to award to either political branch the right unilaterally to call early elections under the condition that the elections always be bilateral, or for both branches. Thus, the branch exercising the constitutional prerogative would have to pay the price of running the electoral risk.

This second set of innovations is the hardest to achieve in the American context given the cult of the Constitution. However, its effect may be at least in part replaced by a change of attitude and practice under current arrangements.

A third set of innovations would better tap the experimentalist potential of federalism. It would do so, on the one hand, by facilitating cooperative federalism—joint initiatives by different parts of the federal system, including both vertical cooperation among the three levels of federation and horizontal cooperation among states and among municipalities. It would do so, on the other hand, by enabling particular parts of the federal system to secede from widely prevailing national solutions and to develop in different parts of the country countermodels of the national future. This prerogative of divergence must be conditioned on its not being used to entrench any form of social exclusion or oppression. The experiments must be experiments in freedom broadly understood.

The cumulative effect of these three sets of innovations would be to deepen democracy: to enhance the power of democratic politics to master the structure of society and overthrow the rule of the living by the dead. A vital attribute of the arrangements of a deepened democracy is that as they enable change in the arrangements of each area of social life, they also facilitate their own transformation. In this sense, they represent the political embodiment of an experimentalist ideal, just as knowledge-intensive production and the democratized market economy are the economic embodiment of that ideal.

The deepening of democracy is a concern intimately related to the themes of this book and to my earlier argument in the introduction. It is also a practical requirement for advancing beyond their initial stages the other two directions of cumulative institutional change discussed here—democratizing the market and empowering the individual.

EMPOWERING THE INDIVIDUAL: FROM RIGHTS TO POWERS AND ENDOWMENTS

To democratize the market and to deepen democracy, we must also enhance the powers of the individual. No aim has been more central to the ideas of personal and social liberation that for more than two centuries have aroused humanity than the ideal of selfconstruction: the making of a person who is bigger than her circumstance. Such a person is not the slave of collective formulas. She does not reduce her life to the enactment of a script that she is handed by the family, the class, the community, and the age into which she was born. She asserts her prerogative to judge the world—her world—and to turn the tables on it. She will not surrender to the conformity of routine or bear submission to another.

This ideal is the ideal of the American prophets Ralph Waldo Emerson, Walt Whitman, and Abraham Lincoln, and it has never ceased to have the most intimate bond with American democracy. In each democracy everywhere, such prophets have spoken this message in a language resonating with the experience of their nation.

This ideal may seem remote from the practical problems of financial and economic reform addressed in the first two chapters of this book. Nevertheless, proposals like the ones explored in those chapters are meant to exemplify in the area with which they deal—finance—a practice of radical reform, undertaken in the light of structural vision, that can apply to any part of social, economic, and political life. In every domain, they mark a direction of cumulative institutional innovation. The practice of radical reform cannot flourish without its agents—people equipped and empowered in a certain way. And the reforms brought about are unlikely to advance beyond their initial steps unless they form part of the larger project that this third agenda helps define.

We realize this ideal by ensuring every citizen's and every worker's endowments: the means with which to make something of their lives and to resist their circumstances. Such endowments must consist in both material assets and educational opportunities.

The material endowment is the existence of a social inheritance—a minimum stock of resources settled on each individual that she can draw on at turning points in her life or, alternatively, a minimum guaranteed income on which she can rely independently of any part she plays in the production system. The point is independence: the ability to venture her life in one direction or another rather than to be driven by material dependence into a course of life in which she has no interest.

The educational endowment is a form of education, both in youth and throughout life, enabling her to enhance her powers of initiative and invention. Such an education must be dialectical in its approach to received knowledge, presenting every subject from contrasting points of view. Insofar as it is practical, it gives pride of place to generic and flexible capabilities rather than to job-specific and machine-specific skills. Insofar as this education is general, it prefers selective depth to encyclopedic coverage in the choice of contents that provide a context for the acquisition of analytic capabilities (given that such capabilities cannot be acquired in a vacuum of content but that no particular content enjoys precedence). And whether it is practical or general, its social setting should be marked by cooperative teaching and learning rather than by the juxtaposition of individualism and authoritarianism in the classroom. Assurance of such material and educational endowments gives effect to the ideal of self-construction.

To define the practical means for enacting the ideal of self-construction is to describe some of the most fundamental conditions for the existence of the individual worker and citizen who can be the protagonist of the democratized market and the deepened democracy. The definition of this material and educational equipment supplies one among many standards by which to judge any proposal for the reformation of finance and of its place in the economy: how useful the proposal is to the funding of these material and educational endowments and more generally to the flourishing of a society that can create and support such an individual.

An outpouring of decentralized innovative activity, supported by society's accumulated capital as well as by the assurance of material and educational endowments, is what would link the role of finance to the development, en masse, of people who have ceased to be puppets of their circumstance.

THE ALTERNATIVE FUTURES OF CAPITALISM SEEN THROUGH THE LENS OF FINANCE

Suppose a future for "capitalism" (if by that we mean the established form of the market economy, viewed in light of the idea of structure not system discussed in the introduction) in which the most advanced practices of production remain quarantined in insular vanguards, weakly linked to other parts of each national economy, and excluding most of the labor force. In such a future, most firms, especially small and medium-size businesses, will have little or no engagement with productive vanguardism.

Productivity growth for the economy remains limited by failure to radicalize and to disseminate knowledge-deep, experimentalist production. Productivity outside the insular vanguards either stagnates or declines. Wage labor continues to be the predominant form of free labor. Most workers languish in the performance of repetitive and tedious tasks. Large and successful firms continue to accumulate huge reserves of capital. As a result, much of production undertaken by large, established firms remains internally financed by retained and reinvested earnings, while most small businesses continue to rely on family savings and self-exploitation to remain viable. Only big business, organized in the corporate form, can bring large numbers of workers together with sophisticated machines under the aegis of the corporate form.

In such a future, finance can turn in on itself. It can use the transactions of the real economy as a pretext rather than as a focus. It can absorb large portions of the talent of the society in an activity that may be extravagantly remunerative but that has little connection to society's agenda of production.

Now suppose an alternative future of capitalism in which the most advanced practices are widely disseminated in the economy and the gateways of access to them are opened to larger portions of the labor force. New regimes of private and social property begin to coexist experimentally in the same market economy and make it possible to combine decentralized economic initiative with large-scale production. Scale no longer requires big business operating in corporate form. Wage labor eventually ceases to be the predominant form of free labor and gives way little by little to the combination of self-employment with cooperation.

In such a future, finance can and must draw closer to the real economy. Its fate becomes entwined with the future of production in ways that I explored earlier in this book. Its dangers are contained, although they can never be suppressed, and its constructive potential is more fully realized.

Beside lending to individuals and lending to firms, finance lends to groups organized by contractual relations outside one of the limited forms that the law allows to a firm. It supports cooperation, organized through contractual arrangements to bring people, resources, and projects together and aggregate resources. However, it no longer requires the legal device of the company to remain the primary device of resource aggregation.

Such a possibility is already prefigured in present experience by collaborative relational contracts in advanced manufacturing—for example, in the biotechnology and pharmaceutical industry. Its further development, however, remains stymied by the seemingly perpetual infancy of the law of relational, incomplete contracts. It remains confined as well by the preeminent importance of firms' retained earnings to the funding of production and by the nearly exclusive reliance of autonomous finance, including venture capital, on firms to which the law grants corporate personality. In coming closer to production and in contributing to the economy-wide spread of knowledge-intensive, experimentalist production, finance can begin to be reconciled with democracy.

Described in such terms, many moves ahead, this better future may appear too good to be achievable. If we misrepresent it as a blueprint, it may seem to offer yet another of the imaginary, insubstantial alternatives into which progressives were accustomed to pack everything that they found missing in the world around them before they learned to mistake disappointment for growing up, myopia for realism, and surrender for responsibility. If, however, we see this better future for what it is—the provisional and corrigible account of a direction, it invites our attention to the steps by which we might begin to move in its direction. To accept that invitation is what I have attempted to do in the earlier parts of this book with regard to finance and what I try to accomplish in the remainder of the book with respect to the economy as a whole.

CHAPTER FOUR

The Democratized Market Economy in Latin America (and Elsewhere)

An Exercise in Institutional Thinking Within Law and Political Economy

BY EXTENDING OUR SIGHTS to the experience of our sister republics in the Americas, we can help clarify the character and content of the institutional innovations that would open the way to a productivist and democratizing reform of finance. The development experience of Latin America over the past century supplies a vast historical laboratory in which to grasp the nature of the institutional innovations that can best democratize the market economy, enlist finance in the service of production, and reconcile it with democracy. Instructed by comparison and history, we can forge better tools for institutional thinking in law and political economy.

The historical period on which I focus is the extended second half of the twentieth century from the Second World War to the financial and economic crisis of 2007–2009. In particular, I address the moment when in the 1980s and 1990s what came to be described as neoliberalism or the Washington Consensus became a predominant influence on the course of economic policy and institutional design in one major Latin American country after another. This orientation marked a change from the more autarchic, corporatist, or statist orientation of the immediately preceding period, closely identified in its strategy of economic growth with import-substituting industrialization. Because the neoliberal doctrine of that time represented the circumstantial form of beliefs that continue to be entrenched in economics and in legal thought, an understanding of its momentous career and effect in a large and distinct part of the world holds enormous interest. Long after this idea turns into others or loses its power, it will continue to pose questions central to the argument of this book: Can we have only more or less of a market economy and therefore more or less of governmental intervention in economic life? Or does economic reality allow us and do our interests and ideals command us to develop different kinds of market order, each with distinct institutional form, productive of different social and economic consequences? The theme guiding my analysis is the nature of the institutional ideas and arrangements that inhibit or facilitate the deepening and democratization of finance and the organization of socially inclusive growth.

Chapter 3 placed my narrower argument about the reform of finance and its relation to the real economy in a broader programmatic context by exploring the institutional content of a democratized market economy, understood as the institutional setting of socially inclusive economic growth. In this chapter, I confront the ideal of a democratized market economy with the byways of historical experience. Although my argument here begins with comparative history, it concludes with proposals for institutional reconstruction. Informed by comparative historical study, it gives institutional detail to the broad ideas about a democratized market economy presented in chapter 3. We need both programmatic vision and historical insight to find a path from here to there.

THE THEMES: NEOLIBERALISM, THE IMAGINATION OF AN ALTERNATIVE, AND THE RESPONSIBILITIES OF LEGAL ANALYSIS

In the 1970s and 1980s, Latin America became a stage for a vast institutional and ideological experiment: a turn to more liberal economies as they were and are understood and organized in the United States and western Europe. This neoliberal experiment amounted to a variation on the dominant mode of institutional and ideological change in the world today. Thus, a critical understanding of this event may shed light on similar changes occurring now almost everywhere. To outline such an understanding and to suggest an alternative trajectory of change are the major concerns of this chapter. The minor theme is the role that a suitably reoriented style of legal analysis can and should play in the interpretation of institutional changes such as those discussed here as well as in the conceptual and practical development of alternatives to those changes.

The method I employ combines a normative vision and a descriptive and explanatory approach to a complex circumstance. It thus differs from both positive social science and Anglo-American political philosophy: the former is marked by its emphasis on a sharp distinction between fact and value, whereas the latter is characterized by its quest for a foundational standpoint of impartial judgment and its demotion of institutional concerns to a secondary, merely technical or tactical stage of reflection. Here, by contrast, I begin with and seek to illustrate (rather than to demonstrate) the hypothesis that thinking about ideals and thinking about institutions are overlapping endeavors.

Although the situations and proposals I discuss are drawn largely from Latin America, my working hypothesis is that the substantive ideas as well as the method of argument have some value for basic issues of reform in market economies and representative democracies anywhere. The American reader should frequently note the analogies connecting the Latin American experiences and possibilities explored here to suppressed American debates. The practical problems and the institutional and ideological repertories of different societies around the world have become bound together in something analogous to the Wittgensteinian metaphor of the rope: just one rope, but none of its countless strands runs from end to end.

Thus, the vision outlined here has no simple geographical domain of application; it can readily be modified to apply to the problems of other contemporary societies, rich and poor alike. Each of these "applications" requires a deepening of insight as well as a revision of proposals. But no one who understands the problems and the alternative solutions in one place would be at a loss to understand them in any other place. New turns in the conversation would remind her of turns she had already taken.

THE POLITICAL-ECONOMIC BACKGROUND: PROTECTED FORDISM AND PSEUDO-KEYNESIANISM

Protected Fordist Production

Before the neoliberal changes are examined here, it is useful to recall the background against which these changes react. Although there is some measure of consensus among scholars about how to characterize the background, there is much less agreement about the true nature of its deficiencies. Slogans about the evils of "statism," "economic nationalism," and "populism" cannot stand in the place of real analysis.

Two main elements compose this background: the strategy of autarchic industrialization, oriented to the development of Fordist mass-production industry through import substitution, and pseudo-Keynesian governmental finance.

The core of the industrialization strategy was governmental support in the form of planning initiatives, overt and covert subsidies, and protectionism to set up a Fordist-style industrial complex.[1] In the most developed example, Brazil, state-founded and state-owned industries produced inputs for private firms—the largest of which were multinationals. Although this strategy has often been described and justified as import substitution,[2] its driving economic feature was a governmental guarantee of the profit margins of private firms in the subsidized sector. On this basis, there developed a style of economic growth that associated a strong measure of internal dualism with a specific position of the national economy in the world economy.

This autarchic style of industrialization deepened the internal division of the economy and the society between the favored, newly industrialized, and market-oriented sector and a second economy bereft of favors and with marginal access to capital, technology, and markets.[3] The vast majority of people remained imprisoned within this second sector. Autarchic, import-substituting industrialization led to the aggravation of internal dualism by many intersecting routes.

The Fordist-style industry established in the favored sector of the economy was equipped to reproduce in Brazil many of the consumption goods enjoyed by the inhabitants of the developed countries. But it was ill suited to produce the inputs and the machine tools needed by the small and medium-size firms of the second economy. Today, a post-Fordist industry with flexible machines and flexible production practices would, as a technological vanguard, serve as the indispensable partner of the technological rearguard that accounts for most economic activity in countries such as Brazil. Organizational and technological stagnation—the failure to develop an array of firms capable of accelerated learning—underlies blanket accusations of inefficiency that conventional economic thinking has traditionally directed against the inward-turning, import-substituting style of industrialization.

If a constraint upon innovation was the first sin of this style of stateprotected economic growth, the second was the stark disparity in the distribution of government favors—a mounting disparity between the need for governmental support and its availability. As the favored sector—both a social and a geographic reality—became richer, the disfavored sector became ever more needful of public investment. But the government had already committed its resources and energy.

As inequality between classes and regions grew, politicians spoke of the need to expand compensatory entitlement programs. Entitlement mechanisms, however, cannot succeed when faced with extreme degrees of wealth and income inequality rooted in an entrenched economic dualism. Long before the transfer of resources from the first economy to the second economy were to reach the size necessary to deal with the problems of the majority of working people caught in the second economy, the transfer would begin to disorganize the first economy, killing the goose that lays the golden eggs.

In fact, this massive transfer never occurs: the same alliances that helped produce the import-substituting strategy in the first place and that were immensely reinforced by the adoption of that strategy inhibit a major assault upon the first economy's prerogatives and resources. The disfavored sector may strike back through the vote—especially the vote in plebiscitarian presidential elections. But in the age of dualistic, import-substituting industrialization, the characteristic expression of this electoral revenge has been a self-defeating economic populism. By printing and borrowing money, the government attempts to achieve what it has failed to accomplish by redistributing resources.

The counterpart to the deepening of internal dualism is the pegging of the national economy in a belated Fordist niche of the world economy. The industrial base of the favored sector gets caught over time in a competitive squeeze. It cannot compete with high-skilled post-Fordist industry. At the same time, it is beset by the emerging, lowest-wage platforms of exportoriented, Fordist-style industry (on these platforms today, countries such as Malaysia and Indonesia have succeeded countries such as Taiwan and South Korea, which have moved to a more-advanced technological frontier). As a result, wages in the favored sector of the national economy face a continuing downward pressure, for which the national government is expected to compensate.

Recent international trade theory has emphasized how, contrary to the standard Ricardian doctrine of comparative advantage, small national handicaps or successes may develop into continuing advances or setbacks up or down the evolutionary ladder of productivity.[4] Once a country gets caught in an unfavorable niche, escape is possible but difficult and costly. The escape from the squeeze of protected late Fordism requires, among other initiatives, massive investment in people, especially in their educational capabilities. Such investment, however, proves a daunting task for governments under the conditions against which the neoliberal project is reacting in contemporary Latin America.

Pseudo-Keynesian Public Finance

To understand why the urgent investment in people turns out to be so difficult to make, it is necessary to take a second element of the background into account: the dominant practice of governmental finance accompanying import-substituting industrialization.

This practice has often been labeled populist, but it might more accurately be called "pseudo-Keynesian." It is a policy of cheap money, subsidies for consumption goods as well as for favored production sectors (including the use of public enterprises and public banks to help private firms), overvalued exchange rates, and, above all, massive public borrowing, both foreign and domestic, as well as large-scale and continuing monetization of governmental deficits.[5]

The essence of pseudo-Keynesian state finance is the national government's inability to impose the cost of public investment in infrastructure and people upon the country's propertied classes. The government instead generalizes this cost to the whole society through inflationary finance. This policy superficially resembles Keynesianism in its use of governmental deficits to raise the level of growth and employment beyond the limits that would be imposed by a "low-level equilibrium trap." Original Keynesianism, however, served as both an expression and a reinforcement of governmental strength; by weakening the hold of sound finance doctrine, it diminished, if only for a while and in certain circumstances, the dependence of governmental policy upon the state of business confidence.[6] Pseudo-Keynesian state finance, by contrast, betrays governmental weakness: a failure of power and nerve of central governments in confronting the interests of entrenched elites.[7]

The elementary legal requirement for the practice of pseudo-Keynesian public finance is a remarkable and remarkably universal instance of what Marxists would call fetishism in legal thought: the failure of the law, in Latin America as everywhere else, to consider the seigniorage earnings of the government taking of private property subject to compensation. My point is not to advocate that seigniorage earnings should be so taken. Such action would result in the creation of a functional equivalent of the gold standard and would drastically diminish democratic control over the course and consequences of economic progress. The point is rather to observe how vastly influential styles of political economy may depend on very specific, controversial, and perplexing legal concepts. The noncompensated and incontestable character of the earnings that an executive or a central bank may secure by debasing the currency, without legislative support or judicial scrutiny, may coexist under the same legal regime with the most severe restraints upon those expropriations that are classified as takings.[8]

In fact, a very large part of the political and economic life of many Latin American countries today can be explained by examining the cumulative effect of only three legal rules: the almost unlimited right of inheritance (reproducing extreme inequality), the mandatory vote in the context of a strong presidential regime (ensuring that the economically disenfranchised can strike back through politics, although the politicians, thanks to the right of inheritance, will usually be serving two masters), and the noncompensated character of seigniorage earnings (enabling the government to find a way between the people's cries and the propertied class's vetoes by printing money). Jeremy Bentham would here have his work cut out for him. Pseudo-Keynesian state finance has a typical history that economists have only recently begun to understand. This history has both a cyclical and a sequential aspect. The boom–bust cycle of economic populism coexists with a slow progression toward circumstances that diminish the benefits and increase the costs of pseudo-Keynesianism. The cyclical aspect is the now familiar cycle of economic populism. Demand-led inflationary growth produces a short-lived boom and a substantial increase in nominal wages. The boom comes to an end with a balance-of-payments crisis brought about by an overvalued exchange rate and an unsustainable rise in imports. Disinvestment and capital flight finish what the balance-of-payments crisis began. In the end, the government finds itself driven to adopt an austerity program that depresses the real wage and the overall level of economic activity, sometimes to a point below where the cycle began.

The sequential aspect of the recurrent history of pseudo-Keynesianism is the progressive undoing of a state's ability to mask its weakness by borrowing and printing money. At the outset, massive borrowing at home and abroad may enable the government to maintain economic growth and wage levels even in the face of major economic shocks, such as massive increases in the price of an essential import—oil, for example. But foreign borrowing requires the government to accumulate a substantial internal debt, which inevitably leads it to print the money with which to buy the private export earnings needed to service the foreign debt. As confidence in government paper diminishes and maturities shorten, the effects of borrowing money come to resemble those of printing it.

The government forces the typically large public sector to pay a disproportionate part of the cost of inflation containment, limiting the tariffs and prices of the goods and services that public enterprises produce and using them as instruments through which to continue foreign borrowing. The result is a progressive disorganization of the public sector.

Finally, as inflation increases and reaches its high and chronic stage, just beneath the threshold of hyperinflation, pseudo-Keynesianism begins to threaten the favored private sector. A general cry arises to get rid of it, but it can be discarded only when there is a political force strong and cohesive enough to impose a specific allocation of the burdens of stabilization.

The vital link between import-substituting, autarchic industrialization and pseudo-Keynesian state finance cannot be understood in narrow economic terms. The connection lies in the interests and alliances from which each of them draws life and that each in turn helps to reinforce. The favored sector that the industrialization strategy helps to define is the same sector that pseudo-Keynesianism exempts from paying much of the cost of public investment in people and infrastructure.

THE NEOLIBERAL PROJECT AND THE WASHINGTON CONSENSUS: THEIR CONTENT AND CONSEQUENCES

Influence of the Neoliberal Project

The neoliberal project, as it has been pursued in Latin America in recent years, represents one response to the failures and limitations of autarchic, import-substituting industrialization and pseudo-Keynesianism. Latin American scholars are quick to point out that different countries have pursued different routes to economic stabilization and liberalization. Chile, Argentina, and Mexico, to take the most significant examples, have indeed diverged in many of their policies, as they differ in many of their circumstances. But an overriding direction, a body of ideas, and a repertoire of solutions have been repeatedly enlisted in the defense of these distinctive national trajectories.[9]

This shared direction has sometimes been labeled the "Washington Consensus." The label clearly suggests the decisive nature of the American influence on the ascendancy of neoliberal ideas in Latin America and elsewhere. This influence has two overlapping sources: the world of the American technocracy, established in government and in the major multilateral banks, and, more importantly, the world of the American universities, especially the graduate economics departments where so many candidates for Latin American elite status have trained.

In the United States and Europe, neoliberal ideas (with the term neoliberal used in the Latin American and European sense rather than in the American sense) were always kept in their place. Reaganism, Thatcherism, and their continental European counterparts never reigned free, either, because the associated country had powerful social-democratic movements and resistant portions of an organized civil society with which the ideology had to contend or because the national governments they took over had much less effective power over the national economy than did their Latin American counterparts. In Latin America, the weakness of these constraining conditions has been vastly accentuated by the widespread sense of crisis produced by the failure of the inherited strategy of economic growth and by the dominant style of government finance.

But the neoliberal project had one more simple but easily overlooked advantage: it was there. Developed ideas about alternative pathways of institutional change are few and far between. Enormous influence will attach to a body of beliefs that is frequently surveyed and easily defended and that seems to be supported by the example of the successful countries and by the teachings in their universities. No wonder the neoliberal project has had so much going for it.

Content of the Washington Consensus

The Washington Consensus has four main components.

1. Orthodox Stabilization

The Washington Consensus calls for economic stabilization and monetary transparency through fiscal adjustment.[10] Its primary emphasis is on cutting governmental expenditures rather than on increasing tax revenues. The central bank should be made independent, and the treasury should be prevented from financing itself through draws upon the central bank. Wage–price freezes and social compact negotiations may be grudgingly allowed as secondary stabilization devices.

2. Liberalization

Tariff barriers should be brought down, and market reserves (quantitative restraints upon imports) should be abrogated. The internal economy should be exposed to a heavy dose of foreign competition.[11] Free trade should extend to services and intangibles, and the ground rules of world trade (e.g., patent rights), as defined by the leading economic powers, should be fully respected. Much less attention is given to internal liberalization (e.g., antitrust initiatives designed to break up the oligopolies accounting for a large pan of the private sector). The counterpart to liberalization is free convertibility and unification of exchange rates. The achievement of these convertibility goals may be delayed until stabilization is secured. If, however, an exchange-rate anchor for the money supply is adopted, the convertibility measures may be implemented simultaneously with the stabilization program.

3. Export Orientation

The economy should gear up for a sustained export orientation. Because of the antigovernment bias characterizing the Washington Consensus, export drives are supposed to occur spontaneously as a result of free trade and free convertibility in a context of worldwide specialization and comparative advantage rather than as a consequence of strategic coordination. The export orientation is needed to generate the earnings to service the preexisting foreign debt and to sustain an expanded import capacity. It may also be required to create an exchange-rate anchor for the money supply. No special attention is given to the profile of imports and to the priority of technology transfers and machinery purchases. Market forces are expected to take care of such concerns.

4. Privatization

Public enterprises and banks should be privatized—as many and as quickly as possible.[12] If necessary, investors should be allowed to buy public companies with government paper, for this purpose valued more highly than it is valued by existing secondary markets in government paper. The state should get out of the business of production. (Everyone, the votaries of the Washington Consensus repeat, knows that governments are bad producers.) The government should instead devote itself to dealing with social problems and developing the conditions for the profitability of private firms.

Criticism of the Stabilization Component of the Washington Consensus

The truth in the fiscal-adjustment part of the Washington Consensus is just the reverse of the illusions of pseudo-Keynesianism and of the "heterodox" ideas about inflation and its control. These ideas have given pseudo-Keynesian approaches a new lease on life in Latin America by emphasizing inertial forces and inflationary expectations rather than the weakness of the state and its tax revenue. There can be no sustained growth with high and chronic inflation and no way of ending such inflation, in the real conditions of the Latin American economies, that fails to address the persistent fiscal crisis of the state. The flaw in the fiscal-adjustment part of the Washington Consensus is the supposition that fiscal adjustment can be achieved principally by cutting back on government expenditures and privatizing public companies.

In poor and hierarchical societies, people and firms need government. For there to be a democratizing style of economic growth, one that diminishes inequality while creating opportunities for entrepreneurial innovation by many more people, public savings and investment must increase rather than diminish. To this end, the government must be freed from the shackles of large foreign and domestic debt. (In Brazil and several other Latin American countries, the domestic debt, although often small in absolute terms when compared to that of certain industrialized Western countries, became the centerpiece of a system for financial speculation, forcing the state to pay very high real interest rates for the acceptance of government paper.) The cost of public investment in people and in infrastructure must be imposed on the propertied classes through a higher effective tax rate rather than generalized to the society as a whole through inflationary finance.

Criticism of the Structural-Adjustment Component of the Washington Consensus

Three issues with respect to the Washington Consensus are paramount. They intersect at many points.

1. The Washington Consensus fails to have a properly critical attitude toward the private sector as it is currently organized. In its present form in Brazil, Mexico, Argentina, and many other Latin American countries, the private sector, particularly in the protected Fordist part of the industrial system, is tainted by oligopolistic, rent-seeking, and familial nepotistic characteristics. (The largest private businesses that are not family owned and run are typically foreign.) In such circumstances, public enterprises and banks have often provided a valuable countervailing force, both by countering their customers' or suppliers' oligopolistic market power and by creating careers for a technical elite of propertyless, middle-class youth.

2. The Washington Consensus fails to appreciate the requirements for the indispensable investment in infrastructure and people. It is vitally important to increase public savings and public investment. It is also necessary

to have the types of political and social organization that can sustain the pressure to increase public savings and investment while helping to prevent the corrupt, clientelistic use of public funds. Such policy goals mandate rules and practices that heighten the level of political mobilization in society: constitutional arrangements for promoting rapid resolution of deadlocks among branches of government while maintaining the plebiscitarian element of the presidential regime and a preference for forms of social (i.e., union) organization that encourage civil society to organize.

3. The Washington Consensus fails to acknowledge the crucial significance of the partnership between a technological vanguard and the technological rearguard of the economy in order (*a*) to soften internal dualism and (*b*) to escape the late-Fordist niche in the world economy.[13] The technological vanguard must to some extent be in the public sector: public enterprises and public banks can have a longer-term strategic horizon, free from the short-term profit constraint.

But it would be a mistake, characteristic of the thinking that inspires the Washington Consensus, to oppose public enterprise and the market economy. Public firms can compete, have entrepreneurial autonomy, and bear financial responsibility (including the threat of bankruptcy).

Each of these criticisms of the Washington Consensus points in the direction of a series of institutional innovations to be worked out in detailed legal form. The common element in these innovations would be the development of alternative arrangements for the market economy and for its socioconstitutional background. Such arrangements would defy the conventional reduction of the "market" and "democracy" to the present economic and political institutions of the United States and western Europe.

The Work of Legal Analysis

The criticism of the Washington Consensus I have outlined is therefore institutionalist in spirit. Because it is institutionalist, it is also legal. The details of the alternative arrangements are decisive in determining both the practical prospects and the spiritual meaning of any institutional innovations. Practices and institutions are not pieces of social engineering separable from conceptions, interests, and ideals. The style of legal thinking required is therefore one adept at microinstitutional design and at rethinking the links between abstract institutional conceptions and practical arrangements.

THE STRATEGICALLY COORDINATED MARKET AND THE COOPERATIVE-COMPETITIVE FIRM

Standards That a Democratizing Alternative to the Neoliberal Project Should Meet

It is helpful to distinguish general objectives from more specific and circumstantial aims. An alternative to the neoliberal project and the Washington Consensus should reconcile sustained economic growth with continuing democratization of the society. Democratization, for this purpose, should be understood to mean the development of practices of collective deliberation and self-determination in all major theaters of social life, the liberation of the life chances of the individual from predetermination by a rigid, steep hierarchy of inherited economic advantage, and the weakening of the reciprocal reinforcement of political power and economic power to the benefit of privileged minorities. The obstacles to such democratization extend from the extremes of economic inequality (Brazil and Mexico stand at the most unfavorable pole of the Gini coefficients measuring economic inequality[14]) to the clientelistic style of sociability, mixing power, exchange, and loyalty that mark so much of everyday life in these societies.

The idea of an affinity, or an area of potential overlap, between the conditions of material progress and the requirements of individual emancipation is central to the alternative I propose as well as to the normative vision inspiring it. I return to this idea later. For the moment, it is enough to emphasize that a major connecting feature between democracy and economic growth is the capacity for learning. Successful economies are those composed of firms that are good at learning. Democracy, viewed from an inclusive, pragmatic perspective, is a collective practice of learning. An alternative to the neoliberal project and the Washington Consensus, therefore, should provide an answer to the following question: Under what institutional conditions are collective learning activities in the production system and in politics most likely to flourish? Moreover, the question must be addressed not to an abstract and indeterminate audience but to particular countries beset by particular problems.

In addition to these general objectives, the alternative to neoliberalism should offer a response to the twin structural problems that inhibit economic progress and democratization in many Latin American countries: economic dualism and the late-Fordist niche in the world economy. Moreover, the alternative should resolve these problems while both re-creating the capacity for public savings and public investment and deepening the vitality of the market economy. What counts is the market economy in a real sense as a collective experience of economic decentralization, opportunity for individual initiative, and facility for innovation rather than as defined in a formal sense (i.e., conformity to a preset notion of the regime of private property). In such an enlarged alternative system, government and private producers can collaborate. Public enterprises can become competitive market agents. Private firms, as members of "cooperative competition," can cooperate in some respects (e.g., by pooling some of their financial, technological, and commercial resources) while competing in others.

A Method of Contextual Argument

The method I prefer to use in outlining such an alternative is to take certain contemporary regional experiences (that is to say, the experiences of regions of the world economy) as my starting point: to present a controversial interpretation of some of their aspects, to criticize them in light of this interpretation, and to suggest in what respect a revised version of their more promising features would contribute to the alternative I propose. In utilizing this method, I focus primarily on certain aspects of the experience of the so-called East Asian tiger economies. I then complete this critical and reconstructive analysis with a brief, more focused reflection on two other experiences: that of the former Council for Mutual Economic Assistance (Comecon) countries and that of successful regional economies in western Europe (countries in which cooperative-competitive networks of small and medium-size firms have come to play a major role).

In conformity with my context-bound and institution-oriented method of analysis and my skepticism about general justifications, except as they arise from reflection upon historical experience, I prefer to postpone my discussion of the normative vision that underlies my proposal and gives it life.

Although somewhat untidy, this method of proceeding has several advantages. First, it prevents the degeneration of institutional thinking into dogmatic design, undisciplined by the stubbornness of real-world constraints. Fantasies project our prejudices; realities undermine them. Thus, a conception guided less by philosophical preconception may turn out to be of greater philosophical as well as practical interest. Second, by the same token, it allows for a more intimate, continuous, and productive conversation between political-economic argument and social analysis. Third, it helps to explore a hypothesis posited at the beginning of this essay: that we can profitably view the entire world today as a series of analogous theaters of experience, where every basic problem or interesting solution has a counterpart almost anywhere else. We can best approach this worldwide analogy not in the spirit of a quest for universal minima but rather in the spirit of Ludwig Wittgenstein's metaphor of the rope, none of whose strands run from one end of the rope to the other.

General Features of the Alternative

It may help to identify at the outset some features of my proposed alternative that recur throughout its several parts. The alternative explores the institutional means by which strategic coordination, both by governments and subgovernmental organizations and by cooperative arrangements among firms, can be more fully reconciled with market initiative and decentralized economic experimentalism. It sees public intervention in the economy and market decentralization as being capable of mutual reinforcement at many levels. This reinforcement may not come solely in the priority, dear to traditional social democrats, that is given to public investment in infrastructure and in people, but it will also be seen in the direct collaboration between government and public enterprises or banks with private producers in the actual conduct of production and exchange.

The alternative accords a major role to small and medium-size enterprises, often the most dynamic segment of contemporary economies. But it sees the best hope of realizing their productive potential in their association both with one another in regimes of cooperative competition and with a technological vanguard, headquartered in both the public and the private sectors alike. The systematic mixture of competition and cooperation, rather than their allocation to rigidly distinct aspects of economic activity, is a major feature of this proposal.

The alternative sees the need and the opportunity to limit economic inequality as both a condition and a consequence of economic progress. To some degree, such limits are a condition (because of the dependence of sustained economic growth on equalizing reforms such as land redistribution and educational investment) that provides results more secure and dramatic than anything expected from traditional welfare entitlements. At the same time, the acceleration of economic experimentalism, defined organizationally, institutionally, culturally, and technologically, provides an opportunity to carry further the campaign against large and rigid inequalities.

It will always be possible to reconcile accelerated economic experimentalism with stable and entrenched hierarchies of privilege and disadvantage by some variant of social dualism (i.e., the division of society into a class of active participants in the vanguard of production and outsiders marginalized from it). The ultimate constraint upon such a reconciliation lies in the interruption of economics by politics. Thus, for example, a selfdefeating populist political economy, ushered in by populist electoral victories, has in Latin America been the regular response to a style of economic growth that deepens inequality. Nothing, however, in the nature of economic experimentalism requires social dualism. In one sense, the proposal I develop is simply an effort to imagine, in conditions such as those we often encounter today in Latin America and elsewhere, the institutional form of experimentalism without dualism.

Finally, the alternative relates economic change to change in the legal organization of politics and society. The direction of economic reorganization that it sketches both requires and supports a style of politics demanding a higher level of civic engagement. The alternative demands a style of constitutional ordering that facilitates the frequent practice of bold innovation. It mandates a style of organization of civil society that allows people to form and express interests and ideals as members of social organizations put at their disposal by public law rather than just as isolated consumers, self-driven entrepreneurs, or occasional voters. It further requires the development of legal rules and concepts located at two familiar intersections: between administrative direction and private ordering as well as between contract and the corporation.

In short, although the alternative may be criticized as statist, it takes seriously the commitment to a market economy. Moreover, although the alternative implicitly criticizes conventional social and liberal democratic policies and attitudes, it represents an effort to realize the contemporary democratic vision on inhospitable terrain, with the proviso that as we change our ideas about how best to realize the vision, we also revise our understanding of its content.

AN EAST ASIAN STARTING POINT: DEMOCRATIZING HARD STATES AND THE GOVERNMENT–BUSINESS PARTNERSHIP

A Contrasting Historical Sequence

Consider first the experience of the East Asian "tigers"—Taiwan, South Korea, Singapore, and Hong Kong—an experience prefigured by Japan and continued, with different characteristics, by Malaysia, Indonesia, and Thailand. For the moment, I have Taiwan and South Korea especially in mind; they present an instructive contrast while sharing features that Singapore and Hong Kong lack as a result of their histories and situations.

Much of this East Asian experience of successful industrialization and integration into the world economy is not transferable. It depends on an accumulation of unique circumstances: these countries' singular history, including the deeply rooted characteristics of veneration for learning and decisive, one-time upheavals such as the events leading up to the Japanese occupation, the Pacific War, and the American proconsulship; the unique effects of the American and then the shared American–Japanese hegemony; and the state of the world economy when the industrialization of the tigers took place (a circumstance that, following the rise of labor costs in core national economies but preceding the post-Fordist industrial reconstruction, created special opportunities for low-cost producers of standardized commodities).[15]

Even the idiosyncratic, path-dependent evolution of these economies, however, gains a more general meaning when compared to the Latin American experience.[16] In the years after the Second World War, the East Asian tigers passed through an extended import-substituting phase. At this time, their political economies resembled in many respects the Latin American economies in the heyday of autarchic industrialization and import substitution. There were, however, two crucial differences. First, import substitution took place against the background of equalizing reforms, in particular agrarian reform and public investment in education. Second, in the East Asian tigers, foreign direct investment remained low by Latin American standards; there was, on the whole, a reversal of the characteristic Latin American sequence so that an emphasis on loan capital preceded rather than followed a heightening of direct investment. In fact, the tigers' governments generally insisted on national control of the "commanding heights" of their economies, carefully confining direct foreign investment to labor-intensive sectors of industry or to undertakings rich in the potential for technology transfers of strategic value to the national growth path.[17]

This reversal of the Latin American sequence of relations with foreign capital is significant because comparative analysis has repeatedly suggested the existence of a correlation in the contemporary peripheral economies between degrees of economic inequality and levels of foreign direct investment. (The crucial connection may lie in the engagement of multinationals with the reproduction in developing countries of the same standardized goods and services that they sell to the general population in richer countries. The impulse to maintain the consequent profiles of consumption and production turns into a constraint upon macroeconomic policy.)

Just as revealing as these contrasts with the practices of protected Fordism in Latin America is another device by which the East Asian tigers out–"Latin Americanized" Latin America. The tigers inherited from the Japanese a formidable public sector, which they preserved and developed until well into the export-oriented stage of their growth strategies. Two uses of the public sector turned out to be of special importance in laying the basis for this second stage. One was the development of a technological vanguard, generally pioneered by public-sector enterprises and later nurtured by governmental initiative in partnership with private firms.[18] The other was the use of public-sector banks to direct and often subsidize credit allocation.[19] Through these activities, the partnership between bureaucratic and entrepreneurial elites began to develop.

This background makes it easier to understand the nature of the passage from the import-substituting strategy to the export-oriented strategy—the political economy for which the East Asian tigers are now chiefly known. What is remarkable, in light of current policy debates, is that this shift took place under close governmental direction.[20] In some instances, public enterprises themselves spearheaded the export drive, the technology transfers, and the commercial arrangements that made the shift possible. In other instances, the government recruited the new exporters, equipped them, and coached their first steps.

Thus, this political-economic trajectory already serves to dispel two connected illusions: first, that overcoming import-substituting semiautarchy is naturally associated with a withdrawal of government from active involvement in the economy and, second, more generally, that market orientation is inversely related to government activism in the economy. The East Asian experience simply refuses to fit the limits of the contemporary progressive democratic compromise, according to which government leaves production to the producers and limits itself to investing in the conditions of the profitability of private firms.

Background of Equalizing Structural Reform

Which specific features of the new East Asian political economy provide starting points for the development of an alternative to the neoliberal project as it is presented today in Latin America?

The first characteristic is the combination of equalizing structural reforms, such as land redistribution and family-farm support, with large-scale investment in public education. The point is to produce a population of capable and active individuals and not to rely on income-redistribution techniques in the effort to achieve this objective.[21] Government-funded transfer payments are most likely to prove effective within a structure that has already been cleansed of extreme and entrenched forms of inequality and marginalization, but they are no substitute for structural change. Note that investment in people and their educational capital can coexist and in these countries has coexisted with what, by comparison to the European social democracies, are very low levels of government-financed social insurance. Consider also that the fundamental precondition for such investment is the maintenance of a high and stable level of tax revenue and public savings.

The Government–Business Partnership

The second and best-known trait is the development of a series of institutional devices for the operation of a partnership between entrepreneurial and political-bureaucratic elites.[22] The tigers' experience reveals three main patterns in the construction of this partnership. The first, most characteristic of Korea, is the establishment of a few central-government agencies working in partnership with major industrial-financial groups and using largely discretionary policy. The second type, more typical of Taiwan, is the establishment of central-government agencies that work under a combined regime of rule and discretion with a broader, more decentralized array of large, medium, and small firms.[23] The third variant, best typified by Hong Kong, is the negotiation of a trade and macroeconomic policy among the representatives of the major economic interests. This corporatist regime reduces government to a more modest coordinating role than it performs in the other variants.

To characterize the task of this partnership as "picking winners" grossly simplifies and distorts it. The key work of the partnership is, in every instance, that of coordinating the private and public contributions to the delineation of a cumulative investment and trade strategy. Trade theorists have elaborated on the idea that successful changes in the national economy's position within the world economic system depend on persistence on a pathway that exploits cumulative advantages of scale and scope, even in the absence of comparative advantages in particular factor endowments.[24] To increase the likelihood that such an evolutionary pathway can be identified and pursued, the government must undertake two distinct types of coordinating responsibilities. It must induce a critical mass of firms to converge upon the same path (coordination among firms). It must also satisfy some of the requirements and counterbalance some of the risks associated with a novel line of production and exchange (coordination between public and private agents).

If this twofold coordination for the sake of strategies of cumulative advantage in production and trade is the work of the partnership, its single most important instrument is the direct or indirect allocation of credit. Such allocation in turn presupposes the deployment of free-floating resources under the strategic control of the partnership. The essential points of such control are (*a*) that the commitment of these resources not be subordinate to short-term profit considerations and (*b*) that the risk of deviating from such considerations not fall solely upon the innovative firm but, thanks to government action, be broadly distributed among firms.

Hard States

The third feature of general interest is a precondition of the other two: the existence of a "hard state." A state is hard when it enjoys a substantial capacity to form and implement strategies that impose the cost of public investment upon present consumers and the propertied classes as well as a corresponding ability to resist influence by powerful factional interests (including the interests of its own partners in the government–business partnership).

Hard states have been necessary as agents of public investment and structural reform. They have also been required both to make the strategic partnership between government and business possible and to contain its risks. Common sense suggests that in evaluating the costs and benefits of such a partnership, we must balance the burdens of dispersion and interference among productive undertakings (burdens that the absence of such a partnership imposes) against the dangers of rent seeking and clientelism that the same partnership multiplies. The hardness of the East Asian states limits the proclivity toward the cannibalization of government policy by private interests. It cannot ensure strategies against illusion, but it can diminish their vulnerability to corruption by narrow self-interest. Thus, a successful strategic partnership and the performance by government of the twin coordinating roles discussed earlier can work only when the state is hard.

These features of hardness have been associated with authoritarian regimes in the history of the East Asian tigers. There is no necessary relation between hardness, so defined, and authoritarianism; a democratic or even a radically democratic society can certainly be a hard state. It is nevertheless also true that the way in which these Pacific states are hard has been thoroughly shaped by their undemocratic and authoritarian character. This uncontroversial remark introduces the central problem of imagining the revisions the East Asian political economy would have to undergo in order to supply institutional and ideological materials for a democratic and experimentalist alternative to the neoliberal project.

Democratizing the Government–Business Partnership

This East Asian model has to undergo two basic changes if it is to inform an attractive alternative to the neoliberal project. These two changes are connected in several respects: they respond to analogous concerns; they reinforce each other; and the first change is in a certain sense a special case of the second. The first change is an institutionalized broadening of the partnership between business elites and political-bureaucratic elites that has provided the tigers' political economy with its motor. The second change is a style of democracy (in the organization of government, electoral party politics, and large-scale economic power) that makes the state more fully accountable to a more equally organized civil society while ensuring to the state the requisite characteristics of hardness.

The partnership of business and government as developed by the tigers can be faulted on economic as well as political grounds. In broader social terms, it puts government power at the service of the export-oriented firms it supports. Even in Taiwan, which has developed the most broad-based version of the partnership, there seems to be a widespread appreciation of the gap between insiders and outsiders. An incipient dualism grows out of the division between those entrepreneurs and workers who belong to the partnership and those who are excluded from it. The truth in the more focused objection, according to which any such arrangement will likely end up in an attempt to "pick winners" when it does not generate into cruder forms of clientelism and corruption, is that the East Asian variant of the partnership goes but a small distance toward occupying the intermediate space between strategic direction (or coordination) and decentralized market-oriented initiative. The central reason for its failure to achieve such an advance is that it leaves the conduct of the partnership in a highly centralized form. Typically, one elite government agency directs internal industrial policy, while another directs foreign trade.

But we can imagine, instead, the coordinating responsibilities of the government being vested in multiple pairs of agencies with a considerable measure of decision-making independence and financial autonomy. There is no reason to suppose that the benefits of coordination (among firms publicly induced to coordinate and between firms and the public providers of the requirements of efficient production and trade) can be realized only if all firms and authorities converge on a single menu of strategies. The existence of multiple pairs of coordinating agencies will ensure that the coordinating, strategic functions will be performed, albeit in a disjunctive rather than unified form. At the same time, this regime will capture some of the experimentalist benefits of a market order, in particular the realization of multiple trials and the consequent opportunity to observe and to act upon their practical results.

Serendipity and coordination are not simple opposites; the degree of their reconcilability depends directly on their particular institutional forms. That is one of the chief lessons we learn when we subject any programmatic conception to legal-institutional analysis. This principle of imagination shapes many of the arguments in this book.

Democratizing the Hard State

As we pass from the more narrow need to broaden the government–business partnership to the broader objective of democratizing the hard state while maintaining its hardness, the same principle continues to hold. If the pertinent characteristics of hardness are to be maintained, the form of democratization of the state and of its relation to society must respond to certain concerns. Although these concerns can be satisfied by a wide range of institutional alternatives, they are far from being institutionally empty.

1. The Devices for Preventing and Breaking Deadlock

First, the national government must be institutionally capable of devising and implementing strategic initiatives that confront powerful interests and enjoy staying power in the face of opposition. The grant of substantial powers and funds to multiple, competitive, and semi-independent pairs of agencies hardly diminishes the need for this ability to act. The rule regime of the agencies, the basic allocation of resources and responsibilities among them, and the interpretation of the practical results of their actions call out for government action focused on comprehensive national strategies.

Such a requirement is incompatible with an extreme form of divided government, such as the American version of checks and balances under a presidential regime. It is also irreconcilable with a form of the parliamentary regime that fragments political parties, concentrates power in the class of professional parliamentary politicians, allows the election of these parliamentarians to be dominated by local concerns and dependencies, and requires power and policy to develop by a broad measure of consensus (the lowest common denominator) within this political class.

The approach to the organization of government that I defend is compatible with both presidential and parliamentary institutions. Most often, a specific combination of presidential and parliamentary traits may prove most promising (especially one that maintains the plebiscitarian and destabilizing force of presidential elections amid a strong presidency while enabling both the president and the parliament to call anticipated elections for both branches in the face of programmatic deadlock).

Just as important as the ability to break a constitutional stalemate while ensuring the plebiscitarian potency of power is the creation of conditions favorable to the emergence of strong parties. For strong parties to emerge, technical rules, such as a system of lists under a regime of proportional representation, have to converge with arrangements assuring a high level of political mobilization (more on this point later). Such rules must also be able to draw upon a style of national politics focused on debates about structural change rather than on the combination of symbolic cultural issues and marginal redistribution characteristic of the industrial democracies today.

It is interesting in this light to reconsider the ongoing constitutional debate in Latin America. In recent years, political and intellectual elites in several Latin American countries have made a concerted effort to institute a parliamentary regime. The people have on the whole refused to convert to the new constitutional religion. The complaint against presidentialism is that it promotes the election of demagogues unable to deliver on their promises while leaving the political parties in parliament marginalized from power and uninterested in seeing the president succeed. But the proposed solution, the wholesale adoption of parliamentarianism, mistakes a superficial stabilization for a change of the social circumstances that have given rise to political instability in the first place.

When conventional constitutional institutions, such as those of American-style presidentialism, are projected into a world of extreme inequalities and exclusions, some of the consequences of these institutions are exaggerated, and others change their content. In many Latin American countries, the presidential election has been by far both the most important and the least-controlled aspect of politics—the political space least likely to mirror the surrounding social space. The concentration of power in the parliamentary class would indeed be most likely to increase shortterm and superficial stability, but only because it would withdraw the principal instrument for political rebellion by the underprivileged.[25]

The traditional presidential regime, however, suffers from two related disadvantages as a context for the reiterated practice of structural reform and the framing of bold national strategies of production and trade. Although powerful enough to favor friends and punish enemies, a Latin American president is usually too weak to implement structural change. (Mexico, a technocratic dictatorship, is the exception that proves the rule.) Moreover, Latin American regimes encourage the recurrence of political impasse between a populist president and a conservative Congress. These deficiencies account for the importance of arrangements, such as the plebiscite-setting and election-calling powers, that not only break a deadlock but also engage the citizenry in its resolution.[26]

2. The Intermediate Organizations

A second feature of the arrangements needed to democratize states while preserving their hardness is the existence of a level of organization between government and industry. It is at this level that the multiple, competitive, and semi-independent pairs of government agencies responsible for strategic coordination in production and trade would operate. We can imagine several variants of this intermediate level of organization: public entities with substantial decision-making and financial autonomy that are subject to competition among themselves; mixed public–private bodies in which the independence of the organization from central control is counterbalanced by the temporary, inalienable, or otherwise conditional character of the private rights assigned to it; and private bodies that arise from the pooling of resources among private firms and gain public support in exchange for restraints upon the exercise of private property.

The broad significance of the development of this intermediate level of organization is to moderate the tension between decentralized market initiative and strategic coordination between public authorities and market agents as well as among market agents. The point is not that the development of the intermediate organization dispels these tensions but rather that it softens them by altering the institutional form of each of the elements in contrast. The statement of this programmatic goal, however, conceals a daunting task of institutional design and legal imagination. Two bodies of ideas and techniques, one about public accountability and the other about private property and contract, must be mixed together and turned into something novel and different. A theory of restricted and fragmentary property rights, a theory of associational contracts occupying the continuum between contract and the corporation (viewed as a nexus of contracts), and a theory of double accountability (by both political control from above and participatory–proprietary control from below) have something to contribute to such a body of rules and doctrine.

3. The Institutionalized Heightening of Political Mobilization

A third feature of arrangements favorable to the reconciliation of deepened democracy with the hardness of the state is a preference for rules and practices tending to heighten political mobilization and maintain it at a high level. An organized and engaged citizenry, formed by individuals who are reluctant to draw a sharp contrast between the pursuit of their own interests and the redirection of public affairs, is a requirement for the reconciliation of hardness and democracy. The multisided business of a hard state, burdened by strategic responsibilities in a setting of harsh scarcity and unyielding conflict, presents an ever-present danger of authoritarianism of one type or another. It is this risk that must be met by a countervailing rise in the level of political mobilization. Although no one measure can ensure such a rise in political mobilization, a combination of initiatives tend to produce it, including rules of mandatory voting; free access to means of mass communication for political parties and organized social movements; public financing of campaigns, combined where possible with severe restraints upon the use of private resources; and (in most but not all circumstances) proportional representation, with partystrengthening arrangements such as a system of closed lists. That context changes the meaning of each such arrangement when taken in isolation is illustrated by recent events in Italy: the adoption of single-district majority voting promises to allow underlying progressive and conservative coalitions to free themselves from the distracting chicanery of the political class.

Note that just as the legal innovations represented by the development of a level of power between government and industry tends to soften the tension between strategic coordination and market initiative, the practices that promote political mobilization dissipate the force of the supposedly inverse relation between mobilization and institutionalization. The failure to appreciate the concept that sets of political institutions differ, by large amounts, in their hospitality to political mobilization has been one of the abiding illusions of conservative political science.

4. The Public-Law Organization of Civil Society

The fourth characteristic of the democratization of a hard state is the adoption of a legal regime facilitating the self-organization of civil society while ensuring that social organizations remain independent of government control. Society, when organized, can resist, but it can also speak and deal. In counterbalancing the increased power of the hard and active state, an organized civil society also provides the state with the interlocutors it requires both to identify coordinating strategies with broad appeal and to implement them effectively. I have described elsewhere a particular instance of such an institutional approach: the combination of the contractualist type of union organization, independent from government, with the corporatist type of automatic unionization of everyone within a comprehensive union scheme, open to internal factional struggle and governed by the principles of democratic representation.[27]

THE LAW AND CONSTITUTION OF ECONOMIC VANGUARDISM: LESSONS FROM RUSSIA AND NORTHERN ITALY

Two Themes to Be Developed

In this subsection and the succeeding subsection, I develop two aspects of the alternative outlined in the preceding pages. One theme to be developed is the contribution that public–private organizations between the government and the firm and more generally that a highly organized civil society can make to the partnership between a technological vanguard and a technological rearguard. Such a partnership is crucial to both self-sustaining economic innovation and the acceleration of learning in production. It requires, especially but not exclusively in backward economies, a legal-constitutional framework departing in significant ways from the traditional structure of the regulated market economy.

The other theme to be developed is the relationship between the raising of fiscal resources uncommitted to government operations and social entitlements and the creation of a credit and finance system that makes these resources available to firms, entrepreneurs, and workers. This fiscal-financial nexus depends on changes in the tax laws, in the law governing capital markets, and even in more basic rules and ideas about private property.

The theme of economic vanguardism and its constitutional framework is developed here through reflection on a few elements of the current Russian and northern Italian experience. The theme of the fiscal–financial nexus is presented without any suggestive historical context. If one were desired, the closest approximation might be debates and experiments about tax reform and capital-market reform in the European Union.

Economic Vanguardism and Legal Reorganization: A Russian Lesson

The circumstances of Russia and other formerly Communist countries are very different from those of Latin America. It is therefore all the more interesting that certain basic structural problems and possibilities that become clear in a Russian context suggest how some aspects of the alternative I have begun to outline can best be developed. Here again, the metaphor of the rope holds good: the strands of substantive analogy in political economy and legal organization run from everywhere to everywhere else. Differences in national circumstance simply bring into stronger view the extent to which what at first appear to be incomparable problems and solutions turn out on closer view to be variations on common themes.

The reader should bear in mind two rudimentary features of the industrial structure that present-day Russia inherited from the Soviet Union. The first feature is a striking economic dualism, different in content but no less marked in force and effect than the economic dualism characterizing many Latin American countries. This Russian dualism is the division between the relatively advanced technology and production styles of the military-industrial complex, on the one hand, and the hyper-Fordist and largely autarchic character of the general production system—protected Fordism with a vengeance—on the other. Foreign experts dismiss many of these hyper-Fordist producers as "value subtracting." But the more significant and more general fact is that hyper-Fordism imposes a severe constraint upon productivity-raising innovation. Similarly, although it is true that much in the Russian military-industrial complex is as worthless for production as it may have been for warfare, there are also islands of technological sophistication, many of them informed by advanced science.

The second feature of the Russian industrial structure is the combination of extreme horizontal concentration with pervasive, episodic, and small-scale vertical integration. The production of key inputs and standardized commodities is often dramatically concentrated in just a few producers. These producers then attempt to diminish their dependence on each other by producing some of their own key requirements in-house, without orientation to the market.[28]

Any promising path of industrial reconstruction in Russia must include an effort to spin smaller, more flexible firms out of the archaic, oversize production complexes. Such a reconstructive program should also relate regionally or functionally defined groups of such firms to the technological vanguard, which remains largely imprisoned within Russia's military-industrial complex. In Russia, as in Latin America, accelerated growth requires the establishment of a vital link between the technological vanguard and the technological rearguard of the production system.

In the past, debates about economic development have often been misdirected by the false idea that countries must choose between emphasis on a capital-intensive, high-skill, low-job type of production and a labor-intensive, low-skill, high-job alternative. In fact, the evolution of technology and of organizational forms in this age of post-Fordist industrial reconstruction and numerically controlled machine tools has made it ever more apparent that a technological vanguard and a technological rearguard are natural partners. The vanguard can produce in customized fashion the machines and inputs that the rearguard needs if it is to increase and improve production. The vanguard can produce according to the growing capacity for assimilation that the rearguard acquires.

The partnership between the vanguard and the rearguard is a device to create an economy of learners, and learning is the heart of production. The trouble is that the forging of such a partnership is not a technological operation; it is to a very large extent a legal-institutional operation.

To understand this legal-institutional imperative, it is useful to consider another aspect of current Russian experiences and debates. One of the chief ideas commanding the great debate over the future of Russia caricatures a conception that also influences the advocacy of the neoliberal project in Latin America. Modern societies, according to this idea, could develop along two different routes: the command-economy route and the market-economy route. Russia took the wrong turn. It must go back to the fork and take the other road. The shift is cumbersome and costly, but about the direction of the path there can be little dispute. (By contrast, the implicit central theme of this book is that there are no such predefined roads. The illusion that there are such predefined roads begins to dissipate as soon as one starts to investigate the detailed legal materials that must be used to build these supposedly well-mapped routes.)

Under the shadow of illusion cast by this idea, one group (now precariously in power) offers an extreme and even reckless version of the neoliberal program. This version offers no distinct strategy of economic growth or industrial reconstruction; rather, it claims that the stabilization of the money supply, the clarification of property rights, and the tightening of economic relations with the West will suffice to ensure growth. It holds that a sharp decline in production is unavoidable and even beneficial given the nature of the industrial system inherited from the Soviets.[29] Out of fear and self-interest, the other faction clings to the defense (and private appropriation) of the existing production system; its self-interest becomes by default entangled with the popular interest in defending production. What is missing from this Russian debate and to a lesser extent from its Latin American counterpart is the development of a realistic and democratic program of industrial reconstruction, with a strategy of growth and a proposal for the favorable positioning of the national economy within the world economy.[30] The newly liberal legal elite, prominent in the political class and in the intelligentsia, witness this contest with painful passivity. Many believe any form of politicized organization of civil society to be an unaffordable luxury for the country at a moment of transition.[31] They acquiesce to practices that permit rule by decree and leave civil society largely shapeless and voiceless. Yet it is precisely this lack of social organization as well as the lack of the institutional arrangements and legal rules that would foster organization in civil society that stand as the greatest obstacles to the development and expression of programmatic alternatives.

In this circumstance, one institutional idea stands out as an involuntary institutional invention of potential significance: the commitment to develop a popular capitalism based on universal distribution of shares in privatized state enterprises and the pooling of these fragmented shares by investment funds or holding companies (an idea with which both Poland and the Czech Republic are also experimenting in quite different forms).[32]

Note that this institutional innovation arises from the difficulty of clinging to a conventional sale-and-auction mechanism for mass privatization. With such a scheme, no one other than foreign investors, the nomenklatura, and black-market speculators would have money to pay. Even to the last two groups, firms would have to be sold for a song. Thus, a substantial part of ownership (the part not sold and not reserved for the workers and managers) must be distributed universally and gratuitously. The resulting fragmentation of ownership, however, would leave managers without effective control unless these popular shares were pooled in investment funds and holding companies.

What only now begins to be appreciated, however, is that these funds, a would-be example of the intermediate organizations I have already discussed, can become effective agents of a truly democratic market economy if reformers satisfy two fundamental conditions. First, there must be an industrial policy to save and reconstruct the production system, most especially by establishing a partnership between the vanguard and the rearguard. In the absence of such a policy, vast expanses of the industrial system become worthless, except for the firms that domestic entrepreneurs may, with the help of foreign capital, spin off. Second, the funds must benefit from a legal structure that both stabilizes them and makes them accountable to the regions and populations among which they operate as well as to the investors whose shares they pool. Without the fulfillment of these conditions, the rapid concentration of ownership will gradually overtake the system of popularly distributed ownership and holding companies. The recipients sell their shares, like peasants who have been given a little land and no support, and the funds become instruments of a new speculative finance capital rather than the agents of democratically organized regional economies.

Thus, there can be no stable diffusion and pooling of ownership without a successful strategy of industrial reconstruction. Conversely, however, it is hard to see how such a strategy could advance far, in a direction consistent with democratic experimentalism in society as well as in production, without a legal-institutional framework empowering workers, regional governments, and social organizations. In a large and complex country, prosperous industry requires vital regional economies—economies in which local populations and governments are willing and able to invest in the material and human infrastructure of production, and gain, in turn, some influence over the social forms and consequences of production. One can imagine that workers, regional governments, and social organizations, together with individuals, would become stakeholders in the investment funds and that the funds, although specializing in different sectors of production, would also compete with one another for investors and for capital.

The general point is that technological-organizational innovation and legal-institutional innovation depend on each other. The more specific point is that the organizations between government and industry come to life in the environment of a regional economy organized to take account of the claims of many different kinds of stakeholders.[33] It is an ideological dogma, which the contemporary experience of the peripheral economies is helping to discredit, that the law should use one set of rights and arrangements to organize the market and another set to organize society. The legal structure of a democratized market economy can be stretched—it increasingly must be stretched—until it becomes as big and as diverse as civil society itself.

Cooperative Competition Among Firms and Its Legal and Cultural Framework: A Lesson from Northern Italy

Much of the recent literature about industrial reorganization has been dominated by discussions of the possible sequel to Fordist-style, mass-production industry.[34] This style of production is characterized by the large-scale manufacture of standardized commodities by rigid machines and production processes, with sharp hierarchies of distinction between nonroutinized supervisory activities and routinized practices of implementation as well as an equally sharp contrast between the domain of cooperation (within firms) and the domain of competition (among firms). Students of industrial organization have shown how the economic success of the advanced economies is closely related to their varying ability to make the transition to a post-Fordist style of industrial organization—namely, one that achieves substantially higher levels of productivity and, above all, a stronger capacity for ongoing innovation by deploying flexible machinery and processes to develop a more continuous interplay between task definition and task execution and by jumbling up the categories of cooperation and competition.[35]

Networks of small and medium-size firms or semi-independent divisions of large corporations can continue to compete while cooperating through the pooling of financial, technological, and commercial resources. The boundaries between what is inside and what is outside a single contractual-corporate structure can be softened. The coexistence of cooperation and competition makes it possible to combine, to a greater degree, economies of scale with decentralized initiative. It also extends opportunities for learning in production. Under a regime of cooperative competition, invention through imitation now has two tracks on which to move, each with distinctive costs and benefits.

Certain regional economies in western Europe, such as that of northern Italy, have proved thus far to be the most successful theaters of this brand of industrial restructuring.[36] A pre-Fordist craft tradition and the developed set of associational structures with which it has historically been connected have offered a favorable environment for the development of post-Fordist industry.[37]

As the rich industrial democracies struggle half-consciously with the problems of industrial reconstruction and deal with the demands of a labor force stuck in either the declining mass-production sector of the economy or in its penumbra of joblessness, Fordist industry is transported to the leading tier of the peripheral economies, especially to its biggest members: China, Russia, India, and Brazil. In these countries, Fordist industry continues to be profitable, thanks to the repression of internal wages. Many a receiver of discarded Fordism, however, finds itself caught in a tightening grip between the high-skill, high-value-added industry of the successful restructurers and the even lower wages of the endless reserve-labor army of the world economy.

I have already observed how mass production in the typical social and cultural conditions of the peripheral economies helps to reinforce dualism as well as prevent a productive partnership between the vanguard and the rearguard of the economy. One of the main concerns of the institutional program developed in this book is to describe a trajectory of institutional change along which developing countries might escape the niche of discarded Fordism that they are now invited to occupy within the world economy.

However, the northern Italian example suggests a major obstacle in the path of post-Fordism for peripheral economies such as those of Latin America. This obstacle is the absence in those economies as well as in those of most of the world, including much of the United States, of the rich texture of craft and associational traditions (the guilds and schools, clubs and leagues, family and neighborhood-based apprenticeships) that have so immensely benefitted an old regional economy, such as northern Italy. On this problem, of such crucial importance to the developing world, the literature on industrial reorganization has thus far had little to say.

For there to be post-Fordism in the absence of this background, some functional equivalent has to be created through collective action and political initiative. There must, at the outset, be massive investment in education and in the social-support systems that make it possible for children to attend school. To be sustained in conditions of extreme inequality, this investment requires hard states capable of securing high tax revenue and escaping the disintegrative cycle of pseudo-Keynesian public finance.

More difficult to identify is the character of the associational equivalent to the traditionalist background of post-Fordism as found in an economy like that in northern Italy. A network of cooperative competition ordinarily thrives in a regional economy and depends invariably on a supporting structure of local government and community life. The reasons for this dependence are both practical and cultural. The practical reason is the need of cooperative-competitive firms to supplement the economies of scale achieved through cooperation. Help comes from the investment in material infrastructure and people that the existence of strong local government, sustained by a vital civil society, makes possible. The cultural reason is the need to encourage trust, especially trust among relative strangers, which is the single most important resource of a regime of cooperative competition. Trust flourishes when people not only live but also act together in civic life and social organizations. It is not irreconcilable with conflict; it is incompatible with anomic fragmentation and distance.

Among the contributions that legal-institutional innovations can make to cooperative competition in industry, two are particularly significant: one relates to the legal form of cooperative competition and the other to its social framework. The first is the development of a wider repertory of contractual-corporate forms that equip the network of cooperative competitors with many legal options along a continuum that goes from allowing contract between separate firms to allowing management decisions within a single firm. Similarly, there must be ways to recognize legally the varieties of stake holding now developing within these networks of cooperative competition.

The second key legal-institutional contribution is the invention of legal forms facilitating the creation of intermediate organizations,[38] especially organizations involving some combination of public and private investment and activity. The cooperative arrangements set up by otherwise competitive firms are themselves examples of such organizations. Other examples are investment funds, development banks, labor exchanges, technical and technological assistance programs (on the model of agricultural extension), retraining and continuing-education facilities, and regional health-care and daycare alliances and cooperatives. Particularly intriguing and delicate is the problem of finance; I discuss later the role of special banks, charged with a mission both supportive and reconstructive.

These organizations prosper, in turn, in a setting of strong and strongly participatory local government and in a setting of public law that facilitates the organization of civil society. The associational structures created by public law (such as a structure of automatic unionization within which different labor movements compete for position) may remain empty shells or be captured by activist minorities. But when taken over and inhabited, these associational structures may also make possible a valuable economy of organizational effort, counteracting the tendency toward fragmentation and passivity. Where the pre-Fordist conditions for post-Fordism are missing (and they are almost universally missing in Latin America), their counterparts must be created by politics and imagined by law.

THE FISCAL-FINANCIAL NEXUS: MAKING RESOURCES AVAILABLE FOR INVESTMENT AND INNOVATION

The Fiscal-Financial Nexus

The Latin American economies have been characterized by the combination of capital scarcity and extreme inequality. They have also been governed most of the time by soft states, which are hamstrung in their efforts to impose the cost of public investment upon the propertied classes, prodigal in the distribution of subsidies to the strong, and fatally attracted to inflationary sleight of hand. In such a circumstance, both the quickening and the democratization of economic growth require an enlargement of the fund of resources available to the government for investment in people and infrastructure and available to innovators for innovation. These must be resources that are not under the command of existing property owners in a society in which the inheritance of capital and economic advantage remains the overriding mechanism for generating extreme inequality. There must also be resources whose commitment will not be driven by the logic of short-term profit maximization, unrelated to productive contribution.

A long-standing dispute in the theory of economic growth centers on the relative importance of savings and technological innovation as conditions of growth. For the purposes of my institutional argument here, these categories are both too narrow and too crude. We may need to think of the kind of savings that can put resources at the disposal of productive experiments and experimenters—in other words, make them available to people with energy and ideas but without capital or patrons as well as to the public agencies that can help supply the experimenters with the physical and cultural apparatus they need. In a democratized market economy, the struggle to increase the amount and to accelerate the circulation of free-floating resources ("free floating" in the precise sense just defined) is the object of a fiscal-financial nexus.

The legal-institutional development of this nexus includes three sets of arrangements. The first set concerns the reform of taxation, expanding the means for both public investment and venture capital. The second set concerns entitlements ensuring people access to educational capital. A third set concerns the legal framework for socially funded and socially oriented banking and venture-capital operations.

The Tax System of a Democratized Market Economy

In many Latin American countries, the estimated tax revenue is low by comparative standards. It is, above all, highly skewed in its actual incidence. The two major departures from the professed aims of most tax systems are the heavy reliance on regressive indirect taxes and the disproportionate contribution of salary earnings within the area of direct taxes. The very high real rates of return to capital, especially to speculative finance capital, increase the significance of this substantial fiscal immunity of non-work-based earnings.

Massive tax evasion, particularly by those who operate in the gray economy or move finance capital around, magnifies these distortions. The paralyzing result of this evasion is to superimpose upon the insolvency of the government a widespread sense of the illegitimacy of taxation.

The recent experiences of Mexico and Argentina demonstrate that relatively modest investments in the tax-collecting apparatus can produce a substantial rise in tax revenue and eventually in voluntary tax compliance. Such investments could be followed by the exemplary indictment of rich and powerful tax evaders, a measure that would itself do much to signal the hardening of the state. All such initiatives, however, would fall short of the tax reform that a democratized market economy needs in conditions like those of Latin America today; a radical reform of the tax laws is also indispensable.

In the outline of such a reform, redistributive commitments must be tempered against realism about the demands of reliable revenue collection. The tax system must have a reliable base in an indirect tax that is relatively neutral in its economic impact and is capable of raising large amounts of revenue with modest distortion and disruption of economic activities. Comparative experience and analysis suggest that such an indirect tax is a comprehensive, flat-rate, value-added tax. In a federal state, the valueadded taxes imposed by state and local governments can piggyback on the federal value-added tax.

Once a sound basis of revenue collection is assured, the government can experiment in the redistributive direct taxes without fiscal danger.

The mistake is to try hitting the funding and the redistributive targets with the same tax tools. The most attractive direct tax system is one that relies on the combination of a Kaldor-style expenditure tax (taxing each individual the difference between income from all sources and savings) with a wealth tax (to which the gift-and-estate tax can be assimilated).[39] Such a system applies specialized tools to specialized targets: one tax for the hierarchy of standards of living and another tax or group of taxes for the restraint upon economic power. The income tax, combining as it does these two objectives, characteristically achieves both badly. Moreover, the replacement of the income tax by the Kaldor tax has a special interest for a capital-starved economy because it helps put taxation on the side of savings and investment.

My proposal is that a generic connection be established between the sources and the uses of revenue. The funds produced by a comprehensive, flat-rate, value-added tax go to public investment in the cultural and physical infrastructure of production and to the capital accounts of the socially and strategically oriented banking and venture-capital operations I describe later. The economically neutral tax funds the improvement of the production system and the labor force. The funds generated by the redistributive direct taxes finance the core operations of government and those entitlement or welfare programs that are not directly linked to basic or continuing education.

One rationale for this system is to guarantee a relatively secure source for public savings and strategic investment. A tax comparatively neutral in its redistributive and cost-shifting effect finances the development of the overall productive capacity of society. The fiscal mechanism of this financing remains relatively disentangled from the politics of redistribution. It does, however, fund what the experience of developing countries has shown to be the single most important redistributor: investment in an education system that is open to everyone in fact as well as in form. However, the redistributive taxes count among their objectives the funding of the most controversial redistributive programs: those unrelated to the collective interest in education.

A secondary rationale for this system is that the self-interest of the state's political and bureaucratic apparatus becomes tied to the success of redistributive taxation, for it is from the redistributive direct taxes that the funding for the government's operational expenses must come.

Educational Capital

Investment in education enjoys a special status among the commitments and techniques of a democratized market economy, especially one whose installation must move forward through the disruption of extreme privilege and inequality.

Comparative research has shown that no other form of public investment is more important in diminishing inequality. Thus, in the East Asian countries, beginning with Japan from the time of the Meiji restoration onward, heavy and persistent educational investment, rooted in social traditions as well as in political decisions, has helped equip and more nearly equalize the population. Even in Latin America, political economists have shown how countries like Colombia, which has invested more heavily in education, have seen their investment translated into the descent of a few notches down the ladder of Gini coefficients, which measures economic inequality.

In addition, the economic and political institutions I have proposed require if not a definite repertory of knowledge and skill then at least a strengthened capacity for experimental learning. The political and economic agents of such a society must have learned to learn early on. Moreover, these institutions aggravate a problem that European social democrats are only now beginning to discuss in earnest: the incompatibility of strong and widespread claims to job tenure with a quickened economic experimentalism.

Job security has played a prominent role in the historical agenda of working-class movements, especially in countries such as those of central and northern Europe, in which social-democratic parties have enjoyed power for long periods and in which corporatist styles of political economy have flourished. (In Japan, the lifetime employment system has evolved as a result of a very different form of oligopoly in markets, dualism in the labor force, and business unionism in labor–management relations.) Even in many Latin American countries, including Brazil and Argentina, workers in the protected Fordist sector and civil servants in the enormous apparatus of central and local government have achieved a degree of job tenure that the neoliberals are now trying to revoke or to loosen. But the emphasis on job tenure depends for its realization on particular political and economic conditions—the same conditions guaranteeing the stability of a Fordist mass-production sector of industry—that are able to distinguish between a core of stable workers from a periphery of temporary workers and subcontractors at home and abroad.

If by both necessity and design firms must have ample room to hire and dismiss workers and to rearrange people and machines, states must satisfy in other ways the concerns underlying the struggle for job security. These concerns go to establishing trust and cooperation in the production system and to developing practical bases for the individual and collective empowerment of workers. A major part of the compensation for the loss of nearly absolute job tenure should be a claim to continued retraining and reeducation throughout a lifetime as well as a claim to an original educational endowment.

What legal-institutional form should this claim take? Consider first the original education of the individual and then consider continuing education and reskilling.

The effective provision of basic education in very unequal societies, such as those of Latin America, is a many-sided task. The experience of countries as different as Uruguay and Costa Rica demonstrate that such a task is feasible. The school must have a physical support structure, including food and health assistance, that keeps children there. It must also develop a pedagogic orientation privileging capacities to analyze and recombine. It must have community engagement but also a nationally set agenda. Localism in school organization is incompatible with the central educational mission to rescue the child—any child—from his family, his class, his community, and even his country, giving him access to remote forms of experience and standards of judgment.

In light of this ideal, there is every reason to supplement public schooling with an educational capital account set up by the state for each individual. The points in this account could be applied to payment for nonstate educational institutions or could be contributed to independent public schools that, exempt from the nationally set educational agenda, try to pursue distinctive directions.

For the provision of continuing reeducation and reskilling throughout a working life, such a government-funded account for payment to experimental private, public, or mixed public–private educational facilities may be the sole and sufficient mechanism. Moreover, these organizations should occupy all points of a spectrum going from practical reskilling to more comprehensive education. The system may require some measure of paternalism. Thus, substantial drawing upon this account may require the agreement of trustees, who are recruited from both public counseling services and union or professional associations. The core idea is that whatever the differential transmission of economic advantage through familial gifts and inheritance, every worker would continue to inherit from the state the equipment she needs to reinvent a little bit of herself from time to time.

The Financial Agents of Economic Experimentalism

I complete the institutional definition of the fiscal-financial nexus with a sketch of the financial agents of innovative investment. It may help to begin this sketch with a few remarks about the history of banking in Latin America and elsewhere, for these remarks will help to clarify the central problem and mission of finance in a democratized market economy.

Discussions of banking in Latin America often begin with the observation that banks there fail to perform their standard and necessary role of mediating between individual savings and productive investment. They instead have frequently become enterprises almost entirely devoted to financial speculation and to the easy gains made possible by the government's financial dependence. This observation, in its first part, presupposes an idea about banking that has in turn been given historical validation.

Alexander Gerschenkron conducted a famous study of the transition in nineteenth-century Europe from commercial banks of the early Rothschild type, dealing in short-term commercial credit and sovereign lending, to universal banks, committed to long-term industrial investment and heavily involved in the management of enterprises in which they held equity stakes.[40] If the Credit Mobilier was the prototype of the investing and entrepreneurial bank, the German, Austrian, and Italian banks completed the development. They were able to establish their investing activity upon the solid basis of short-term credit activities and consumer banking. Bankers like J. P. Morgan demonstrated how such a universal bank could be used to turn around failing enterprises and to capture the benefits of hidden synergies.

If, however, we look further ahead, we see that what at first seems to have been a progressive and irreversible transition in the history of banking turns out in retrospect to be a brief interlude between long periods of financial passivity and short-term vision. Recent studies, for example, suggest that German banks, despite their vaunted ascendancy over industry and their industrial cartel-building proclivities, increasingly fail to exercise any real supervision over the firms to which they loan money or in which they hold equity.[41] The post-Keynesian economists have studied how firms struggle to free themselves from capital markets by generating investment funds internally. And even merchant banks, on the old European model of a Julius Baer or a Warburg, seek to prosper as intermediaries of corporate finance and markets in corporate control rather than as primary investors and industrial reorganizers. Like the American investment-banking houses, they find themselves running after the latest opportunity for arbitrage in financial intermediation. The decried hegemony of finance capital, as theorized by Rudolf Hilferding, has not survived this retreat.

It seems that the most powerful obstacle to the execution of the larger investing and reorganizing mission of the universal bank is cultural rather than narrowly economic or legal. Given who they are and what they know and want, the bankers are wholly unable to serve as the superentrepreneurs, the shakers and recombiners of industry, that they were invited by that mission to be. They more regularly stand at some point on the continuum between accountants and gamblers, with all the points of the continuum equidistant from the world of production.

This involution, fortunate as a diminishment of unaccountable economic power, is unfortunate to the extent that it represents a withdrawal of agents capable of investing and reorganizing with a long-term strategic perspective. Public development banks have very modestly filled the vacuum in Latin America. These banks are now under attack by the champions of the neoliberal project and under attack in the world economy generally by multilateral public institutions such as the International Financial Corporation. The central problem highlighted by this continuing lack of capable agents is the relative absence of a form of finance that is liberated from the constraint to ensure short-term profits and that is able to nurture and deploy a long-term strategic approach to industrial investment.

A democratized market economy, established under conditions of capital scarcity, must rely on financial agents that are able to make socially useful investments over a broad range of sectors and in a rich diversity of forms. These agents must be able to perform two functions in addition to the functions now performed by conventional commercial and investment banks. One is the public venture-capital function: to make capital available and to take equity stakes in firms and projects in a fashion that is liberated from short-term vision. The other is the superentrepreneurial function: to take the lead in pressing for the reorganization of production and corporate control whenever such a reorganization seems a promising way to capitalize on unexploited productive possibilities.

Conventional economic analysis will object that market forces and market forces alone can be fully capable of producing the agents best suited to perform these two functions, rewarding those who guess right and punishing those who guess wrong. This objection raises a central implicit theme of my argument. The program I outline is predicated less on a belief that the market is inadequate than on a belief that the market needs to be defined institutionally and can be so defined in different ways and with different consequences. In this argument, each proposal has to meet a double test, showing signs of being located in a zone of overlap between the conditions of economic growth and the conditions of the progressive democratization of society. Every banker and manager understands the severe although varying restraints that reinforce short-term vision in the dealings between the world of finance and the world of industry in the existing regulated market economies. These constraints have been the primary motor driving successful firms to generate investment funds internally.

Three kinds of financial agents can perform the two functions I have identified: independent public banks (modeled on the International Finance Corporation arm of the World Bank and on the Banco Nacional de Desenvolvimento Econômico e Social of Brazil, with special responsibility for investment and superentrepreneurship at the frontiers of production); mixed public–private banks (specializing in large-scale projects of strategic interest to the national economy in the style of the joint ventures of European Union governments and private firms in the airplane industry and other high-technology areas); and private banks (linked to a network of cooperative-competitive firms as their financial arm and brain in the fashion of the banks that have already developed special relations with such firms in northern Italy and elsewhere).

The public banks and the mixed banks would differ from network-oriented private banks in two respects. First, in their investment-making and creditgranting work they would go beyond freedom from short-term vision to occasional financial initiatives that cannot be justified on a pure calculus of profit and risk but that nevertheless satisfies some perceived strategic or social interest. Second, they would count upon as a major source of capital the funds generated by the comprehensive flat-rate, value-added tax, which through their activity would circulate in the economy. This circulation is what justifies the claim that this tax represents a levy on production for the sake of production. For the use of these moneys, the public and mixed banks would have to pay a return to the government or to the higher-level public banks responsible for administering such funds.

The most important legal innovations in such a scheme lie in two areas. One area is the definition of a framework within which public and private banks can be independent from government tutelage, competitive with one another, and financially responsible while nevertheless remaining ultimately accountable to elected governments. A natural starting point for thinking about such an arrangement is the experience accumulated in the relations between democratic governments and independent central banks. Another point of departure is the record of some of the more successful public banks or public enterprises in Latin America itself. It is sheer legal superstition, arising from a failure to grasp the diversity of possible market forms, to mistake nonprivate ownership for lack of competition.

The other area for legal innovation lies in the relationship between the public or mixed banks and the government that makes funds generated out of the value-added tax available to them. It is doubtful that standard contract and property norms would suffice to inform this relation. These rules would have to be supplemented by forms of personal liability, both civil and criminal, of both the bureaucrats and the bank managers under broadened standards of fiduciary responsibility. In fact, a predictable legal consequence of any economy that joins public and private activities more intimately rather than segregates them rigidly is to require a great expansion of fiduciary principles and sanctions.

THE ANIMATING VISION: DEMOCRATIC EXPERIMENTALISM IN AN AMERICAN KEY

Justification of This Alternative Approach

The alternative to the neoliberal project presented and developed in the preceding pages draws life from a reinterpretation of the democratic vision. Faithful to my method, I shall not pretend that this vision is neutral in its consequences for different conceptions of the good or different ways of life. The vision has developed in the course of a political tradition that, although many sided and inclusive, is nevertheless specific. Moreover, I express it in a vocabulary that is characteristically American (and in certain respects also Latin American) and connected with the most persistent anxieties of American democracy.

The vision can be justified in one way by the help it provides both to the imagination and to the defense of trajectories of institutional change possessing two connected features. First, these directions of change must be promising in their ability to satisfy (better than the alternatives one can think of and hope to advance) the recognized interests of the broad masses of ordinary working people. Second, they must also prove superior to their rivals in dealing with the fundamental structural problems of the society (in Latin America today, problems such as the persistence of economic dualism, the continuing fiscal crisis of government, and the inadequacy of an entitlements-based style of redistribution). Such problems regularly impede a fuller realization of recognized interests. The basic difference between these two standards of judgment—the reason why they may occasionally diverge—is that the second, unlike the first, allows for the possibility of ignorance or "false consciousness."

A conception such as the one I invoke can also be justified in a more general way: by its capacity to help inform vocabularies, attitudes, and ideas that maintain a living bond between aspirations and practical desires over a broad range of changing circumstances. Here the standard bears some kinship with the "wide reflective equilibrium" discussed in contemporary Anglo-American political theory. The point is to describe the contours of an imaginative space in which some roughly stable relation between what people really feel, really want, and really need and what they believe ought to be the case becomes feasible. The historical testing that such a standard invites is never direct, unambiguous, or conclusive. Nor, however, is it wholly elastic. The untidiness of the view of justification resulting from these premises may be disconcerting to the rationalist. It is nevertheless better in its consequences and more realistic in its claims than the familiar oscillation between hyperrationalistic pretenses to impartiality or objectivity and the inhibiting or complacent skepticism to which such pretenses so often give way.

The Search for an Area of Overlap Between the Institutional Conditions of Economic Progress and the Conditions of Individual Emancipation

The essence of the normative vision I propose is the commitment to search for the area of potential overlap between the conditions of economic progress and the conditions of freedom from subjugation. This quest has oriented many of the arguments and much of the theorizing about the democratic project over the course of the past two centuries. The conception of economic progress to which I allude is straightforward. It is a self-sustaining increase in output and productivity, counting among its principal instruments a strengthened capacity for learning, a persistent power to innovate, and a broadened freedom to recombine organizational arrangements as well as factors of production.

More subtle is the conception of the good of emancipation. I prefer to interpret this good as a lessening of the tension between the demand for self-direction and self-expression, on the one hand, and the need for solidarity and engagement in group life, on the other. The tension diminishes to the extent that group life loses some of the terrors of practical and spiritual oppression. These terrors have the effect, as they mount, of exacting a marginal price in autonomy for each strengthening of community. To disrupt this equation is the work of emancipation.

The radical-democratic doctrines of the past differed from the academic democratic theories of today in, among other things, their insistence on keeping in focus the relation between the requirements of prosperity and the demands of emancipation. They would have no truck with a view of democracy as remorseful idealism carping at the heels of the devotees of worldly success. Their frequent error was a dogmatic optimism, supported by a deterministic view of history, according to which economic progress and individual emancipation naturally and necessarily converge. But we would be just as dogmatic and misguided as they were if we were merely to invert this conviction and subscribe to the belief that freedom and prosperity are doomed to conflict.

The proposed revision of the classical doctrine is the belief that the conditions of economic progress can, although they need not, overlap with those of individual liberation. Each of these two goods can advance through alternative sets of institutions and practices or alternative pathways of change. The point is to identify an intersecting (and available) subset of each of the two sets.

The deep reason to believe that such an area of overlap exists is the affinity between the increased power to recombine things and people that continuing economic progress requires and the demand, implicit in the agenda of emancipation, to disengage the life chances and social opportunities of the individual from predetermination by inherited advantage or stereotyped roles. To state the same affinity in another way, a strengthened capacity to learn (to learn more and to learn more quickly) is the most powerful unifying thread in the pursuit of economic progress and antisubjugation. Both an engaged citizen of a democratized hard state and a successful economic agent in a democratized market economy must be quick studies; they must also have at their disposal the instruments and materials of organizational transformation.

No belief is more characteristic of the old (and now downtrodden) American hopefulness than the hope that the road to collective riches may also become the path to individual liberation. In fact, in the American vision this belief stands on an equal footing with our other great hope: that the development of originality among individuals can increase the opportunity rather than diminish the chances for solidaristic cooperation in social life (the central hope of an Emerson or a Whitman). In labeling these beliefs "hopes," I mean to suggest that they are more than reasonable gambles; they are attempts to exploit a possibility that by being believed in and acted upon becomes more likely to be realized. By drawing attention to the special status these hopes enjoy in American culture, I want to emphasize not their dependence on a particular national tradition but rather the openness of this tradition to aspirations that have become increasingly worldwide and now exercise a revolutionary influence everywhere.

Cooperation and Competition, Strategic Coordination, and Market Initiative

The search for the common ground of the conditions of economic progress and individual emancipation describes only the most general aspect of the vision animating the alternative to neoliberalism outlined earlier. At a lower level of generality, this vision includes a conception connecting these general concerns to the preferred direction of institutional change explored earlier in the essay. The main idea here is that the most promising route to making good on the common ground is a form of economic organization and legal ordering that combines strategic coordination, decentralized initiative, cooperation, and competition more fully than most present political economies allow.

In the programmatic argument of this book, I have emphasized the practical advantages and institutional vehicles of such a combination. But I also believe that this effort holds a larger political and spiritual promise as well. This promise relates to the value that I described in the preceding section as exercising among American beliefs an authority coequal with the commitment to make economic progress and individual emancipation converge: the impulse to develop a form of genuinely common life that is nevertheless able to forgive, to use, and eventually to inspire the originality of individual people.[42]

The point is to build a bridge between originality and solidarity. Such a bridge is more likely to be built in a society where people experience frequent and easy passage between the cooperative and the competitive aspects of their workaday lives.

The thesis that market initiative and strategic coordination, competition and cooperation, can and should combine stands opposed to the idea, familiar today in debates about the meaning of the failure of state socialism, that all varieties of "third wayism" have been discredited. If institutional innovation or the lack of it is political fate, third, fourth, and fifth ways are not only possible but also unavoidable. The real question is, Which ways are the best? Indeed, the experience of the formerly Communist countries, as my earlier discussion of Russian industrial reorganization implies, suggests the need to resurrect and reconstruct some of the undeveloped ideas of "market socialism." We need to distinguish the bad part of these ideas, the equivocation about political constraints upon economic experimentation, from the good part, the insight into the diversity of possible market arrangements.

However, the commitment to combine cooperation with competition and strategic coordination with market initiative more fully and continuously is reminiscent of some of the familiar slogans of present-day European social democracy in which the call is made for more of the market in the state and more of the state in the market. The difference lies in the conviction, central to all my arguments, that this more energetic synthesis requires a sequence of legal-institutional inventions that change the practical forms of both government activism and market decentralization. Institutional conservatism taints the solutions of European social democracy, severing them from the democratic experimentalism I have advocated.

Contrast with the Dominant Perspective of Anglo-American Legal and Political Philosophy

The way of thinking that produces the vision I have outlined differs in several respects from the habits of mind and modes of argument characteristic of much contemporary Anglo-American political and legal philosophy. First, it treats relative impartiality, the distancing of oneself from one's own circumstance, as the horizon rather than as the starting point of inquiry. Second, it takes legal and institutional analysis to be an integral part of the imaginative development of ideal conceptions rather than a tactical or empirical afterthought. Third, it focuses on institutions and practices as well as on the varieties of social activity and relations they favor or discourage rather than on distributive ends as the ultimate objects of political-legal argument and action. Fourth, it refuses to organize thinking about democracy around an overriding value such as equality of resources or respect, preferring to explore the reciprocal connections between practical economic success and rescue from oppression.

The Twin Disciplines of Institutional Thinking

Two disciplines would be most important to the systematic development of the way of thinking I advocate: an institutionally oriented practice of political economy and a style of legal analysis devoted to an understanding of the legal agenda of alternative pathways of institutional change. These two disciplines would be so close in subject matter and method that each would simply designate a different region of a continuous imaginative space. In fact, however, neither of these disciplines now exists in other than a fragmentary form.

Dominant macroeconomic theory deals with institutions episodically or indirectly as a shadowy background to the phenomena that it studies when it does not identify the idea of a market economy with the version of a market economy that it finds established. As a result, it has trouble avoiding halftruths, circumstantial truths, or temporary truths of the kind exemplified by the Phillips curve or the Laffer curve. It often fails to rise above misleading trivialities of the type that holds that unified party governments are better at keeping down government deficits than coalition or divided governments are. In the following section, I argue that the conventional forms of policy analysis in legal thought are equally unsuited to the task of achieving the diagnosis and developing the program I advocate here.

In the absence of ready-made disciplines and methods, we have to work with what we have, using programmatic proposals as occasions to try out ways of thinking and talking that join empirical understanding and normative visions more intimately than we are accustomed to joining them in either positive social science or political and legal argument. If one does not believe in the value of institutional alternatives, one would have reason, out of sheer intellectual curiosity, to pretend that one does.

THE TASK OF LEGAL THOUGHT

Legal Thought as Vehicle and Obstacle

What style of legal thought is needed to inform the kind of structural diagnosis and programmatic argument to which this essay points? Before addressing this question, consider a few characteristics of legal culture in Latin America. These observations have a twofold relation to my theme. First, they describe a typical way in which legal culture comes to impede the work of understanding, reimagination, and reconstruction. Second, they serve as a second-hand commentary on some of the problems of American legal culture; in this, as in much else, Latin American traits represent a lopsided exaggeration of flaws that continue to afflict American legal culture.

The dominant legal culture of Latin America is marked by an ever-widening opposition between doctrinal formalism of a very conventional nineteenth-century sort and a demand for the creative, ad hoc reinterpretation of law by judges and other professional law appliers. In Brazil, for example, there is a well-established movement of "alternative law," complete with its own journal, collective meetings, and a degree of influence upon the judiciary as well as with a legal academy that far outreaches the American critical legal studies movement and its European counterparts. The proponents of this alternative law demand, in a manner most reminiscent of the free-law movement of early-twentieth-century Germany, an ongoing reinterpretation of law. This reinterpretation should attend to the needs and expectations of the marginalized and the disadvantaged, and it should resist the crushing of what Jürgen Habermas would call the "life world" (the fine structure of moral reciprocities in everyday life) by the wooden and violent generalities of state law. In societies in which the oppressed form the vast majority of the population, such a mission represents a formidable undertaking. It in effect changes the judges and other law appliers from government officials into mediators between the government and ordinary people—Trojan horses who through competitive examinations wheel themselves into the walled space of state power.

The underlying political-professional context in which this contest between a reaffirmed doctrinal formalism and the alternative-law movement takes place is one in which legal professionals have been dramatically pushed aside by technocrats, especially economists, as the experts with the most to say to power holders and the strongest claim to the *arcana imperii*. Until the 1960s, lawyers remained the dominant segment of the political and economic elite in Brazil as in all Latin America. For most of the history of Brazil, legal education has been the generic form of elite education. Similarly, in Mexico until recently, political and economic leaders as well as even writers and philosophers have commonly been *licenciados*. This predominance has now been undone with a vengeance as the lawyers seem to have increasingly less to say about the real problems of their societies.

Faced with this abrupt and decisive fall from influence, lawyers have responded by alternatively reaffirming the constraints of the rule of law upon technocratic policy making (the reassertion of doctrinal formalism) and engaging in guerilla warfare against the episodic interpretation and application of law (the alternative-law movement). These responses have in common the lack of any structural understanding or proposal. They fail to respond to the technocrats at the level at which the technocrats operate: the level of understanding an institutional system and its requirements of successful management and improvement. To answer that legal thought by its nature has less to say than other disciplines about structural issues and alternatives is to beg the conclusion in a particular way. It is to assume that detailed institutional understandings and proposals of just the sort that a reformed style of legal thought should be good at generating form no part of the alternative message.

There is little in this description that readers will find unfamiliar in the present U.S. legal culture. The only substantial difference is that for the American jurists the fall from influence has been less marked. Much of the mainstream legal culture has moved toward a functionalist or policy analysis that shades more continuously into the methods and ideas of the nonlegal technocrats. The invocation of routinized sets of countervailing policies in each legal discipline, however, often resembles nineteenth-century formalism, albeit with a different vocabulary. It typically remains as bereft of a sense of structural alternatives as it is disconnected from sustained empirical study of the consequences of different rules and arrangements. The truth is that practical American legal culture has escaped the fate of its Latin American counterpart only in part and only to the extent that it has surrendered to what the Latin Americans try, albeit ineffectively, to resist. What we miss in Latin America, in the United States, and in every other place is a practice of legal thought that can speak structurally about structural problems and that exploits the hidden strengths of a legal imagination—the reciprocal probing of ideal visions and practical arrangements and the discovery of real and potential institutional diversity, contained, suppressed, and concealed under the lid of power, tradition, and dogma.

In the following pages, I present in the form of a small number of dogmatic theses possible starting points for a legal culture that could work as an active contributor to debates such as those considered in this book. They describe some beginnings and presuppositions of an approach equipped to escape the Hobson's choice of doctrinal formalism and alternative law without turning legal analysis and legal thought into an institutionally conservative policy science.

Rejection of Legal Dualism

The belief that structural alternatives need not and should not hold the attention of legal thought has sometimes been made plausible by the idea that the reexamination of basic practices, arrangements, and assumptions takes place in certain culminating foundational or reconstructive moments of social life. Thus, the normal legal science of the nonrevolutionary moments takes its agenda from the most recent reconstructive movement. American legal thought, for example, would still be bound to complete the unfinished work of the New Deal. Bruce Ackerman has recently developed this essentially Durkheimian notion of the rhythm of collective enthusiasm and prosaic reality as the basis of an approach to law and legal history.[43]

There is a truth in legal dualism: the basic truth of discontinuity in institutional and conceptual change. The political economy of autarchic import substitution and pseudo-Keynesianism, discussed here, was indeed a political invention with large and long-lasting consequences. But the thesis of legal dualism goes wrong when it overestimates the determinacy of each foundational settlement and underestimates the endless opportunities that practical problems present to reopen the ambiguities and refine the direction of the settlement. For example, are the privatization of public services by local governments impatient with welfare bureaucracies, the development of a common market with Canada and Mexico to increase the mobility of capital while maintaining the immobility of labor, or the enshrinement of affirmative action based on formal group classifications rather than on real and varying circumstances of disadvantage for or against the New Deal settlement? Would it be for or against the New Deal settlement to express skepticism about the efficacy of tax-andtransfer programs as the principal device of egalitarian redistribution?

At a more fundamental level, the thesis of legal dualism errs insofar as it implies that there is an inalterable or uncontrollable rhythm of structural stagnation and innovation requiring us to wait, should we be born at the wrong time, for the next wave of enthusiasm and restructuring. Moreover, by pushing the structural themes back to the exceptional revolutionary interludes, legal dualism makes it seem that, with respect to basic arrangements and conceptions, there can be no science, normal or otherwise, only prophecy. Thus, what should have been an opening risks becoming an alibi; if structural change or thinking is not in the cards, the best we can hope for is to humanize what we have.

The Opportunity-Creating Translation of Legal Conceptions Into Legal Details

Every time a legal conception, in particular the legal conception of an institutional regime, gets translated into a detailed set of arrangements and rights, we find that the conception admits alternative possibilities of imaginative and practical development. This is the truth in legal skepticism or indeterminacy. From this truth arises the possibility of a mutually subversive and progressive interaction between legal-institutional conceptions and their detailed legal translations. Far from being a species of reflective equilibrium, this interaction is a kind of permanent disequilibrium. The disequilibrium keeps legal and political thought on the run when they do not surrender to some fetish about the necessary or final institutional form of their preferred conceptions.

The model of protected mass production and pseudo-Keynesian government finance, the neoliberal project, and the alternative to both outlined here are all interpretations of a regulated market economy and a constitutional democracy. But as each of them adds legal-institutional detail, each develops these conceptions in a distinct direction.

Moreover, choices about alternative developments of both the conceptions and their practical forms continue to be made at every turn. We may find solace in the thought that once we have made the big selections (among models of political economy or legal-constitutional regimes), the remaining options will be of a more contained technical character. But we shall find that we have bought this solace at a heavy cost if it obscures the recurrence, within the work of defining a regime in detail, of choices as significant in their reconstructive potential as those that led us to the regime in the first place.

Thus, to be developed in legal detail, the fiscal-financial nexus, which I have presented as an important but technical part of my alternative to the neoliberal project, requires a series of conceptual and institutional innovations in the structure of the tax laws, the arrangement of welfare rights, and the organization of capital markets. Although each of these innovations is in itself modest, each requires us to make choices about some feature of economic and political pluralism. The legal definition of a regime is just an accumulation of such decisions, repeated many times across a wide range of concerns. What seems to be a technical afterthought, like the material about the fiscal-financial nexus, could equally well serve as the starting point for the whole proposal of a political and economic regime.

Structural Solutions to Structural Problems

Every society has problems that, remaining just beyond the horizon of active concern, doom to frustration a host of recognized interests and professed ideals. These problems characteristically have to do with the institutionalized organization of social life and with the social understandings that this organization enacts. The pieces that make up this background form no indivisible system, but nor are they readily separable. They become entangled with one another. The combination of the features of entanglement, of distance from everyday action, and of influence upon what people can do and how they can connect is what defines an arrangement or a conception as "structural."

To bridge the gap between this opaque structural background to social life and its surface of need, demand, and difficulty is the ambition of every form of legal and social understanding that wants to be more than a technique. A style of legal thought that is more than a technique of social compromise and rights assignment must try to grasp the legal-institutional aspect of the structural problems besetting a society. It must also identify the legal-institutional element in the possible solutions to the problems. In this enterprise, legal analysis finds a natural ally in a certain kind of political economy, one attentive to institutions and their consequences.

It is the failure to take seriously the responsibility of structural analysis that makes inadequate the conversational focus of much recent legal and political theory. For this theory, a democratic legal order is one that ensures a widening conversation in which more voices can be heard and heard with more nearly equal time. The problem, however, lies in what is left unspoken: the structural restraints and assumptions that, unchallenged, come back to shackle the conversationalists. Thus, the conversational focus may lend a philosophical halo to the dominant style of American progressivism with its "What about me?" perspective and its difficulty in addressing the reorganization of society and its institutions.

Legal Pluralism

In another piece, I explore in the setting of disputes about the sovereign debt of developing countries a principle that ranks high among the central ideas of contemporary legal thought: the idea that individual and collective self-determination depend on factual and defeasible conditions and that we cannot ensure freedom merely by clinging to a predefined system of rights without worrying whether or how these rights can be exercised.[44] Some things have to be withdrawn from the area of free choice to make free choice real. Remarkably, contemporary legal thought has on the whole failed to draw from the idea that self-determination depends on empirical conditions what would seem to be an inescapable corollary: that such conditions can always be defined and satisfied in different ways. Which of these different ways of defining and satisfying the requirements of effective freedom and effective rights holding we accept ends up shaping the constitutional democracy and the regulated market economy that we have. The point is that the choices we make about these matters need not and do not converge in the same direction.

If we were to give freer reign to such experimentation with different ways of defining and satisfying the requirements of individual and collective self-determination, we would have legal pluralism. We would realize that different systems of market-defining contract and property rights can coexist in the same economy, different arrangements for accountability (ranging from the most indirect to the most direct forms of democracy) can coexist in the same polity, and different ways of mixing private initiative with public coordination can coexist within the same state and the same society—all to a much larger extent than we now imagine possible. (In my proposal for a democratized market economy, I have tried to turn some of these possibilities of coexistence to advantage.) We would be unembarrassed in our experimentalist eclecticism because we would be free at last from the residual illusion of nineteenth-century legal science: that regimes of rights and institutional orders lose integrity and efficacy if they fail to coalesce into a master scheme.[45]

From the standpoint of the thesis of legal pluralism, it is interesting to reconsider one of the seminal developments of modern legal thought: Wesley Hohfeld's attack on the idea of a single logic of rights.[46] The meaning of the Hohfeldian analysis has usually been understood to be the discovery that rights and their counterparts (powers, privileges, and immunities) may conflict and that nothing in the real logic of rights guarantees them a preestablished harmony. The conflicts invite "balancing" according to policies and interests. However, this reading robs the Hohfeldian analysis of half of its force, the undeveloped constructive half. A different reading would emphasize that alternative systems and logics of rights (and their counterparts) can coexist within the same legal order and that the coexistence we see and have is only a small part of the coexistence we can imagine and construct.

Comparative Law: Trading Influence for Insight

A major obstacle to the development of a style of legal thought with the characteristics and ambitions I have described is that it requires the lawyer to assume a perspective distancing her from her political society and legal culture. It may distance her from the ongoing conversation, depending on the extent to which that conversation lacks structural focus. It will in any event distance her from the focused work of policy-making and adjudication. The distancing may pay off; it can produce insight.

One of the most promising vehicles for such insight through distancing is comparative law. The point of comparative law, practiced in this light, is to force us to think beneath the surface, to think structurally, because we are thinking about an experience remote from our own. We have no influence to lose among these faraway peoples and readily renounce what we never really possessed. Then we bring our discoveries home to the space that we remain anxious to influence and in which our anxiety for influence threatens to undermine the reach of our insight.

Viewed in this light, comparative legal study can share in the power of storytelling to free us from seemingly insuperable constraints. By giving us a glimpse of an exercise, far away, of freedom to change, it can both encourage and instruct us in the exercise of such a freedom close at hand. Politics is about the struggle over the future, and law turns temporary victories into temporary rules.

CHAPTER FIVE

Economic Progress and Structural Vision

We lack a comprehensive social, economic, and legal theory to guide our efforts at understanding the problems and opportunities addressed in this book. We need not and cannot wait for such a theoretical system. The elements for a different way of thinking—one meeting the imperatives of structural vision and institutional imagination—are already at hand, even if its expression as systematic theory is not. Once seen from the perspective of this way of thinking, we can begin to envision how finance might be reconciled with democracy. We can then hope to apply the same method, proven in the study of finance, to other, less-recalcitrant parts of our social experience. We should stop using our ideas to demonstrate the futility of attempts to overcome the constraints that we have imposed on ourselves. We can use them to gain more freedom and power than we now possess.

TOWARD A WAY OF THINKING

The first two chapters of this book dealt with the workings and reform of finance as a wedge into a larger program: the reimagination and reconstruction of the market economy. Chapter 3 addressed this larger program directly. Chapter 4 confronted the direction and the ideal proposed by this program with the realities and convolutions of historical experience. It did so by seeing American developments in the mirror of experiences in Latin America and other parts of the world.

Implicit in the arguments of the previous four chapters are some of the elements of a way of thinking about economies and about how they can and should change. The aim of this last chapter is to make this way of thinking explicit. Once made explicit, it can elucidate a broader range of problems. It can also inform the imagination of alternatives to the political and economic arrangements of contemporary societies.

In the way of thinking that I defend and exemplify here, law and legal thought play a central role. They allow us to reckon with the present organization of the economy, the state, and society as a structure of institutions and assumptions that is resistant to change but susceptible to revision. Structural change is no less consequential for being piecemeal, as it almost always is and must be. To be practiced in this spirit and to this end, legal analysis needs a partner: a way of engaging economics that allows us to profit from the power of present-day economics without surrendering to its limitations.

The argument of this chapter speaks to a widely experienced but rarely remarked challenge faced by those who think critically of established economic, political, and social arrangements with a view to institutional innovation. How do we engage in criticism with intellectual tools bearing the marks of the realities and arrangements that we set out to criticize? We must use the instruments of thought available in our circumstance. We should not pretend, as Karl Marx and his followers did in the past, that there exists a ready-made and reliable alternative to the ideas dominant in the economics and legal thought of our time.

To renounce such a pretense, however, and to recognize the power and uses of the existing practice of economic and legal analysis, need not be a prescription for intellectual abdication. We can begin to redress the deficiencies of this practice with equipment that it provides as well as with the inspiration offered by ideas in law and economics that have been marginalized, forgotten, or simply left undeveloped.

There are two ways to advance in this spirit. One way is to address directly the foundational issues in economics and legal thought. Another way, no less useful for being less ambitious, is to provide a developed alternative approach and apply it to particular problems: an approach showing how in practice we can use established methods and conceptions critically and selectively, the better to begin redressing their defects while continuing to profit from their capabilities. An advantage of this second approach is that it lends itself more easily to cooperative intellectual effort, offering examples on which many can build. I take here the second approach.

The aim of this chapter is not to offer elements of a systematic theory. It is to draw out the message and the implications of my argument for our thinking about institutions and institutional alternatives beyond the boundaries of the issues—about finance and its role in national development—that have been at the foreground of my argument.

I proceed in two steps. I begin by discussing four major themes in the view for which I have argued. These themes do not add up to a theory. They do, however, suggest an approach to thinking about the reconciliation of the market economy with democracy and democratic ideals. They explore such an approach from a perspective that refuses to acquiesce in the limitations of institutionally conservative social democracy. They reject the social democrat's preference for the pietistic over the transformative—her attempt to humanize a world that she has ceased trying to reimagine and remake. Moreover, they contradict the classic leftist-Marxist view, which social democracy implicitly accepts, that there is a "capitalist system," understood as the unalterable economic logic and legal architecture of a market economy under conditions of scarcity. According to that view, if we cannot replace the capitalist system by another system—the revolutionary substitution of socialism for capitalism—we must resign ourselves to sweetening capitalism's social and economic effects by recourse to regulation, progressive taxation, and redistributive social spending. If progressives are not revolutionaries, they must, this conception implies, become institutionally conservative social democrats.

In the second section of the chapter, I turn from animating ideas to telling historical experiences. I invoke some episodes of the history of the past hundred years in which we might hope to find new meaning and guidance. To find them, we must be able to see these episodes not blinkered by some of the beliefs that have been dominant in the discourse of politics, policy, and social science. Just as the statement of the general themes is not meant to propose a systematic theory, so, too, these historical allusions are not intended to stand in the place of historical analysis. They recall in a few sentences widely known events of the past hundred years that can acquire new significance for us when read with the help of the ideas explored in the first half of this chapter.

We live in an age when a continuing scientific and technological revolution coexists with a counterrevolutionary impulse in our thinking about society and its future. Whether we embrace belief in cumulative institutional convergence or not, we tend to see the pursuit of large-scale institutional alternatives as a mark of the dangerous illusions and calamities of the twentieth century. We are inclined to view the defeat of the maximalist ideologies of the Left or the Right as a gain in realism as well as in humanity. We may then, from the perspective of our present disillusionment, interpret the historical record backward as an overcoming of false options and as an awakening to inescapable constraints.

Once we have freed our ideas about structural change and structural alternatives from their contamination by an unwarranted belief in the existence of supposedly predefined and indivisible systems such as "capitalism," we can begin to see these events with new eyes. We can view them not as foreseeable moments in a long descent into our present poverty of available or imagined alternatives but as a storehouse of examples of change as it really happens. Change of institutional and ideological regimes—"structural change," as I call it—is fragmentary, piecemeal, and reversible. It must work with the institutional and ideological materials available to the agents of change.

Structural change is not, however, condemned to remain within the gravitational field that these materials mark out. It is drawn but not confined to the path of least resistance—the solutions least disturbing to powerful interests and entrenched preconceptions. Its significance always depends on what happens next. It bears the mark of our highest aspirations and our most prosaic anxieties. Structural change in the economy is not just about making people richer or poorer, as individuals or as a society, but also about making them bigger or smaller.

Some of the episodes of piecemeal structural change or of the avoidance of such change discussed in this chapter were more successful and are more worthy of emulation than others. None of them deserves to be mistaken for the wave of the future or as a model to follow. Nevertheless, all of them suggest a world richer in the possibilities of institutional innovation than the reality pictured by long-dominant ideas in social science and politics.

In each of the historical episodes that I recall in the following pages, finance played an important role. It never just played the role of dream breaker and enforcer of constraint. It always also played the role of creator of new possibilities—desirable or undesirable, tightening or loosening the relation of the capital markets to the real economy, and more inclusive or restrictive in the distribution of opportunities and capabilities.

Ideas become powerful when they are married to the interpretation of tangible experience: how we see our options and prospects in the light of how we understand what has happened in one country and in the world. The aim of this chapter is to suggest how this marriage can provide insight into opportunities for structural change rather than confer on established arrangements an undeserved halo of necessity and authority.

FUNDAMENTAL THEMES

Institutional Variance in the Relation of Finance to the Real Economy

Central ideas in this book are that finance can be related more closely or more loosely to the real economy and that institutional arrangements, expressed in law, are decisive in determining whether the relation will be closer or looser. I have given the name "financial deepening" to the act of enlisting finance in service to the real economy and in particular to the production of goods and services—the expansion of output and the improvement of productivity. The concept of financial deepening describes a direction or a level, not an end state that we either reach or fail to achieve. By contrast, the name "financial hypertrophy" describes the circumstance in which the financial sector increases its share in profits and talents even as its connection to the real economy weakens. The transactions of the real economy become triggers or pretexts for trading and speculation rather than the chief object of interest. (Financial hypertrophy might also be called by the familiar name "financialization," except that this name has been used to describe vaguely a wide range of ways in which finance displaces productive activity instead of supporting it.)

At stake in the idea of financial deepening is the mobilization of a society's economic surplus over current consumption—that is, its saving—for the creation of new wealth. To render the idea more precise, it is important to be clear about the relation among the overlapping or internally related concepts of capital, saving, and finance.

Saving is surplus over current consumption. The cumulative product of this surplus over time is capital. Three elements enter into the definition of capital. The first element is that capital consists of man-made things. The second element is that these man-made things can be used to produce other man-made things or to extract resources from nature. The third element is that things can be converted into money by being sold and can command an income stream. The concept of capital has only tenuous sense in a barter economy or in one that, lacking money or its equivalents, drastically restricts exchange under a division of labor.

The relation of the stock of capital to opportunities for gain is one of the basic constraints on economic growth. The interest rate in principle provides a picture or a proxy for this relation. However, it is an increasingly misleading one to the extent that—as happens in all contemporary economies—national governments and their central banks influence the interest rate to serve objectives of public policy, such as the relation of the level of employment to inflation and deflation.

There are three crucial influences on the relation of the stock of capital to opportunities for gainful investment: the available forms of cooperative activity; the technological and scientific resources on which production can draw; and the way in which we combine our experiments in organizing cooperation with our experiments in using science and technology to enhance our powers and to transform nature. Perpetual revolution in the process of production becomes the force driving economic growth, turning capital to greater or lesser effect. In so doing, it also poses the question of the share of each class or group in society in the staging and control of this perpetual revolution as well as in the enjoyment of its benefits.

A mistake common to the pre-Marginalist economists, including Adam Smith and Karl Marx, was to have exaggerated radically the importance of the level of saving as a limit to economic growth. Indeed, for Marx, the chief explanation of class society throughout history was the indispensable role of class power and advantage as an instrument for the coercive extraction of a surplus over current consumption.

Only in the poorest and mainly preliterate societies did the level of saving represent the overriding constraint on growth. As economies developed, saving was soon overtaken by innovation in the arrangements and instruments of production as the overriding constraint on economic growth. It then matters whether power over capital is established and exercised in ways that either inhibit or encourage permanent revolution in the process of production. Capital is dead and voiceless. It requires living agents who will speak for it and make decisions in its name, exercising a power that the law of property, employment, and business organizations gives them.

The questions of how capital is used as well of who decides and under what arrangements bring us to the third of these interlocking notions: finance. The concepts of savings and capital allow for a stable definition, cutting across a wide range of historical circumstances. The concept of finance has a different character, more sunk in the particularities of historical experience and connoting a particular cast of agents. There can be an anthropology of finance (but none of capital or of savings) precisely because finance designates a world inhabited by distinctive organizations and agents.

The world of finance, as it is organized in contemporary economies, has three main parts. The first part comprises the banks and bank-holding companies or equivalents, authorized by law to undertake activities characterized as banking. The second part consists of organizations that although not organized as banks have assumed banklike functions: the now vast realm of what has come to be called shadow banking. It includes professionals of finance who commit other people's money to investment without assuming in law or in fact the core responsibilities of commercial or general banking. Among these professionals are asset managers, hedge funds, private equity, venture capital, and other enterprises and agents. The third part is the financial activity of firms that may control large stores of liquid capital generated by retained earnings. Depending on the rules of each jurisdiction, such capital may be invested in production, in acquisitions or investments, as well as in the buyback of its own shares when they are not distributed to the shareholders. We can add to this three-part structure a fourth element: the individual investor, almost always required to act within the constraints and with the tools supplied by one of the other three parts of the financial world.

To the extent that banking includes the figures of the universal and merchant banks that emerged in modern European history, taking stakes in productive enterprises as well as lending to firms and individuals, the distinction between the first part and the second part of this financial world wanes. There emerges a cadre of financiers who commit capital investment in private enterprise or fund states by holding governmental debt. The impulses and attitudes of this cast of organizations and protagonists in turn influence what firms do with their own liquid capital.

By "finance," I mean the activity of deciding what to do with the surplus over current consumption once the surplus has been turned into liquid capital ready to be invested—that is to say, committed to one or another use. Finance is this activity regarded from the perspective of the agents and organization populating the particular world whose basic architecture I have just evoked. To inquire into the relation between finance and the real production of goods and services is to ask to what extent production is the object or simply the occasion of financial activity. It is to question whether our present arrangements adequately exploit the potential of finance to expand output and enhance productivity or leave this potential relatively untapped.

To suggest that they leave it relatively untapped is to imply that alternative arrangements would tap it better. We cannot achieve an understanding of how such arrangements work without developing ideas or making assumptions about how they might change. And the change that matters for insight as well as for practical effect is the change that we can produce with conceptual and institutional instruments that we either already possess or are able to fashion.

The central thesis around which I organize my treatment of this first basic theme is that different sets of institutional arrangement shape the extent to which as well as the ways in which finance serves or fails to serve productive activity. Moreover, in the spirit of the idea of structure not system (discussed in the introduction to this book), we cannot adequately understand the arrangements shaping finance and its relation to the real economy as the enactment of a preset regime, under labels such as *capitalism* and *market economy*. Such a regime would come replete with its in-built legal architecture. According to the view of structure as system, we must choose between replacing the current system by another system (equally indivisible and resistant to reinvention) and improving it through regulation and redistribution.

The thesis that alternative institutional pathways always shape the relation of finance to the real economy, tightening or loosening it, may seem uncontroversial. However, it contradicts the basic tenet of the dominant approach, which is that the capital markets will automatically allocate resources to their most efficient uses provided two conditions are met. The first condition is that there not be a localized failure in competition, resulting, for example, from oligopoly or asymmetrical information. The second condition is that there not be a localized failure in the regulatory response to the localized market failure. According to this dominant approach, until we can reestablish more perfect competition, we must use regulation to make up for the effects of the market flaw.

What is excluded in the view that the capital markets allocate resources to their most efficient uses (except for failures of competition or regulation) lies at the heart of my thesis: the claim that at any given level of decentralization or competition, a market economy can be arranged, legally and institutionally, in different ways. Such alternative directions will, for example, deal differently with the task of reconciling our stake in the wide dispersal of initiative with our interest in the aggregation of resources and the achievement of economies of scale. Some of these differences will bear on the commitment of capital and the tapping of the economic surplus over current consumption for the financing of growth and innovation.

Historical experience should teach us the significance of such alternatives even before programmatic imagination enlists them in the widening of our present political and economic horizons. At each crucial moment in the formation of the United States, there was a struggle over alternative institutional directions in the organization of the economy. It happened in the foundation of the republic, with Hamilton's organization of the national debt in the context of a top-down mobilization of physical, financial, and human resources for national development. It happened some decades later with Andrew Jackson's dissolution of the Second Bank of the United States, followed by the emergence of a network of local banks that, together with the organization of family-scale agriculture, played a major part in the early economic empowerment of Americans. It happened at the turn of the twentieth century, when this decentralization of finance was overwhelmed by an intimate partnership between financial and industrial concentration. The progressives and nationalists of the early twentieth century then responded with an inconclusive attempt to tame the alliance of high finance with big business rather than with what would have been a bolder attempt to reinvent in the new circumstance the Jacksonian democratizing of finance. And the struggle happened during the Depression, the New Deal, and the war, when public investment, the organization of paragovernmental entities (the GSEs), and the creation of conditional deposit insurance reshaped the terms on which capital was mobilized for economic recovery and world war.

Today these lessons of historical experience have renewed and pressing significance. We have recently lived through an event, the financial and economic crisis of 2007–2009, reminding us of the harm that finance can do to the real economy. It is a harm that results from the economic and political arrangements that allow financial hypertrophy to prevail over financial deepening: first, the arrangements of the capital markets; second, the institutional form of the market economy; and third, the organization of politics and of the state. The greatest harm of failure to act on this thesis is the squandering of transformative opportunity, or the chance to turn finance from enemy to friend of socially inclusive economic growth.

At the time of the writing and publication of this book, we witness a prolonged slowdown of growth in the world economy. All around us we hear talk of secular stagnation, of the scarcity of radical technological innovations, and of a worldwide savings glut, marked by an increasing ratio of the stock of capital available for investment to opportunities for that capital's gainful deployment.[1] Historically low rates of interest seem to confirm the narrative of diminished possibilities.

In this context, it may seem paradoxical or anachronistic to argue that the productive potential of capital remains underutilized but for institutional innovations that we have failed to implement or even to conceive. This objection, however, fails to do justice to the role that the reforms discussed here can play in the creation of new opportunities for gainful investment. Each of the episodes in the history of American finance that I have just recalled exemplifies the way in which finance can help provoke as well as fund the technological, organizational, and institutional innovations without which capital alone would remain sterile.

A clear contemporary instance of this active role of finance in generating new, gainful opportunities for investment is venture capital. A venture-capital firm does much more than passively fund start-up enterprise. It brings together the finance, the business model, the technology, and the talent on which the prospect of success in the emerging enterprise depends. Yet venture capital, defined broadly to include everything from "angel" investing to private equity, remains a small part of financial activity, even in the few countries in which it has developed most. Moreover, its present outcomes and future fate remain tied to a narrow slice of the economy, employing an even smaller part of the labor force: the vanguards of production, especially in high-technology manufacturing and services.

One of several simple and partial ways in which to define the task of advance is to ask what it would take for finance to do the work of venture capital for the wider economy and labor force, not just for the technological and entrepreneurial elite with which venture capital habitually works.

The Alternative Institutional Forms of Market Economy

The mainstay of ideological controversy over the past two centuries has been the choice between market and state: more market, less government; more government, less market; or a synthesis of market and government, as in the conception of the regulated market economy or the social market economy. This organizing belief gains support from the impulse of practical economics in its central post-Marginalist iteration to swing between a complete institutional skepticism (in its purest analytical versions) and an unwarranted and largely unspoken identification of the abstract notion of a market economy with a particular set of economic institutions that became prevalent in the history of the North Atlantic countries.

An extreme instance of this view—which merely exaggerates a widely accepted conception—is the view, associated with thinkers like Hayek, that a system of exchange among free and equal economic agents automatically generates or requires the same set of arrangements. These arrangements are characterized as the pure core of the law of private property and contract. Much of what passes for institutional economics lends a semblance of justification and respectability to the belief that a market economy has a predetermined legal and institutional form, within a very limited range of permissible variation.[2] To transgress the boundaries of this range is to undermine or to pervert the market, resulting in an inevitable loss in the efficient allocation of resources.

This belief in a predetermined form of the market economy is not confined to conservative thinkers. It has also been a major premise of Marxist thinking, enshrined in the concept of capitalism—an economic and legal regime whose regular operations under the laws of historical change account for its rules and institutions, including private property and the right to buy and sell labor. For Marx and his followers, it was only under the radically different circumstances of communism, when the reign of scarcity had come to an end, that a decentralized economic regime different from capitalism could take form. In that regime, money would no longer buy labor.

A recurrent idea in this book is that a market economy has no single natural and necessary form, not even a closely restricted set of feasible variations on its supposedly constant themes, such as the set studied in the literature on "varieties of capitalism." In contemporary societies, we do indeed find a relatively narrow range of institutional arrangements in the organization of the market economy; its architecture is expressed in the rules and doctrines of private law. The comparison of civil-law and common-law regimes of market order as well as of the modest differences among, for example, the German, French, and Italian versions of civilian private law or between the British and American developments of private-law doctrine suggests functional similarity under the disguise of doctrinal difference.

According to one influential species of this faith, differences in doctrines and doctrinal categories among contemporary legal systems are misleading; they distract us from appreciating the extent to which alternative sets of doctrinal categories, rooted in the legal traditions that have been influential in different parts of the world, may achieve the same or similar goals by different means. Once functional analysis has been added to the comparative lawyer's repertory, significant difference in private law among the contemporary societies will strike us as even more restricted than it at first seemed to be. Thus, comparative law appears on the scene ready to do service for theories of institutional convergence among contemporary societies and economies.

The comparison of "varieties of capitalism" joins the conversation but does not change it: the comparison qualifies the convergence claim without challenging its core message. That it fails to do so is already implied by the use of the term *capitalism*, associated in Marx's social and economic theory with one of the "modes of production" that emerge in history. That theory represents each of the modes as an indivisible system, born with a preset institutional and legal logic and fated to play its assigned role in the evolution of humankind.

We owe to the history of modern legal thought an insight that has never fully penetrated the discourse of politics or the theory and practice of economic analysis: there is no natural and necessary way for a market economy to be organized and no prospect of inferring from the abstract conception of a decentralized economic order any particular set of market rules. We may be able to explain why some ways of arranging such an economy prevailed over others at particular times and places given how different classes and groups understood their interests, the ideas available to them, and the characteristic path dependence of institutional innovation.

At any time, the stock of institutional arrangements and ideas—including arrangements and ideas about production and exchange—is severely restricted. It expands by analogical extension, selective borrowing, and the marriage of social conflict to political prophecy. To recognize, however, that it is limited is not the same as to attribute its restraints to conceptual or practical necessity, bestowing on it a semblance of lawfulness or rationalization that it does not deserve.

Over the past century and half, the cumulative discovery by legal thought of the institutional indeterminacy of the abstract idea of a market economy has long seemed to have only skeptical or negative implications. At each step on the march from legal conception to institutional embodiment in working out the detailed legal form of the market economy, jurists found, often against their own initial inclinations, that there were choices to make. They could not settle the matter simply by referring back to the abstract idea of coordination among free and equal economic agents, as Hayek and others implied. Different ways of putting institutional flesh on legal and political ideas have consequences—the jurists discovered—for the shape of production and exchange as well as for the distribution of economic advantage. The alternative ways of shaping the market order presented at each turn a contest among interests and among visions, the perception of which was suppressed by the false assumption that a market economy has a single natural and necessary institutional expression within a small range of successful variance.

It fell to a later moment in the history of economic and legal thought to dismiss and trivialize the significance of this hard-won discovery by claiming that legal and institutional differences in the organization of a market economy were insignificant for a reason that the jurists had failed to appreciate. Whatever the economic arrangements that private law appeared to establish, interested parties could contract around them, negating their supposed consequences. At most, those to whom the law awarded an initial advantage in this game of musical chairs might reap an ephemeral benefit. "Transaction costs" might slow the reallocation of resources to their most efficient uses and users. Nothing, however, justified the idea that different ways of shaping the market economy, expressed in law, really mattered.

Yet these different ways did and do matter, as history—including some of the historical experiences discussed earlier in this book and later in this chapter—shows. The argument for their insignificance suffers from a fatal circularity. It supposes the existence of a space of free and equal coordination and assumes that the contract regime has a natural, uncontroversial form. It lends to these assumptions a superficial plausibility by repeating a characteristic move of nineteenth-century legal thought: the treatment of the core doctrines of the established body of private law as a perfectly elastic natural language in which we can express any transactional or institutional thought and then go on to implement it in practice.

What seems at first to carry only skeptical or negative implications in the tradition of legal thought turns out to have a positive programmatic significance. It supplies one of the elements of the approach to institutional history that this book exemplifies. Once we stop seeing that history under the lens of the preconception of relentless institutional convergence, we can approach the limited institutional diversity in history, as I have in this book, as a foretaste of wider possibilities: not the hypothetical and remote possible but the proximate, adjacent possible—the *theres* that we can reach from *here*.

With this reasoning, we begin to equip ourselves with the means with which to explore alternative forms of the market economy. We start to turn what seemed to be the skeptical, negative idea that the market has no single natural or necessary form to affirmative, programmatic use. In this book, three areas of institutional innovation have served as focal points for this conversion of a negative legal analytics into a positive programmatic argument.

The first focal point—the foreground theme of my argument—is the role of institutional arrangements, set in the law, in shaping the relation of finance to production. A major assumption of my treatment of this theme has been that if we fail to shape finance, we allow it to shape us: it sets the pace as well as the direction of our efforts to grow the economy. Arrangements that fail to tighten the link of the capital market to the real economy do not simply threaten to squander the productive potential of saving—the surplus over current consumption— but also risk allowing finance, unmoored from production, to contaminate and compromise activity in the real economy. And they entrench a class of moneyed interests that may corrupt democracy, thus bending governmental power to the interests of financial rentiers and speculators.

The second focal point, which has figured in the background argument of this book, is the contrast between initiatives influencing the primary distribution of economic advantage and opportunity and those merely attenuating inequalities generated in the market *after* they have arisen, thanks to progressive taxation and social spending. The former have causal priority over the latter. The latter are most effective when they complement rather than replace the former.

Institutional and legal innovations that reorganize the supply side of the economy rather than simply redressing inadequate demand, in the spirit of vulgar Keynesianism, require intellectual tools and political attitudes largely alien to our present circumstance. They contradict the spirit of institutionally conservative social democracy—the residual program of a Left that has retreated from transformative ambitions. Moreover, they rely on an approach to institutions—the conception that I have called "structure not system"—for which both the contemporary social sciences and classical European social theory fail to provide a basis.

The third focal point is the one at which our stake in economic growth most directly intersects our interest in inclusion, empowerment, and the containment of inequality. It is the extent to which the most advanced productive practice of today, the experimentalist knowledge economy, remains confined to insular vanguards or is widely disseminated in the economy. Its dissemination would require a broad range of institutional and educational innovations to satisfy the cognitive, moral, and social conditions of the advanced practice of production outside the narrow slices of economic life where they now flourish.

Consider, as one of these requirements, the role played by a heightening of trust and discretion and by collaborative competition on the spread of knowledge-intensive, experimentalist production. Highly specialized and hierarchically ordered work roles have marked previous styles of production, including industrial mass production. A wide margin of discretionary authority was reserved to the firm's managerial elite. Cooperation and competition were consigned to clearly distinct areas of economic life: cooperation within firms and competition among them.

A modicum of trust sufficed for this model to work. Classical European social theorists, such as Max Weber, saw in the universalization of a modest level of trust among strangers a distinctive and indispensable trait of the rational or capitalist economy. Such an economy requires strangers to be able to trust one another but not too much. Trust is incompatible, these social theorists argued, with a feature of the moral culture of many earlier economies and societies. That earlier culture tolerated a contrast between high trust within an in-group held together by ties of blood and shared experience, on the one hand, and distrust toward strangers, on the other. The new order demands the generalization of trust—of low trust as opposed to either distrust or high trust—across group boundaries.

The market, according to this view, is unnecessary when there is high trust and impossible when there is no trust; it operates on the basis of moral middle distance. Even within the firm, because cooperative activity remains organized on the basis of rigid hierarchy and specialization and of coercive cooperation, it places little trust in the workers and requires little trust among them.

Such an economic world could live with a duality of power and contract. It could take the arm's-length bilateral executor contract as its model of contractual relations. Consider collective bargaining. That labor-law regime was designed to reestablish the reality of contract amid the stark disparities of power in the employment situation. Yet within the broad framework of rights that the regime set up, managers representing the rights of property continued to give orders, and workers continued to obey or occasionally to resist those orders.

The knowledge-intensive, experimental practice of production allows and requires all its participants to take initiative and to work, to a greater or lesser extent, as coauthors of the plan of production.

Within the firm, this practice heightens the threshold of discretion and trust among workers. Among firms that continue to compete in their sector against one another, it benefits from the circulation of people, resources, practices, ideas. The result is a practice of cooperative competition.

A legal expression of cooperative competition is the relational contract. The bilateral executory promise, standing at the center of classical contract theory, is an arm's-length, fully articulated bargain that is instantaneously exhausted at the moment of performance. By contrast, the relational contract governs a continuing reciprocal relation, often between firms or other organizations. It seeks less a particular performance than an open-ended series of reciprocal benefits. The nature of these benefits changes as the relation evolves. Moreover, it is only partly bargained out; its terms continue to develop over its life. Because it is only partly articulated, it demands and fosters a heightened level of reciprocal trust, sustained by engagement over time.

The placement of relational contract at the center rather than at the periphery of economic life would in turn exercise its full effect only in an economy in which decentralized initiative could more readily be combined with economies of scale. The use of disaggregated, fragmentary property rights might allow different categories of stakeholders to hold joint stakes in the same productive resources. Such stakeholders may include workers, local communities, and national governments as well as investors. The easier it is to combine scale with decentralization, the more favorable becomes the legal and institutional background for the development of networks of small and medium-size firms. These firms would no longer need to work as satellites of major corporations in order to operate at the front line of advanced production. In such a setting, transformed by a change in both institutions and consciousness, the reorganization of finance, to enlist it in the service of production, can achieve wider effect.

This example brings us back to the central point: the institutional indeterminacy of the market economy is no mere negative and analytical proposition. Properly understood, it opens a gateway to a programmatic imagination and a transformative practice interested in reshaping the market order rather than just regulating it (to counteract localized market failures) or humanizing it (through progressive taxation and redistributive social spending).

Alternative Globalizations

We can reshape the market economy by innovating in its legally defined institutional arrangements instead of simply altering the division of responsibility between government and market. We can respond to globalization in a similar spirit. Instead of having more or less globalization, we can have a *different* globalization. The contest over the institutions of the domestic market has as its global counterpart a struggle over the arrangements of the world economy and the world order.

In this book, I argue that financial deepening can help countries engage the world economy without relinquishing strong national projects. Such projects mobilize the physical, economic, and human resources of the nation in favor of the development of a distinct form of life, expressed in institutional arrangements that sustain it. A democratized market economy represents a species of these strong national projects. "Active globalization" is the name that I have given to such engagement with the world economy but without surrender of the prerogative of developing strong national projects.

Two distinct but complementary ideas combine in my development of this theme. The first is that the constraints imposed by the present form of globalization admit a wide range of responses. Some of these responses are much more promising than others. They help set the basis for strong national projects, including those that give priority to socially inclusive economic growth or to the broadening of opportunities and capabilities. Thus, they can enhance individual and collective agency: our power to act and to change the circumstance in which we find ourselves.

The second idea is that the class of alternatives for which I argue in this book cannot advance beyond their initial steps without a change in the path that globalization is taking. To say that the constraints of the present global regime admit of a wide range of responses is not to see these constraints as either neutral or indefinitely elastic.

These two ideas do not contradict each other. The effort to create alternatives must begin in the space of regions, nations, and local governments and communities. It must proceed until it hits against the limits imposed by the present world order, especially the regime of world trade and world finance. The conflict between the globalization regime and the forces that it frustrates can then motivate an effort to change the regime. In the absence of such a contradiction, there would be no force pressing to redirect the arrangements of the world economic and political order.

The significance of the first idea becomes clear in the contrast that I have drawn between the responses of the Latin American and East Asian economies to globalization in the second half of the twentieth century. The major Latin American countries opted for submission to the discipline of world capital and to the ideas, policies, and institutions recommended by the political, economic, and academic authorities of the North Atlantic countries. Mental colonialism supplied the climate in which national surrender came to seem reasonable.

The collection of polices by which this result was achieved amounted to a functional equivalent to the late-nineteenth-century gold standard. Like that standard, it made the level of economic activity depend on the level of business confidence. Its ideologists regarded the tying of the hands of national governments in fiscal, monetary, and trade policy as a solution rather than as a problem. The collection of policies prevented national governments from embarking on what those ideologists regarded as nationalist and populist adventurism by strengthening the veto power of domestic and international finance.

This syndrome of policies included a relatively low tax take (often replaced by rents from the extraction of natural resources as a source of funding for the government), acquiescence in a low level of private and public saving, a consequent reliance on foreign capital as a source of investment, an opening of the capital account to make such reliance feasible, and a willingness to let foreign capital occupy strategic positions in the production system, including the manufacture of intermediate goods and consumer durables. Obedience to foreign interests and ideas has rarely been so complete. For much of the history of Latin America, such obedience has generally met, as obedience generally is met throughout history, with exemplary punishment: slow or fitful economic growth in the context of some of the most extreme forms of inequality and exclusion that the world has seen in recent decades.

An alternative direction was the one taken by the Northeast Asian economies in the second half of the twentieth century—Japan, South Korea, Taiwan, and then, on different terms, mainland China. Here the state played a central and overt role in the creation of new comparative advantage. It insisted on a high tax take early on, spurning the dependence of governmental finance on rents from natural resources, even when such rents were available. It worked to require a high level of private and public saving. To this end, it often sacrificed recourse to the conventional devices of fiscal and monetary policy—especially deficit-financed public spending in response to an economic slump—the better to arm the state with the means with which to finance a rebellious strategy of national development. As a result, it created a basis on which to use foreign finance and investment without allowing them to penetrate and dominate national production.

From this orientation, there resulted in the early stages of the strategy a preference for loan capital without ownership of major productive assets. Only later, after new comparative advantage had been won in strategic sectors—typically industrial manufacturing in this historical period—did government allow foreign direct investors to own major productive resources. Even then, the takeover of pieces of the production system by foreign capital remained subject to governmental veto. A premise of such arrangements and policies was tight control and gradual opening of the capital account. The purpose was to protect national sovereignty while empowering national producers to create new comparative advantage in the world economy.

We need not treat these orientations with apologetic sentimentality to perceive their advantages. In practice, they were often associated with favored deals between the masters of political power and a cast of favored industries and entrepreneurs. This association was more inclusive and open in some countries (e.g., Taiwan) than in others (e.g., South Korea). Moreover, the forced mobilization of national resources in pursuit of national development often provided occasion for an authoritarian politics, which in turn proved hostile to the diffusion of a radical experimentalism in the economy and the culture.

The result has been favoritism and dogmatism to the detriment of democracy and experimentalism. Nevertheless, even in this perverse or truncated form, this direction in development preserved the possibility of national divergence and rebellion, allowing for the relatively greater success of the Northeast Asian economies in their effort to catch up to the Western powers.

The characteristic impulse of each of these two pathways shows in the role that each development strategy accorded to finance in its conception and strategy of economic growth. Some variant of what I have described as "financial deepening" in this book was essential to the East

Asian direction. One of its consequences was the subordination of rentiers and financiers' interests to producers' interests—at least among the producers who could count on the authoritarian state's favor. By contrast, the Latin American direction was more likely to treat the capital markets as the arbiter of sound policy. The more it gave the domestic and above all the international capital markets this arbitral role, the more likely it was to identify the financiers and rentiers' interests with the national interest.

It did so under either a general or a special pretext. The general pretext was a principle based on standard economics: insofar as the capital markets suffer no taint of market failure, they allocate resources to their most productive uses. The special pretext was the one resulting from the threat that democracy presented to the views pressed on developing countries by the academic and political authorities as well as by the North Atlantic powers' financial interests: the hope that national governments' dependence on financial confidence would make them less likely to sacrifice economic orthodoxy (as it was then represented) to popular appeal.

It is no part of this argument to suppose that countries must choose or ever had to choose between the two directions that I have just summarily described. We can best think of these directions as two development routes among many. Each expressed the marriage of reigning interests with ideas that seemed to serve those interests. They were the ideas that happened to be available and influential in that milieu. No regime of globalization allows for a unique response to the constraints that it imposes.

Globalization has become a generic alibi for national surrender. The diversity of responses to it, however, shows that the equation of globalization and national surrender is baseless. The countries in which the alibi was made to sound most plausible were those that, like the Latin American republics of the turn of the twenty-first century, embraced ideas and policies giving to the constraints imposed by fuller engagement with the world economy a force and a consequence that they would otherwise lack. These countries chained themselves or allowed themselves to be chained by their governing elites. Many then attributed their submission to the blind forces of globalization rather than to the initiatives and beliefs of those who governed them.

The clearest expression of this reversal of causation was the role attributed to capital. Institutional alternatives such as those that I have proposed in this book were dismissed as certain to produce capital flight and disinvestment, even early on the road from proposal to implementation. Yet vulnerability to a capital strike was more the consequence than the antecedent condition of policies that included low domestic saving, dependence on foreign capital, and an openness to capital flows enabling this dependence to produce its effects.

The idea that the present regime of globalization or any regime that may replace it allows for alternative responses to its constraints has as its complement the idea that globalization, like the market economy, takes many different forms. Just as finance performs different roles in each way of responding to the constraints of the established form of globalization, so too it changes in each approach to the reform of the world economic order. To be caught in debate about the advantages of more or less globalization is to risk accepting the premise that the present course of globalization is natural and necessary. Anyone who accepts this premise is likely to unwittingly mistake opposition to the present form of globalization—especially to the world trade and monetary regime—for hostility to an open world economy.

A discussion of the world trading system, one of the most important forms of globalization, shows what is at stake. One feature of this system is its tendency to incorporate into the rules of world trade the requirement that participant countries accept a particular version of the market economy. The result is to outlaw or restrict the kinds of institutional experiments that have figured in my argument, including experiments in the reshaping of the relation between finance and the real economy. The multilateral treaties concluded under the aegis of the World Trade Organization prohibit, as forbidden governmental subsidies, the practices of strategic coordination between governments and firms or the use of governmental power to develop new comparative advantage. Rich Western countries now want to deny the latecomers the right to do what they did in the course of their ascent. Similarly, they seek to incorporate into the trade rules the arrangements of intellectual property, developed at the end of the nineteenth century, which leave technological innovations vital to the cure and empowerment of millions of people in the control of a small cast of Western multinational businesses.

The regional trade pacts—such as the Transpacific and Transatlantic trade deals that were proposed in the second decade of the twenty-first century and that have now become the forward line for the development of the global system—go further in the same direction. They do so, for example, by allowing private businesses to sue sovereign states in the defense of the interests that these regional treaties protect and promote.

There is nothing necessary or self-evident in this relentless maximalism of institutional restraint: the effort to build the maximum of restraint on institutional divergence into the arrangements of an open world economy. The regime that preceded the World Trade Organization, under sponsorship of the General Agreement on Tariffs and Trade, was marked by an institutional minimalism, seeking economic openness with a minimum of institutional restraint rather than using the development of trade arrangements as an occasion to impose a particular species of the market economy and to proscribe the institutional and legal innovations that would depart from it.

The result of the maximalism is to risk turning the enemies of such prescriptions into opponents of economic openness. It is also to undermine the sole basis on which democracy can be reconciled with free trade. This basis is the design of arrangements that empower states and their citizens and entrepreneurs to try out new ways of organizing themselves rather than putting them in a straitjacket made to suit the interests and opinions of those who happen to be in command.

A country interested in the narrower financial or the broader economic innovations for which I have argued must resist the maximalist direction and defend the minimalist one, even as it takes advantage of the multiplicity of ways of responding to a regime of globalization antagonistic to democratic experimentalism.

Another feature of the developing world trade regime presents the international implications of financial arrangements more directly. A striking and ever more pronounced feature of the predominant direction of globalization, expressed in the arrangements of world trade as well as in their broader political and legal setting, is the contrasting treatment of the mobility of goods, services, and capital on one side and of people on the other. The owners of things and money enjoy increasing freedom to move them. People must remain confined to their state or at most their bloc of states.

There is no sound basis in either economic theory or democratic doctrine for such a stark opposition between allowing mobility to the inanimate (whether capital or tradable goods) and denying such mobility to the living. The inclusion of services provided by firms among the beneficiaries of mobility shows that the real line of division implied by this principle in the trade regime is the difference between the treatment accorded to the products of firms—goods or services—and the treatment accorded to workers.

A standard proposition in practical economics is that capital moves so that labor need not move. Theoretically, if enough capital moved, labor productivity among different economies would tend more rapidly to converge. Repeated empirical study, however, has shown that to this day only a relatively small proportion of funds available for investment moves among economies; most capital stays at home. The part that does move may exert a destabilizing influence out of all proportion to its size.

No initiative even remotely rivals increased mobility of labor in its potential to attenuate inequalities among economies: the most salient form of inequality in the world, overshadowing by far the admittedly vast inequalities that continue to exist within economies. No sudden and radical worldwide advance in the mobility of labor could be achieved without massive destabilizing effects. Each step would have to be measured and subject to qualifications and compensations: safeguards for the countries receiving foreign workers and restitution to countries losing skilled labor. Progress in the mobility of labor implies as well a reinvention of the role of the nation-state and of national differences. It is incompatible with the idea of the nation as a large family or a tribe, united by blood as well as by shared experience, commitment, and belief.

As always, what matters is the direction of movement. There is a straightforward alternative to the radical contrast between unlimited mobility for things and for money, achieved as soon as possible, and the denial of the prerogative of movement to people. The alternative is incrementalism: labor and capital gaining the freedom to move across national borders in small, cumulative steps.

The established direction—the one denying to people what the global regime allows to business products and capital—can more readily be reconciled with autonomous finance: with forms of thought and of practice viewing the capital markets as they are now organized as a machine for the efficient allocation of resources. They may suffer from localized flaws (in which case we require an equally specific regulatory response to those localized flaws). On this view, however, we cannot conceive and design the financial market in any fundamentally different way.

By contrast, the view that the living should gain freedom of movement together with the inanimate, step by step, draws on an idea central to the argument of this book: that the usefulness of finance lies in the density of its engagement with the real economy. The dangers of finance multiply, and its potential goes to waste, to the extent that it becomes unmoored from the real economy. We come to mistake its present form for the providential device of efficient resource allocation, occasionally flawed in its details but incapable of fundamental rearrangement.

Different national responses to the constraints imposed by the present form of globalization prefigure a larger contest over alternative globalizations. In each of these two moments of the discovery of collective possibility, finance plays a revealing role. We are accustomed to think of finance only as the enforcer of unyielding constraint. We do so, however, out of sheer lack of insight and imagination: properly understood, its problems and possibilities anticipate larger contests over the path of national development and the organization of the world economy.

A Revised Practice of Economic and Legal Analysis in the Service of Institutional Imagination and Reconstruction

One of the aims of this book is to exemplify a practice of economic and legal analysis useful to institutional imagination and reconstruction. Before addressing the hallmarks of that practice, I pause to consider different ways in which we can hope to advance such a practice and the relation of my argument to these alternatives ways of thinking.

The most straightforward approach to the advancement of such a practice is *the formulation of a comprehensive theoretical view and the explication of the method that the theory implies and deploys*. The scope or subject matter of such a theory and method relate most directly, among all fields of social study, to economic and legal analysis. These fields are or should be the twin disciplines of the institutional imagination, dealing with the established arrangements of the economy and the state as well as with the penumbra of accessible institutional possibility surrounding those arrangements.

The deeper and more inclusive such a theory and the method serving it are, the more it will represent an intellectual engagement with the institutional and ideological presuppositions of a regime of social life. It will be comprehensive social theory even if pursued under the label of economic or legal thought. A view of this kind works in two registers: as general social and historical thought and as economic and legal analysis. Marx's theory of capitalism, in the context of his broader account of the history and logic of modes of production, is the most important example of a conception that is at once economics and comprehensive social theory. Smith's economics share this double nature.

We must resist the temptation to identify such a theoretical project with the particular ways in which European thinkers of the eighteenth and nineteenth centuries undertook it. In the hands of the European social theorists of that time, the ambition to develop theories of structure and structural change most often took a form that we have reason to reject: the conception of a closed list of social regimes, each of them an indivisible system, operating in lawlike fashion and driven forward by high-order laws of historical change in a foreordained historical sequence.

A comprehensive theory of this order can take forms radically different from those it took in the work of the classical European social theorists and economists. Whatever form it takes, it cannot, given its high ambitions and extraordinary demands, be a normal intellectual practice. A view of structure and structural change in the mode of comprehensive social and economic theory requires vast learning, prophetic insight (given the relation between understanding of the actual and imagination of the possible), and genius. It defies the intellectual division of labor. I argue here, however, that in failing to meet these tests, as almost all of us must, we are not therefore condemned to accept an intellectual practice—such as the one now established in the social sciences, in economics, in law, and in the discourse of politics and policy—that is bereft of structural vision.

A second approach, at the opposite pole of self-consciousness in theory, is *tacit insight revealed in innovative action*. Here there is no explicit view whatsoever. Nevertheless, innovation in the institutional arrangements of society implies or enacts an understanding of structural change and discontinuity. There is no institutional life in society without a representation of this life in belief. There is no way of innovating in our institutions and practices that fails to enact an understanding of what is possible and what is real in social and economic life.

An example invoked in the introduction to this book helps show what is at stake in this claim. In the first half of the nineteenth century, Americans innovated in the organization of agriculture and finance. They developed family-scale agriculture of unprecedented efficiency on the basis of what we would today describe as decentralized strategic partnership between producers and governments as well as cooperative competition among producers. They suppressed the national bank and established the most decentralized system of finance at the service of the local producers that had ever existed. The creation of this national network of local banks is an example of financial deepening if ever there was one.

According to present beliefs, the two basic initiatives that we can take with respect to a market economy are either to regulate it or to attenuate the inequalities generated by the market. To soften inequality, we rely on compensatory and retrospective redistribution by means of progressive taxation and redistributive social spending. However, there is also a third class of initiatives, with more transformative potential than these two: to innovate in the arrangements defining the market economy.

That is what the Americans did in agriculture and finance in the early nineteenth century: they were reshaping the institutional and legal form and therefore the economic, social, and political consequences of agricultural and capital markets. Their method had the potential to transcend the limits of the relatively modest differences discussed in the current literature on "varieties of capitalism."

If Americans had been restrained by the now prevailing preconceptions about the natural form of a market economy, they would not have not taken these formative initiatives. Tacit insight informed their reconstruction of the institutional setting of agriculture and of finance. Failure to make this insight explicit and to develop it in the form of actionable understandings of social life has exacted a price: the difficulty of resisting the illusions shared by the two major traditions of progressive reform in subsequent American history.

One of these traditions, reaching from Thomas Jefferson to Louis Brandeis and beyond and expressed in the vocabulary of property-owning democracy, sought to defend small-scale enterprise and property against the forces of economic concentration and the dominating influence of big business. The other tradition, associated with the two Roosevelts, accepted the occupation of the commanding heights of the economy by big business. However, it sought to bring big business under the restraint of regulatory power, exercised by a strong national government. Neither of these two reform traditions committed itself to what had distinguished the early-nineteenth-century reforms in agriculture and finance: the remaking of the market economy in its legally defined institutional arrangements.

As a result, the most important impulse in the American project of national development remained buried under a veneer of superstition. That impulse was the dialectic between the mobilization of national resources from above and the democratization of opportunity down below, achieved through institutional and legal innovation in particular sectors of the economy. The two traditions of progressive reform did little to renew the life of this dialectic at later moments of U.S. history. How could they? They lacked an understanding of its nature.

So each time this dialectic recurred in some more limited form—during Reconstruction in the aftermath of the Civil War, during the heyday of early-twentieth-century progressive nationalism, and during the New Deal—it operated more weakly than it had before. We may attribute this cumulative weakening of the interaction between developmental mobilization from above and democratization down below to the combination of two main causes. One cause comprised the restraints that the proto-democracy character of American constitutional democracy placed on the moneyless classes' ability to challenge the moneyed interests. The other cause was the naturalization of the established institutional arrangements by the ideas prevailing in practical politics and policy as well as in the high culture. The failure to make explicit the insight underlying the reconstruction of agriculture and finance exacted a price: the misrepresentation of American experience helped weaken American democracy.

With each successive decline of the vital interplay between mobilizing resources above and democratizing opportunities below, democracy became weaker and finance stronger. Instead of marrying the real economy, finance married political power.

There is a third approach to the understanding and proposal of institutional innovation: *the association of fragmentary theory with radical reform*. We might view this approach as intermediate between the other two approaches—comprehensive theorizing and tacit insight—

except that we cannot achieve it by splitting the difference between the other two or by simply combining them. It makes its own demands and has its own distinctive dangers and benefits.

By "radical reform," I mean piecemeal change in a society's institutional and ideological regime. Almost all structural change in history happens in the form of radical reform. The revolutionary substitution of systems continues to be an extreme exception or hypothetical limiting case rather than the standard mode of structural change that Marxism and other social theories have cast it to be.

By "fragmentary theory," I mean a way of thinking that is structural in its explanatory and programmatic interests without being systematic in form and comprehensive in its scope. Rather than seeking to tower above the specialized social sciences and branches of policy discourse, it raids them in search of intellectual tools for the pursuit of its structural interests, in the hope of converting to another use the ideas and methods often employed to naturalize an established institutional and ideological regime. It has most reason to engage the two disciplines that bear most directly on the institutional order of social and economic life: legal thought and political economy.

Fragmentary theory does not profess to turn economic and legal analysis into the instrument of a systematic view of structure and structural change. Nor does it claim to possess an alternative theory of economics and law, ready to challenge the ideas and procedures dominant in each of those disciplines. Rather, it explores the storehouse of legal and economic ideas as well as their hidden and forgotten history, the better to develop a way of thinking about institutions that is free from the impulse to treat their established forms as natural and necessary. It refuses to treat legal thought and political economy, as they are now practiced, on a take-it-or-leave-it basis. Thus, it carries the spirit of radical reform from politics to thought.

As an intellectual practice distinct from systematic theorizing about structure and tacit insight into structure, fragmentary theory has three distinctive features. Its first trait is its view of society's institutional and ideological regime as decisive in influence and resistant to challenge and change yet susceptible to part-by-part, step-by-step reconstruction. Its second characteristic is its association with radical reform—that piecemeal and cumulative change of the regime. Radical reform represents both its subject matter and its goal. Its third attribute is its critical engagement with the received practice of economic and legal analysis.

I now address that engagement in both its general form—its working assumptions about institutional structure and change—and its specific form—its relation to economics and law.

Fragmentary theory makes up as best it can for the absence of a usable view of structural change in contemporary social science, economics, and legal thought. Such a view would be one capable of informing our imagination of accessible institutional alternatives: the alternatives that we can hope to develop with the institutional and conceptual materials at hand. Unlike much of contemporary social science, it recognizes the decisive influence of institutional arrangements and ideological assumptions. To account for their emergence and transformation requires distinct ideas and methods. We can explain an institutional and ideological regime in the same way we explain the activities that take place within the framework that it establishes.

Unlike the central tradition in classical European social theory, however, fragmentary theory denies that such regimes form a small, closed list of recurrent options (of which "capitalism" or the market economy is one). It rejects the idea that each regime represents an indivisible system that must be either managed or replaced, thus negating the possibility of radical reform, which is of central interest to transformative practice and its partner, fragmentary theory. It contradicts the thesis that laws of historical change govern the evolution of such regimes. Despite their power, tenacity, and their variable recalcitrance to challenge and change, these institutional and ideological orders are makeshift constructions, put together in times of crisis and heightened strife with the institutional and ideological materials that happen to be available to the people who made them.

Faithful to the character of fragmentary theory, my arguments in this book make use of this understanding of structure—of what in the introduction I called "structure not system"—without formulating or defending it in the language of systematic theorizing. My arguments instead exemplify it by the way in which they deal with the past and possible futures of finance and the market economy in the context of alternative pathways of national development.

I now consider in turn the relation of my argument to the prevailing ideas and methods in these twin disciplines, economics and legal thought, qualified above all other branches of social and historical study to serve our institutional understanding and our imagination of institutional alternatives.

The central tradition in economics since the last decade of the nine-teenth century has been the one that the Marginalist theoreticians—Léon Walras, Karl Menger, and Stanley Jevons—inaugurated. It has never been the only tradition of economics. From the outset, even in Great Britain, it had rivals, such as Alfred Marshall's conception of economics as a context-bound, natural-historical science like the science of tides or the science of the weather or Francis Edgeworth's approach to economics as a systematic psychological science. These and other rival paradigms have continued reappearing, often in compromised and less self-conscious forms, in the subsequent history of economic theory. However, they have never expelled the Marginalist conception of economics from its central place. Even Keynesianism, the most important economic heresy of the twentieth century, did not challenge that tradition in many of its most central tendencies. In some ways, it accentuated them.

The post-Marginalist practice of economic analysis has exercised immense influence and continues to be useful to even the most radical critics of established economic arrangements. Its great value has been to serve the cause of analytic clarity as a science of trade-offs and constraints. It exposes confusion and self-deception. Its achievements, however, have been bought at the cost of four defects.

The first and fundamental defect of post-Marginalist economics is the absence of any properly causal theory at its core. What the Marginalists created was, as their Austrian disciples understood, more a form of logic than of causal science. The analytic practice established by Marginalism worked by a hypothetico-deductive method that avoided controversial empirical, normative, or causal assumptions. In its most rigorous forms, it was not even a psychological science that made contentious claims about rational behavior. It could operate only by making its analytic apparatus run on the fuel of the factual stipulations, causal theories, or normative concerns supplied to it from the outside. It was in this sense wholly unlike the physics that its practitioners were often said to emulate. If an economic model failed to account for the facts, the solution was not to change the underlying theory but to build another model by adjusting its assumptions or the values of its parameters.

The empirical investigations that occupy so much of contemporary economists' time can mislead us into thinking that economics pursued in the post-Marginalist tradition has undergone a character change and become an empirical science. Its basic nature, however, remains unchanged. There is theory, and there is empiricism, but they have little to do with each other. Insofar as economics has causal conjectures, they are either formulated ad hoc or imported from some other social, behavioral, or psychological science.

This practice of economic analysis confronts an intractable dilemma. To the extent that it remains rigorous and faithful only to its own assumptions, it is empty of causal or programmatic consequence. It acquires causal or programmatic power only by taking on extraneous baggage: factual stipulations, normative commitments, and causal theories imported from another field or stipulated ad hoc. It must either compromise its analytic purity or settle for causal and programmatic impotence.

A second weakness of post-Marginalist economics is its lack of institutional imagination. The most important expression of this deficiency is the tendency to naturalize the established form of the market economy. Such an economics fails to appreciate the extent to which a decentralized regime of market exchange can take radically different institutional forms, with major consequence for the arrangements of production and exchange as well for the distribution of economic advantage.

A third flaw in this dominant tradition is its lack of any proper view of production. It is at its core a theory of competitive selection through market-based exchange. From the outset, the most characteristic and undisputed achievement of Marginalism was to rescue economic analysis from the confusion about value and prices that had plagued classical economics. It represented the economy as a set of connected markets. It took as its commanding problem an approach to the elucidation of relative prices that would require no scholasticism about value or about the relation of value to prices.

However, in this undertaking Marginalism discarded what had always been central to classical economics: a view of production. It came to see production as a shadowy extension of exchange. It found opportunity for this narrowing of horizon in a fact about the economy that has no necessary relation to the tenets of economics: the prevalence of wage labor among the forms of free work. Because in these economies labor could be bought and sold, it became easier to see the world of production through the lens of relative prices. There was nothing natural or inevitable in this circumstance: it was only late in the nineteenth century that the predominance of economically dependent wage labor among the possible forms of free labor (including self-employment and cooperation) began to be seen as natural or inevitable.

The fourth defect in this dominant tradition of economic analysis may be the least obvious, but it is the most surprising: the absence of any account of the diversity of the material on which the mechanisms of competitive market selection operate. Economics takes for granted the degree and quality of this diversity.

One of the most basic sources of diversity in economic life is the division of the world into sovereign states. At least in principle, states can establish different arrangements for production and exchange, subject to whatever constraints engagement in the international trading system may impose. The division of the world into sovereign states is the key premise of the theory of trade and therefore of the doctrine of comparative advantage, which Paul Samuelson described as the single most powerful insight of economics. It nevertheless lacks any status or explanation in established economics. From the standpoint of received economic theory, humanity might just as well be united in a single state, with a uniform and universal set of economic institutions.

An analogy to the neo-Darwinian synthesis in evolutionary theory suggests just how strange this situation in thought is. The fecundity of a mechanism of competitive selection, whether it is Darwinian selection in nature or competition among firms and their products in a market, depends on the richness of the material on which the procedure operates. It is as if we were to have a view of the evolution of life that includes the half about natural selection but excludes the other half about genetic mutation and recombination. The workings and significance of the former would remain uncertain without the presence of the latter.

These four limitations of what has become since the Marginalist turn the main line of economics are closely connected in many different ways. For example, the deficit of institutional imagination, with its consequent impulse to naturalize the familiar arrangements of the market economy, would be harder to support were it not for the sacrifice of a view of production to a theory of exchange. The realities of production are tangibly shaped by the available stock of ways of organizing capital and labor, including the grant or denial of legal personality to different types of business organizations. Moreover, both of these limitations can survive more readily in a discipline that borrows from other areas of thought its causal theories as well as its factual stipulations and normative commitments.

My focus here is on the second of the four limitations: the poverty of institutional imagination. Any attempt, however, to redress this poverty, even by my chosen procedure of fragmentary theory in the service of radical reform, requires us to resist the other three faults. We may resist them without doing so in the mode of systematic theorizing.

No one whose method of economic analysis remains tainted by these four defects can hope to make progress with problems like those lying at the center of this argument. One such problem is the variable relation of finance to the real economy. Another is the fate of the most advanced practice of production of a given historical period: To what extent and under what conditions is the most advanced productive practice either confined to insular vanguards or, on the contrary, widely disseminated within the economy? Yet another is the nature of the political arrangements that can best facilitate innovation in the institutional arrangements of the economy. Of these three questions, the first lies in the foreground of my argument here. The other two remain in the background. They come to the fore in the companion volume to this book.

Both the foreground and the background issues require us to think about the workings of the economy and its piecemeal reconstruction (in the spirit of radical reform) in ways that defy the limits of the tradition inaugurated by the Marginalists—all the limits, not just the lack of institutional imagination.

We need not and must not wait until we have another economics to begin thinking in this way. We can do it in pieces with the instruments that current economics provides as well with the resources of other disciplines. Of these other disciplines, the one with the most to contribute to an agenda like this one is legal thought.

Legal thought has the most intimate relation with the argument of this book and with the effort to contribute ideas and proposals like the ones discussed here. However, it is not legal thought or its applied form, legal analysis, as they have been commonly understood, that we lack in the present debate. It is a revised practice of legal analysis seizing on an intellectual potential that ideas long dominant in legal thought have wasted. A revised practice of legal analysis, developed in the spirit of fragmentary theory associated with radical reform, serves as the natural partner of a practice of economic analysis responsive to the criticisms laid out in the preceding pages.

One way of understanding the legal analysis that we need is to contrast it with what legal thought has traditionally been in its long history as well as to what it has mainly become in recent decades. The legal thought that we require is not legal doctrine as it was understood in the major jurisprudential traditions of world history: the development of a set of legal conceptions and categories representing a whole world of social practices as an intelligible and justified ordering of human life and its continued care and refinement by jurists. Nor is it what has been the main rival to the doctrinal pursuit of immanent normative order in the history of legal thought: the work of jurists as interpreters of state-made law. Jurists have wanted to represent the will of the sovereign translated into law as a system animated by interests and ideals described in the language of impersonal policy and principle.

Throughout its history, much of legal theory—the most abstract department of legal thought—has tried to manage the apparent conflict between these two ideas of law and legal method. It has done so with a practical responsibility in mind: to apply the law, whether legislated by the state or found and made as doctrine by judges and other jurists. To guide the official who decides what the law means in a particular case, committing the power of the state in the exercise of this rights-declaring role, has been a large part of the whole exercise. It is as if discourse about law were simply a source of instruction to official interpreters of the law—judges or the counselors or academics who try to think of themselves as judges in the hope of fulfilling their professional responsibilities.

A momentous by-product of this combination of assumptions and concerns has been the understatement or denial of what law ultimately is: the detailed expression in rule, doctrine, and conception of "the institutional form of the life of a people," as Hegel and the German historicists described it. Law represents the institutions and practices of society, defined in legal detail, by reference to the interests and ideals that make sense of them. This view of law differs from the doctrinal pursuit of immanent normative order in social life as well as from the effort to represent state-made law as an evolving plan. It renounces the attempt to represent the law as an idealized and harmonious system.

It is not that this approach forswears a practical stake in how we think about law and in what we do with it. It is that our practical stake has ceased to provide guidance for the official who sets out to understand and apply law in particular disputes. It has become instead a way to use the contradictions and variations in the established law, whether in one country or around the world, the better to enlarge the stock of the institutional alternatives available for the governance of different parts of social and economic life. Among such alternatives are arrangements bearing on the relation of finance to the real economy. The practical goal is not to speak in the voice of the judge or in that of the judgelike official or expert. It is to inform the activity of radical reform—the piecemeal but potentially cumulative revision of the established institutional and ideological regime.

If radical reform is the practical aim, fragmentary theory is its intellectual instrument. Fragmentary theory as legal analysis is free from the impulse to understate legal difference, revelatory of institutional variation in existing or past societies. It therefore represents law as what I have called "structure not system."

The law is not a formless heap of rules that can be made to mean whatever the interpreter wants them to mean. Nor is it the preset content of a supposedly consistent and recurrent type of social organization such as "capitalism" or the market economy. In each area of law and social practice, dominant institutional models coexist with others that differ from them or even contradict them outright. These odd pieces are the vestiges of rejected solutions or the prophecy of possible futures. We can see what such an approach to law implies for our methods by considering its consequences for a branch of legal thought that holds special interest for the fragmentary theorist and the radical reformer: comparative law.

Take two conceptions of comparative law. One has lived in school textbooks and in the writings of conventional comparative lawyers. The other was embraced in the later part of the twentieth century by much of the intellectual elite in comparative law. Both are defective: they misrepresent the law and fail to exploit adequately the insights that comparison make possible. The criticism of these two approaches helps show the way to a revised comparative practice that offers a context in which to pursue the association of fragmentary theory with radical reform.

The first of these two approaches in comparative law is literal and taxonomic. It divides the world map into a few legal systems, mainly variations of Anglo-American common law and continental European civil law. It surveys the doctrinal content of each of these variations. It registers the legal-process characteristics that may be associated with each legal tradition: whether, for example, judge-made or statutory law prevails. It is more interested in classification and genealogy than in the way law and its consequences are transformed by their setting. It ignores, for example, that German private law in China bears only a shallow resemblance to German law in Germany.[3]

This taxonomic literalism provides no reliable ground on which to explore the consequences of legal differences. If the comparative lawyer seeks to establish correlations between some of these differences and any number of social and economic consequences, the correlations will be haphazard and fanciful, based as they are on misunderstandings.

In the history of comparative law, rebellion against this literalism led to its overthrow in the second half of the twentieth century and its replacement by another hegemon: a functionalism in the service of belief in strong practical convergence under the disguise of doctrinal divergence. A defining idea of the functionalist comparative lawyer is that the same or similar functional outcomes are achieved by alternative doctrinal means in contemporary legal systems. The rules and vocabulary of contract formation, for example, may differ in the common and civil law. Nevertheless, the interests or "policies" in contention and the way of reconciling them in each of these doctrinal settings may point in the same direction. And so it happens, the functionalist argues, in one branch of law after another.[4]

The ulterior subject matter of the functionalist thesis is an institutional and legal regime—in particular an economic regime, such as the regulated or social market economy. Contract law, for instance, must ensure predictability in the understanding and enforcement of contracts. Alternative sets of rules and doctrinal categories can produce the same effects; doctrinal diversity is the outward cover of functional similarity.

The part of truth in this practice of comparative analysis is the uncontroversial observation that alternative doctrinal means can have similar consequences. Nothing, however, justifies the maximalist proposition with which this minimalist thesis is commonly associated: the idea of strong institutional convergence. That conception is an ideological or metaphysical gloss on the findings of comparative legal analysis.

The similarity of consequence, obtained by a diversity of doctrinal means, may have another meaning: that there is now available in the world a very limited stock of living institutional and legal options for the arrangements of different parts of social life. But the composition of this stock has resulted in great part from choices made in moments of institutional change and social and ideological conflict—the path least disturbing to powerful interests and entrenched preconceptions. Solutions to some of the pressing problems of contemporary societies require us to enlarge the fund of available institutional alternatives, defined in the details of law. For example, we need to enlist finance more effectively in the service of production and free the new, knowledge-intensive practices of production from their confinement within exclusive vanguards.

If such an enlargement is our purpose, we cannot rest content with the dismissal of doctrinal diversity as the veil of functional convergence. We must take an interest in the anomalies and contradictions of established law, in its vestiges, countercurrents, and prophecies, for they may serve as instruments for the development of institutional alternatives with the materials of law. By this means, we begin to turn comparative law into an expression of the marriage of fragmentary theory with radical reform.

I have not offered in this book a theory of this practice of comparative analysis and programmatic argument, but I have tried to show it at work: in the first two chapters of the book through ideas about the reshaping of finance and of its relation to the real economy and in the third chapter through examples of the wider institutional reconstruction of the market economy, involving relations both between governments and firms as well as among firms.

Consider now another example having to do with the legal treatment of the relation between capital and labor. (I address this example in detail elsewhere.[5])

In the rich North Atlantic democracies and in the countries that have successfully emulated them, the dominant labor-law regime has been one or another variant of collective bargaining. Call it the contractualist regime. Its core motivation is to reestablish the reality of contract under the conditions of extreme inequality of bargaining power that characterize the employment relation. This labor-law regime has two major organizing principles, the character and significance of which become clear only when we contrast this regime to its only major contemporary rival. A first principle is that within the procedures established by law, workers are free to organize or not and, having organized, to strike and to negotiate. A continuing controversy in contemporary labor law addresses the scope of the matters reserved to managerial discretion, given the coexistence of contractual and hierarchical arrangements for production. A second principle of the labor-law regime is that the organization of workers and the practice of collective bargaining belong to the private legal sphere. They are independent of the state, save for the right that the law may reserve to government to intervene when industrial strife threatens a grave national interest.

An alternative to the contractualist labor-law system is the corporatist regime disseminated in Latin America in the middle and later part of the twentieth century. The labor laws of authoritarian European states, especially Italy under fascism, provided the original inspiration for the corporatist order. Nationalist-populist governments, such as those of Cárdenas, Vargas, and Perón, changed its meaning. Its two commanding principles are the inverse of those of the contractualist system. The first principle is that all workers will be automatically unionized according to their positions in the economy. The second principle is that the unions must be under the tutelage of the state, exercised typically through the Ministry of Labor. The corporatist labor-law regime served as a tool of controlled popular mobilization.

Experience has shown that the contractualist option has a series of political consequences, which those committed to a democratizing of the market economy have reason to resist. It favors a centrifugal tendency in the labor force, tracking and reinforcing the hierarchical segmentation of the economy. Relatively advantaged and secure employees in the capital-intensive sectors of the economy find it easier to unionize and strike. At the same time, they share interests with their employers, given the relatively small part of the wage bill in the overall cost of production. This divergence of interest works to the detriment of the vast majority of less-advantaged workers. Trade-union militancy consequently declines, except in public employment: where it is most needed, it is hardest to establish. Moreover, the contractualist regime favors an economistic tilt in the agenda of the labor movement: a single-minded focus on wages and benefits to the exclusion of economic and political arrangements that have decisive influence on welfare and opportunity.

The corporatist labor-law regime works in the opposite direction. Because it provides for the automatic unionization of all workers and fosters the creation of an economy-wide union movement with national leadership, it counteracts the hierarchical segmentation of the economy. The tilt to inclusion and national organization in turn favors concerns that transcend a narrow economism: labor's legal and institutional status, the arrangements that shape its relation to capital, and its influence on political power as well as its claim on national income.

This example of the legal treatment of the relation between capital and labor discredits, at least in this setting, the notion that functional convergence is predestined to advance under the appearance of doctrinal difference. Nevertheless, the pure corporatist alternative has no place in a democratized market economy because of its second organizing principle, which subordinates the union movement to the state. The comparative analysis suggests, however, another possibility: to recombine the two regimes. Why not take from the corporatist regime the principle of the automatic unionization of all workers and from the contractualist regime the principle of the complete independence of the unions from the state? The law would in effect create a structure parallel to the state, albeit independent from it, granting every worker a second citizenship in the production system, Different labor movements would compete for position in this law-made structure, just as political parties compete for office in the democratic state.

Such a labor-law regime would provide a counterweight to the hierarchical segmentation of the economy. By economizing on the effort to unionize in the first place (because unionization would be a gift of the law), it would concentrate attention on what to do with this collective power. It would encourage workers and their unions to look beyond the narrow economistic issues that commonly monopolize concern under a contractualist labor-law regime.

Such a hybrid system is no mere speculation. It has in fact been proposed and to some extent implemented in some of the countries whose labor laws were shaped in the corporatist mold. The hybrid is a telling example of the benefits of comparative law liberated from the stranglehold of functionalist convergence in the spirit of the association of fragmentary theory with radical reform (i.e., the piecemeal revision of any part of the institutional and ideological framework of social life).

Meanwhile, however, a change is taking place in the condition of labor. These proposals for a hybrid labor-law regime fail to address it. Let us see, as another example of a reoriented legal analysis, how a revised practice of comparative law might cast light on it.

Both the contractualist and the corporatist labor-law regimes take for granted a certain picture of the circumstance of labor: the existence of a relatively stable labor force working in large productive units, such as factories and factory-like offices, under the aegis of big corporations or governmental bureaucracies. In no economy has this image ever described the situation of the majority of workers: most workers have always worked in relatively small shops. Nonetheless, the picture does capture the situation of labor under Fordist mass production: the large-scale production of standardized goods and services by hierarchical firms. It also describes a form of public administration that continues to operate as an administrative Fordism. This public administration specializes in the bureaucratic apparatus's provision of standardized, low-quality public services for the state—that is, services of lower quality than the quality services that might be purchased by people with money. The labor-law regimes that I have just compared take this picture for granted, but it is fast losing its hold on reality.

The picture does not describe how work has always been organized. This way of organizing it was preceded by several centuries in which work was done on the basis of decentralized contractual arrangements rather than internalized in the firm. Such was the "putting-out" system that Marx discusses in detail in the early chapters of *Capital*: the capitalist provided the workers with machines and materials for them to use at home with family and associates and contracted to give them a part of the gains.

A new putting-out system now emerges on a global scale. One of its by-products is the abandonment of vast numbers of workers to economic insecurity. They are the new "precariat" in the occasional labor or gig economy: the victims and at times the beneficiaries of the worldwide contracting out of one part of production after another. What we regard as the natural way of organizing work may come to seem in retrospect as a brief interlude between two longer periods in which work is organized around decentralized contractual arrangements.

This momentous change has been justified in the name of economic necessity and flexibility. Whether it consigns the majority of workers to radical economic insecurity depends on the political and legal response that it elicits. Here our fragmentary theorist and radical reformer as insubordinate comparativist must become both a historian and a visionary, reaching back into past legal variations as well forward to institutional alternatives made possible by legal innovations.

If the new putting-out system is not to result in universal economic insecurity for the precariat, we must create alongside the traditional labor-law regimes, whether contractualist, corporatist, or hybrid, a new set of rules and doctrines designed to protect, organize, and represent them. Such a complementary legal regime may provide for a sliding scale of protective intervention by the law in the employment relation. The greater our success in organizing and representing these workers (by means made possible by the new technologies of communication), the less the need to afford them direct legal protection. The more we succeed in organizing and representing them, the weaker the case for direct intervention in the employment relation. Such intervention would be designed to keep the new putting-out system from cheapening the cost of labor and sharpening the contrast between a minority of relatively secure employees and a majority of precarious workers.

Legal innovations like these are unlikely to prosper unless they have as their counterpart progress in the attempt to give a socially inclusive form to today's knowledge economy. The advancement of such an inclusive vanguardism may require decentralized, pluralistic, and experimental partnership between governments and firms as well as cooperative competition among firms.

Such practices may in turn need to rely on forms of contract and property departing from traditional contract and property doctrine. In contract, they may require relational contract to usurp the central place traditionally accorded to the bilateral executory promise. In property, they may demand the development of disaggregated property rights, the better to reconcile decentralized economic initiative with economies of scale.

To take such a direction is to breathe new life and meaning into a conviction shared by nineteenth-century liberals and socialists: that economically dependent wage labor is not the natural and necessary embodiment of free labor. It is a defective and transitory form, retaining some of the features of slavery and serfdom. Over time, wage labor should give way, they believed, to the superior varieties of free labor, self-employment, and cooperation. It was only relatively late that the predominance of wage labor among the forms of free work came to seem natural and even inevitable. The earlier hope could be sustained only if it found expression in a socially inclusive version of productive vanguardism and in the legal innovations, including innovations in the contract and property regimes, that would make such a rearrangement of production feasible.

It is only in such a context of radical democratization of the market economy that the tightening of links between finance and the real economy can realize its full potential. We can now look back on my discussion of the reform of finance in the first two chapters of this book and understand its method as what in this chapter I have described as the association of fragmentary theory with radical reform. The further we go in the use of this method, the less reason we have to conform to the ideas dominant in contemporary social science.

THE THEORETICAL ARGUMENT IN HISTORICAL CONTEXT: THE SURPRISING LESSONS OF HISTORICAL EXPERIENCE

Character and Aims of the Subsequent Discussion

In the preceding section of this chapter, I outlined and connected the most general ideas informing the argument of this book. In this section, I seek to show that these ideas can help us recover aspects of the history of our institutional arrangements and ideological assumptions that established beliefs disregard or distort. There is more in historical experience than these beliefs are able to understand or even to acknowledge.

Once we recover, with the help of fragmentary theory, the suppressed or forgotten aspects of our economic and political past, we can confront the problems addressed in this book with new confidence in our powers of reconstruction. Past variations suggest future possibilities and discredit the restrictive formulas that have continued to narrow our imagination of the accessible possible.

I offer here a simplified comparative-historical contextualization of my argument—both the narrower argument about finance and the broader argument about the alternative futures of the market economy. I make no claim to new historical discovery. I allude to well-known events in the history of many of the countries that have appeared in these pages. I suggest how the explanatory and programmatic approach for which I have argued enables us to see more in these events than we have been accustomed to discern. At the same time, I use the compressed historical narrative to suggest the limits that the poverty of our ideas about institutional alternatives has imposed on the reconstruction of our arrangements.

A first working assumption of this historical coda to my theoretical argument is that our present and past experience contains a much richer storehouse of institutional experiments than the most influential ideas in social science and politics today allow us to recognize. The impulse to naturalize the existing arrangements and to see institutional evolution from the perspective of a doctrine of convergence is so powerful that it tempts us to bring the past down to the level of our preconceptions.

A second working assumption is that the institutional variation we discover in history represents only a subset of a wider penumbra of opportunities for change: *theres* that we can reach from any given *here*. The range of institutional alternatives that has been produced in history is not a neutral trial of what works better and worse for the largest number of people over the largest array of circumstances. It is a contest among the institutional conceptions that happen to have been available at each moment and in each circumstance. So the institutions we have before us are the result of rearrangements that served a pressing practical need (economic prosperity or national defense) with minimal disruption to the interests and preconceptions that are most entrenched and powerful in the circumstance. Path dependency carries enormous weight: societies develop institutional variations with the materials at hand, residues of past changes and conflicts.

Fortunately, interests never speak with a single voice. There may, for example, be a contest between the interests of financial rentiers and the interests of producers, such as industrialists or farmers. And whether the interests of producers are understood to be more deeply and closely aligned with those of financial rentiers or workers may depend on the course of politics and of thought.

A third working assumption is that the path of least resistance is never the only path. To create alternatives to the path of least resistance is the work of transformative insight and practice. They relate the understanding of the existent to the imagination of the proximate possible. They challenge pieces of the institutional and ideological framework of social life rather than taking that framework for granted.

The two greatest enablers of our power to create alternatives to the path of least resistance are the deepening of democracy and the demystification of the established institutional and ideological regime: the degree of our success in depriving social arrangements and their history of their specious semblance of naturalness, necessity, and authority.

Democracy grows deeper when the level of organized popular engagement in political life strengthens together with the ability to subject social and economic arrangements to deliberate and experimental revision. The deeper democracy becomes, the better our chance against the path of least resistance.

The less our ideas about society have the character of a retrospective rationalization of present arrangements and insist instead on representing the actual from the standpoint of its proximate possibilities of transformation, the more useful they become as a basis for the understanding of our circumstance. An institutionally informed political economy, working in combination with a revised practice of comparative law, can play a decisive role in the fight against superstition disguised as reason.

The role of democracy and of transformative insight in serving as a counterweight to the path of least resistance is no mere speculation. Limited, compromised, and often defeated, democracy has nevertheless been a presence in each of the historical episodes to which I next allude. It is in our interest to arrange our ideas and institutions in such a way that they rob the path of least resistance of its advantages.

It follows that although the range of institutional variation that we observe in history is much richer than what our conventional discussion of regulation and institutionally conservative reform is able to envisage, it is much narrower than what an informed institutional imagination might take to be appealing and feasible.

A fourth working assumption of this comparative-historical discussion is that a subset of the institutional innovations undertaken or rejected in the course of the historical experiences invoked in the following pages holds special interest. These innovations exhibit three distinct but related traits. The first characteristic is that they broaden access to the economic, political, or educational instruments of agency: the ordinary man and woman's capacity to act and share in the making of new things and new states of affairs. The second feature is that they facilitate further innovation, which has the enhancement of agency as one of its conditions. The third trait is that they make possible a process of collective decision—such as the definition of a national development of agenda—that is not under the control of a foreign economic or political power. Such innovations strengthen conditions for collective as well as individual agency.

The cumulative outcome of this class of innovations satisfies some of the practical conditions that enable a society to define a pathway of change without embracing a fixed formula for the direction of change. It also gives more people the practical equipment they need to make something of their lives.

These criteria may seem so abstract that they have no tangible meaning. Yet in each domain of social and economic life they do acquire a meaning in a particular historical circumstance, given the problems at hand and the institutional and conceptual resources available to deal with it.

In finance, the innovations satisfying these criteria have been those that combine financial deepening with active globalization. They tighten the link between finance and the real economy, avoiding or mitigating financial hypertrophy—the expansion of an autonomous financial sector with an oblique, episodic, or parasitic relation to the transaction of the real economy. To that end, they may increase the level of domestic private and public saving and multiply the vehicles channeling long-term saving into long-term productive investment. They may also establish public or quasi-public financial entities such as the postal banks found in several of the countries and mentioned in the historical examples here.

At the same time, innovations of this kind help the national economy access foreign capital without surrendering to the doctrines and interests of international financial markets. For example, they limit the penetration of the national economy by foreign capital, allowing it to take equity stakes in major productive assets only after assuring overall national control of development strategy and of the "commanding heights" of the production system. They struggle to engage in the world trading system on terms that preserve the power to experiment with the institutional arrangements of the market order. Moreover, they commit to building organizations such as national development banks that increase national governments' and firms' ability to develop new comparative advantage and to resist the short-termism of the financial interests at home and abroad.

The reach of this class of financial innovations depends on the larger national project of which they form a part. The innovations will mean more and go farther to the extent that they form part of an agenda of reconstructing the market economy. Such an agenda will not be content to regulate the established market order or to attenuate its inequality by compensatory and retrospective redistribution through tax and transfer. It will innovate in the arrangements defining the market economy so that more people have more access to more markets in more ways. It will seek to fulfill some of the conditions that allow the most advanced practice of production to be widely disseminated in the economy rather than remaining confined to productive vanguards from which the majority of the labor force remains excluded. Movement in such a direction will also require innovations in the way that governments can work with firms (decentralized pluralistic coordination rather than either arm's-length regulation or imposed, unitary trade and industrial policy) and that firms can work with one another (cooperative competition).

The history of radical reforms, almost invariably practiced in opposition to the interests and ideas informing a path of least resistance, is full of contradiction and surprise. At many points along the way, finance has appeared in two opposing roles: as the enforcer of constraint and as the breaker of constraint. The course of politics and thought has always been decisive in determining the outcome of the contest between the path of least resistance and alternatives to it. So it remains today.

From the recurrent themes in the historical commentary in the remainder of this chapter there emerges a view of the institutional element in economic growth and the evolution of finance. This account proposes explanations in the mode of fragmentary theory, not in the manner of systematic theorizing. It takes as a defining feature of each of the moments that it discusses the practice or the avoidance of radical reform: the way of dealing with the institutional context of economic activity that gave shape to the economy and to the place of finance within it in each of these episodes.

I discuss here five moments in economic history: the development of the American economy in the period between independence and the

Civil War; the Great Depression of the 1930s in the United States and Germany; the American war economy during the Second World War; the Northeast Asian experience of economic growth in the decades after that war; and the comparative and interconnected economic evolution of the United States, China, and Brazil in the years immediately before and after the financial and economic crisis of 2007–2009.[6] My procedure in discussing each of these five episodes is to use the interpretation of each as a point of departure for the discussion of some aspect of the institutional element in economic growth. These aspects form fragments of a way of thinking, presented successively and related to historical experience.

In the following pages, then, I offer an example of fragmentary theory at work, dealing with its most important subject matter: the institutional and ideological regime and its reconstruction. In the economy, as in all parts of social life, a regime becomes fate until people defy and remake it. Radical reform is, by its presence or absence, my foreground subject matter in these pages. My background concern is our struggle to recover structural vision when we no longer believe ourselves entitled to rely on its inherited forms and methods.

In seeking to recover structural vision, we face a characteristic predicament. We can no longer believe, as nineteenth-century liberals and socialists did, in definitive institutional and ideological formulas. We must find a way to achieve structural insight and to develop the imagination of structural alternatives without succumbing to structural dogmatism. One of the most important attributes of the institutions and practices that we adopt must be to allow and indeed provoke correction in the light of experience. We need these institutions and practices to offer not a resting place but a setting for organized and fertile unrest.

The United States as a Developing Country: The American Reform Traditions and the Real Dynamic of Nation Building in America

Central to the development of the United States in the decades between its foundation and the Civil War was the combination of two ways of developing the country.[7] One way was a national development project led by the federal government. The other was a series of institutional innovations designed to democratize two sectors of the market economy:

agriculture and finance. We can think of them as a movement from the top down and a movement from the bottom up, although both of them required an interaction between governmental initiative and collective action or private enterprise. In the introduction, I briefly addressed the dynamic that these movements jointly produced, with the aim of suggesting how my argument seeks inspiration in American experience even though it contradicts ideas long dominant in the United States. I now discuss this double movement in greater detail for the light that it throws on the relation between a misunderstood past and a possible future.

The mobilization from above had in Alexander Hamilton its first major exponent and organizer. Its goal was to build the country, both literally and figuratively, by engaging the government of the newly established republic in the mobilization of physical, financial, and human resources for national development. Its method was a flexible association of the state and private enterprise. Its agent was an informal network of officials, entrepreneurs, and speculators.

No obstacle was allowed to stand in the way of the nation-building program, which generated countless opportunities for private enrichment as well as collective gain. In almost every respect, it represented an inversion of the tenets that were later to be considered sacrosanct to the American market ideology. It was planning by the state, unrestrained by the dogmas and procedures of a planning bureaucracy. (The mid-twentieth-century war economy, set up to prosecute the Second World War, represented an even more dramatic form of such an inversion.)

We can distinguish four pieces in this development strategy orchestrated from above. The first was a series of initiatives designed literally to open up the country by organizing the transport routes necessary to westward expansion: first roads and canals, later railways. Various forms of association or partnership between government and the relatively large-scale private entrepreneurs of the period carried these initiatives forward. They were all the more remarkable for taking place in a country in which the overwhelming majority of free white men were self-employed smallholders, craftsmen, and proprietors rather than wage laborers.

A second component of this approach to development was trade protectionism. With its ups and downs, protectionism continued throughout the nineteenth century and well into the early decades of the twentieth. The South, with its slavery-based, export-oriented economy, provided the exception, favoring free trade under British auspices. The case for protection or free trade can never be more than circumstantial: it depends on what, when, how, by whom, and to what end.

Moreover, any policy requiring governmental selectivity, such as the imposition of restraints on trade, can never be better than the state that does the selecting. A weak, low-energy democracy, like all the democracies that have yet been established, will be porous to the organized and the moneyed as well as vulnerable to capture by them. An authoritarian state, employing a technocratic apparatus that claims to float above the divisions of society, will be hostage to its own stake in the preservation of power and will soon corrupt and be corrupted by the translation of political power into private advantage.

Only the radicalization of both democracy and experimentalism has any prospect of avoiding these perversions and allowing selective policies such as circumstantial restraints on trade to escape the twin evils of dogmatism and cronyism. There is nevertheless a higher goal that even imperfect policies may serve: to enhance collective agency under the shield of economic sovereignty, thus strengthening the conditions to embark on a rebellious strategy of national development, as the United States did in the nineteenth century.

A third part of this movement from above was the organization of the public debt. The public debt became the master instrument for the financing of the national development strategy as well as for the short-term and long-term funding of government. Hamilton and his successors made ample use of techniques for the management of the public debt that had a long previous history in Europe. Well before later nineteenth-century conflicts over the relation of fiat currency to bullion, political and business leaders used the First Bank of the United States, chartered by Congress in 1791, to help organize the economic life of the country.

The fourth part of this national strategy was the most important and the least explicit. It defined the agent of the movement from above: a loose clique of politicians, bureaucrats, financiers, and entrepreneurs who dealt with one another to mutual advantage. They assigned tasks and distributed opportunities among themselves. The idea that the institutions of a market economy are political artifacts open to variation would have struck these agents as too obvious to require statement.

The prominence of countermajoritarian or frankly antidemocratic elements in the constitutional arrangements and political practices of the United States and the domination of politics by an elite of moneyed notables, who joined political power or influence to economic advantage and cultural authority, formed the social backdrop to this movement from above. This backdrop helps account for the relatively informal or noninstitutionalized character of the association between officials and entrepreneurs that directed the development of the country between the War for Independence and the Civil War.

If we were to describe the Hamiltonian movement from above in a contemporary vocabulary, we might characterize it, in the manner of Alexander Gerschenkron, as the use of government to overcome relative backwardness or as a developmental state or as a Nasserite program or even, given the informality of its arrangements and its pervasive confusion of governmental activism and private advantage, as crony capitalism.

However, if this project were all that the early American republic relied on, the United States would never have developed as it did. The deals struck inside the governing elite, within the framework of the protodemocratic liberalism of the Constitution, would not have allowed for a sustained broadening of economic opportunity. The funnel of economic opportunity would have narrowed rapidly. And the result of such a narrowing in a society in which most men were either self-employed or slaves would have been the imposition of a higher barrier to economic growth as well as to social inclusion. That barrier would have made it harder to tap the constructive energies of the majority and to engage the mass of free workers in the development of the country.

What prevented this outcome was the interaction of the Hamiltonian project of national development, conducted from above by governing and moneyed elites, with a movement to democratize two vital parts of the American economy: agriculture and finance. This movement reshaped the institutions of the market. It did not do so comprehensively in every sector of the economy. Nevertheless, what it accomplished in the two sectors that it mainly touched proved vital to the subsequent course of American history. We can understand the fragmentary, sector-specific character of this democratizing impulse as both cause and consequences of limitations of thought and of democracy. The intellectual and political limitations converged to limit the scope and undermine the force of the double movement.

No doctrine represented the institutional and legal innovations in agriculture and finance as partial expressions of a comprehensive project: democratizing the market, which would ultimately require deepening democracy. It is we who in retrospect can see the innovations in the arrangements of agriculture and of finance as possible points of departure for such a comprehensive program. To that end, we need the general ideas about a democratized market economy that the nineteenth-century architects of those initiatives lacked.

The failures of democracy joined the limitations of thought. A doctrine alone, no matter how appealing, would not have sufficed to support a more comprehensive democratization of the American market economy. It would have required as its ally an organization of democratic politics that overstepped the limits of the protodemocratic liberalism set out in the Constitution. Such a deepening of democracy would have brought the ideas about the democratization of the market to life by making them actionable, for it is in politics and in thought, expressed in law, not in the economy, that we set the institutional presuppositions of the market. In chapter 3, I explored the institutional direction and content of such a deepening of democracy.

Consider the specific character of the early-nineteenth-century American innovations in agriculture and finance.

Americans rejected the dynamic of agrarian concentration that many, including Marx and his followers, believed to be intrinsic to the growth of a capitalist economy. They did much more than distribute land to smallholders on the agrarian frontier. They took initiatives that would turn the new agrarian economy into the most efficient family-scale agriculture that had ever existed rather than allow it to slide back into inefficient subsistence farming.

These arrangements included many elements of partnership between the central and local governments and family farmers: land-grant colleges, agricultural extension, and, little by little, the apparatus of food stockpiles, minimum prices, and crop insurance that would protect family-scale agriculture from the lethal combination of climate risk and economic risk. They also encompassed the development of practices of collaborative competition among family farmers, who pooled labor, technological, and commercial resources without relinquishing private property or ceasing to compete against one another.

In finance, the struggle over the Second Bank of the United States culminated in the dissolution of the bank during Andrew Jackson's presidency. More significantly, it resulted in a long-standing prohibition of interstate banking and in the creation of an unrivalled network of local banks, without precedent anywhere in the world, at the service of local producers as well as consumers. It was a striking example of financial deepening, accomplished by the indispensable means of institutional innovation.

The Second Bank of the United States, a reincarnation off Hamilton's First Bank of the United States, was understood to be the heart of the arrangements by which the governing circles of the early republic managed both the business of the state and their own business.[8] Its dissolution was an antiplutocratic move.

One effect of the dissolution was to neutralize, for better and for worse, the use of the public debt as an instrument of national planning—something that is supposed not to exist in the United States but that has existed at crucial moments in the national history, such as the times of the two great wars in the twentieth century. Rather than reinventing the management of the public debt as the instrument of a democratizing, antiplutocratic political economy, the authors of the dissolution prevented it from being used in the plutocratic interest by destroying it. They tied the monetary hands of their class enemies only by tying their own hands.

Another, lasting consequence of the disbanding of the Second Bank was to set the stage for the development of the country's unrivaled network of local banks at the service of producers as well as consumers. The prohibition of interstate (and sometimes even intrastate) banking was a blunt instrument for containing the power of large financial organizations and their influence on government as well as on the economy. It laid the basis for the development of a network of local banks that has ever since remained one of the main strengths of the U.S. economy and American democracy.

However, the prohibition of interstate banking could not prevent the emergence of large banks, notably in New York. Long before the prohibition was lifted, the major New York banks had in effect become national banks, controlled by financiers such as J. P. Morgan who wielded enormous economic and political influence.

A more effective way to serve the twin goals of financial deepening and broadening access to capital—especially capital for production—would have required an entirely different approach to the problem of scale in finance. Such an approach would have combined a commitment to the defense and sharpening of competition with the development of alternative mechanisms for ensuring decentralized access to capital. It would also have demanded ideas and rules distinguishing the varieties of finance, including speculative finance, that are useful to production from those that are not. Such innovations would have in turn required what has always been so difficult in the United States, even more than in many other countries, given prevailing ideas as well as dominant interests: experimentation with the basic legal machinery of the market economy, including its regimes of property and contract.

The initiatives in agriculture and finance, despite their severe limitations, exemplified innovation in the legally defined institutional arrangements of the market economy. They did much more than regulate agriculture or finance; they reorganized it. They influenced the primary distribution of economic advantage rather than seeking only to correct it retrospectively through progressive taxation and redistributive entitlements.

These initiatives were not the gift of a public-spirited political and bureaucratic elite to a needy citizenry. They were the outcome of popular struggle. Although the course and outcome of this struggle remained limited by both the undemocratic elements in the arrangements of American democracy and the deficiencies of legal and institutional imagination in the populists' and progressives' ideas, they nevertheless created room for the broad-based engagement that brought wealth, power, and a measure of shared freedom to the American people.

Yet these initiatives were confined to specific sectors of the economy. They never became points of departure for an economy-wide refoundation of the market order. They touched only white men, coexisting with the grinding incubus of African slavery. Moreover, they were undertaken without being expressed as an explicit program. As a result, they failed to provide a basis for self-conscious resistance to ideas that made the inherited institutional forms of the market and democracy seem natural, as if these institutions defined the uncontroversial form of economic and political pluralism.

The limitations of American democracy aggravated the consequences of the lack of programmatic and ideological clarity. The constitutional arrangements of the United States established a protodemocratic liberalism. They helped keep the citizenry at a low level of engagement in political life, the better to filter out popular passions and leave representative institutions in the hands of enlightened notables. They were designed to perpetuate rather than to resolve rapidly any impasse between the political branches of government. They slowed the pace of politics even as they cooled its temperature. And they established a version of federalism that by its rigid assignment of powers among the parts of the federal system inhibited states and towns from becoming the laboratories of experimentation that canonical doctrine proclaimed them to be.

The limitation of American democracy and the failure to develop ideas that could challenge the superstitious naturalization of the country's institutional framework worked fatefully together. Together they help explain the weakening of what had been a combination crucial to building the United States: the alliance between governmental initiative to open up the frontier by mobilizing public and private resources for national development, on the one hand, and institutional innovation to broaden opportunity, on the other. The dialectic of government-led mobilization from above and democratizing institutional innovation from below in particular sectors of the economy took place many times. It recurred in later formative moments in American history: during Reconstruction and industrialization after the Civil War, during the progressive reforms of the early twentieth century, and during the early New Deal. However, it never again achieved the forcefulness that it had enjoyed in the formative years of the republic.

One of the consequences of its weakening was a change in the economic and political status of finance. High finance regained in steps the power to operate nationally and exercise a controlling influence on the economy: first on the basis of New York banks that exercised national influence from their local base until the restraints imposed in the early nineteenth century were repealed. With financial concentration, justified as always in the name of indispensable scale, came a slow, persistent change in the relation of finance to the real economy. Financial deepening gave way to financial hypertrophy.

Freed from its restraints, high finance married political power. Its masters bought and exercised political influence. They did so increasingly with the blessing of economic ideas that portrayed the capital markets, when they came to be organized, as a machine for the efficient allocation of resources, susceptible to being tainted only by localized defects in market competition. Localized defects in the capital markets (competitive failures or asymmetries of information) were to be addressed by similarly localized regulatory responses. Under the dominant legal and economics ideas, such defects never called for an institutional program to redesign the relation of finance to the real economy. Gone were the radical innovations of the Jacksonian period. High finance helped corrupt the representative institutions that had failed to tame it.

The two traditions of progressive reform that later came to prevail in the United States share a failure to acknowledge the vital significance of this formative dialectic in American history. Instead of breathing new life and new meaning into the dialectic, they disregarded its message: that we change the market order rather than just regulating it or attenuating, through retrospective correction, the inequalities resulting from its operation. In each of these traditions, finance played a diminished role in a different way.

The tradition of property-owning democracy, of the defense of small business against economic concentration, might seem to have been vindicated by the agrarian and financial examples with which I have illustrated the interplay between developmental resource mobilization and democratizing institutional innovation. What is the family farmer or the local bank but a tangible embodiment of this creed? However, to identify those agrarian and financial innovations with the preference for the small over the big is to miss their larger significance.

For agriculture, the larger significance was not just the establishment of family-scale farming, or farming on the scale of an independent proprietor working with family and friends, with little or no wage labor. It was the development of a series of connected innovations in agricultural markets establishing a decentralized partnership between farmers and governments as well as cooperative competition among farmers. For finance, the larger significance was not just the advancement of a network of local banks that continue to serve the country and local communities as an extraordinary resource to this day. It was the dismantlement of a center of financial power that threatened American democracy and risked subordinating the interests of producers to those of financial rentiers and speculators. It was the more effective enlistment of finance in the service of the productive agenda of society.

The other major tradition of progressive reform accepted the leadership of the production system by big businesses that never employed more than a minority of the labor force. This reform tradition made explicit what remained implicit in the work of the champions of small, independent property: resignation to the basic institutional and legal form of the market economy, including the regimes of property and contract established in private law. This basic form's favored instrument, from the first Roosevelt to the second and beyond, was the strong regulation of big business by national government. Its assumption was that the terms for reconciling decentralized economic initiative with imperatives of scale in the aggregation of resources cannot be fundamentally altered. These terms resulted from characteristics of the market order as basic as the acceptance of the unified property right (vesting all the constituent powers of property in the same right holder, the owner) as the key legal device for the organization of a property regime.

An additional assumption of this second reform tradition is that regulation begins where reorganization stops. Regulatory policy corrects for the consequences of inadequate competition or for asymmetries of power and information that result in a misalignment of incentives. Its premise, however, is that the contest over the organization of market order has ceased or been interrupted.

The truth is just the opposite. There are always alternative plausible responses to a problem that is described as a market failure requiring a regulatory response. Each such response can represent the first move in reorganizing the regulated industry. (The question of institutional competence—who should decide the reorganization—may in turn prompt radical reform in the organization of the state and democratic politics.) The frontier between institutionally conservative regulation and institutional change (radical reform) is open rather than closed. It is a frontier drawn in the mind, not in reality.

In the first two chapters of this book, I traced the consequences of these premises for the U.S. response to breakdowns such as the financial and economic crisis of 2007–2009. I considered the proposed agendas of financial regulation: the resuscitation of the old New Deal barriers between federally insured deposit-taking banks and proprietary trading, the creation of new powers of resolution and liquidation in the executive branch, the proposal of more stringent standards of capital adequacy by the more scrupulous and frightened section of the international financial elite, and the commitment to greater consumer protection in the use of retail financial services.

All such initiatives shared a failure to pursue financial deepening over financial hypertrophy. In fact, they even failed to challenge and change the strategy of regulatory dualism that had been most directly involved in the genesis of the crisis: the contrast between the world of thickly regulated bank-holding companies and a vast penumbra of thinly regulated, speculative finance and "shadow banking." In the approach to finance, these successive and combined abdications represented the specific expression of a more general failure to reinvent and continue the dialectic between Hamilton's developmentalism and the attempt to democratize the market economy one step and one piece at a time.

One of the major American traditions of progressive reform defends small-scale property and enterprise against economic concentration. The other tradition resigns itself to the commanding role of big business in the economy so long as the corporate power can be subject to vigorous regulation by government. Neither tradition recognizes the extent to which the institutions that define the market economy, including the arrangements governing the relation of finance to production, can be reimagined and reshaped. For this reason, neither provides an adequate basis for reform today.

I have argued that American history provides clues to what overcoming the limits of these two traditions of progressive reform requires. The most important clue is the double movement that I discussed earlier in this section. Americans would need to reimagine and reinvent that double movement, freeing it from the taints and illusions that circumscribed its reach and made it susceptible to the cumulative weakening that it suffered in the course of U.S. history.

The Hamiltonian movement from above—governmental activism to mobilize physical, financial, and human resources for national development—can no longer remain the prerogative of a plutocratic elite, which is inclined to identify the national interest with its self-interest. The democratizing movement from below to renovate and diversify the institutional forms of economic decentralization in one part of economic life after another can no longer be either sector specific or devoid of a doctrine. Its doctrinal explication is one of the requirements for its transformation into an economy-wide agenda of change.

We must understand and practice the democratization of the market and the deepening of democracy as reverse sides of each other. Now, as then, finance remains a crucial theater of conflict and invention: decisive for the American economy and decisive for American democracy.

Lessons of the Great Depression: The United States and Germany in the 1930s

The Great Depression of the 1930s was the last major period of institutional innovation in the richest countries of the world. I discuss here some of the implications of this experience for the radical reform of the market economy as well as for the role of finance. I do so chiefly from the perspective of the United States, contrasting at certain points American developments with simultaneous events in Germany.

The innovations of this period were often bold, but they were also narrow in scope. In the context of an economic slump of vast proportion, they created safeguards against economic insecurity and redressed the failings of the market order by decisively expanding public investment and governmental initiative, especially to employ the jobless. However, they brought about only limited change in the legal arrangements of the market economy. To the extent that they reshaped the relations between governments and firms, between the private and the public domains, they did so mainly through policies and arrangements emphasizing managed competition or concerted action under the eye of the state. Instead of democratizing access to the resources and opportunities of production, they restrained economic competition as well as social conflict.

What happened and what failed to happen to finance reflected this agenda. The government responded to the banks' failure to fund recovery by organizing public investment rather than by seeking to reshape the capital markets and to influence the relation of private finance to the real economy. The government's limited initiatives with regard to the reform of finance focused on avoiding bank panics and containing the dangers of financial speculation.

The basic shape of this agenda, both in what it accomplished and in what it left untouched, was remarkably similar in two countries as radically different as Roosevelt's America and Hitler's Germany. In each instance, the reform of the market order and of finance remained hostage to thought and politics. Democratic leader and brutal dictator alike were at the mercy of the ideas available to them: the stock of institutional conceptions, especially conceptions of the arrangements of the market order, was then, as it has almost always been, relatively inelastic. The extremities of the historical circumstance were not enough to ensure its enlargement. We do not find the ideas that we need and want just because we need and want them.

The organization of politics under democracy as well as under dictatorship reinforced the frailties of the institutional imagination. The American president found himself hamstrung by a constitutional plan designed to inhibit the political transformation of society, even in the favoring circumstance of national crisis, by multiplying the obstacles to any reform plan in proportion to its transformative reach. The German dictator, supposedly free from all constitutional restraint, had to reckon with the ancient double bind of revolutionary despotism: to compromise with the established powers, including the interests of big business and high finance, or to arouse a wave of popular mobilization against the financial and corporate interests, a popular agitation that he might not later be able to quiet and to master.

In the United States, as in any country, democratizing the market beyond initial steps in a program of economic reform would have required the deepening of democracy as its political basis: the creation of a high-energy democratic politics. The arrangements of such a politics raise the level of organized popular engagement in political life. They resolve impasse among the parts of the government while continuing to host multiple centers of powers. In a federal system like the American, they turn federalism into the machine of experimentation that it was proclaimed to be but has never become.

The "long New Deal," was the entire period from Franklin Roosevelt's coming to power at the beginning of 1933 to the immediate aftermath of the Second World War. We can distinguish four periods in its evolution. The first was the early New Deal, the first year and a half of the new order, with its restless but narrow institutional experimentalism and its emphasis on public investment as a circumvention of private finance. The second was the mature New Deal, from the end of the first period to the entrance into war at the end of 1941. The third was the war economy. The fourth was the turn to mass consumption and eventually to the broadening of access to credit as a substitute for the property-owning democracy that had failed to result from the earlier innovations and abdications. Although this turn came into its own only after the war, the mature New Deal prefigured it, and the war economy made it possible.

In the next few pages, I address the first two stages of the long New Deal. I follow this discussion by a summary treatment of the startling and misunderstood episode of the war economy.

The early New Deal was the heyday of institutional experimentalism. Roosevelt said: "The country needs and, unless I mistake its temper, the country demands bold, persistent experimentation. It is common sense to take a method and try it. If it fails, admit it frankly and try another. But above all, try something."[9] The experimentation turned out to have a narrower focus than these words implied.

The emergency experiments of the early New Deal fell under two main headings. The first was employment of the jobless by the federal government in public works under the aegis of the Works Projects Administration and regional development projects such as the Tennessee Valley Authority. Rather than force the hand of private capital to invest, the government extended its own hand. It put people to work on government building projects. The immediate aim was not support for demand, as the later consumption-oriented popular Keynesianism proposed; it was investment, with intended effect on both the supply and the demand sides of the economy.

The second set of institutional innovations enacted an idea so alien to present fashion in economic policy and political economy that we may be tempted both to slight its importance and to mistake its character. The idea was that the response to the collapse in the real economy must begin in the management and containment of competition and conflict rather than in the inspiration of new creative and entrepreneurial activity. Recovery, according to this view, was ancillary to stability. Such stability was to rely on reciprocal accommodation among firms, between business and labor, among classes more generally, and between private interests and state power.

Hugh Johnson, head of the administrative vehicle most closely identified with this project—the National Recovery Administration— summarized its central theme: "The very heart of the New Deal is the principle of concerted action in industry and agriculture under the supervision of government."[10] That meant in practice an abundance of initiatives imposing restraints on price competition or creating price supports as well as license for cartels or oligopolies to form under governmental monitoring. It meant more generally what political science would come to describe as corporatism: the normalization of corporate power (and of the power of organized labor by analogy to it) under rules and restraints imposed by the state, expressed in law, and adjusted through ongoing negotiation between corporate leaders and public officials.

The larger ideological and institutional program of corporatist reorganization and stabilization of the economy was attacked and discredited. However, its handiwork survived in the detailed legal architecture of a regulated "capitalism," organized to moderate competition and risk, to preempt or soften class conflict, and to give each organized interest both a stable place in the economy and a series of channels through which to strike deals with the state.

The vision enacted in these two categories, if not explicitly and fully formulated, was one in which the federal government compensated for the limitations of the market through public investment and governmental employment. What it did not even propose to do was to reshape the market, except to the extent that the institutional arrangements of corporatism, concerted action, or managed competition and the formation of cartels represent such a reshaping.

The nature of this project becomes clear in its characteristic legal expression. A new body of public law—of administrative regulation and coordination of private enterprise and governmental activism as well as of limited compensatory redistribution through progressive taxation and social entitlements—came to be superimposed on a largely unchanged body of private law. The terms on which people could gain decentralized access to the resources and opportunities of production, set out in the law of contract and property, as well as in corporate and labor law, remained largely unchanged.

The banking and securities legislation bridging the early and the mature New Deal made no significant exception to this model. The Banking Act of 1933 (Glass–Steagall Act), establishing the FDIC, provided a powerful safeguard against bank runs. That erected a wall between the commercial banks taking federally insured deposits and the investment banks engaged in proprietary trading. In a major advance for transparency, the Securities and Exchange Commission was established in 1934 to implement the new securities laws. One of the goals of these laws was to diminish the ability of financial and corporate insiders to put outsiders to disadvantage in the capital markets.

What tied these legislative initiatives together and connected them with the salient trait of the mature New Deal—its struggle against economic insecurity—was anxiety over the dangers of unregulated finance: vulnerability for the individual depositor or investor and instability for the economy as a whole. The rules governing bank-holding companies and stock markets were amended to tame the wildness of finance rather than to broaden access to it or to make it more useful to production.

The character of the New Deal's financial reforms becomes clear in their failure to address, other than obliquely and accidentally, two goals central to the argument of this book. The first aim is to strengthen the contribution that finance makes to production. Nothing in the New Deal reforms or in the ideas supporting them (save for the special role of finance in the reconstruction of the housing market, addressed later here) was designed to tap more effectively the dormant productive potential of saving. Nothing was calculated to widen or multiply the channels through which saving turns into investment capable of expanding output and enhancing productivity.

The financial reformers of the New Deal, including their most visible and radical exponents—Louis Brandeis and William O. Douglas—passed in silence over the central enigma of modern finance: that the vast stores of liquid capital held in the banking system as well as the capital "invested" in the stock market—that is, used to trade shares—has only an indirect, episodic, or theoretical relation to the funding of production.[11] The reformers did nothing to exploit the opportunity for a reform of finance at once more growth oriented and more friendly to democracy that an effort to address this enigma would have presented. That such an enlargement of vision lies within the reach of what is imaginable—and even doable in America—had been demonstrated unequivocally by the Jacksonian reformation of American finance in the early nineteenth century.

The second large goal in which the New Deal reforms failed to share was intimately related to the first: the democratization of finance. Its deeper meaning is not the broadening of access to financial services and to credit in the absence of a change in the arrangements of production. It is the role that finance can play in the development of an economic regime affording more opportunity to more people in more ways and consequently diminishing inequality in the initial distribution of economic advantage (the distribution prior to the corrective work of tax and transfer). Among such arrangements today are those that support the economy-wide spread of knowledge-intensive, experimental production.

There is, we have seen, an asymmetrical relation between deepening finance and democratizing it. We may be able to deepen it, up to a point, without democratizing it: by multiplying channels between finance and productive investment without broadening access to the resources and opportunities of production. However, we cannot democratize finance without deepening it: increasing the extent to which it serves production rather than serving itself.

The New Deal and its European equivalents in the 1930s pursued economic recovery chiefly through public investment and the direct employment of workers by the state rather than though a reconstruction of the market order. Stability was the byword of the concerted action to be achieved between government and business. Had the New Deal embraced the aim of creating an economic regime that privileged innovation over stability, while refusing to leave innovation in the control of an entrepreneurial and technological elite, it would have had to rethink the private-law basis as well as the public-law setting of the market economy. It would have had to ask itself how to enlist finance in this program. Its interest in democratizing finance would have forced it to take an interest in deepening finance.

As a consequence, the New Deal could not have remained content with its solution to the problem of investment that combined expanded investment by the state with the reinvestment of retained earnings by large corporations. This solution left the vast majority of smaller businesses in the country, responsible for most of output and for the vast majority of jobs, starved of access to advanced practice and technology as well as to capital. Reliance on the duo of government investment and earnings retained and reinvested by big business had consequences for the future. When the crisis and the war passed, the first basis of investment—government spending—would shrink. Only the second— retained earnings in large firms—remained.

The limitations of the New Deal approach to the reform and regulation of finance presaged the direction taken by the mature New Deal. We can date this mature New Deal from the middle of Roosevelt's first term to the country's entry into the Second World War. Its hallmark was a narrowing of focus. The broader scheme of concerted action or corporatism—associated with the National Recovery Association (dissolved in 1935)—gave way to what is retroactively viewed as the greatest achievement of the New Deal: protections against economic insecurity. The Social Security Act of 1935, with its provisions for unemployment insurance and pensions, was its most characteristic program, alongside the financial reforms discussed in the preceding paragraphs.

There was, however, one sector in which the institutional experimentalism of the early New Deal not only persisted but advanced beyond the limits of the corporatist vision: housing. The National Housing Act of 1934 and the Housing Act of 1937, followed by the creation in 1938 of a government-sponsored enterprise (the Federal National Mortgage Association, or Fannie Mae) set the institutional foundations for wider access to housing. The initial drive to support local governments' public-housing efforts gave way to a bolder emphasis on the creation of a secondary mortgage market, intended to provide affordable housing for working families. It was an advance easy to accommodate within the mature New Deal's commitment to economic security. It is in this way, rather than as an example of an attempt to give substance to the ideal of property-owning democracy, that we can best understand the appeal of these innovations in the legal arrangements of the housing market.

The housing-market initiatives nevertheless contained all the elements of institutional innovation that the administration might have deployed in other areas of public policy. One such element was the use of law and policy to develop a new kind of market (as the early-nineteenth-century Americans had done in agriculture and finance) rather than just to regulate the market as it was then organized or to soften its inequities through compensatory redistribution by means of taxation and entitlements.

A second element was the enlistment of finance in the execution of the task. The secondary mortgage market—a product of these innovations—became one of the foundations of the capital market, drawing capital into a form of activity and investment that touched the lives of millions of people. The later abuses in the secondary mortgage market resulted from failure to uphold and deepen the initial project. The securitization of housing loans was later allowed to serve as pretext for the development of financial products with little or no connection to activity in the real economy. What had been the target turned into a pretext.

A third element was the making of a new institutional vehicle for what was in effect a public–private partnership. The GSEs may have been conceived by the light of a corporatist imagination. They nevertheless embodied a principle of institutional design that could have been used to begin broadening access to the resources and opportunities of production as well as to protect against economic insecurity.

This principle was not so used: the impulse to democratize the market and to enlist finance in the effort remained confined largely to the housing market. It failed to figure within a larger movement in thought and in politics that could replace corporatist stabilization with democratic reinvention of the market economy. This sector-specific institutional innovation became on its own home ground vulnerable to subsequent perversion and dismantlement, according to the inverse of Nietzsche's principle regularly exemplified in the history of institutions and institutional ideas: what does not make me stronger begins to kill me.

Now let us step back briefly to compare the shape of the early and mature New Deal with the direction taken by Nazi Germany in the years before the war. The circumstances of the two countries and the character of their governments could hardly have been more different. Yet the basic direction of their respective responses to the slump of the 1930s was nevertheless astonishingly similar. In Hitler's Germany, as in Roosevelt's America, the main line of response to economic crisis and mass unemployment was direct public spending and the hiring of workers by government.[12]

Hitler's "labor fronts," set up by the state for road and home building, paralleled the public-works projects of the early New Deal. In both countries, the hiring of large numbers of workers by government attenuated the sufferings of the jobless but proved insufficient to bring about economic recovery. The Nazi regime claimed to have taken the German economy out of the slump. Closer study, however, shows that despite massive public spending, free of many of the legal and constitutional restraints with which the federal government contended in the United States, output increased only modestly.

Fiscal stimulus would have needed to be massive to produce the requisite outcome: in effect, a war economy before the war, which neither the Americans nor the Germans established. In both countries, large-scale and general recovery happened only through war. In both countries, resort to public spending and direct employment of workers by government had as its counterpart an unwillingness to reshape the private-law foundations of the market economy. The contract and property regimes setting the terms of access to capital and economic opportunity remained intact, with the exception of enhanced opportunity to work for the state. A corollary of this orientation was failure to reshape or to attempt to reshape the relation of finance to the real economy.

In both countries, such institutional and legal innovation as took place in the arrangements of the market economy occurred under the guidance of corporatist ideas of concerted action and negotiated accommodation between the state and big business. The American democracy and the German dictatorship gave different meanings and support to these ideas. Practice, however, differed less than doctrine. In both countries, the goals of security for the individual and stability for the economy prevailed over any more radical aim of either economic recovery or broader opportunity for working people.

How are we to account for this surprising parallelism? (We might extend it to include most of other advanced economies of the day. I have selected my example to sharpen the point that I use it to illustrate.) No economic or technological determinism can persuasively explain the outcome. Any number of differences in economic circumstance, geopolitical context, and national circumstance might have suggested greater divergence in direction. To understand the parallelism, we must look to thought and politics: the places in which the institutional presuppositions of the market economy are set.

Crisis facilitates change. The political and economic arrangements of contemporary societies may indeed make significant change in their structure all but inaccessible without the advent of crisis. However, crisis gives no direction to those who must respond to it. They find themselves at the mercy of the ideas that happen to be available to them.

In the 1930s, the ideological options visible to practical statesmen were starkly drawn: to cling to the essentials of the market order as it had evolved in the North Atlantic world, freeing it from the rent-seeking concessions to organized interests that its most uncompromising advocates denounced; to follow Soviet Russia in placing the economy in the hands of the state, with limited space for small-scale private production and exchange in the spirit of the New Economic Policy; or to enlist the state in the restabilization of the economy and the creation of safeguards against radical economic insecurity.

The domination of the economy by big business and high finance seemed unavoidable, unless government were to take their place. What remained was for the state to bring economic competition and class conflict under control, subjecting them to the authority of its laws and policies. In return for agreeing to play its part in a project defined by government, each organized interest would have a chance to turn its advantages into vested rights. The mass of ordinary workers would be rendered less vulnerable to the loss of job, income, home, and prospects. In this vision, social solidarity was corporatism by another name.

These ideas were so widely influential as markers of an alternative to classical-liberal privatism and to state socialism that they informed the practical teachings of movements and organizations that did not participate directly in the contest for state power. For example, institutionally detailed corporate communitarianism distinguished even a papal statement of the social doctrine of the Roman Catholic Church such as *Quadragesimo anno* (Pope Pius XI, 1931).

The high culture of theory did little to expand the conversation. The most influential of the academic orthodoxies, the post-Marginalist practice of economics, was deficient in institutional imagination. Keynes's new heresy accentuated the poverty of the Marginalist tradition in institutional ideas and its lack of any view of production (other than as a shadowy extension of exchange, viewed under the lens of relative prices) rather than redressing it. Marxism, the leading doctrine of the Left, shared with its right-wing adversaries the view that capitalism is capitalism (or that a market is a market): a system with a preset legal and institutional content. It could be replaced only by another equally indivisible regime—socialism. Its instabilities and cruelties might even be softened by "reformism." What we can never accomplish, according to this view, is to reimagine and remake the legal and institutional core of the market system.

Legal thought failed to defy these assumptions. In this period on both sides of the Atlantic, it remained largely occupied with the effort to free legal analysis from the shackles of traditional approaches to legal doctrine. It failed to take the discovery of the legal and institutional indeterminacy of the market order, made slowly and cumulatively by several generations of jurists, as an invitation to explore institutional alternatives to the established economic and political arrangements.

Consider the example of the American legal realists, who came to prominence in this period and helped design the New Deal programs. They struggled in the academy, the courts, and the national debate against "Lochnerism," the constitutional entrenchment of understandings of private rights that would result in the invalidation of a broad range of government regulatory and redistributive initiatives. Yet they developed no alternative vision of the legal foundations of the market order: the different ways in which decentralized access to productive resources and opportunities might be reconciled with the need to aggregate resources and achieve scale in production. Narrowing their program to the truncated institutional experimentalism of the New Deal, the legal realists exempted themselves from the need to propose a more far-reaching one.

Politics, together with thought, was the other decisive constraint on the shape of the agenda that I have discussed. How the politics of a flawed but vibrant democracy and of a brutal dictatorship could have supported such similar responses to the economic crisis of the 1930s is what I next explore.

The protodemocratic liberalism established in the United States set formidable obstacles in the path of any practice of radical reform by multiplying intermediate levels of representation and by allowing political activity, including access to the means of communication, to depend on private money. It set up these obstacles most directly through constitutional arrangements (Madison's plan of checks and balances) that fragmented political power only by also simultaneously slowing down politics. Separation of powers in its Madisonian mode perpetuated impasse rather than resolving it quickly (through early elections, for example, or comprehensive programmatic plebiscites). It did so even by failing to give greater practical effect to the experimentalist ideal of federalism—the states as "laboratories of experimentation"—in the actual organization of the federal system.

Roosevelt had a depression of unprecedented proportion and a world war as his allies. He had as well the support of the people, reaffirmed in successive elections. Even then he struggled with the consequences of a constitutional system that had been designed in part to inhibit structural change. The problem was not that the constitutional regime made it possible to challenge his proposals, as any democracy would have had to do. It was that the regime turned the mounting of such challenges into a way of slowing politics down rather than of speeding it up. To speed up politics would have meant to settle the conflict quickly by engaging the people through, for example, early elections or plebiscites and referendums about whole sets of initiatives rather than single issues.

I remarked earlier that the semidemocratic arrangements of the United States help explain the failure to renew the life and the meaning of the interplay between resource mobilization from above and democratization of opportunities down below, pursued before the Civil War in agriculture and banking. That dialectic, which had proved so decisive in the early history of the republic, reappeared in diminished form during the Depression. The emphasis on stabilization and concerted action took the place of Hamilton's national-development project, while the reorganization of the housing market became the last refuge of the impulse to democratize the market economy.

Under the German dictatorship, a more ancient and fundamental influence reinforced the poverty of available institutional ideas in excluding from consideration any significant reshaping of the market economy. In its early years, the Nazi regime had revolutionary pretensions. The "state of exception" as an enduring untying of political power (as Carl Schmitt had theorized it) might be thought to provide a constitutional basis for a practice of radical reform. In fact, the regime confronted the dilemma of revolutionary despotism, which long before the age democracy, nationalism, and world history had beset the rulers of the agrarian-bureaucratic empires. On the one hand, they needed to support independent smallholders in the struggle of peasants against dispossession by landowning magnates. To give into these oligarchs and warlords would have been to lose the source of taxes and soldiers and to destroy the foundation of commercialized agriculture and the money economy. On the other hand, to pit the people against the magnates would have been to arouse a tension that no ruler could hope to control or even to direct. He could expect soon to become its victim.

The circumstances of a twentieth-century European society prevented the periodic breakdown of the market economy and political order that those empires had suffered throughout their history. However, these circumstances could not resolve the dilemma of revolutionary despotism; they could only delay or ameliorate its consequences. To incite or to please his base in the petty bourgeoisie and the less-organized part of the working class, the dictator would have had to wage war against big business and its plutocratic chieftains. He would have had to design, with the help of class traitors, an alternative basis for the organization of production. Corporatist accommodation between the state and the organized interests would have had to give way to a more fundamental remaking of the market economy. Such a remaking would have in turn required another way of organizing the state and the representation of interests in society. In revolutionary dictatorship, there existed neither the political will nor the institutional ideas to support such a project.

The sole way of loosening the constraints that afflicted both the American democracy and the German dictatorship in the formulation and enactment of institutional alternatives would have been to radicalize democracy. It would have been to create the institutions of a high-energy democracy capable of making the structure of society subject to the law in fact and not just in constitutional theory. What has instead prevailed in the compromised democracies of modern history as well as under the dictatorships that arose in this historical period is law as episodic intervention in an inherited and largely unquestioned order.

The War Economy

The war economy, the reorganization of the American economy during the Second World War, deserves separate treatment. I deal with it here in summary fashion in the hope of bringing out the significance of this astonishing and misunderstood experience for the subject matter of this book. My remarks address the United States. However, each major claim I make applies, often with only slight modification, to the other major belligerent powers, with the exception of the Soviet Union.[13]

It has long been recognized that it was the war rather than the supposed proto-Keynesianism of governmental spending before the war that took the United States and some of its European enemies and allies out of the slump. Yet we have formed no clear and agreed-upon picture either of the economic consequences of the war effort or of the means by which they were achieved.

In four years, from 1941 to 1945, U.S. GDP more than doubled. Under the pressure of war, the country cast aside many of the economic dogmas to which it was devoted, as if they were a mask that Americans could take off when circumstances required them to discard it. Americans continued to exhibit their knack for cooperative activity across class and even race lines in production as well as in warfare. However, they did so on the basis of institutional arrangements that contradicted, often starkly, the supposedly sacrosanct principles of the U.S. market economy and American constitutionalism. These heresies extended, for example, to taxation: the top marginal rate of the personal income tax exceeded 90 percent.

The institutional vehicles of the war effort had antecedents in earlier twentieth-century American history. The War Production Board, the agency centrally responsible for coordinating the effort, was modeled on Bernard Baruch's War Industries Board and the War Finance Corporation of the First World War. It also, however, continued and in some ways radicalized practices of many of the failed, disbanded, or marginalized agencies of the early New Deal. Its work was complemented by governmental organizations. Some of these organizations, such as the Supply Priorities and Allocation Board and the Office of Production Management, were absorbed into the War Production Board. Others survived to play distinct roles. Among them was the War Manpower Commission, authorized to allocate labor between military and civilian uses; the National War Labor Board, empowered to impose binding arbitration in conflicts between capital and labor; and, most tellingly, the Office of Price Administration, which had a broad mandate to fix prices.

The most important of these governmental agencies, including the War Production Board, were run by some of the leading business executives in the country. Their profession did not stop them from adopting practices in such manifest conflict with free-market ideology that the general in command of Army Special Forces could describe them as instruments for "Henry Wallace and the leftists to take over the country."[14] What did these agencies do to deserve such a description?

To understand the organization of the war economy and the basis of its extraordinary success, we must distinguish its two axes. The first axis was massive mobilization of the physical, financial, and human resources of the country to produce for war. The second axis was loosely planned and sometimes anarchic institutional innovation, primarily in the dealings between government and business and secondarily in the relations among firms. Without the second element, the first would not have worked. Each of the agencies that I mentioned earlier performed a double role: it shared in the work of resource mobilization while forming part of the administrative redesign of the market order.

Forty-five percent of the cost of the war was financed by current taxation; the remainder was financed out of borrowing, especially through the purchase of Treasury bonds by the general population. The powers vested in the war agencies enabled them to mobilize labor, capital, and productive apparatus on a scale of which Hamilton could not have dreamed. The value of military procurements in the first six months of 1942 exceeded GDP for the whole of 1941.

This extraordinary heightening of national savings and investment largely bypassed the capital markets. Indeed, the market in corporate securities shrank dramatically, while saving and investment increased exponentially. The chief instruments of the substitute saving–investment process were the procurement arrangements and the reinvestment of retained earnings by major firms.

Production was orchestrated on a basis that cannot be accurately described as either market competition working through relative prices or state planning. Reciprocal consultation between the government and the firms, constantly revised in the light of experience, took the place of both the traditional market and the plan. The main burden of production rested squarely, as it did in Germany, on a small number of the largest corporations in the country.

This fact reveals the limits of the institutional innovations embraced in the war economy; these innovations failed to democratize the production system even as they mobilized its potential. Oligopoly advanced under the cover of wartime mobilization.

The war economy nevertheless illustrates the crucial significance of the relation among three elements to a quantum leap in economic growth: the voluntary or forced heightening of savings; the immediate conversion of available capital into productive investment outside the established capital markets as well as through them; and the role played by ways of organizing production that cannot be reduced to the familiar choices between market and plan. The reshaping of the market could have gone farther and had greater exemplary significance if mobilizing resources had been used to democratize access to productive opportunities. The conviction that finance would have to form part of any such democratizing movement inspired laws such as the Small War Plants Corporation Act of 1942, passed to provide working capital to smaller firms.

To the extent that the war economy is remembered at all, the bias of subsequent thought has been to treat its arrangements as irrelevant to the peacetime economy. In some respect, however, the institutional alternatives for which I argue in this book could be described as a war economy without a war, in which mobilizing resources becomes the occasion for democratizing opportunities and capabilities.

To grasp the deep basis for the wider pertinence of this experience and to refute its confinement to the exceptional circumstance of total war, we must confront a basic problem in economic theory. An understanding of this problem sheds further light on the vision that I have sought to advance in this work and on the role of finance in its advancement.

We have seen how a crisis beginning in the capital markets may end up damaging the real economy. One of the reasons to value financial deepening is the reasonable hope that the multiplication of channels between finance and real economic activity may help contain, although it cannot abolish, the dangers of finance. It may help prevent finance from acting as a "loose canon," driven by impulses and perceptions that are not chastened and guided by engagement with the need to produce real goods and services to meet real needs. Thus, financial deepening helps twice: by enhancing the contribution of finance to production and by moderating the risk that financial volatility will periodically and unnecessarily interrupt economic activity.

Among the possible ways of promoting economic growth, one of the most important is the avoidance or mitigation of its interruption by financial crisis. A crisis that begins in finance may soon spread to the real economy. One of the worst variants of this peril is the one that we in fact repeatedly encounter: finance may be relatively indifferent to the real economy in good times (thanks to financial hypertrophy without financial deepening) but destructive in bad times. Overcoming this imbalance by enlisting finance more effectively in the service of production should be one of the chief aims of the reform of finance.

The instability of finance is, however, only the secondary cause of the periodic downswings studied in writings about the business cycle. The primary cause emerges from the heart of economic phenomena: the relation between supply and demand in a market economy. Marginalist economics and its successors took the explanation of relative prices as their defining task. It approached that task by viewing the whole economy as a set of connected markets. Nothing was more fundamental to its concerns than, first, the relation between supply and demand and, second, the idea that in the absence of some market defect (such as the downward rigidity of wages, later to be emphasized by Pigou and Keynes) supply would elicit demand and demand would elicit supply. Nevertheless, the logical formalism of this analytic tradition and its hostility to qualitative distinctions prevented it from appreciating a disturbance in the relation between supply and demand that rendered the economy vulnerable to perennial instability: one even more basic than that which results from the troubled and variable relation of finance to the real economy. The interpretation of the nature and achievements of the war economy provides an occasion to incorporate an understanding of this basic truth about the market economy into a view of the institutional element in economic life and economic growth.

The fundamental cause of economic crisis is the lack of reciprocal reinforcement between breakthroughs in the constraints on supply and breakthroughs in the constraints on demand. Demand and supply develop discontinuously in ways that have greater or lesser promise to produce subsequent lasting advance. An advance on one side—either supply or demand—cannot ensure an advance on the other side. As a result, the economy is subject to repeated maladjustments of supply and demand, with detrimental consequences for employment and growth.

Consider first the demand side of the economy. Imagine three bases for the expansion of demand. The most fragile basis is a strengthening of demand supported by an increased access to credit without a corresponding rise in the income or wealth of the borrowers. At the next level of advance, an increase in aggregate demand may result from tax-and-transfer exactions and payments by government: retrospective redistribution by means of progressive taxation and redistributive entitlements. As the less well off spend proportionately more of their income than the relatively well off, an attenuation of inequality will strengthen demand. At its most consequential, the expansion of demand may result from the enhancement of individual capabilities and productivity thanks to institutional and educational innovations. Such changes may improve the original distribution of economic advantage before its correction through tax and transfer.

An economist formed in the tradition of post-Marginalist economics may object that aggregate demand produces effects proportionate to its quantitative level, regardless of its causes. However, to disregard the qualitative distinctions and causal differences is to miss features of economic life that, together with the troubled relation of finance to the real economy, make it susceptible to recurrent breakdown. It also misses the quantitative implications of qualitative and structural distinctions: the shallower the basis for the expansion of demand (credit rather secondary redistribution, secondary redistribution rather than primary redistribution), the less likely is the prospect that it can last.

Now consider the economy from the supply side and from the perspective of the actions of a firm or a producer. Such a firm provides, for the simplifying purposes of this argument, the modal or typical response to the provision of supply in the light of actual or expected demand. Imagine five stages in the depth of a breakthrough in constraints on supply.

At the first stage, the producer (that is to say, the modal firm in this thought experiment) waits for demand before building up inventory or deciding to expand production. At a second stage, the producer builds inventory without significant expansion of output in anticipation of future demand. At a third stage, the producer expands output without substantially altering his technologies and practices. At a fourth stage, the producer innovates in practices and technologies, enhancing his productivity. Such innovations typically increase efficiency and spare capital. At a fifth stage, the producer marries new technologies to new business models to create new products and services and a kind of demand that did not previously exist. This activity is what Christensen has labeled "disruptive innovation."[15] Such innovations tend to demand more capital rather than to spare capital by increasing the efficiency of its use.

This double list of levels of advance in breakthroughs in constraints on supply and demand provides a basis on which to present the problem. A given level of advance on one side, supply or demand, fails to ensure a corresponding advance on the other side. For example, the move from credit-fueled expansion of demand to a heightening of demand through retroactive redistribution need not translate into a move from an expansion of supply without innovation to one based on such productivity enhancement.

Keynes's *General Theory* presented a view of slumps that seized on only one variant of these failures in the correspondence between supply and demand: the role of swings of mood and attitude and of rigidity in the price of labor in undermining the operation of Say's law, according to which supply generates its own demand. Keynes's theory is the theory of a special case: a particular failure in the correspondence between demand and supply, viewed from a perspective that is psychological or behavioral rather than institutional. The substitution of a theory of the special case for a general theory of these failures of correspondence has decisive consequences for our understanding of how best to respond to slumps or to prevent them from occurring in the first place.

Consider three ways of dealing with the failure of correspondence between supply and demand. Each response has implications for our foreground theme of the role of finance in the funding of production and in the institutional reshaping of the market regime.

The first approach is that of the war economy, viewed now not as a particular event but as a situation that might happen in the economic history of humanity even without an actual war. In the war economy, there can be no fundamental failure of correspondence between supply and demand. What prevents such a lack of correspondence is the radical simplification introduced by the role of the state. The state works with big business to orchestrate supply. At the same time, the state guarantees demand. Under the conditions of total war, demand is close to being unlimited for all practical purposes. A failure of correspondence between supply and demand cannot arise except as a result of inefficiencies intrinsic to a method of production or of warfare that makes up for defects of quality with the rapid expansion of quantity (a characteristic of the way in which both American government and American industry dealt with production targets during the Second World War).

In the war economy, financial deepening is assured not by the multiplication of new ways of channeling capital into productive investment but rather by a circumvention of the capital markets. The procurement process mobilized forced saving, while administrative prices were used to negotiate profit margins with business—mainly big business.

This solution of the problem of correspondence between supply and demand through the simplification of the task, on the one hand, and the simplifying role of the state in orchestrating its execution, on the other, goes a long way to explaining the spectacular economic growth that the war economy can deliver.

The second way of dealing with the failure of correspondence between supply and demand is "disruptive innovation": the fifth and most far-reaching mode of breaking through the constraints on supply. The disruptive innovator finds adequate demand not because demand results spontaneously from supply (according to Say's prescription) but because he creates the demand that he needs. Such demand creation forms part of what disruptive innovation means: the arousal of new wants for new products and services in markets that may also be unlike any that existed before.

Disruptive innovation is capital intensive rather than capital sparing. As a consequence, it requires finance to do in fact what finance ought to do but in reality does only episodically or obliquely: direct capital to the expansion of output and the enhancement of productivity. If retained earnings are insufficient to finance producers' plans, as they will be for start-up or emerging enterprise and even for more mature companies engaged on a plan of radical change, producers must consider the full range of forms of debt and equity as well as strategic partnerships, mergers, and acquisitions. If financial deepening remains exceptional in the economy at large, producers must nevertheless find a way to make external finance work for them.

The disruptive innovator solves the problem of the lack of spontaneous reciprocal reinforcement of supply and demand only at the level of the firm, the microlevel, to the extent that he solves it at all. We can interpret disruptive innovation as a way for firms to respond to the challenge that the failure of supply to create its own demand in the general economy presents to them. Even at the level of the firm and even in the best of circumstances, however, disruptive innovation can make up for that failure only imperfectly and for a while. Sooner or later the disruptive innovator will face the limits imposed by the failure of spontaneous correspondence between supply and demand in the economy as a whole.

Henry Ford famously quipped that he liked to pay his workers well so that they could buy his cars. Of course, they could take the higher, "efficiency" wage that he paid them (made possible by the declining part that the wage bill represented in an industry that was relatively capital intensive) and use it to buy his competitors' cars or no cars at all.

We might imagine, as another thought experiment, a contract between capital and labor—all capital and all labor. Under the contract's terms, capital would agree to pay workers more. Labor would agree to use its higher pay to buy more of what capital produces. Is this not what happens in fact in any process of economic growth?

The truth is that it happens only precariously and to a limited extent. Such a deal cannot be closed because of the failures of correspondence between supply and demand that I am now discussing. There is no contractual or social-contract solution to this problem, none at least that is compatible with a market regime premised on a wide decentralization of initiative. The idea of a contractual solution to it is a political and economic fantasy. The solution, if there is a solution, can only be institutional: the adoption and development of arrangements that mitigate the failures of spontaneous reciprocal correspondence between advances in supply and deepening of demand.

Thus, we come to the third way of addressing and overcoming the uncertain and unstable responsiveness of supply to demand and of demand to supply. The third and most far-reaching level of the expansion of demand, as I described it earlier, signals the character of such an alternative. This heightening of demand results from reforms that increase the opportunities, capabilities, and advantages of a broad mass of people—citizens, workers, and consumers—before redistribution through tax-and-transfer payments. The same features of this movement that heighten demand will also tend to strengthen supply. More people can buy more because more people also have the economic and educational equipment—opportunities and capabilities—with which to produce more and better goods and services.

The difficulty here is no longer, as in disruptive innovation, that the response remains a microsolution without a macrobasis—a basis pertinent to the general workings of the economy rather than to the gainful strategies of innovative firms. Here we have a macro- rather than a microresponse. The problem is that this response exists only as an unrealized possibility. As conception, it is no more than a sketch. As practice, it is a political and economic project, not the description of an existing economy.

This project is the same one that I have explored throughout this book under the name "democratized market economy" as a setting for the economy-wide diffusion of the most advanced practice of production and the tightening of the links between finance and the real economy. It gives practical content and effect to the goal of socially inclusive economic growth. Recall some of its most general traits.

There would have to be an enlargement of the stock of legally defined institutional arrangements for the relations between governments and firms as well as for the arrangements among firms. Such changes would allow for cooperative competition among firms. They would also make possible a practice of industrial policy—or of strategic coordination between governments and firms that is decentralized and pluralistic. The emphasis would fall on expanding access to means for creating new comparative advantage through mechanisms such as multisector technologies and access to venture capital rather than on government choice of the most promising lines of production.

Such an expansion in the repertory of arrangements for the relations among firms or between firms and governments would need to be followed by innovations in property and contract regimes that allow more decentralization of initiative to be reconciled with more aggregation of resources. Among the means to promote that goal would be property and corporate laws facilitating the coexistence of fragmentary and conditional claims in productive resources by different tiers of right holders: workers, technical staff, local communities, and local governments as well as outside investors. Disaggregated property and relational contract—marginalized in established private-law theory—would play a central role.

A vital complement to these economic and legal changes would be the development of a style of both general and technical education that is analytical rather than informational. Technical education would replace job-specific and machine-specific skills with the higher-order abilities required by numerically controlled machine tools. In its use of information—given that no analytical capabilities can be acquired in a vacuum of content—this style of education would spurn encyclopedic coverage in favor of selective depth. It would want teaching and learning to be based on cooperative practices by teachers and students alike rather on the juxtaposition of individualism and authoritarianism. And it would approach all received knowledge dialectically, through a contrast of views. In this way, it would oppose the naturalization of the marriage of method and subject matter—the mistaking of dominant ideas for the way things are—that descends from the university system to poison education and emasculate the young in preparation for a lifetime of intellectual servility.

Such changes can begin, but they cannot advance far without an energizing of democracy. They require a democracy that is able to subject increasing parts of the structure of the economy and society to challenge and change. Such a democracy would need institutions that raise the level of organized popular engagement in political life, resolve impasse quickly to facilitate the practice of radical reform, and empower pieces of the economy as well as parts of the country to experiment with alternatives to the current path taken by the state and the society.

It is only in such a context of a generalized democratic experimentalism that the deepening and democratization of finance can move beyond their initial steps, produce their larger effects, and demonstrate their full value.

To move, even haltingly and by initial steps, in such a direction is to solve in practice rather in theory the problem lying at the heart of the periodic economic slumps and breakdowns that interrupt economic growth. It is to do for the economy at large what disruptive innovation does only for the firm and its milieu. And it is to apply the formula of the war economy—mobilizing resources and innovating in institutional arrangements—while dispensing with the costly simplifications of such an economy and its circumstance of armed conflict.

The East Asian Development "Miracle"

The rapid ascent of the Northeast Asian economies in the decades following the Second World War is the single most striking instance of economic growth in the second half of the twentieth century. In this section, I define the geographic scope of this ascent narrowly to include Japan, Korea, and Taiwan. I address China in the next subsection of this chapter, together with Brazil and the United States. Japan's economic transformation has a longer historical background, going back to the reforms following the Meiji Restoration in 1861. In this section, however, I refer to Japan from its mid-twentieth-century defeat in war to its reemergence as one of the richest and most productive economies in the world. The conventional grouping of Japan, South Korea, and Taiwan remains useful given the similarities in their development paths.

From the beginning, there have been two major clashing accounts of the main basis and lesson of this development experience. We can follow the common practice of calling these accounts the "orthodox" and the "heterodox" interpretations. However, we must be careful to note that the orthodox account describes a trajectory that was never followed by the older developed countries and that the heterodox account is closely related to the orthodoxy of late-twentieth-century development economics.[16] In my subsequent remarks, I take the heterodox view as a point of departure but argue for its inadequacy both as an interpretation of historical experience and as a guide to future transformation.

On the orthodox view, there was no "East Asian miracle." The Northeast Asian countries succeeded by dint of hard work; sound management of public finance, including a commitment to fiscal responsibility and price stability; openness to the world economy; and investment in human capital. They prospered despite occasional attempts by the state to select and to support particular sectors of the economy and lines of production, not because of those attempts.

This view fails to do justice to the pervasive character of governmental involvement in setting the development strategy of these economies. It also disregards the central role of what I earlier described as active globalization in this development experience: selective integration into the world economy. Such an integration advances by steps designed to maintain and enhance national governments' and entrepreneurs' ability to develop new comparative advantage within the world economy. It saves them from passively accepting the niche to which established comparative advantage consigned them. Moreover, the orthodox view fails to address the important political and social background in East Asia: a relatively unified political and bureaucratic elite and a highly organized, albeit poor, population.

The heterodox approach to Northeast Asian success assigns a central causal role to what the orthodox account slights. Its focus is a developmental state's achievement in three areas that proved decisive to economic growth.[17]

First, government worked with firms, especially in the industrial sector, to give them access to capital as well as to technology and advanced practice, using subsidized credit to gain new comparative advantage. The range of businesses benefited by such governmental activism in industrial policy varied from the relatively narrow, tilted to big business (as in South Korea), to the relatively broad, with more space for small and medium-size firms (as in Taiwan). A salient feature of this approach was the preference given to manufacturing, in the mode of Fordist mass production, with its demonstrated potential to support rapid convergence with the richest countries in the world.

In an economy that continued to be divided into clearly distinct sectors, industry offered a combination of advantages as a basis for such convergence. It made tradable products. Its productivity could be enhanced by successive applications of capital, embodied in technology.

Above all, it lent itself to the use of a package of simple standardized machines and labor skills that could be easily imitated and reproduced.

Second, government adopted laws and policies designed to raise the level of private as well as public saving, sometimes to higher than 40 percent of GDP. This forced heightening contradicted the Keynesian teaching that the savings level is more the consequence than the cause of economic growth. That teaching failed to grasp the strategic reason for a high saving level in the early moments of a rebellious strategy of national development—a strategy that refuses to accept the place assigned to a country in the world economy by its established comparative advantages. To resist and ascend, government must not remain on its knees, beholden to the prejudices and interests of finance, especially from foreign sources. It must be able to act on the principle that foreign capital is the more useful the less you need it: you do what you must to bring about growth. Foreign direct investment comes later, attracted not by the religion of high finance but by the reality of economic growth and the opportunities for profit that growth generates.

Third, government worked to integrate the national economy into the world economy by steps ensuring that integration would happen on terms useful to the national development strategy. In chapter 4, I showed that such steps included not only protection for local industry but also dosage and selection in the penetration of the local economy by foreign capital: loan capital before direct foreign investment and gradual, controlled opening of the capital account. Export-led growth could make up for the thinness of the domestic market, allowing the economy to grow quickly without major internal redistribution of wealth.

Let us complement these emphases in the heterodox interpretation of the East Asian development experience with other features that either go unmentioned or are habitually misrepresented. They form the subtext of this account; they are no less important to an understanding of that experience.

The educational and cultural background to state-guided and export-oriented industrialization included schooling oriented to mastery of received, conventional knowledge, to the competitive discrimination of success and failure, and to disciplined obedience. It was low in creativity, in critical distance, and in an appreciation of the variety of contradictory methods and conceptions that might be brought to bear on any given subject matter. Those individuals formed in such a system were generally better at emulating than in inventing. *Literacy, numeracy*, and *conformity* were its watchwords. The heterodox account, like the orthodox account, recognized the importance of investment in people but had little to say about the character of education. The education in fact provided was good enough for a Fordist factory or a Weberian office but inadequate if permanent innovation were to be both the goal and the method.

The political and legal background to these initiatives included the establishment of property rights in the form that property took in the civilian private law of continental Europe. The legal transplants included a private-law system centered around the unified property right, vested in an absolute owner, rather than around any idea of multiple stakes held by different kinds of stakeholders in the same productive resources. By the same token, these transplants denied legal significance to the incomplete and half-articulated relational contracts that are central to societies and economies rich in social capital. They organized contract law instead around the bilateral executory promise, as prescribed by the standard version of classical contract theory, with its sundering of legal obligation from social reciprocity.

Security in property, reduced by law to the nineteenth-century European form of the unified property right, had as its political counterpart a state that was either openly authoritarian or run on the basis of limited, controlled democracy. At its best, such a state resisted outright capture by the moneyed interests and allowed a professional, competitively chosen economic bureaucracy to design and implement selective industrial policies, regulations, tariffs, and subsidies. A state of this kind was, however, unable as well as unwilling to engage the country in debating and building alternative pathways of national development. Its practice of rational deliberation and expertise presupposed the effective disenfranchisement of ordinary citizens and workers. It rendered the state less porous to capture by moneyed interests only by also making it less capable of serving as the site of a national self-reinvention and redirection. Guided democracy comported with an economy oriented to standardized production and with schools that prized passive learning and uncomplaining obedience over inspiration and disruption.

The heterodox account of East Asian success, without the critical tilt introduced by the preceding remarks about education and politics, amount to a straightforward application of the central message of development economics in the second half of the twentieth century. A critical understanding of that message can show us how to correct the heterodox view of the East Asian development experience. It can contribute as well to my argument about the institutional conditions of economic growth in the spirit of the association of fragmentary theory with radical reform.

The classical development economics to which I refer had its heyday in the forty-year period between the Second World War and the sovereign debt crises of the 1990s, from Arthur Lewis to Albert Hirschman. It saw itself as diverging from the practice of post-Marginalist economics both in its concern with the structure and structural transformation of the economy and in its acknowledgment of the state's central role in economic development. It took care, however, not to challenge directly the dominant style of economic analysis. It pursued instead a strategy of peaceful coexistence with the established analytic practice. We should attribute the later waning of its influence to its evasion of conflict rather than to its inadequate devotion to mathematical model building (a by-product of its interest in structure and structural change).

Classical development economics had a core doctrine. It taught that development depends on fundamentals and structural change, by which it meant primarily a change in the allocation of workers and capital from one sector to another.

The fundamentals are education and institutions. Education determines the skill set that workers bring to production. Institutions expressed in law determine the rules of the economic regime. Most important are the rules setting the terms on which individuals and firms can command resources and governing the relation of the state to such nonstate actors. In the long term, according to this core doctrine, fundamentals constrain economic growth.

A weakness of this part of the classical developmental message is that it had little to say about the content of either of the two categories of fundamentals. As a result, it failed to confront the troubling relation of each to the development experiences that it studied and sought to influence.

Standardized, Fordist mass production, the benchmark of economic advance for the central tradition of late-twentieth-century development economics, required little by way of formal education other than basic literacy and numeracy. What it chiefly demanded was hand–eye coordination and a willingness to take orders. It was only in the transition to a later experimentalist, knowledge-intensive practice of production that higher-order capabilities would become vital. Those capabilities could take hold outside a technological and managerial elite only if the experimentalist impulse set its mark on culture and politics, not just on the curriculum and the school.

Similarly, this development economics said both too much and too little about the institutional requirements of development. It said too much in accepting, as a requirement of development, the combination of a conventional market regime (organized on the basis of absolute property rights) and a state that intervened in this economic order to help create new comparative advantage. It failed to recognize that the market could be organized in different ways (as it later was, for example, in China). The most effective governmental activism might consist in the pursuit of such alternative regimes for the sake of a broadened access to opportunities and capabilities (as in the democratizing of agriculture and finance in early-nineteenth-century America).

The homage that classical development economics paid to the importance of education and institutions was no more than a preface to its chief message. In the log run, the fundamentals set limits to development. But in the short term development might be ignited and accelerated by transferring workers and resources from relatively less-productive to relatively more-productive sectors of the economy. "Less productive" largely meant agriculture. "More productive" meant industry.

The message had five parts. The first part of the message advised taking people and resources from agriculture and putting them in industry, which, in this historical context, was mass production. The second part of the message said to use the power of the state to orchestrate and accelerate this process. (Historians such as Alexander Gerschenkron supplied a demonstration of the central role that the state had always played in overcoming relative economic backwardness.[18]) The third part of the message counseled embedding the state-led transfer of workers and resources from agriculture to industry in a broader project of creating new comparative advantage in the world economy. As a consequence, the world economy was to be guardedly engaged in successive and deliberate steps and on terms that advance the power to create new comparative advantage. The fourth part of the message warned that the labor force must pass the modest educational threshold required by mass production. The fifth part of the message instructed that a state be established that is resistant enough to capture by the organized interests and supported enough by a professional bureaucracy to orchestrate this development process.

From the outset, there was a puzzle. Why accord exclusive priority to the transfer of workers and resources to industry rather than to the generalization throughout the economy of practices and technologies associated with the most advanced practice of production? In the aftermath of the first Industrial Revolution, such widespread dissemination had taken place. Every sector of production, including agriculture, had been changed on the model of the then most advanced practice, mechanized manufacturing.

Now, however, there is a more immediate objection to the favored prescription of development economics: it has simply stopped working. That prescription made two factual assumptions. Both have ceased to be valid.

The first assumption was the division of each economy into sectors, clearly separated from one other and distinguished by their relative productivity. Each sector was defined by a combination of what it produced with how it produced it. Manufacturing stood at the top of the hierarchy of productivity, thanks to the marriage of advancing technology with large-scale, standardized production.

The second premise provided the international counterpart to this view of the domestic economy. It described a world in which production was hierarchically distributed. Capital-intensive production, exemplified by industrial manufacturing, took place in the central economies. Labor-intensive production, represented by agriculture and low-level services and shops, was the business of developing economies.

The distinctions among sectors have begun to break down. Much of advanced manufacturing in the emerging, experimentalist knowledge economy represents crystallized services, and its products are often sold bundled together with services. The most productive agriculture has absorbed more and more science, as even the distinction between the natural and the synthetic becomes blurred. Yet this waning of the distinctions among sectors has so far failed to be followed by an economy-wide spread of the most advanced practices and technologies. In each of the traditional sectors—manufacturing, services, and agriculture—there emerges instead a vanguard of production, surrounded by a large periphery of more backward productive activity.

This vanguard has remained relatively insular. In even the richest countries, it excludes the vast majority of the labor force. It fails to export its practices and technologies to the rest of the production system.

Such a vanguard is present in all the major economies: China, India, and Brazil as well as the United States, Japan, Germany, and Britain. In each of them, however, it remains confined largely to an advanced network of firms. These firms exchange ideas, practices, and people with their counterparts around the world. However, although they sell their products and services widely, they fail to become, as mechanized manufacturing had been in the early industrializing countries, a model for the transformation of the whole economy.

Knowledge-intensive, flexible, experimentalist production should in principle be capable of even more rapid and universal propagation than mechanized manufacturing enjoyed in its day. It is not intrinsically connected to any sector. This universality, however, is deceptive.

The new advanced practice of production depends on a host of cognitive and social-moral conditions. Among these conditions are an education and a culture hospitable to permanent innovation and a high level of discretion and trust, sustained by cooperative competition among as well as within firms. Where these conditions are not spontaneously present, as they are not in most of economic life and in most places in the world, a combination of collective action and governmental initiative must create them or their functional equivalents. Part of such an initiative may consist in legal innovations. For example, laws exploiting the use of relational contracts and disaggregated, fragmentary property rights may be better suited to the forms of entrepreneurship and investment required by knowledge-intensive production.

In this context, the question suppressed by the orthodoxy of development economics becomes crucial. The relevant question is no longer how to transfer workers and resources from a less-productive sector to a more-productive one but how to generalize in the economy today's most advanced practice of production. The ideas that can help us in this project must do for us what Adam Smith's and Karl Marx's ideas did for their contemporaries: use the study of the most advanced practice of production as a provocation to revise and deepen the understanding of how the economy works and how it can change. For Smith, the most advanced practice of production was incipient mechanized manufacturing. For Marx, it was mass production in its earliest stage. For us, it is a form of production that transforms productive activity into a practice of permanent innovation and narrows the difference between the best firms or producers and the best schools.

This productive practice may loosen what has seemed to represent the single most unyielding constraint in economic life: the "law" of diminishing returns. In idea-filled, experimental production, this supposed law may be suspended or even reversed. It is a productive practice requiring a form of the technical division of labor that softens the distinctions among specialized roles at work as well as the contrast between making the plan of production and implementing it. The plan must be revised continuously in the course of being implemented. We have come to appreciate that this economic practice demands a moral culture of productive experimentalism, reflected in cognitive capabilities and reciprocal trust.

The study of this way of producing goods and service gives us reason to change our ideas about what in general makes one practice of production more advanced than another. In every historical epoch, the most advanced practice of production is not necessarily the most efficient one right now: the one that produces the greatest output with the fewest resources. It is the one that is most mindlike, that most enlists and resembles the imagination (the mind in its nonformulaic mode and in its capacity to outreach its habitual methods and defy its settled presuppositions), and that because of its imaginative character has the best chance of enhancing productivity and increasing output over time. In Smith's period, the most advanced practice of production was the mechanized manufacturing that he observed in the pin factory. In our age, it is the form of production that we mistake for high-technology industry but that has a potential home in every department of economic life.

Suppose that the knowledge-intensive economy remains confined, as it now is, to an insular part of each national economy, employing a minor part of the labor force. Imagine as well that each such vanguard continues to be dominated by a relatively small number of large firms surrounded by a periphery of smaller businesses that grow, fail, or are acquired. Then finance may continue to play a secondary role. The large firms will continue to fund production largely on the basis of their retained and reinvested earnings. Smaller advanced firms will continue to be supported by a venture-capital industry accounting for only a minute part of the activity of the capital markets even in the countries in which it is most developed. The great mass of backward small businesses will continue to rely on self-exploitation and family savings.

If, however, we suppose that the task is to spread the advanced practice of production widely throughout the economy for the sake of both growth and inclusion, finance will have a vital role to play: finance reimagined, reorganized, and enlisted in the service of production. Part of the programmatic aim of this book is to describe that role and to place its performance in the context of a broader set of institutional ideas and innovations.

The proximate target of the preceding criticism and revision of the message of twentieth-century development economics is the heterodox interpretation of the East Asian miracle. The ulterior target is the East Asian development experience itself: the revelation of its limits as a model to be emulated. The heterodox account was always a defense as well as an interpretation. If it departed from the free-market antistatist orthodoxy, it did so to vindicate what the East Asians had accomplished and to use their example in a worldwide polemic.

In his *Discourses*, Machiavelli deals with the relation between character and power. A leader may rise because his character—the rigidified form of his self, his habitual way of being and acting—suits the circumstance in which he finds himself. Then circumstances change, and he proves unable to change his character accordingly.

If for character we substitute the institutional regime and the conceptions of social life that it enacts, we can translate Machiavelli's problem about character and circumstance into a problem about the relation of a society and its development trajectory to the institutional regime in which it operates. Three crucial limitations in the Northeast Asian countries' development experience in this historical period need to be identified if we are to take that experience as an example to be emulated. All three limitations express the same problem anticipated in Machiavelli's remark. Moreover, for all three the task of organizing a transition to the knowledge economy gives to the problem a tangible focus.

The first limitation lies in the conception of industrial policy embraced by the Northeast Asian economies as an alternative to passive acceptance of the existing distribution of comparative advantage in the world economy. The state placed bets on the most promising sectors and conferred favors on firms in those sectors, typically in the form of subsidized credit. Taiwan, for example, placed bets on a broader ranger of businesses, including small and medium-size firms, than South Korea did. Even when the net was cast more widely, however, the state chose the way, albeit in consultation with the companies that it favored. To the extent that it chose the way rather than supporting a way chosen down below by the firms, it laid itself open to the twin evils of cronyism and dogmatism.

The more radical and accelerated the process of production becomes, the less we can hope to plot its course before it happens. Governmental initiative may be needed to help satisfy the conditions on which the knowledge-intensive economy depends; to broaden access to this economy's instruments of credit, technology, advanced practice, and knowledge; to bring this economy into closer contact with the markets around the world that will test it by a world benchmark; and to identify and help spread the organizational and technological innovations that have proved most successful. What the government should not do, on this understanding of its role, is to choose the sectors in which the advanced practice can take hold, except insofar as the new must be based on the available. The state should be bold about procedures but agnostic about sectors.

Industrial policy reinvented along the lines suggested by this criticism should be neither the arm's-length regulation of business by government (proposed by free-market ideology) nor the choice of direction favored by the Northeast Asian model. It must develop the way along the way, experimentally. Its outcome will not be a unitary trade and industrial policy, following a preset track. It will be pluralistic, resulting in a series of divergent experiments. It will be applicable to every part of the economy rather than to industry alone. And its appropriate agents on the side of government will be quasi-governmental organizations, professionally staffed and shielded from short-term, direct guidance by the political forces in power.

It follows that in finance such a practice of industrial policy cannot use subsidized credit as its preferred tool. Every form of credit rationing or credit dualism (separating a pool of benefited recipients from the rest, who must face the harsher terms of the general, residual capital market) imposes the preconceptions of the present on the unforeseen possibilities of the future. In so doing, it also opens itself up to a collusion between political and economic power that is threatening to democracy.

Financial deepening in all its forms must take the place of subsidized credit. That may include not just the active promotion of private venture capital and its kindred forms but also the mimicking of those forms by public and paragovernmental entities. Public or private ownership matters less than independence from political control; a pluralistic, experimentalist orientation; and testing by competition in the market. Prospective encouragement of entrepreneurial initiative must have as its complement competitive selection of the results of such entrepreneurial fervor. The fiercer the competition, the better. The agents of the state must not conduct themselves as long arms of the government in office. And the market whose competitive testing we should most value is the market democratized by institutional innovations like the ones explored in this book.

The deep problem underlying these criticisms and proposals is their dependence on a democratic state and a democratized market that do not yet exist. They need to be created as well along the way. The reinvention of industrial policy and the reorientation of finance invoked in these pages represent incidents in this larger project.

Two hundred and fifty years of ideological debate have led us to believe that the proper and inevitable axis of ideological controversy is a contest over the relative importance of the market and the state. The result of this debate is the thesis of institutionally conservative social democracy (in the European idiom) or of the regulated market economy (in the American one): the flaws of the market must be corrected by the state's regulatory and redistributive activity. The deeper, latent ideological contrast, the one on whose explication our economic and political progress depends, has a different character. It is the opposition between the market and the state as they are now established and the alternative economic and political arrangements that we are able to imagine and fashion with the institutional and conceptual materials at hand.

Faced with the claim that the market order embodies the virtues of experience, found through decentralized initiative, we must ask: Which market order? The relation of the market to the ideal of competitive searching and selection is not established by analytic inference; it is established by institutional reality and variation.

To the claim that the democratic state is, alongside economic and political thought, the legitimate locus for defining the institutional framework of the market economy and for expressing it as law, we must respond: Which state, and which democracy? To perform this role, the state must not be a dictatorial state in the grip of an authoritarian cadre, claiming to speak in the national interest, committed to its own power interests, and held at the mercy of its prejudices about the possible. Nor can it be a low-energy democracy that, because it keeps the populace at a low level of political engagement, inhibits the practice of radical reform and prevents local experiments from creating counter models of the national future. Such a low-energy democracy is porous to capture by organized interests, especially when they have money. The state's authority to revise the market economy's institutional framework is proportional to the deepening of democratic politics.

These remarks signal the other two major deficiencies of the East Asian development experience as a model propitious to the experimentalist knowledge economy and deserving of emulation. They have to do with education or, more broadly, with consciousness and culture and with democracy or the lack of it. For the development model to be self-correcting rather than a straitjacket rendered costly and dangerous by changing circumstance, an experimentalist impulse must take root in every department of social life.

This impulse must have a friend in education: not any education, but the analytical, selective, cooperative, and dialectical education to which I earlier referred. As technical schooling, its focus falls on generic capabilities rather than on job-specific and machine-specific skills. As general education, it approaches every field from contrasting points of view the better to dissolve the forced marriage between method and subject matter and to free the mind from the stranglehold of academic orthodoxy. Intellectual conformity is poison to practical innovation.

The political limitation of the East Asia development experience was its association with tame, guided democracy or outright authoritarianism. The constraint on the deepening of democracy supplied the political basis for the imposition of unitary industrial and trade policy and for collusion between the state and business. Indeed, the dependence of this practice of economic policy on the containment or suppression of democracy has often been invoked, in the open or under veil, as reason to keep democracy in check.

Our progress in economic life, as everywhere else, depends on relativizing the difference between habitual action within an institutional and ideological framework and the piecemeal but cumulative remaking of the framework. As a consequence, the radicalization of democracy, despite its short-term costs and dangers, becomes the indispensable counterpart to the quickening of practical innovation. Part of the core meaning of democracy is to prevent the structure of society from remaining beyond the reach of collective challenge and choice. It is to carry the experimentalist attitude from the micro to the macro and to create a politics designed to unfreeze both the state and society.

It has formed no part of my purpose to argue that the Northeast Asian countries of today, authors and beneficiaries of a mid- and late-twentieth-century development "miracle," remain wedded to the formula explained and defended by the heterodox account of their success. In all of them—certainly in Japan, South Korea, and Taiwan—the inadequacy of the previous model as a basis for the knowledge economy was widely recognized at the time this book was written. The clash between the orthodox and the heterodox explanations of their recent ascent no longer speaks to their predicament.

These countries see the revolutionary potential of the knowledge economy diminished by its confinement to vanguards excluding the vast majority of the labor force. They must face the limitations that a surplus of conformity and a deficit of democracy place on their hopes of national renewal. In all these respects, they have become like the rest of us in other parts of the world.

The United States, China, and Brazil in the Early Twenty-First Century: The Evasion of Structural Change and Its Consequences for the Real Economy and for Finance

I conclude these re-readings of history in the light of the ideas developed in this book with a comparison of some aspects of Chinese, Brazilian, and American economic experience in the early twenty-first century, in the years immediately before and after the financial crisis of 2007–2009. The central theme of my remarks is the way in which each of these countries has evaded the task of changing its economic institutions the better to achieve the widely professed goal of socially inclusive economic growth. In each of these countries, the failure of finance to serve the real economy more fully exemplifies and reinforces this evasion. In each of them, the limitations of politics and thought have proved decisive in accounting for the result.

The evasion of structural change exacts an immeasurable toll in the belittlement of humanity. Economic growth over the past two hundred years has improved human life to an extent that is hard to overstate.

Nonetheless, every society continues to witness a tragic mismatch between the intensity of human ambition and the severity of the belittlement to which most people remain subject. Part of this belittlement consists in the diminishment of their ability to reshape their own circumstances. Each of the three countries compared here, with respect to certain aspects of their recent economic evolution, is a world seething with initiative and vitality. In each of them—even the richest and the freest—the great majority of ordinary men and women find themselves confined and dragged down. They lack the equipment and the opportunity to build a larger life.

What results is a squandering of human potential on a massive scale. This dissipation is an economic calamity as well as a moral and political evil. To limit agency, or the power of constructive initiative, of the mass of ordinary people is to deprive us all of what they could have accomplished with adequate equipment and opportunity. Here, rather than in a blind clash of ideological commitments, lies the significance of the evasion of structural change.

I approach the Chinese, Brazilian, and American variants of this evasion in four steps: from the perspective of trade and each country's place in the world economy; from the standpoint of the institutional and educational requirements of socially inclusive economic growth and of the economy-wide spread of the most advanced practice of production; from the angle of the role of finance in the evasion and its avoidance; and from the vantage point of the sources of the evasion in politics and in thought.

Trade as an Escape from Structural Change

Integration into the world economy and the consequent expansion of trade can serve to strengthen the institutional innovations—democratizing the market and tightening the link between finance and the real economy—for which I have argued. In China, Brazil, and the United States, they have on the contrary provided a temporary reprieve from the need to undertake such innovations.

The export-led growth strategy pursued by China in recent decades has made it possible to postpone the deepening of the internal market. In principle, no opposition exists between production for the home market and production for the world, just as there is no contradiction between export-oriented growth and growth reliant on import substitution. Production for the world market, however, can also compensate for the thinness of the domestic market.

So it has happened in contemporary China. However, the use of foreign trade has depended on the suppression of internal demand and on the willingness of foreign countries to continue to engage with China, even when trade productive of massive imbalances in the current and capital accounts is not economically or politically sustainable. For the United States in the recent historical period of the early twenty-first century, it has meant compensating Chinese trade and capital surpluses with American trade and industrial deficits. For Brazil, it has meant exporting to the Chinese relatively untransformed agricultural and mining commodities and receiving manufactured goods in return.

The reorientation of China's growth strategy to producing for internal consumption is no mere technical reallocation of resources. It cannot be achieved suddenly and by decree. It requires large-scale redistribution among classes, regions, and sectors. The resulting distributive conflict needs to be politically managed. The precise trajectory of national development has to be debated and discovered. Such a collective process strains the limits of an authoritarian state, uncertain of its ability to contain or guide strife. The export orientation of economic growth, while it lasted, had allowed the masters of the state to exempt themselves from the demands of this work.

For the past several decades, Brazil has pursued a development strategy with two bases: the popularization of consumption and the production and export of commodities. Millions of people were lifted out of poverty thanks to rises in the real wage, conditional cash-transfer programs, and the expansion of consumer credit. Agriculture, ranching, and mining paid the bill. China became Brazil's biggest foreign market as the Brazil suffered, like many another middle-income developing economy, what has come to be described as "premature deindustrialization."

It was an old story in Brazilian history: looking in nature rather than in the mind for easy riches. Nothing prevented the production and export of commodities from helping finance a redirection of the economy or from absorbing increasing amounts of science and technology. In fact, the country used them as an easy way out.

I remarked earlier on the asymmetry between democratizing demand and democratizing supply. The former can dispense with institutional innovation; the latter, because it deals with the organization of economic opportunity and educational empowerment, cannot. Thus, the export to China (as well as to other parts of the world) of relatively untouched natural resources and agricultural produce became part of the background to a national abdication: the failure to follow the democratization of demand with the democratization of supply.

In the United States since the late 1970s, there has been a severely regressive redistribution of income. The country had developed, especially since the Second World War, a market in mass-consumption goods. Mass consumption drove economic growth. There was a manifest contradiction between these two historical tendencies. The contradiction was resolved by a massive expansion of credit, especially to households. A fake credit democracy usurped the place of a property-owning democracy.

There was extraordinary innovation in the vanguard of production, much of it identified with high-technology manufacturing and services. Most of the economy, however, failed to share in this culture of innovation, even when it used the gadgets and services produced by high-technology industry. The country had simply stopped producing enough goods and services that the rest of the world wanted.

Just as the massive expansion of internal debt reconciled mass consumption with regressive income redistribution, trade and capital deficits—especially in the relation of the United States to China—sustained consumption. Possession of the world's reserve currency made it easier than it would otherwise have been for the United States to maintain these deficits.

The confinement of the most advanced practices and technologies of production to a relatively small part of the economy and the aggravation of inequality condemned the country to a debt-based and credit-fueled course of economic growth. Financial hypertrophy, preying on the opportunities that exuberant leverage permitted, rendered the economy more susceptible to breakdowns, such as the financial and economic crisis of 2007–2009.

The alternative would have been a national agenda addressed to the supply side of the economy rather than just successive doses of stimulus administered to the demand side. If such a program were designed to enhance the productivity of the economy by democratizing access to economic opportunities and educational capabilities, it would have reversed the regressive redistribution of income at the same time that it increased the productivity of labor.

For the United States, as for Brazil, the character of its integration into world economy, most acutely revealed in its trading and capital relation to China, served to avoid confronting the work of structural change.

Economic Growth and the Failure to Spread the Most Advanced Practice of Production

In this same period, a debate took place in the United States about the slowdown in the rate of growth and, most momentously, in the rise of both labor productivity and total factor productivity. This discussion renewed Irwin Fisher's thesis of "secular stagnation" in the 1930s. As in that decade, many causes were cited; to a large extent, in fact, they were the same causes. Among them were the declining rate of population growth, the inadequacy of demand, and, most insistently, the slowing of technological evolution: the alleged lack of inventions comparable in the reach of their consequences to those made in earlier periods of economic growth. The outcome was overdetermined, according to these accounts, and made to look natural—that is to say, independent of political choices and institutional directions.

The invocation of technological slowdown failed to reckon with the changing relation between technology and its context of use. Mechanized manufacturing, the technology and practice of the original Industrial Revolution, served as a model that rapidly left its imprint on every part of the economy. It consisted of a small set of machines, such as machine-cutting lathes, performing repetitive operations. Under mechanized manufacturing, the worker was set to work as if he were one of his machines, performing a highly specialized task repetitively. It was a characteristic that industrial mass production, the immediate sequel to early mechanized manufacturing, preserved.

This model was easy to imitate and to reproduce in one part of economic life after another. It demanded from the mass of workers little by way of discretion or capability. Hierarchical discipline and obedience could take the place of trust. Command and control preempted the space of discretion. In his machinelike role, the worker needed hand–eye coordination and a willingness to obey and suffer silently more than he required ingenuity or flexibility. These facts also explain why well into the twentieth century a reliance on manufacturing seemed able repeatedly to help an economy perform the miracle of rapid convergence to richer countries.

As technology advances, it ceases to lend itself to the standardized simplification of machine tools and the capabilities of those who use them. Its characteristic machines, such as the robots and three-dimensional printers of the present, as well as its information and communication devices have a much more indeterminate use. The more the worker becomes the opposite of the machine, the better he can realize its potential. What we have learned to repeat we express in a formula. What we have expressed in a formula we embody in the machine. It does what we have already learned how to repeat, so that we who use the machine can focus on the not yet repeatable. Then and only then can the combination of worker and machine become immensely more powerful than either the worker or the machine alone.

The more technology advances, the more it becomes an open-ended materialization of science rather than just a set of rigid gadgets, the physical residues of past discoveries. Its relation to its social and cultural context becomes more intimate. Its dependence on higher-order cognitive capabilities and on a distinctive moral culture resembling the moral culture of science grows. At their best, the cooperative practices for using technology in production begin to resemble the cooperative practices for inventing and developing it.

In such a circumstance, the economic significance of technology depends on the fulfillment of the cognitive and social conditions for its full use. Workers must be able to profit from a wide margin of discretion. They must share in the ongoing revision of the production plan and rearrange with their work teams both the plan's practices and its machines. Production must take place in a collective setting dense enough in the bonds of association to permit a heightening of reciprocal trust. There must be a legal framework useful to cooperative competition within and among firms and to decentralized strategic coordination between firms and governments. Such a legal framework will, for example, develop the law of disaggregated property rights and relational contracts.

The more such conditions are satisfied, the greater the ability to achieve the potential of the practices and technologies of experimental, knowledge-intensive production. The same conditions that make it possible to realize the potential of the most advanced practice of production also facilitate its propagation beyond the boundaries of an isolated vanguard to wide parts of the economy. A close connection exists between the radicalization of a new paradigm of production and the scope of its application: the more radical the realization, the wider the scope.

We are then driven to inquire into the features of society, culture, and politics, making it more or less likely that these conditions will be fulfilled. To make it more likely, there must be a change in the character of education for the mass of ordinary people, not just for an elite. An experimentalist attitude must be promoted and established in every part of social life. And democracy must be deepened through the development of political institutions exposing the structure of society to challenge and revision.

The motivation for these wider changes lies in the appeal of socially inclusive economic growth. It also lies more fundamentally in the enhancement of agency: ordinary men's and women's power to make more of their lives. The commitment to strengthen agency is the point at which the economic goals of a democratic society most clearly join its political and spiritual aspirations: prosperity becomes part of a larger attempt by the mass of ordinary men and women to lift themselves to a higher level of capability and experience.

The new technologies and practices were less revolutionary than the inventions of earlier historical periods; they were more revolutionary. It is that the new practice of production was neither radicalized nor widely disseminated in the American economy. It remained arrested within the confines of a productive vanguard that exchanged people, resources, and practices with similar vanguards in other parts of the world. In the absence of the conditions that I have described, it failed to serve as a model for the transformation of the whole economy.

The United States was at this time the most important base of knowledge-intensive production in the world. The confinement of this knowledge-rich productive practice to a relatively insular part of the economy was not a uniquely American failing. It was the American expression of a worldwide problem. The solution to this problem, through cumulative institutional innovations and redirections of policy, would have provided the heart of a strategy of socially inclusive economic growth. It would also have given direction and focus to the loose set of ideas about investment in infrastructure, education, and renewable energy that have stood as proxies for a national strategy of economic growth in recent American history.

To the extent that the United States had any realized strategy of economic growth in this period, it was easy money. Its agent was the central bank rather than the national government. Successive doses of expansionary monetary policy had increasingly less effect on economic growth. The Federal Reserve pursued its heroic effort to wring short-term benefits out of cheap money. It did so even at the cost of indifference to the term structure of the interest rate; a flattened yield curve added to the obstacles in the way of sustainable and broad-based economic growth. The most tangible consequence of easy money was to inflate asset values, all to the benefit of the moneyed classes. There was no structural project, no progressive approach to the supply side of the economy, and therefore no attempt to give socially inclusive shape to the knowledge economy.

In a different form and setting, China in this period also saw the emergence of experimentalist, knowledge-intensive production. Advanced manufacturing, together with the services that it used, produced, or sold, represented a small part of the production system. It absorbed an even smaller portion of the labor force. It existed as a satellite of the defense-industrial complex, as a minor participant in the export zones, and as a provider of services to the richest part of the population. At the margin, it entered into standard areas of industry, as with the mini–steel mills. Much of the service economy, agriculture, and even industrial production remained almost entirely untouched by the most advanced productive practice.

In becoming the industrial workshop of the world, China had mainly placed its bet on belated Fordist mass production for the making and export of tradable goods. It therefore continued to rely largely on routinized, machinelike labor, profiting from a real wage much lower than the return to labor in the rich North Atlantic economies.

Yet there was a vast low-level institutional experimentation in the country: countless instances of new ways of associating the public and private sectors as well as of associating firms with one another. These innovations were incongruously forced into the private-law vessels that China had imported wholesale from Germany. Many of these institutional experiments were motivated by the attempt to reconcile the realities of an economy in which the central state and local government played a major role and the market order and private law were built on the conventional Western model. As time went on, the tendency was for these experimental anomalies to wane. They could have served as points of departure for the development of a market economy organized differently from the North Atlantic system. They instead served for the most part as a way to grant corporate personality to entities, like the township–village enterprises, with no close counterparts in European market economies. Having been incorporated under the law, these entities could trade in the market. The agents were new. The market regime in which they traded was not.

Much of the transformative opportunity presented by China's turn to the market was wasted. In another political and intellectual context, the experimental forms of economic activity (such as township–village enterprises) that abounded in China could have been used to build a different kind of market order. Chinese arrangements could have provided initial institutional equipment for the organization of cooperative competition among small and medium-size firms as well as for stake holding by local governments and collective organizations in productive enterprise. Such legal and institutional innovations could have served as points of departure for the construction of a democratized market regime in the interest of the majority of the Chinese people.

One of the goals of such a regime would have been to prevent the turn to the market in China from resulting in extreme concentration of income and wealth. Another would have been to begin creating the conditions under which a larger part of the labor force could participate in the most advanced practice of production. That would have meant avoiding the confinement of knowledge-intensive production to insular vanguards, associated in China with export-oriented advanced manufacturing.

Such alternatives would not have suppressed the market economy. They would have created from the bottom up, piece by piece and step by step, a different market economy, just as the Americans had done in agriculture and finance in the first half of the nineteenth century. The path to alternatives of this kind, however, was barred in China by limitations on politics and on thought, to which I return at the end of this chapter.

In Brazil, as in the United States and China, the future of socially inclusive economic growth depended on a progressive approach to the supply side of the economy. The heart of the industrial system, established in the southeastern region of the country in the middle of the twentieth century, was an instance of belated Fordist mass production. Although the state had a major position in basic industry, foreign multinational firms dominated the consumer-goods industries. These firms copied, without radical innovation, products that they already produced at home and in other parts of the world. They sold those products to the relatively privileged part of the population. Brazilian industry remained competitive only on the basis of restraints on the return to labor and produced mainly for the domestic market.

I earlier described the growth strategy that Brazil adopted in the early years of the twenty-first century—one driven by mass consumption and paid for by the production and export of commodities. When commodity prices were high, there was a costly appreciation of the currency; when prices collapsed, growth stalled. Monetary and fiscal stimulus, provided under the aegis of vulgar Keynesianism, gave only brief reprieve.

The exhaustion of this approach to economic growth presented the country with the task of reinventing its industrial base in a circumstance in which the rigid hierarchy of sectors favored by classical development economics no longer made sense. Instead of the distinction, presumed by that economics, between a relatively more-productive and transformative industry (mass production) and a relative less-productive and more-retrograde agriculture and services, there was now in every part of the Brazilian economy a distinction between a front line of production, working at the global benchmark, and a vast periphery of more backward production.

The vanguard had achieved a relatively greater presence in scientific, precision agriculture than in industry or services. Advanced manufacturing and the services from which it could not usefully be distinguished existed in a small number of firms in a few places in the country as well as in the technical schools of a quasi-governmental system, devoted to the skills required by advanced manufacturing. Such economic and educational initiatives remained barely more than an elite fringe.

There were then two tasks of industrial reconstruction. The first, easier, and more familiar job was to hasten the passage beyond belated Fordism to experimentalist, knowledge-intensive production in the industrial heartland of the country. Central and local government could help provide access to capital as well as to advanced technology and practice. In the absence, however, of more radical institutional

innovation, the result of such efforts would have at best been to reproduce in Brazil something like the relatively quarantined vanguards
established in the richest economies—their Silicon Valleys.

The other, less-familiar, and more-difficult task was to organize
outside the industrial centers of the country a direct passage from pre-
Fordist to post-Fordist production, without the need to pine in the pur-
gatory of belated Fordism. The rest of the country did not need first to
turn into the Sao Paulo of the mid–twentieth century in order to become something else later. The areas with the best chance of enlisting
in such a movement were those in which property was more widely
distributed, local government had most strongly committed to an an-
alytically oriented education, general and technical schools were oriented to analytic capabilities, and a small-business culture coexisted
with a tradition of craft labor. The agent would then not need to be
invented, only to be equipped.

The Brazilian state and its paragovernmental extension, inherited
from the Vargas period, had instruments to support such a transformation of practice (SEBRAE, the small-business organization), of technology (EMBRAPI), of technical education (the SENAI system as well
as the network of Federal Technical Schools) and of finance (the public
banks, including the enormous National Bank of Economic and Social Development). These and other instruments, however, had so
far failed to be brought together under the umbrella of an attempt to
build a socially inclusive form of experimental knowledge-intensive
production.

To develop beyond its initial stages, such a project would have required an institutional content of the kind outlined in my discussion
of the East Asian development experience. The firms would have needed
to be able to compete and cooperate with another at the same time.
They would also have had to work with local and national governments
acting as enablers of experimentalism, organizing access to capital, technology, and advanced practice, and spreading the example of what had
worked best.

What began as a change in policy could continue beyond its initial
stages only through institutional reconstruction. The task was to reshape the market economy in its legal vocabulary and syntax as well as
in its social and economic consequences. Such changes in law would
have included innovations in public law that converted the corporatist
legacy of the Vargas years (such as the entrepreneurial associations and

their technical schools), originally designed to organize society under the guidance of the government, into an instrument of uncontrolled experiments in production from below, anchored in the world of small and medium business.

They would also have required innovations in private law. Some of these innovations would have developed the law of incomplete relational contracts, central to the practices of cooperative competition. Others would give form to disaggregated, fragmentary property rights, facilitating the coexistence of multiple stakes, held by different kinds of stakeholders (investors, workers, social organizations, and local and national governments) in the same productive resources. Institutional innovation expressed in law is the chief tool of radical reform.

Squandering the Productive Potential of Finance

I now use a comparative discussion of the role of finance in recent American, Brazilian, and Chinese experience as an opportunity to bring together the main elements of the discussion of finance in this book. It is a view calculated to seize a transformative opportunity. I begin by returning, in the light of the arguments of this book, to the three enigmas about finance that I first described in the introduction.[19] I then go on to consider the recent financial experience of these three countries in the light of ideas about the most promising solution to these enigmas in practice as well as in theory.

The first and fundamental enigma is the surprisingly loose relation of finance to the real economy. One hundred years ago in the United States as well as in Germany and other major European economies, high finance and its masters played a leading role in the control and sometimes the development of big business. In *The Theory of Economic Development*, Joseph Schumpeter described the banker—by which he meant the European or American merchant banker—as the "ephor" of the economy: a magistrate deciding the path of economic evolution. "The money market," he wrote, "is always, as it were, the headquarters of the capitalist system, from which orders go out to its individual divisions."[20] In retrospect, we see that this description was always exaggerated; it disregarded the extent to which, even then, the production system was largely self-financed.

Now, however, a hundred years later, in all the largest economies in the world, including the American and the European, even the semblance of such a role has dissolved. The share of finance in profits and in talents has increased. Autonomous finance—the world of the investment and commercial banks, private-equity firms, hedge funds, and asset managers—answers for a major portion of business profits and attracts a disproportionate part of the graduates of the elite universities.

Yet every empirical study has confirmed that well more than 80 percent of the funding of production is internally generated. Private firms' retained and reinvested earnings largely finance productive activity in every developed contemporary economy. The production system and autonomous finance are separate worlds that intersect at particular points and moments. The intersection is just as likely to be driven by a large firm's attempts to share in the gains of autonomous finance or to limit its exposure to the capital markets as it is by an effort to obtain external funding for the creation of new assets. If, for example, a company issues bonds or otherwise borrows to finance the buy-back of its own stock and even to take the business private, it does not go to the capital markets to finance production.

Some financial activities (such as initial public offerings, venture-capital investment, mezzanine finance, and bond issues for the purpose of financing new capacity) may make direct contributions to the expansion of output or the enhancement of productivity. However, they represent a very small portion of financial activity. However, the financial activities that make no such direct contribution, such as the trading of shares in the stock markets, are alleged to make an indirect contribution: for example, by establishing a benchmark of value by which companies might borrow for production if they need and want to do so.

This theoretical invocation of indirect effects conceals the enigma requiring explanation: that the preponderance of financial activity does not have the growth of output or productivity of firms and workers as either its purpose or its consequence. On the contrary, it uses productive enterprise as an occasion or as a basis for financial gain. What is the point of all of that capital stored in the banks, stock markets, and pension systems if not to finance production as well as consumption, supporting successive breakthroughs in the constraints on supply and on demand?

The default way of explaining and defending this reality is to insist that productive enterprise depends on capital markets that establish value in productive assets even when they fail directly to support the expansion of output or the improvement of productivity. The extravagant development of autonomous finance is, on this account, a price that we pay for the setting of a price on such assets. Its dangers are to be mastered by appropriate regulation.

The weight of this defense, however, rests on denying the possibility or the usefulness of arrangements that would enlist finance more effectively in the service of production. Such arrangements would, in the language that I have used here, make finance a good servant rather than a bad master. The response to the enigma, in practice as well as in theory, lies in changing the arrangements that govern finance and shape its relation to production. The thesis of wide and decisive institutional variation in the organization of finance and its relation to the real economy is not simply a programmatic and conjectural idea about the future; it is also a descriptive and explanatory view of the past: events such as the development of a local banking network in nineteenth-century America or of universal banks in nineteenth-century Europe changed the relation of finance to the real economy.

The first enigma, like the other two and like every conception or conundrum about the arrangements of society and the economy, has to do with something that people made and that they could make differently. We do not fully understand our own creations and often fail to grasp their unintended consequences or their unrecognized conditions. To treat them, however, as if they were natural phenomena that we are powerless to change, mistaking the local for the universal and the circumstantial for the eternal, is to reenact the essential form of mystification in our ideas about the economy and society.

A second enigma is the seemingly asymmetrical relation of finance to the real economy. When finance has a loose relation to production, the exaggeration that finance is largely indifferent to the real economy in good times but destructive in bad times takes on a disconcerting truth. When financial activity is not shaken by crisis, it contributes less to the expansion of output and the enhancement of productivity than the supposed function of finance would lead us to expect. When, however, there is a financial crisis of significant scale, the crisis regularly harms real economic activity. How are we to understand this apparent contradiction, and what are we to do about it?

There are three main mechanisms by which turmoil in the financial system may depress real economic activity. The first two mechanisms are relatively straightforward; the third is more diffuse but may have the greatest impact. None of the three contradicts the thesis that finance makes only a limited contribution to production under current arrangements.

The first mechanism is the deleveraging effect. During the many financial crises that have as a cause the run-up of household and corporate debt, households and firms try to improve their balance sheets by rapidly deleveraging, with the foreseeable impact on consumption and investment.

The second mechanism is the asset effect. The restraint on demand and investment, together with the fall in confidence among both consumers and investors, will result in a sellout in the stock market. The fall in the market value of firms and consequently in the retirement accounts and portfolios of individuals will in turn tend to result in higher unemployment and lower consumption and investment.

The third mechanism is what we might call the context-of-doing-business effect. If the crisis is significant enough to cause the occurrence or the prospect of the failure of major financial organizations, all business activity, by firms and households alike, will come under a restraint of caution and retrenchment. The flow of funds as well as the circulation of goods and services will be disturbed and inhibited.

All three mechanisms can exert an influence without negating the limited nature of the help that finance may give to productive activity. Finance in such a circumstance enjoys a destructive power that is disproportionate to its constructive uses.

Like the larger conundrum of the relation of finance to the real economy, this second problem must be solved in practice, not in theory, and must be solved in the same way. No change of arrangements will ever altogether suppress financial volatility. Finance works in an institutional context that it may barely shape and is exposed to political and economic forces that it cannot control. The resource with which it works, liquid capital, lends itself, by virtue of its liquidity, to bearing the imprint of swings of fear and greed, despondency and hope, anticipations of calamity and prophecies of enrichment.

Nevertheless, it has been a recurrent thesis of this book that financial deepening moderates the susceptibility of finance to periodic breakdown. Real economic activity in a complex economy is by its nature broken up into a world of many parts and many agents, with their own trajectories and circumstances. At any moment, some of these parts and agents prosper and others fail. It is a diversification imposed by economic reality. But the more finance retreats from the discipline and the diversity of the real economy, the more unstable it becomes.

A preliminary to this solution is the rejection of the strategy of regulatory dualism—the dominant approach to the regulation of finance in the past few decades: the division of financial activity is divided into a thickly regulated sector and a thinly regulated sector, the latter also known as shadow banking. We have seen that the supposed justification for this approach is an argument about the appropriate and inappropriate occasions for legal paternalism: the financial professionals and high-network individuals who populate the thinly regulated sector can take care of themselves. The consequence, however, is the reappearance in the thinly regulated sector, under different labels, of the products and services forbidden to the thickly regulated sector.

The repudiation of regulatory dualism would need to be accompanied by regulatory and tax changes discouraging or prohibiting financial activities that make no plausible contribution to the expansion of output or to the improvement of productivity while encouraging those that do. (For example, option contracts in commodity markets help solve practical problems: continuity of supply and liquidity. But what practical problem of the real economy do option contracts in financial markets help solve?)

A third enigma concerns the paradoxical relation between the relative indifference of much financial activity to the real economy and the vital importance of finance to the creation of the new: new assets, especially when they are made in new ways. The established production system may to a large extent be able to finance itself on the basis of the retained and reinvested earnings of established firms. Innovators cannot. For them, finance is indispensable. As our economic prospects come to depend ever more on the rapidity and reach of innovation, the organization of finance becomes even more important than it is in an economy in which most of production can take financial care of itself— where firms treat external finance as a source of additional gain rather than as a requirement for continuing to do business.

A reading of economic history helps bring this third enigma into focus. In the first period of economic history, the main constraint on economic growth was the size of the surplus over current consumption. Adam Smith, Karl Marx, and many other thinkers treated this constraint as decisive even in the economies that they observed around them. For Marx, the need for the coercive extraction of a surplus over current consumption was the basic reason—reason as explanation and reason as justification—for the existence of a class system. Only when economic progress overcame scarcity would the coercive extraction of a surplus cease to be necessary.

Smith and Marx were mistaken. Only in the most primitive societies is the size of the surplus the overriding constraint on economic growth. Very early in the economic history of humanity, the principal constraint became the level of technological, organizational, and institutional innovation. We can think of technology itself as the combined expression of our experiments, supported by science, in harnessing nature and our experiments in changing the way we cooperate in work. It was not because Britain saved more than, say, Ming–Ching China (historical evidence suggests that it saved relatively less) that it became the first seat of a revolutionary acceleration in economic growth that has since come to embrace most of the world. It was because Britain underwent innovations that began vastly to increase its capabilities of production. (Keynes was later to teach that savings is more the consequence than the cause of growth, a teaching that in turn needs to be qualified by recognition of the strategic role that a heightened saving level may play in allowing a country to embark on a rebellious course of national development.)

In the second period of economic growth, which encompasses almost the whole history of civilization, economic life is under the constraint of diminishing returns. If any regularity of economic life, in which everything is mutable because dependent on structures of our making, deserves to be considered lasting and universal, it is the constraint of diminishing returns.

We may now have reached the threshold of a third period in economic history, in which production, rather than just being supported by science and embodied in technology, begins to become the materialization of our scientific insights. The three-dimensional printer, drastically shortening the distance between conception and execution, is a telling example of this change. That most constant feature of economic law, the law of diminishing returns, is suspended or even reversed as the knowledge economy comes to be characterized by expanding returns: the more ideas are materialized in experimentalist, knowledge-rich production, the easier it may be to come by even more such enacted ideas.

From this perspective, world economic history is the history of innovation resulting or failing to result in the acceleration of economic growth through the quickening of growth in productivity.

Now suppose that by a rough approximation we divide the economies in this period of economic history into two worlds with respect to the role of finance. What these two worlds have in common is that both depend only modestly on the support of what I have called autonomous or external finance: lending or investment by lenders or investors external to the firm. There is the world of large established firms, reliant primarily on their own earnings for the financing of production. And there is the world of small business, dependent on self-exploitation and family savings.

These two worlds may be able to operate with a modicum of access to external finance. But something remains outside of them, as I argued in the introduction: the new businesses that would create new assets in new ways, the agents of innovation. It is these new businesses that can least dispense with external finance. They can rely neither on retained earnings (which do not yet exist at all or exist in the requisite amount) nor on self-exploitation (because the translation of science into new technology, wedded to new business models, to make new products and services requires capital). It is not efficiency-enhancing, capital-sparing innovation that concerns them. It is productivity-raising, capital-intensive innovation.

External finance may be replaced over much of economic life largely by the internal funding of production in established large firms and by self-exploitation and family savings in small business. It cannot, however, be replaced in the funding of innovation, at least insofar as innovation is made by emerging firms—start-ups and other young businesses. Schumpeter saw monopolies and oligopolies as the chief agents of innovation in the economy. A simple inspection of historical stock-market charts, however, shows that most of the innovative large firms of today did not exist fifty years ago or were then struggling small young firms dependent on external finance.

Yet the financial activities devoted to innovation by emergent firms, such as venture capital, represent a tiny part of finance as a whole. The enigma, restated, is why the part of finance most important to the future represents in the existing economies an inconsequential portion of financial activity.

Let us now connect this observation with the earlier argument about the overriding significance of propagating the most advanced practice of production—now the practice characteristic of experimentalist, knowledge-intensive production—throughout the economy. Such a diffusion has to be organized, and it has to be financed by some combination of private and governmental initiative. That combination must in turn be given institutional and legal form.

The estrangement of finance from production matters in the end for this reason: it leaves unaccomplished the task that I have just described. A simple criterion by which to judge the benefits of innovation in the law governing finance and shaping its relation to the real economy is that it helps do this indispensable work.

Neither the state nor the market, including the capital market, as now organized, is designed to accomplish this task. The state is prey to dogma and easily bent to the promotion of the powerful private interests that may hold it captive. It is tempted, for example, to decide which lines of production may represent the future or serve as a basis for new comparative advantage in the world economy. The market is oriented to existing firms, demands, and opportunities and heavily discounts the future.

Our best chance is to work on the problem from both ends. At one end, we may develop liability, tax, and regulatory rules discouraging trading and speculative activity unrelated to production and to innovation. At the other end, we may use the state's power and resources to establish quasi-governmental entities, under professional management and subject to the market's competitive discipline. Such entities would mimic private venture capital and its kindred forms, partner with private firms when feasible and useful, take equity stakes in businesses to the point that these paragovernmental funds become self-financing, and resist the pull of short-term gain. In such initiatives and inventions, our principle will be the same as our method: devotion to a radical experimentalism.

Consider now, in the light of these reflections, some aspects of the recent history of finance in the United States, Brazil, and China.

In 2006, in the run-up to the subsequent crisis. the financial sector was responsible for 8.3 percent of U.S. GDP. It had been 4.9 percent in 1980 and 2.8 percent in 1950. At the high point in the early 2000s, it absorbed around 40 percent of all corporate profits earned by American business. Even now it takes about 30 percent. In 2008, with the crisis already in full swing, 28 percent of the graduates of Harvard College went into financial services upon graduation. A similar development took place in other North Atlantic economies, especially the United Kingdom and Canada. Yet as the British regulator Adair Turner, with intimate knowledge of finance, wrote later, "There is no clear evidence that growth in the scale and complexity of the financial system in the rich developed world over the last 20 to 30 years has driven increased growth and stability, and it is possible for financial growth to extract rents from the real economy rather than to deliver economic value."[21]

Nevertheless, as the size of the financial sector grew and it absorbed more and more of the nation's talent, its influence on the direction of the economy and the organization of big business diminished—strikingly by comparison to what it had been a hundred years early at the time of J. P. Morgan and the trusts. Private equity developed as a means to profit from the undervaluation of corporate assets rather than as an instrument to open up new ways of making and delivering goods and services.

The largest and most successful corporations in the country maintained vast pools of liquid capital at home and abroad. They financed their development by drawing on that ever replenished reservoir of earnings. They went to the capital markets for the most part to share in the profits of finance external to nonfinancial firms or to diminish through buybacks of their stock their future exposure to the market in corporate control. From the standpoint of big business, autonomous or external finance—finance not internalized in the firm— became a sideshow offering additional opportunities for gain. It did little to contribute to the expansion of output or the improvement of productivity.

Small businesses continued to turn for credit mainly to the country's remarkable network of local banks, the legacy of a much earlier historical period. These local commercial banks were generally unable and unwilling to provide long-term finance to innovative, risky start-up business. They were forbidden by law from taking equity stakes in them.

As in the whole world and throughout history, small enterprise continued to depend largely on self-exploitation and family savings even more than on bank credit. Those who worked in small business typically faced extra hours at lower pay (than for comparable work in the economy at large). Self-exploitation did for small business what retained and reinvested earnings did for the large established firms.

There was a vibrant culture of emergent firms—start-ups and young, smaller companies—marrying advanced technology to new business models and requiring external capital for their development. They occupied an insular vanguard of knowledge-intensive experimental production thinly linked to the rest of the economy and the labor force. Moreover, they dealt with a part of finance—venture capital, including venture capital run by the large firms themselves (e.g., Google Ventures) that amounted to a minute portion of overall financial activity.

The venture capitalist might claim that there was, if anything, an excess of venture capital looking for opportunities of gainful investment in radically innovative and promising enterprise. That answer, however, only begged the question of the role that finance might play in giving a socially inclusive form to the new advanced practice of production by supporting the economy-wide diffusion of its methods, culture, and conditions. That was a task that the venture capitalist could not execute. Its execution depended on institutional and educational innovations beyond his grasp and in the hands of the state and the law.

In a sense, the commitment of the most innovative firms to disruptive innovation (as it came to be called)—working to create new markets, demands, and consumers as well as new products and methods of production—represents an adaptation at the level of the firm. It was a response by such firms to the lack of policies and institutions that could help break through the supply-and-demand constraints on economic growth. The disruptive innovators tried to achieve at the microscale what only an institutional reshaping of the market economy could accomplish at the macroscale.

In a situation characterized by the coexistence of these three worlds—large firms reliant on internalized finance; retrograde small businesses dependent on self-exploitation, family savings, and commercial banks; and the advanced start-ups married to venture capital—autonomous finance turned its relation to the real economy upside down. It used the transactions of the real economy less as the genuine object of its work than as the pretext for the development of successive layers of financial engineering. Each layer offered new opportunities for financial arbitrage, speculation, trading, and gain.

The chief setting in which finance caused this reversal of the canonical relation of finance to the real economy was the expansion of consumer rather than producer credit, most notably for housing. The proximate condition was the dominance of regulatory dualism and the expansion of shadow banking. The underlying functional prompt was the need (and for the financiers the opportunity) to reconcile, thanks to the expansion of consumer credit, the regressive redistribution of wealth and income in the country with the maintenance of a market in mass-consumption goods. The broad social and economic consequence was the embrace of a fake-credit democracy standing in the place of a property-owning democracy and a democratized market economy. And the specific effect on finance and its role was to bloat finance rather than to deepen it, creating a financial regime that became more susceptible to breakdown as it became less rooted in the real economy.

As the roots of finance in the real economy thinned, its potential to damage the real economy through financial crisis increased. To the paramount evil of wasting much of the potential of finance for prosperity and democracy were added the destructive consequences of financial crisis. The events of 2008 and the subsequent slump in real economic activity, followed by slow and defective recovery, demonstrated the cost to society.

The response of government to the circumstance and to the crisis took three forms, further discussed in the appendix to this book. I address them briefly here because an understanding of them is necessary to complete the picture of the situation of finance in contemporary America.

One response was the often half-hearted and inconclusive promotion of a series of reform projects: the reinstatement of the New Deal divisions between government-guaranteed deposit banking and proprietary trading by financial organizations; the strengthening of authority in the executive branch of the national government to liquidate and turn around failing banks; the tightening of capital-adequacy requirements for banks as recommended by the Bank of International Settlements and other vehicles of the international financial elite and its technical cadres; and the establishment of an agency responsible for the protection of consumers of financial services.

What these reform programs had in common is that neither none of them nor all of them together addressed the basic arrangements shaping the relation of finance to the real economy. They failed to exemplify what I have described as the practice of piecemeal and gradualist but nonetheless radical reform because they attempted no change in structural realities. They even failed to challenge and dismantle regulatory dualism, the division between the thickly regulated sector and the thinly regulated sector of finance. Such a dismantling would have been a preliminary to radical reform. It is therefore unsurprising that these reform efforts bore only a tangential relation to the facts that had helped trigger the financial crisis of 2007–2009 in the first place.

Fiscal stimulus represented a second response. The American disciples of Keynes, raised in the intellectual climate of the "neoclassical synthesis" in economics, announced what was supposed to be the permanent truth about such breakdowns: a slump brought about by too much credit and confidence could be overcome only by more credit and confidence.

The fundamental difficulty was the typical insufficiency of fiscal stimulus to overcome a major decline in real economic activity. The experience of the Depression of the 1930s had been repeated at other times and in other parts of the world: to be effective against a major slump, a fiscal expansion must be large—large enough to provoke fierce political resistance (because of the danger that it will shift the power relation between government and big business by increasing governmental influence over the investment decision) and large enough to threaten provoking a crisis of confidence in the sovereign debt.

As an antidote to a major decline in economic activity, fiscal stimulus would have to serve the function of a war economy without the motivating force of war. Not even the Nazi government, determined to achieve recovery and enjoying dictatorial powers, could reach this goal. As in the United States, the stimulus that really worked was actual war. The crisis of 2007–2009 remained beneath the threshold beyond which any politically and economically feasible stimulus would have proved ineffective. Thus, the stimulus exerted only a modest influence.

Here, however, another problem arose. Just as the re-regulation of finance might have been designed in a way that represented an initial step toward arrangements better enlisting finance in the service of production, so the fiscal stimulus might have been designed in ways that anticipated a strategy of inclusive economic growth. (See the appendix to this book.) Instead, most of the fiscal stimulus consisted in the bailout of failing financial organizations to the primary benefit of the financiers themselves rather than of homeowners and workers. The modest New Deal–style public-works programs and the tax breaks to the general population did little to alter the situation. Thus, the fiscal stimulus confirmed the rule of thumb that in the low-energy democracies of today, whose states are beholden to moneyed interests and whose academic culture and political discourse are bereft of transformative ideals, expansionary fiscal policy is likely to be too limited to make a difference. It is also likely to be too misdirected to make the right kind of difference.

A third response outreached the first and outlived the second. It was the policy of easy money, or very low interest rates, crafted and implemented by the central bank. The clearer the relative inefficacy of the reregulation of finance and the fiscal stimulus became, the heavier was the reliance on expansionary monetary policy. It became, more than a response to the slump, a proxy for a missing national strategy of economic growth, whether socially inclusive or not. Convinced that little could be expected from the sitting government or from any administration that would replace it in the foreseeable future, the central bankers made money cheap and kept it cheap. They hoped that easy money would result in more consumption, especially of homes and automobiles, and that more consumption would cause higher employment. They experimented with ever bolder ways to prevent deflation and maintain the interest rate close to zero before they began to "normalize" it.

Experience demonstrated in the United States, as in many of the rich industrial democracies, the intractable limits to the use of monetary policy as a substitute for a missing growth strategy. The pursuit of cheap money *à outrance*, without a realistic grasp of the way finance works, resulted in a flattening of the yield curve, bringing the long-term interest rate close to the short-term rate. This derangement of the interest rate's term structure deprived finance of its role in maturity transformation. The shedding of this role was not an unintended consequence of the policy of cheap money; it formed part of its goal. The central bankers pursued this goal in the misguided belief that low long-term as well as short-term rates would result in a higher level of activity in the real economy. The foreseeable result, however, was that they depressed the supply of credit. No wonder that well into the flawed recovery the overall level of credit remained lower than it had been at the lowest point in earlier slumps.

The statutory mandate of the Federal Reserve failed to justify these abdications. In the forgotten and crucial part of its language, the Federal Reserve Act, as amended in 1977, charged the central bank with maintaining "long-run growth of the monetary and credit aggregates commensurate with the economy's long-run potential to increase production" (sec. 2A). In their choice of language, the authors of the statute had proved indifferent to the foreseeable complaint of the post-Marginalist economist: What is production?

Cheap money cannot substitute for a growth strategy, much less for a strategy of socially inclusive economic growth, committed to institutional and educational innovations designed to support the economy-wide diffusion of the most advanced practice of production. It is to politics and thought, expressed as law, and not to central banks and to monetary policy that we must look for a progressive approach to the supply side of the economy.

The financial experience of Brazil in this same period shows the usefulness of state-controlled or state-owned banks. They prove valuable as an instrument to continue investing in production when a domestic or international crisis has resulted in an investment-discouraging slump. They are useful as well in focusing investment on the long term when the market's culture and practice, incited by a high real rate of interest, remain fixed on the short term.

However, the Brazilian experience exemplifies as well the limits to any attempt to use this public channel of investment as a substitute for reform of the arrangements governing finance and organizing its relation to the real economy. It is less important to circumvent private investment through the use of state banks than it is to change the arrangements under which any investment takes place.

I earlier discussed the exhaustion of the Brazilian growth model based on mass consumption and on the production and export of commodities, especially relatively untransformed agricultural, ranching, and mining products. Its cardinal sin was failure to democratize the economy on the supply side, which would have broadened access to economic opportunities and educational capabilities.

In the Brazilian model, finance played a key role on the demand side through the popularization of consumer credit, provided largely by private banks with governmental encouragement. The encouragement included legal facilities allowing worker's salaries to serve as collateral, even to the extent of being partly deposited in escrow for the comfort of creditors.

In the provision of credit for production, however, the state and its banks took the leading part. They did so under a lending regime characterized by a stark form of credit dualism and credit rationing. The state banks, beginning with the BNDES, the National Bank of Economic and Social Development, provided subsidized credit. As credit was subsidized, it was also rationed. The justification for this arrangement was the persistence of a very high real rate of interest, against the background of an oligopolistic banking industry and a history of high, chronic, and unstable inflation, only recently tamed. As a consequence, no market in long-term lending existed. Its absence served to justify the subsidization of credit for the favored few. The distinction between subsidized and nonsubsidized credit in turn inhibited the lowering of the interest rate for the latter and the development of the long-term lending market.

Moreover, despite all protestations to the contrary, the lion's share of state credit, especially in the loan portfolio of the BNDES, went to a handful of big businesses rather than to the thousands of small and medium-size enterprises that produced most of the national output and created the vast majority of jobs. As the crisis of 2007–2009 drew near to Brazil and threatened to destroy a cycle of economic growth that had not yet been halted by the collapse of commodity prices, the state used its banks to sustain a forced march of investment. In so doing, it illustrated both the benefits and the dangers of the circumvention of private investment.

There were two key flaws in the use of this shortcut. The first was the continued slighting of small and medium-size business. The second was the absence of a larger project to change and democratize the economy on the supply side and to lay the basis for the creation of new comparative advantage. These two flaws turned out to be connected.

Even when the state banks tried to reorient their loan portfolios to small and medium-size business, the attempt either failed outright or fell far short of its goal. It is not simply that most of the state banks (with the exception of the oldest, the Bank of Brazil, which had helped build Brazilian agriculture) had no practice and culture of dealing with smaller firms and that such fragmented lending was inherently more costly. It was also that in an economy in which there was wide dispersion between the most advanced firms and other, more backward businesses in every sector, the vast majority of smaller firms lacked the collateral, track record, skills, and prospects to satisfy a prudent lender. The reorientation of the loan portfolios of the state banks therefore depended on the cumulative effect of initiatives that could lift up the vast rearguard of the production system.

In such an effort, access to capital represented only one of several elements. These elements, combined, would have meant much. They included the organization of access to more advanced technology and the capabilities that it presupposes, to advanced practice and the social capital that it assumes, and to domestic and international markets and the benchmarks of quality that they demand. But implemented alone and without such complements, access to capital meant little. Once banking crossed the threshold of microlending to very small enterprises, backed by family and community networks, it found itself dealing with a world of businesses that were not primitive enough to be the beneficiaries of such varieties of social finance but were too primitive to meet the tests of a contemporary banking system. Moreover, the Brazilian economy was notably lacking in an entity that habitually plays a strategic role: the medium-size firm at the front line of production, able to measure itself against a world benchmark.

One way to approach the requirements for the uplift of the immense rearguard of such an economy is to consider them from the perspective of the agent capable of fulfilling them. Who will see it to it that these requirements are met? Who will, in the name of the state (given that private capital had no interest), coordinate access to capital with access to advanced technology, practice, knowledge, and markets in favor of small and medium-size firms?

Brazil was a test case because the Brazilian state, unlike most states in the world, could count on organizations designed to promote several varieties of access. Not only did each such governmental body operate separately from the others—lending separately from transferring technology, from consulting about practice, from helping firms gain access to markets—but no single state organization could be expected to perform the orchestrating role. To attempt to perform it would have been to transplant the Northeast Asian model of a unitary trade and industrial policy to a historical and social setting to which it was unsuited.

It is a characteristic conundrum. The market as now organized cannot do the needed transformative work because the market by its logic channels advantages to the advantaged. The centralized state, operating through the top-down imposition of its choices, cannot effectively accomplish it either because it operates within the straitjacket of universal rules and specialized agencies.

We are accustomed by two hundred years of debate to take as the axis of ideological controversy the contest of the market with the state: more market, less state; more state, less market; or some balance struck between market and state. The programmatic argument of this book stands for the proposition that the task is less to dose market and state than to change both state and market and consequently the relation between them: deepening democracy and democratizing the market. A deepened democracy and a democratized market economy converge on a radical experimentalism.

There are two broad directions by which to change finance in Brazil: through the reconstruction of the market or through the reconstruction of the state. What began with a change in the market would end up requiring innovation in the way the state works. What started as a governmental initiative would result in the creation of new market agents.

An example of a market-based approach would be to extend radically the authorization to lend capital. Individuals could be allowed to incorporate and lend their own capital—not other people's money—to small businesses under a simplified tax and regulatory regime. By a single stroke, this reform would begin to disrupt the banking oligopoly and to promote the deepening of finance. Moreover, it was an initiative already foreshadowed in Brazilian law by allowance for special-purpose financial organizations. Such organizations were set up by small groups of private investors to compete with the banks in certain services as well as in lending through the use of their own capital and without taking deposits.

A state-based approach would be for government to establish a range of organizations, under professional management and market discipline, to do the undone work of coordinating access to capital with access to technology, practice, and markets. In one form, this approach could mimic private equity and private venture capital, taking stakes in the business that it supports. In another form, it could work under contract to render services to both the state and private businesses. Compensation for these services would be tied to performance across the relevant criteria.

In each country, the point of departure would be different, according to the path-dependent materials at hand. In Brazil, it might be the quasi-governmental organizations formed in the corporatist past of the country. In the United States, it might be a development of the GSEs—the government-sponsored organizations precariously surviving today as vestiges of the New Deal. In China, it might be the many ad hoc institutional experiments formed, as the township-village enterprises were, to reconcile the strictures of a statist framework and doctrine with the demands of a market economy.

Whatever the point of departure for each of these initiatives, the state would cease to operate in a centralized and unitary manner. It would be organized to experiment in divergent and competitive directions. In the light of such broad-based and fast-paced advances, the significance of ownership—public or private or organized on the basis of multiple fragmentary stakes by different tiers of stakeholders as disaggregated property rights—would pale in significance and lose its ideological potency. The principle of competitive discovery and experimentation would take its rightfully paramount position in institutional design.

The situation of finance and especially of banking in China during this period might at first seem to represent an exception to the thesis that in contemporary economies the production system largely finances itself while finance mainly serves itself rather production, using real economic activity as a pretext for successive layers of financial engineering.

The largest banks in China remain state-owned and state-controlled banks. Their primary activity is to lend capital cheaply to state-owned enterprises (SOEs). Many of the SOEs are either barely profitable or value subtracting. Instead of the credit dualism prevailing in Brazil—the division between subsidized long-term credit made available to a handful of big businesses in the name of a national industrial strategy and more expensive credit or no long-term credit at all for the vast majority of firms—there is overt credit rationing in China.

The basis of credit rationing is massive financial repression: the imposition of a very low real rate of interest by state policy. One consequence is to establish a lasting imbalance between the supply of capital and the demand for it. Another is to shield SOEs, which are often too unproductive to generate the large pools of retained earnings that finance production by big firms in the United States and other contemporary rich developed economies. (Even so, retained earnings in China have been calculated to have financed 40 to 50 percent of capital expenses in the period from 1992 through 1998. This ratio rose to 71 percent in the period from 2000 through 2008.)

Large private companies then try to share in the bonanza of what is, thanks to financial repression, subsidized credit. They too seek access to the state banks' loan portfolios, even when the companies' earnings make them less dependent on external credit. As in Brazil and many other countries, small and medium-size firms enjoy no such favor. They have little access to either the general or specialized state banks. Nor can they count on any equivalent to the American network of local banks. They must rely on the chief mainstays of small business throughout the world—self-exploitation and family savings—or, as I discuss next, must turn to shadow banking.

The seeming Chinese exception to the worldwide estrangement of finance from the real economy confirms the rule. The significance of state finance to SOEs is it preserves enterprises and forms of production that in the absence of the de facto subsidy might not exist at all. What results is the pseudoperformance of banks' canonical role in the financing of production. Cheap capital, controlled by the state and made possible by financial repression, replaces the retained earnings that unproductive firms are unable to generate in sufficient quantity. And private firms that may suffer from no such lack of economic viability then try to share in the benefit.

What appears to be the financing of production by the banks is more tellingly described as finance ordered by the government to deal with a permanent emergency under conditions that make the normal practice of the self-financing of production impossible. The fragility of the subsidized firms compromises the quality of the lending banks' balance sheets. As the banks are made to save the SOEs, the state may find itself driven to save the banks, until it reshapes the whole national strategy of development and, with it, the organization of finance.

That is only half of the story. Outside the state-owned banks, there has emerged in China a vast realm of shadow banking.[22] Imperfectly understood albeit widely studied, shadow banking's assets have been reckoned to amount to anything from 40 to 70 percent of GDP. Shadow banking—financial intermediation and liquidity or maturity transformation by entities that are unregulated or underregulated and that lack access to the central bank's lender-of-last-resort facilities—has developed in response to two main prompts. The first prompt is a desperate search by Chinese household and corporate savers or investors for yield and wealth protection in an economy under the shadow of severe financial repression. The second prompt is the attempt by small and growing firms to obtain the credit denied to them by the credit rationing practiced by the government-owned banks.

Here we see, under the lens of Chinese circumstances, another general feature of finance and its potential. Dynamism in production such as exists on tremendous scale in China will always incite new forms of financial activity. It would take a much greater measure of financial repression than the state already imposes to stamp out shadow banking. The practical result would be to leave China much poorer, denying it alternatives for investment and lending that the state banks fail to provide.

The spontaneous exuberance of shadow banking, however, is no substitute for a financial system that has been designed as an integral element in a national development strategy. Like credit rationing in the state sector, shadow banking represents a circumstantial adaptation: the filling of a vacuum rather than the pursuit of a goal. The Chinese shadow banks have proven more likely to lend to real estate developers than to take up the undone work of venture capital in supporting innovative emergent enterprise. They have done little to advance experimentalist, knowledge-intensive production outside a few large firms and nothing to help establish it in socially inclusive form. Finance can serve production, innovation, and inclusion. It cannot serve them, however, unless the idea of such an activity takes hold in thought and politics.

Thought and politics. The market economy does not create its own presuppositions. Politics and thought create them and express them as law. It is by their influence on law that these two great formative forces shape the institutional arrangements of the market order. Law also embodies the ideological assumptions that make sense of those arrangements, inform their interpretation, and guide their development.

Law is not a separate part of society—the part cared for by judges and attorneys. What judges and lawyers do amounts to only a small part of the law. Law is the detailed expression of the structure of society, its institutional and ideological regime.

Do not mistake the thesis that politics and thought shape through law the presuppositions of the market economy for the conventional idea of legal constructivism. By "legal constructivism," I mean the notion that the market economy relies on legally constructed entities, such as private property, freedom of contract, and the legal forms that a firm can assume, with their distinct consequences for investment, authority, and liability. The conventional idea of legal construction makes this claim only to rob it of the better part of its potential significance. It does so by combining the notion that economic activity requires legal vehicles with a particular understanding of the institutional structure of the economy and of its genesis.

According to this understanding, an institutionally defined economic regime is a system. All of its parts fit together. Because they fit together, they stand and fall together. There is a small number of alternative forms of economic organization. Capitalism or the market economy is one of them. Its arrangements are subject to some diversity at the margin, but these variations are relatively minor changes in the constant institutional traits of the regime wherever and whenever it recurs in history. For example, the institutional differences studied in the contemporary literature on "varieties of capitalism" are concerned largely with the relatively limited distinctions among the North Atlantic market economies of the second half of the twentieth century.

The underlying conception in this approach is the idea that in the introduction I called "structure as system." The idea of structure as system is invariably associated with a view of strong functional imperatives leading to institutional convergence. It always relies on an explicit or implicit social theory invoking forces and constraints that explain the composition of the narrow range of institutional options in history and the systemlike character of each of these options.

In the history of social thought, the most famous instance of such a theory and its reliance on the notion of structure as system is Marxism. Marxism had at its core the idea of a small, closed list of "modes of production," of which capitalism is one, each with its characteristic institutional and legal form, governed by laws of historical change. Much of conservative economic and legal theory over the past 150 years has also embraced this vision of indivisible institutional systems. "Capitalism," as one of the regimes or modes of production, has an innate legal and institutional content, allowing for only a modest range of institutional variation. Each such regime evolves under the influence of powerful functional imperatives: the requirements of what works to produce the material and ideal benefits (e.g., economic growth, national power, individual freedom) that society needs and prizes. Such was the conception informing much of the project of nineteenth-century legal science, misrepresented in the twentieth century as crude conceptualism and mechanical, deductive inference in reasoning about law. Such is more recently the "new institutional economics," with its signature conception of a quasi-Darwinian winnowing out of suboptimal ways of organizing a market economy.

It is from this background of influential ways of thinking that the thesis of legal constructivism has gained its meaning and drawn its practical message: stick to the straight and narrow! In this intellectual context—the context of the conception of structure as system—thought and politics have only a supporting role to play. Their primary role is to recognize reason and necessity in the form of institutional evolution and convergence, to explain, and (unless, as in Marxism, a better system awaits us next) to help uphold the integrity of the regime. Such surrender to historical fate is supposed to rescue us, whether we are leftists or rightists, from a futile and self-defeating voluntarism in our reform efforts.

The thesis of the indivisibility of structures fails to take account of the piecemeal way in which they almost always get made and remade. The claim of institutional convergence fails to do justice to a striking feature of institutional history: history is full of examples of how the same functional imperatives can be met by alternative institutional arrangements. That such alternatives often result from the recombination or analogical extension of established institutions does not belie the point; it grounds it in historical reality.

People work with what they have by way of institutional legacies and conceptions. They work under the constraint of ruling interests and entrenched preconceptions and often at the provocation of crises, which require response without providing inspiration. But they do not work by selecting ready-made, indivisible systems from a closed set of institutional options or by being forced to embrace the sole possible institutional response to a practical challenge.

The idea that the law, moved by politics and by thought, defines the institutional presuppositions of the market economy takes on significance for transformative practice when it is associated with the conception that I labeled "structure not system." Once again, in this contrasting conception we can distinguish a view of the character of such regimes and a way of understanding how they get made and how they change.

Institutional regimes have far-reaching effects on social and economic life. The institutional architecture of the market economy shapes the forms of production and exchange as well as the distribution of economic advantage and disadvantage. It molds the answers given in practice to questions that have been central to the argument of this book, such as the relation of finance to the real economy and the extent to which the most advanced practice of production will either spread throughout the economy or instead remain confined within insular vanguards.

Moreover, an institutional and ideological framework may resist challenge and change, though how much it resists them and in what way depends on its nature. Although regimes have been traditionally designed to bar themselves against transformation, they might instead be designed to invite it, as the radicalization of both democracy and experimentalism demands.

Nevertheless, an institutional and ideological regime remains a ramshackle construction. It conforms to no consistent logic, such as it might follow if it were a machine programmed according to an algorithm and designed to perform a repetitious function. When it changes, its changes are piecemeal. Even radical institutional change is ordinarily the result of cumulative fragmentary reform. The wholesale substitution of a regime is a limiting case when it is not a political fantasy.

How should we understand in the most general terms the process by which institutional and ideological orders—structures as I am calling them—get made and remade? A persistent polarity in the making of regimes is the pull between the need to face a practical challenge and the impulse to mitigate disturbance to powerful interests and preconceptions.

The practical challenge or functional imperative—to achieve faster economic growth or stronger military power—may require institutional change. Richer and stronger countries may already present a model of change, tempting emulation. Seizing more fully the potential of a technological or organizational innovation—in production as in warfare—may often require radicalizing such innovations: developing them in forms that tap the energy and expand the capabilities of more people in more ways.

On the other hand, the groups best placed to take the lead in such innovations have a stake in preserving the essentials of their position and more generally in minimizing disruption to the established assignment of advantage and opportunity. To the way of practicing the innovations and reforming the regime that circumscribes the disturbance to powerful organized interests and entrenched preconceptions I have given the name the path of least resistance.

The path of least resistance is the most probable one taken. It is never the only one. We can arrange our institutions and practices, including our discursive practices, in ways that make the path of least resistance either harder or easier to defy and replace. The path of least resistance has on its side, by definition, the force of reigning interests and prevailing ideas: until we organize a social and economic world to ease its own transformation, the established regime will be organized to reproduce itself.

However, the path of least resistance also has a key weakness: in limiting disturbance to dominant interests and beliefs, it also limits our ability to exploit our innovations. It makes each organizational or technological innovation less productive. If innovations could take a more socially inclusive form, we would reap more of the benefits for which they are valued: growth, productivity, and creativity. It is the business of the critics and enemies of the established order to exploit this weakness. By doing so repeatedly, they can work toward a future in which more people have the ability and the opportunity to innovate.

An example is a problem that I have addressed repeatedly in this chapter: the extent to which the experimental, knowledge-intensive style of production, which is now the most advanced productive practice, will remain confined in relatively isolated productive vanguards of the economy or on the contrary be widely disseminated in economic life. The prevailing, insular form is the path of least resistance: it requires no more far-reaching changes in the economic and educational arrangements or their political and constitutional setting. The attempt to enlist finance more effectively in the service of production becomes more appealing and feasible to the extent that it serves as an incident in larger endeavors such as the development of the knowledge economy in socially inclusive form.

The confinement of the knowledge economy wastes immense opportunity. It is not only an economic opportunity. It is also, more generally, an opportunity for the empowerment of ordinary men and women, for the enhancement of agency. A simple interpretation of the progressive cause reads it as the project that deals with every practical task, such as the tasks of achieving broad-based economic growth and of creating new assets and winning new comparative advantage in the world economy, from the vantage point of a larger aim. This greater goal is the strengthening of the agency of ordinary people: of their ability to make more of themselves while continuing to ask, Where are the others?

In this view, offered as an alternative to conventional legal constructivism and to the idea of structure as system, thought and politics no longer perform a merely supporting role. They and the relation between them exercise a decisive influence on law, understood as the expression of the institutional and ideological regime, including the arrangements and assumptions of the market order. A species of politics and a practice of thought hold special importance for the creation of alternatives to the path of least resistance.

The species of politics is a deepened democracy: one that is organized to master the structure of society and to enhance the agency of ordinary men and women, beginning with their political agency. Such a democracy raises the level of organized popular engagement in political life; the structural fecundity of political life is related to the level of political mobilization. It quickens the place of politics, facilitating frequent structural change. To this end, it establishes in both the state and society multiple sources and occasions of political initiative while arranging for stalemate to be avoided and impasse to be resolved quickly through the engagement of the electorate—for example, through early elections or comprehensive referendums. And it makes possible decisive initiative at the center of power. However, it also taps the potential of federalism, or of devolution in a unitary state, to allow local governments to diverge from the path taken by the national government and to create countermodels of the national future.

Such a political vision does not understand democracy as simply majority rule, qualified by minority rights. It also views democracy as a collective device for opening a pathway of structural change when we no longer have reason to believe in a definitive institutional formula, as the liberals and socialists of the past did.

Just as there is a species of politics conducive to the creation of alternatives to the path of least resistance, so too is there a practice of thought. This practice is an understanding of social and economic life that recognizes the centrality of structure and structural change. It does so without misrepresenting structure as system or mistaking the accidental course of our past experience for the demarcation of the range of structural alternatives that are open to us.

Such a practice of thought imitates natural science only in its most important attribute: the dependence of insight into a phenomenon on the imagination of its transformative possibilities, given that everything changes into other things under certain conditions and provocations. It works on the assumption that a science lacking an account of change is a pseudoscience. In social and historical study, such a pseudoscience amounts to an obfuscating rationalization of experience.

At the same time, a practice of social thought responsive to this conception will be wholly unlike natural science in another respect. It will view its most important subject matter—the institutional arrangements and ideological assumptions of society—as a human creation, which we can know from within, as we cannot hope to know natural phenomena. It will understand that such structures as well as the practices and beliefs with which they are connected may be arranged in different ways. Some of these ways may make them appear to be like the natural phenomena that they are not, beyond the reach of the transformative will. Others may result in structures announcing themselves to be the collective artifacts that they are and prompting us to treat them as ephemeral instruments of our agency. A deepened democracy needs such an understanding of our institutional creations.

Consider now, in the light of these ideas and in relation to the problems discussed in earlier sections, some features of recent American, Brazilian, and Chinese experience.

No democracy that has yet existed has been organized to expose the structure of society to challenge in the absence of crisis. In every democracy law making has continued to amount to a series of episodic and localized interventions in social and economic arrangements. The electorate has consented to these arrangements only in the sense that silence is equivalent to consent, in the spirit of the legal principle *qui tacet consentire videtur*. Such democracies—the only ones that we have—are not equipped to serve as the collective instruments for setting a direction of structural change.

Each contemporary democracy falls short of this standard in its own way. In the United States, structural change is inhibited by the form given to the separation of powers in the constitutional design established at the foundation of the republic, the relation of money and media to politics as well the avoidance of measures favorable to a higher level of popular engagement in political life, and the failure to give to federalism a form useful to experimentalism. Only crisis in the form of war or ruin can ordinarily counteract the inhibiting effect of these arrangements.

There is a familiar discussion of the undemocratic elements in the American Constitution, such as the Electoral College or the role of the Senate, traditionally justified either as checks on the passions of the majority or as requirements of a federal system. This discussion habitually fails to address the more fundamental ways in which American democracy fails to meet the test of subjecting the structure of society to challenge without the help of crisis. These deeper features of the American constitutional arrangements perpetuate what I earlier described as a protodemocratic liberalism in the organization of the state and politics. The protodemocracy is set up to inhibit structural change, shielding the established structure, including the economic regime, from challenge.

One element in protodemocratic liberalism is the institutionalized confusion, produced by Madison's scheme of checks and balances, of the liberal fragmentation of power with the conservative slowing down of politics. A fragmentation of power among parts of the state (the three branches of government) need not result in impasse so long as there are constitutional mechanisms to resolve impasse quickly. The Madisonian plan, however, is calculated to perpetuate impasse rather than to resolve it, as if the danger to avoid were the transformation of society by politics. No intrinsic relation exists between the liberal fragmentation of power and the conservative slowing down of politics; the Constitution of the United States combines them by intention and design rather than by necessity.

A second element in protodemocratic liberalism is a set of rules and practices that works to depress the level of popular political engagement and to make political activity hostage to the moneyed interests. These rules and practices include the lack of gratuitous access, in favor of political parties and social movements, to the means of mass communication as well as the arrangements that leave democratic politics in the shadow of private money.

A third element in protodemocratic liberalism is the failure to realize the experimentalist conception of federalism—the states as "laboratories of experimentation"—in the organization of federalism. The constitutional, legal, and ideological restraints on vertical cooperation among the levels of the federal system as well as horizontal cooperation among states and municipalities work against the attempt to tap the experimentalist potential of federalism.

A fourth element in protodemocratic liberalism is the high threshold of constitutional change. It is aggravated by reverence for the Constitution as a sacrosanct institutional invention of the founders of the republic. The cult of the Constitution chills a providential irreverence: the institutional form of democracy must always be a priority subject matter of democratic politics, setting as it does the basic terms on which all other parts of social and economic life are open to change.

No less formidable than the restraints on democratic experimentalism, wrongly imposed in the name of political freedom, are the prevailing tendencies in the high academic culture of the United States. In the academy, each branch of the study of society and history severs in its own fashion the vital link between insight into the existent and imagination of the adjacent possible: the states of affairs that are accessible through some sequence of feasible transformations of the present circumstance. Each area of study suppresses in its own manner the understanding of structure, of institutional change, and of institutional alternatives. This failing is clearest in the two disciplines to which democracy can best look to envision its alternative futures: political economy and legal thought.

The practice of economics inaugurated by the Marginalist theoreticians of the late nineteenth century suffered, I argued earlier, from a disconnection between analysis and empiricism. If a model fails, an economist develops another one, adjusting the parameters or the assumptions. No accumulation of contrary facts can impeach a form of analysis that was never meant to be descriptive in the first place and that was designed by its inventors to be empty of contentious normative commitments or causal conceptions. This form of analysis lacks a view of production other than as shadowy extension of market exchange and sees the realities of production from the perspective of relative prices. It offers an account of competitive market selection that is unsupported by any view of the creation of the diverse stuff from which competitive selection selects.

Most significantly for the topics addressed in this book, the tradition of economic thought is deficient in institutional imagination, especially imagination of the alternative institutional forms of the market economy itself. It fails to appreciate that regimes of property, contract, and corporate organization can take radically different forms. For this reason, unless it is restricted to its most rigorous and austere form, it can easily suggest the idea that Hayek made explicit and radicalized: a system of coordination and exchange, free from state inference, spontaneously generates the same rules of contract and property if not also of corporate organization and liability. The result is to deny what I have argued throughout this book to be the fact: no such natural form of coordination and exchange exists.

In the embrace of this prejudice, the dominant tradition of economic theory found reinforcement in two other ideas tending in the same direction. One such conception was the picture presented by the "new institutional economics" in which the established institutional framework of the market economy was represented as the outcome of cumulative convergence to the best practice or the optimal form of a market order. It assumed that the choice of an institutional framework of economic activity can be explained by the same methods used to explain maximizing behavior within such a framework.

The other notion, developed by Ronald Coase and his followers,[23] was that the laws and institutions shaping the market economy do not matter, save for their distributive consequences. It is always possible to contract around them so long as freedom of contract is respected and transaction costs can be contained. This view regards private law as a natural and universal language in which any economic thought can be spoken and realized in practice. It fails to recognize what law really is: the detailed expression of a particular institutional order, viewed in relation to the ideals and interests that make sense of it. Such an order has decisive consequences for economic life.

The leading tendencies in legal thought reached the same result—the insulation of the institutional order against transformative thinking and acting—by a different route. They represented law and the institutional and ideological regime that it expresses in the idealized language of policy and principle. They sought to put the best face on the law in the hope of improving it. Consequently, they understated or denied the element of contradiction and anomaly in the law: the pattern of detailed complication and variation in the details of the law and in each area of social and economic practice that it governs. In every branch of law, dominant solutions are surrounded by countercurrents, vestiges of defeated or rejected alternatives and prophecies of future ones. Such complications and variations supply material for the development of alternatives: small alternatives that we can turn into bigger ones.[24]

The evasion of structure, characteristic of the high academic culture, penetrated the discourse of practical policy and culture. It left undisturbed a model of ideological controversy that had ceased to speak to the real problems and possibilities of social and economic life: the view that the task is to dose the relative presence of market and state rather than to reimagine and reshape both of them.

We cannot fault contemporary economists and jurists for having invented the practice of evading structural vision or of misrepresenting established institutions as the natural and necessary outcomes of convergence to best practice. Such evasion and misrepresentation have long-standing roots in the history of thought and of society. The fault of thinkers and scholars lies instead in their failure to oppose, in the interest of insight as well as of reform, the naturalizing impulse that blinds structural vision.

Remember the two leading American traditions of progressive reform: (1) the defense of small enterprise and property against economic concentration and (2) the acceptance and subsequent regulation of big business. What these traditions have in common is the implicit acceptance of the inherited institutional form of the market order. They therefore naturalize as well the established relation, or lack of relation of finance to the real economy. They recognize no significant room for reconstruction in the terms on which the most advanced practice of production is either confined to an insular vanguard of production or widely disseminated in the economy or in any number of other features decisive for the character and consequences of economic life.

So long as these assumptions prevail, with their life renewed by the experience of living under the arrangements of the prodemocratic liberalism that I described earlier, Americans will remain unable to rediscover and reinvent in their present circumstance the dialectic that built the United States. One side of that vital interplay is the marshaling of resources by government, in Hamilton's spirit, to develop the physical infrastructure, technological resources, and educational equipment of the country. The other side is the democratization of economic opportunity in one part of the economy after another. It can be achieved, in the spirit of Jackson and of the second Roosevelt, by dint of cumulative institutional innovation.

In the China and Brazil of this period, political arrangements and dominant ideas worked together against the practice of structural reform.

China was a collective dictatorship. It reduced democracy to consultation within and outside the ruling party. It tolerated no organized conflict and debate over alternative directions of institutional change. As a consequence, any form of distributive conflict threatened a regime that knew how to manage conflict only by suppressing it. Yet distributive conflict among classes, sectors, and regions was an unavoidable consequence of a change in the model of development that the leadership recognized to be necessary. China, it was widely agreed, had to move away from a growth path in which the manufacture and export of tradable goods served to substitute, as a driver of economic growth, production for a deepened domestic market. It had to move toward a growth strategy in which production for the world and production for the home country complement each other, sustaining successive breakthroughs in the constraints on supply and on demand.

More fundamentally, the denial of democratic freedoms to the Chinese people deprived the nation of a means with which to discover collectively its development path through debate and experiment and to define the institutional implications of the chosen trajectory. The denial reduced the formulation of the national development agenda to the level of technical adjustments to a plan, when the trouble lay in the character and direction of the national project. It abandoned the country to the effects of a crude contrast between anarchy and order, when order was understood as command and control, moderated by co-option and patronage. Its mentors failed to grasp that in political as in economic life the order with the greatest practical fecundity is the one splitting the difference between order and anarchy.

There was no reason for China to reshape its political life on the model of the narrow and defective repertory of constitutional arrangements on offer in the low-energy democracies of the time. There was, however, every reason for it to approach the reconstruction of its development model and its political institutions as two sides of the same refashioning. A strategy of development founded on democratizing economic opportunity and disseminating experimental, knowledge-intensive production has political implications and requirements. It requires a political life that would turn the mass of ordinary Chinese into coauthors of that strategy, assuring them of the basic economic, social, and educational endowments that would render them capable and unafraid in the midst of strife and innovation and reconciling strong governmental initiative with space for a wide range of institutional experiments. Each such experiment amounts to the prophecy of a different national future.

In Brazil of the early twenty-first century, the political obstacle to the practice of structural reform lay in the absence of a capable state. Its flaws stemmed from its character as a democracy organized, like that of the United States (from which it had imported many of its institutions), to tame governmental power only by inhibiting its transformative uses. In the manner inaugurated in Europe after each of the two great wars of the past century, the Brazilian Constitution promised all manner of social and economic rights. It did nothing to establish the forms of economic and political organization that might help keep the constitutional promises.

The vain promises made by the Brazilian Constitution mirrored the central idea in Brazilian politics: the idea of the social. Almost every political force professed to be social-liberal or social-democratic. The social was the sugar of compensatory redistribution and regulation, expected to sweeten the pill of surrender to an economic regime that was imagined to lie beyond the reach of effective transformation. It was the fantasy of a tropical Sweden. Unlike the real Sweden, this fictional land could aspire to the welfare state without having to undergo decades of struggle over the distribution of opportunity and advantage and achieve an uneasy settlement between the social state and the moneyed interests.

If China and Brazil differed in the nature of the political limits that they imposed on structural change, they resembled each other in the character of the intellectual constraints that they suffered. In both countries, much of intellectual life was divided between a fossilized and diminished Marxism and a crude imitation of social science as practiced in the leading American universities. These two modes of thought appeared to oppose each other. In fact, they delivered a similar message: give up on radical reform. The attractions of this message were enhanced and its defects were hidden by the mental colonialism that continued to seduce and corrupt the intelligentsia in the two countries.

The practitioners of shrunken Marxism disbelieved or half-believed in the explanatory claims of Marx's theory of society and history. They nevertheless kept using its categories—capitalism, for example, or class conflict—as if these categories had a meaning independent of their theoretical context. Rather than reinventing or developing the theory, they watered it down.

By the same moves, they abandoned the transformative commitments that had motivated Marxist theory, despite its necessitarian assumptions. They understood the theory as a way of explaining the power of the established structures and of their resistance to change. In their eyes, it discredited programmatic thinking as impotent voluntarism. It reconciled them to fate. They kept the bad part of Marxism—the necessitarian arguments—and discarded the good part—the transformative intention. They learned from Marxist doctrine not to believe in the prospect of piecemeal but cumulative radical reform.

If deep change could consist only of the substitution of one indivisible system for another—socialism for capitalism—and such a substitution was indefinitely delayed as well as manifestly dangerous, there seemed to be nothing left to do other than to humanize the established market regime through regulation and retrospective redistribution by tax and transfer. Thus, fossilized Marxism provided to some a reason to embrace institutionally conservative social democracy as the residual progressive project.

The other and increasingly predominant current in thinking about society and history sought to reproduce the practice of social science as it was studied in the American research universities. Each of these social sciences, under its prevailing methods, cut the link between understanding of the existent and insight into the adjacent possible. The shape of each cut differed, but its effects were the same.

The most influential example was post-Marginalist economics, with its emptiness of causal content, its deficit of institutional imagination, and its subordination of the theory of production to the theory of exchange. The cumulative effect was to naturalize the institutional and ideological regime. Such a naturalization of structures turns ideas about society and history into superstition.

Thus, the two contrasting forms of thought—diminished Marxism and second-hand American-style social science—were represented by their votaries as enemies. They operated instead as alternative vehicles for the same teaching. Rejecting this teaching in favor of a view that puts structural vision at the center of our thinking about society and does so by enlisting fragmentary theory in the service of radical reform of the market order has been one of the major aims of my argument.

Structure, Vision, and Agency

The topics that most demand attention in any study of society are the established institutional arrangements and the ideological assumptions on the basis of which people make sense of them. This structure—"structure" or "regime" is the shorthand name by which I have referred to such a framework for our routine activities—is also the object of greatest ambition in political action: to uphold it and preserve it against attack or perversion if we believe that it is the best available ordering of human life or to change it if we refuse to treat it as the impassable horizon within which to serve our interests and enact our ideals.

There is a tight, internal relation between our cognitive and our practical stakes in reckoning with institutional and ideological regimes. Our understanding of every such ordering of social life is intimately tied to our interest in shaping it. We cannot hope to grasp how regimes work unless we comprehend how they change. We must understand what we can turn them into: not to understand them from the standpoint of transformative opportunity and feasible variation is to give up on understanding them at all. If we hope to change them, we must not allow ourselves to be misled by false ideas about their nature and transformation: for example, the notion that they are indivisible systems that we either replace by another system or regulate and humanize to moderate their inequities.

It does not follow from the primacy of structure as a subject of social, political, economic, and legal thought that we require a comprehensive theory of society to deal with institutional and ideological regimes without illusion. Similarly, it does not result from the overriding importance of such regimes as objects of transformative ambition that we must change them all as one piece or not at all. Our understanding of structure can free itself progressively from the taint of superstition without ceasing to be fragmentary. Our often half-hearted and contradictory attempts to change the institutional and ideological bases of the society and the economy can have radical consequences if these efforts persist in a particular direction, guided by ideas that we revise in the light of our experience. Piece by piece and step by step, we can achieve revolutionary results with gradualist methods and fragmentary ideas.

Without structural vision, even if unfinished in thought and halting in action, we are lost. Structural vision, however, amounts to little if it fails to fix on the detailed stuff of which institutional and ideological regimes are made. To merit being the carrier of our hopes, as theory and as practice, it must engage the details, including those that seem most unyielding: the hard facts of economic life.

The details that have to do with finance and with its relation to the real economy deserve a close look from the friends of structural change. They count among the hardest of those hard facts.

Finance has appeared in the literature of politics, law, and economics as pitiless constraint, a destroyer of dreams, not as a terrain of transformative opportunity. Some among progressive reformers have wanted to extend finance to the poor (microcredit). Others among leftist theoreticians have represented the power of finance as characteristic of a phase in the history of market economies ("finance capitalism" as a stage in the making and undoing of the capitalist regime).[25] Few have seen finance for the complicated and recalcitrant but nevertheless mutable reality that it is. To see finance—and the rest of economic and political life—in this way requires the right kind of structural vision.

As we insist on the centrality of structural vision to both insight and reform, we should not forget the higher purpose of this insistence. Among our interests and ideals, one ideal and one interest command precedence under democracy: the enhancement of agency or of the power of ordinary men and women to act upon their circumstance and to make themselves freer and bigger through such action.

A hallmark of freedom is mastery of the institutional and ideological order of society. We must not serve this order. We must make it serve us. To make it serve us, we must perennially reimagine and reshape it. We cannot enjoy this freedom—the freedom of mastery over structure—as individuals if we fail to exercise it as a people.

Because I believe in our ability to turn the tables on the arrangements and assumptions of society, and to empower ourselves by doing so, I wrote this book.

Crisis, Slump, Superstition, and Recovery*

Thinking and Acting Beyond Vulgar Keynesianism

TAMARA LOTHIAN AND
ROBERTO MANGABEIRA UNGER

The intellectual and practical response to the worldwide financial and economic crisis of 2007–2009 as well as to the subsequent slump has exposed the poverty of prevailing ideas about how economies work and fail. The transformative opportunity presented by the crisis has largely been squandered, but the opportunity for insight has not. Insight today can support transformation tomorrow.

The present debate about the crisis and the subsequent slump has suppressed two themes of major importance. The first theme is the relation of finance to the productive agenda of society. It is not enough to regulate finance: it is necessary to reshape the institutional arrangements governing the relation of finance to the real economy so that finance becomes servant rather than master. The second theme is the link between redistribution and recovery. A pseudodemocratization of credit has been made to do the work of the redistribution of wealth and income in laying the basis for a market in mass-consumption goods. The most important form of redistribution is not retrospective and compensatory redistribution through

---

*Written in 2010. Published here for the first time.

tax and transfer; it is the reshaping of economic and educational arrangements to broaden opportunity and enhance capabilities.

Fiscal and monetary stimulus is rarely enough to redress the effects of a major economic crisis. (It was the massive mobilization and the experiments in public–private coordination of the war economy rather than any proto-Keynesianism that took countries out of the Depression of the 1930s.) The proper role of a stimulus is to play for time by preventing the aggravation of crisis and to prefigure a program of recovery and reconstruction.

The relative success of the major emerging economies in responding to the crisis and in avoiding a slump fails to provide the model of such a program. Many of the policies and arrangements pursued in these countries stabilized markets and created the conditions for continued growth. It would, nevertheless, be wrong to assume that economic recovery in these emerging economies represents the emergence of a superior economic logic. It should be understood instead as a series of second bests. For example, the forced continuation of credit flows through governmentally controlled banks and development agencies has largely reinforced preexisting inequalities rather than democratizing access to resources and capabilities.

A preliminary to a program of broad-based economic recovery is the repudiation of the regulatory dualism that has characterized the regulation of finance: the distinction between a thinly and thickly regulated sector of financial activity. In one direction, such a program must seek the institutional innovations that put finance more at the service of the productive agenda of society. In another direction, it must conceive and build institutional arrangements that give practical effect to the ideal of socially inclusive economic growth. It does so by basing growth on an institutionalized broadening of economic and educational opportunity.

The vulgar Keynesianism to which many contemporary progressives have looked for orientation fails to offer a theoretical guide to such a program of recovery. However, the fault does not lie solely in the vulgarized version of Keynes's ideas; it lies in those ideas themselves and indeed in the whole mainstream of economic analysis that grew out of the Marginalist revolution of the late nineteenth century. The established economics suffers from a deficit of institutional understanding and imagination. Only a broadening of institutional understanding can provide the practical and conceptual materials we need to imagine alternative futures. And although this understanding remains foreign to the main tradition of thinking about economic policy and reform, the same cannot be said of law.

Law and legal thought are integral to the theoretical alternative explored in this essay; they provide the institutional imagination with indispensable equipment.

This book takes a first step in the effort to develop an intellectual alternative. It does so by outlining an approach to our present problems of crisis, slump, and recovery.

THE TRUNCATED DEBATE ABOUT THE SLUMP: WHY THE STIMULUS FAILS

Nothing astonishes more in the present debate about recovery from the slump that followed the crisis of 2007–2009 in the richer economies than the poverty of the ideas informing the discussion. It is as if we were condemned to relive a yet more primitive version of the debates of the 1930s.

On one side, we hear the argument for fiscal and monetary stimulus: the more the better. The intellectual inspiration of this argument is almost exclusively vulgar Keynesianism; with each passing round in the debate, it becomes more vulgar.

The chief opposing conception is a market fundamentalism, the major premise of which is that a market economy has, despite minor variations, a single natural and necessary institutional form. This form supports, according to the market fundamentalists, an economic logic that cannot be defied with impunity: they believe that every attempt to defy it will, sooner rather than later, prove self-defeating. One of the by-products of this market fundamentalism has been a resurgence, in response to the nostrums of the vulgar Keynesians, of the "liquidationist" view of the 1920s (i.e., "purge the rottenness out of the system"): fiscal austerity, monetary common sense, and a return to fundamentals—that is to say, the established institutions of the market economy, with a minimum of governmental action—are supposedly all we need.

The truth is that under the conditions of contemporary democracies and markets no fiscal and monetary stimulus is ever likely to be large enough to help ensure a broad-based and vigorous recovery from a major slump. Long before the stimulus reaches the dimension needed to make a difference, it will encounter difficulties that are hard to overcome. A stimulus big enough to counteract the effects of a major slump is a gamble that will arouse opposition both because of the present interests that it threatens and because of the future evils that it risks producing.

In the practice of monetary policy, it is easy to jump from deflation to inflation and then to see inflation combined with stagnation, as it has been in the past. It is a quandary that has particular relevance to the present situation of rich economies as they suffer the aftereffects of the crisis. The major rich economies are awash in capital that has no place or little place to go. The scarcity of attractive opportunities for capital has helped arouse interest in emerging markets. Nevertheless, most capital remains at home, trapped. This abundance of liquidity coexists with a determined attempt by households and firms to free themselves from the burden of debt accumulated in the years leading up to the crisis. This effort has justified the description of the slump that has followed the crisis as a "balance-sheet recession," driven in part by the desire of both households and firms to reestablish a sustainable level of indebtedness.[1]

The coexistence of abundant liquidity with daunting private indebtedness is only superficially paradoxical. It is itself largely a consequence of the inequality-generating forces that helped shape the precrisis economy. A vast portion of profits was concentrated in financial firms in the decades preceding the crisis. At the same time, in the real economy the most innovative, knowledge-intensive practices, the source of greatest new wealth outside high finance, remained relatively confined to advanced sectors of production. These sectors have become closely linked to similar vanguards around the world. However, they remain weakly linked to other sectors of their own national economies. The inequalities resulting from such forces have become immense. No wonder vast stores of idle capital continue to pile up in economies populated by households and firms over their heads in debt.

In such a circumstance, the expansion of the money supply by central banks (called by a barrage of obfuscating names such as "quantitative easing") may help avoid serious and destructive deflation. It will not, however, help ensure a vigorous recovery in economies full of families and companies anxious to escape an overhang of debt.

Fiscal stimulus faces similar limitations and difficulties. When it takes the form of cutting taxes, the money saved by households (and in effect spent by the government) is likely to go disproportionately into the paying down of corporate or household debt rather than into increased consumption. To the extent that the beneficiaries of tax cuts are cash-rich individuals and companies, the windfall may simply stoke the already vast store of capital with nowhere to go.

Stimulus through spending seems more promising. One route is to put money directly in the hands of those who are more likely to spend it (for example, by extending and increasing unemployment benefits). Another path is to undertake an ambitious program of public works, especially projects designed to enhance the country's transport and communications structure and to promote low-carbon alternatives to present lines of production. These activities are useful, both in themselves and as responses to the slump: they can have an immediate effect on the level of economic activity.

This positive effect, however, is subject to two weighty qualifications that are connected in a way that remains poorly understood.

The first qualification is that the value of such forms of stimulus depends on what comes next. Will the extra money spent by the jobless cause more investment and employment? Will the public-works projects help entice more risk taking and innovation, thus creating a physical basis for the diffusion of more advanced technologies and practices throughout broader sectors of the economy? The relation of cost to return cannot be read off from the public-spending and investment initiatives taken in isolation.

The answers to these questions depend on the role that these initiatives may play or fail to play in a broader process of economic growth. The most important elements of such a process—the ones with the greatest potential to enhance productivity, on the basis of wider opportunities and stronger capabilities—are those that include a combination of technological and organizational innovations. Increased demand, aroused through fiscal stimulus, is far from enough to ensure that such a combination will take place.

The second qualification is that whereas the ultimate effect of such forms of stimulus on economic growth is both speculative and remote, the burden that they impose on governmental finance is immediate. In the presence of a process marked by the mixture of technological and organizational innovations likely to shape a new cycle of growth, the burdens may be wholly justified. In its absence, however, the short-term effect on increased demand may soon wane, and the government's worsened fiscal position inhibits it from undertaking the next round of growth and innovation-friendly measures.

The worsening of the state's fiscal position may in turn arouse the specter of a crisis of confidence in the sovereign debt, the government's ability to repay its obligations over the long term. The United States will continue to be the country least vulnerable to this form of pressure so long as it retains the world's reserve currency, can pay all of its obligations in a currency that it is free to print, and can count on the willingness of cash-rich countries and governments to help finance its profligacy. However, the risk of default is not the sole or normally the most significant form of declining confidence. The outward movement of capital, although less dramatic, can be nearly as decisive.

THE TRUNCATED DEBATE ABOUT THE SLUMP: WHY THE STIMULUS CAN NEVER BE BIG ENOUGH

The intrinsic limitations of fiscal and monetary stimulus as a response to economic slumps are not a reason to foreswear stimulus programs. They are a reason to regard such programs as partial and inadequate responses to severe economic downturns. Moreover, taken together with a second set of considerations, these limitations help explain why the actual implementation of these programs is almost always half-hearted and half-baked, even in the hands of progressive governments intellectually predisposed to vulgar Keynesianism (given the dominant ideas and scarcity of ideas).

The vigorous deployment of expansionary fiscal policies puts the state in more debt and paradoxically makes the state at once weaker and stronger: weaker because it owes more and has in that sense less room for maneuver, but stronger because its influence over economic activity increases and all economic agents' dependence on its actions and inactions becomes if not greater, then at least more obvious. The willingness to risk inflation for the sake of avoiding deflation is similarly an assertion of government's power to influence the terms of exchange in the whole economy and to devalue its obligations to its own creditors.

Fiscal and monetary stimulus taken to the hilt threatens real interests and offends influential ideas. The ideas and the interests, mixed as they always are in real history, conspire to restrain and sometimes to reverse the assertion of governmental power that is implicit in the deployment of stimulus policies. Opponents of fiscal and monetary stimulus are able to exploit to their advantage the inherent weaknesses in its efficacy.

The result is that no fiscal and monetary stimulus, conceived in response to an economic slump, will ever be likely to satisfy the proponents of this policy. Always and everywhere, they will respond with the same litany. It has been done by half, they will complain. Had it not been done at all, the downturn would have been much more severe, but if only there were greater courage and clarity (to inflate or to spend further), the recovery would have come earlier and been stronger.

The exercises of stimulus that the world has seen since the Great Depression almost always appear, both at the time when they were deployed and in retrospect, to have never been enough. Their quantitative inadequacy is so constant a feature of the economic history of the past hundred years that it cannot reasonably be dismissed as an accidental and occasional by-product of misguided beliefs and perverted policies. It forms part of the reality with which we must reckon.

This quantitative inadequacy is not a new reality. Even the briefest consideration of its most famous earlier example helps us to understand what we should and should not expect from peacetime stimulus. Contrary to what is often said, no major Western economy managed to overcome the Depression before the Second World War, with the sole, partial exception of Germany. Franklin Roosevelt, contrary to common latter-day revisionism, had not brought the country to sustained, broad-based recovery by the time he wavered and retrenched in his program of recovery through public spending, as every proponent in power of massive stimulus always has, and through his wavering and retrenchment he in fact helped to precipitate the frightening downturn of 1937–1938.

THE TRUNCATED DEBATE ABOUT THE SLUMP:
THE FORGOTTEN LESSONS OF
THE WAR ECONOMY

What took the advanced economies out of the Depression was the wartime mobilization of people and resources. The war that brought about such massive mobilization has little in common with the costly but limited military adventures of today. It was world war conducted in the spirit of total war. Between 1941 and 1945, U.S. GDP doubled.

The proto-Keynesianism adopted by the United States and other major Western governments during the worldwide depression of the 1930s was largely a failure. The war economy was, in straightforward economic terms, a success. It was not a success simply with regard to the expansion of output but also with respect to conventional progressive redistribution through the tax system as well as to the accelerated technological and organizational innovations that are generally associated with periods of major economic growth. The top marginal rate of the personal income tax, for example, reached levels in the United States that had never been seen before and have never been seen since then—in the midst of extraordinary expansion of output. Necessity, the mother of invention, helped provoke connected waves of innovation in technology, in the organization of work and production, and in the arrangements governing the relations between government and the ways private businesses dealt with one another.

It is important to understand the lessons of the war economy correctly. The radical expansion of output cannot be attributed solely to the forced mobilization of physical, financial, and human resources, massive as it was. Such an extraordinary effort might have come to grief at least in part had it not been accompanied by even more surprising advances in the forms of coordination and cooperation between government and business as well as among firms.

Here was a country that was the world headquarters of free-market doctrine. Its perennial bias was to believe that its founders had discovered at the time of the establishment of the American republic the definitive formula of a free society, enshrined in the rules of contract and property as well as in the Constitution. The formula needed only to be adjusted from time to time under the pressure of crisis and the prodding of changed circumstance. There was room for dispute about the respective roles of the market and regulation. But there was little doubt about the arrangements defining the market economy itself. Any talk of reshaping the institutions of the market economy fell under suspicion of being a disguised form of dirigisme. Such were the beliefs that prevailed before the war and that came again to predominate after the war. Even today the vulgar Keynesians and their conservative adversaries largely share these beliefs.

At their moment of national trial, world war, however, Americans gave these beliefs, supposedly entrenched in their national identity, short shrift. They retook the experiments conducted during the First World War under the aegis of the War Planning Board in an orchestration of productive effort that was neither the market economy as it had been conventionally understood nor central planning. The effort amounted to flexible decentralized strategic coordination between government and firms as well as cooperative competition among firms. It included a willingness to try out whatever way of organizing production at the plant level seemed to promise the most output with the fewest inputs in the shortest time and the greatest prospect of continuing innovation both in products and in the way of making them.

It was as if all the nostrums about the sanctity and the immutability of the market economy were only a mask that could be cast off when it needed to be. These nostrums were not cast off in favor of centralized, coercive direction, although there was some element of such direction as well as of self-serving profiteering. They were cast off in favor of a series of pragmatic institutional experiments defying the supposedly inviolate barrier between market and nonmarket forms of organization as well as between cooperation and competition.

What turned out to be more important than the institutional and ideological dogmas, whether pro-market or dirigiste, was the capacity to cooperate to reach shared and pressing goals. That capacity, already highly developed in the United States as well as in other advanced twentieth-century societies, was not the product of the war. It had roots in a form of social organization and consciousness that had affirmed belief in equality in the midst of tremendous inequality and faith in experimentalism despite an attachment to institutional formulas. However, in the circumstances of the war effort it found occasions for its exercise.

The central attribute of the war economy was the coexistence of a forced mobilization of resources with this quickened pace of bold practical experimentalism in the ways of organizing the effort. That combination—not proto-Keynesianism—was what really worked.

The traditional interpretation of the experience of the war economy, insofar as there is any interpretation at all, is that both its achievements and its methods are to be understood as pertinent only to the extraordinary conditions of wartime and are wholly inapplicable to circumstances of relative peace, such as those that prevail today. This conclusion is unwarranted. Every historical situation on which we can turn the tools of economic thinking is by definition special. Peacetime economies may differ from one another as much as they differ from a particular war economy. If, however, there is any hope of developing a science of economics as anything more than an analytic toolbox empty of causal theories, it can be only by discerning the more general and lasting implications of particular historical circumstances. No other circumstances can serve as the subject matter of economic analysis.

When the lessons of the wartime experience are transported to the conditions of relative peace—the conditions in which we face the slump today—the main lesson to be carried over is that because the forced mobilization of resources is less feasible, the other element—of institutional innovation in the practices of production and in the forms of cooperation and coordination between public and private agents as well as among private ones—becomes all the more important.

Let us take the work of stimulus, especially fiscal stimulus, through public works or through governmental incentives for business investment, as the most plausible counterpart, under conditions of peace, to the all-out mobilization of resources in total war. For all the reasons we have enumerated, stimulus will almost never be implemented in more than half-hearted form. Even when practiced more rather than less, it faces the intractable limitations we described earlier. That is not a reason to foreswear fiscal stimulus. It is a reason not to rely on it as the sole or even as the mainspring of recovery. Rather, the other element of the wartime experience—its institutional innovations in the form of the market economy and in the relation between government and business—deserves and repays greater emphasis. What the monetary and fiscal stimulus does not and cannot do all by itself, such innovations in the organization of production, exchange, and governance must accomplish.

THE TRUNCATED DEBATE ABOUT THE SLUMP: THE MISSING STRUCTURAL AGENDA

In the light of this elementary appreciation of the limits of fiscal and monetary stimulus and of the near inevitability of their truncation, it is possible to understand more clearly what is wrong with the present debate about the response to the slump.

The first thing that is wrong about it is that it consists largely in a polemic between the proponents of more stimulus and the opponents of stimulus. The proponents say, "If only the government had doubled the bet, if only it had shown itself willing to spend more or to put more money in the hands of consumers (by lowering taxes or by expanding the money supply), the slump would already have given way to a more convincing recovery." Their opponents claim that the recovery-producing effects of such measures are at best fragmentary and delayed, and their destructive effect on public finance is certain and immediate, with the future left to pay for the improvidence of the present. The proponents exaggerate and the opponents understate the benefits of the stimulus. Neither offers a realistic view of its uses and limits in the organization of a recovery.

The residue of this debate is what in fact exists today by way of response to the slump and in one or another version has always existed before in earlier instances of crisis and crisis management. It is stimulus by half: halting, compromised, neither here nor there. The defenders of the stimulus are then able to say that their recipe for massive governmental spending or monetary expansion has not been adequately tried. The critics of stimulus can in turn respond that the integrity of public finance has been compromised, with long-term negative consequences for future growth, and that there is little to show for the stimulus. Each party to this contest is allowed keep its prejudices to its own satisfaction, undaunted by the enigmas of the situation.

The second thing that is wrong with the present debate is that it is almost entirely deficient in any view of the institutional innovations that would be required to organize socially inclusive economic growth over the long term. The dominant perspective of the debate—both from the standpoint of the proponents of stimulus and from the perspective of its opponents—is that the slump represents an interruption, a threat, a shadow to be averted. Once it is averted, we can return to how things were before.

However, there is a flaw in the hope of getting back to business as usual. The problem is that things were not well before the crisis and the slump; the crisis and its aftermath are expressions, among other others, of these fundamental defects. The far-reaching estrangement of finance from the real economy and the gross inequalities of the present organization of market economies form a large part of the causal background to the recent crisis. They also help account for the limited efficacy of conventional fiscal and monetary stimulus. These problems were aggravated by the loosening of regulatory restraints on finance in the closing decades of the twentieth century, but they existed before it.

Under the present arrangements of all contemporary market economies, the link between the accumulated saving of society and its agenda of production remains weak. To a large extent, the finance of production relies on the retained and reinvested earnings of private firms, which is to say that production finances itself. Finance is then free to serve itself rather than production and to design successive layers of financial engineering with an ever more tenuous relation to any transactions in the real economy.

A relaxation of regulatory vigilance such as occurred in the second half of the twentieth century merely magnifies these effects. Finance, relatively ineffective in helping support production, may be very effective in disrupting it as its innovations become more and more self- referential and less and less useful to funding the production of actual goods and services. A crisis in finance such as the one we have witnessed will have major effects on the real economy chiefly by dissuading firms and households from running risks and maintaining high exposure to debt.

If the disengagement of finance from production formed part of the causal background to the crisis of 2007–2009 and to its continuing aftermath in the slump, the effect of inequality, manifest both proximately and remotely, formed another part.

As a proximate cause of the crisis of 2007–2009 in its American theater and its appearance in many countries around the world, inequality mattered chiefly as a provocation to put access to consumer credit in the place of redistribution of wealth and income as a basis for a market in mass consumption goods. Mass consumption requires in principle a popularization of purchasing power. Such popularization in turn seems to depend on widespread distribution of wealth and income: either through a broadening of access to economic and educational opportunities that influences the primary distribution of income or through the redistributive effects of taxation and social spending.

The economic growth that the advanced Western economies saw in the second half of the twentieth century relied heavily on the expansion of a market in mass-consumption goods. In this as in many other respects, the United States took the lead. When asked what book he would like to see in the hands of every Soviet child, Franklin Roosevelt answered: the Sears Roebuck catalog.

What real redistribution fails to provide, fake redistribution, in the form of greater access to consumer credit, helped supply instead. Escalating household indebtedness, crucial to the continuing exuberance of the mass-consumption market and therefore to the prosperity of the firms that directly or indirectly produced mass-consumption goods, was in turn made possible in part by the overvaluation of the housing stock as collateral. Such an overvaluation, in the context of widespread abuse and regulatory laxity in the mortgage market, turned out to be one of the immediate triggering mechanisms of the crisis in its American epicenter as well as in many of the countries that suffered most from the crisis, among them Spain, Ireland, and Britain.

Thus did a pseudodemocratization of credit replace a real redistribution of wealth and income. A fragile credit democracy came to stand in the place of the property-owning democracy that many had espoused.

The surplus countries, China first among them, had most of their mass-consumption markets abroad in the countries to which they sold their goods and services. Such countries replaced redistribution not with credit but with exports—exports to countries that had put credit in the place of redistribution.

Inequality matters, however, also in another, deeper, and less-direct way that has more to do with the supply side of the economy than with its demand side and with firms rather than with households. In all major economies in the world, the most important, wealth-creating innovations have come increasingly to be concentrated in advanced sectors of the economy, strongly connected to comparable productive vanguards around the world—with which they trade people, practices, and ideas—but only weakly linked to other parts of their own national economies. The result is that the greatest engine for dramatic rises in productivity finds its potential diminished by the narrowness of its scope of operation and influence. This diminishment is a formidable constraint on any attempt to make the slump give way to a new cycle of enduring and broad-based economic growth.

The established debate about the crisis has left twin imperatives almost entirely untouched: the need to put finance more effectively at the service of the real economy in general and of production and innovation in particular as well as the need to loosen the destructive restraints that inequality imposes on growth. The ideas of regulation and reform that have thus far been presented in the United States and other advanced economies do not even come close to addressing these twin problems, much less to proposing solutions to them. These ideas can be classed under the heading of four main agendas of reform and regulation. Each agenda has been prominently championed by a distinct group of advocates and constituents in the United States and in other rich industrial democracies.

The first agenda is a classic New Deal–style program (as exemplified, for example, by the proposals of the Volcker committee). It wants to reinstate precautions, such as the division between insured deposit taking and proprietary trading, that were prominent in the American and European regulatory response to the Depression of the 1930s but that have since been relaxed. Its characteristic concern is to insulate the part of the banking system on which the general public relies against the excesses of speculative finance.

The second agenda is a new technocratic project. Its sponsors are the high governmental officials in the finance or treasury departments or ministries of the United States and the other advanced economies as well as their academic allies. Its defining concerns are the strengthening of supervisory and resolution authority—that is to say, authority to take over, close down, or turn around failing financial institutions, especially when their instability threatens the stability of the financial system as whole. The goal is very clearly, as one of the favorite metaphors to emerge in the crisis reveals, "to put out a fire." If the crisis is an "eight-alarm fire," the available instruments are regarded as insufficient. Once the fire is put out, everything can presumably go back to the good old days before the conflagration.

The third agenda can be called the "Basel program." Its source is the intellectual and bureaucratic elite of international high finance, as represented by its iconic institution, the Bank of International Settlements in Basel. Its concern is to contain or counterbalance the risks of financial instability. It characteristically proposes to do so by imposing more severe standards on the relation between the capital structure of banks and the risks and liabilities to which they are exposed. It wants, for example, to make the banks conform to more stringent capital-adequacy requirements.

The fourth agenda, the only one with overtly popular concerns, is a consumer-protection initiative. It seeks better to protect the public against the abuses of the finance industry through a combination of regulatory paternalism and mandated transparency. Its favorite instrument is a consumer-protection agency in the area of finance.

Taken together, these agendas of reform fail to deal, even in fragmentary and oblique fashion, with the twin structural problems that are central to the genealogy of the crisis and the slump. They also do nothing to remedy the consequences of the relative inefficacy of monetary and fiscal stimulus. It may well be said that it was never their purpose do so. Their intent, so the argument would go, was to discipline finance and to prevent it from continuing to do or from doing once again the harm that it has just done to the livelihood and welfare of millions of people. It is therefore fair to ask whether any or all of these agendas are in fact able successfully to address the trouble with finance. The answer to this question is no.

THE TWO TROUBLES WITH FINANCE

Grant that the policies of stimulus espoused by the vulgar Keynesians cannot and will not be deployed at the scale that, according to their proponents, would be necessary to ensure a vigorous recovery. Concede that even if they were, they would not all by themselves suffice to secure the benefits that they are hoped to produce. Admit that the agendas of reform and regulation that have thus far commanded attention and authority have little potential to reach the deeper causes of the crisis and the slump.

Even so, you may protest, what has been accomplished is to reaffirm, in practice as well as in discourse, the need to control finance and never to forget that finance is "the squeaky wheel of capitalism," the flaw through which an otherwise vibrant economy may become vulnerable to calamitous disruption. At least here, it might be supposed, there has been success: advance in insight, making possible progress in law and policy.

An indisputable merit of both Keynes's economics and vulgar Keynesianism is to view a market economy as having problems and possibilities very different from those of a barter economy. They refuse to see money as merely a transparent and innocuous instrumentality of real economic transactions. In the academic analysis of the crisis and the slump as well as in the policy debate about how best to respond to them, finance has loomed large. Together with proposals to extend or to retrench fiscal and monetary expansionary policies and ideas about how best to redress the mass imbalances between surplus and deficit countries in world trade and capital flows, the call to regulate or re-regulate finance holds the center of attention in every country touched by the slump and by the crisis from which it resulted.

To no avail. The ruling ideas continue to prevent us from grasping the real trouble with finance. The discussion of finance has followed the psychological bias of pre and post-Marginalist Anglo-American economics, aggravated by the abuse of mathematics (as a substitute for causal reasoning rather than as an expression of it) in contemporary economic analysis.

A characteristic idea emerging from the present discussion of finance is that there is a tendency, entrenched in our habits of mind, to underestimate the significance of uncommon and extreme events. Such events, we are taught, fall outside the established data sets. They occur more frequently than even the most sophisticated observers are inclined to expect. When they occur, they break the bank, literally and metaphorically, and give force to the expression "all bets are off."

The rough and hazy distinction between ordinary and extraordinary calamities bearing on finance gains a specious semblance of theoretical clarity and grounding when it is interpreted in the context of a contrast between quantifiable risk and unquantifiable uncertainty. The distinction confuses flaws in knowledge with features of the world; it trivializes our ignorance as if it were simply a failure to register a natural difference between two classes of economic phenomena. Our quantification of risk can be only as precise and as reliable as our insight into the causal processes that change pieces of reality. If there are changes that seem unexpected and unaccountable on the basis of our established causal ideas about economic activity, they must seem surprising only because these ideas are defective. Whether we are able to correct their defects or not, our first interest is to recognize them.

Both the occurrence and the effects of traumas and catastrophes in the realm of finance are shaped by the institutional arrangements and the enacted beliefs that organize financial activity and determine its relation to the real economy. They are not natural phenomena. For all these reasons, it is safe to say that the trouble with finance is not that we have thus far failed to recognize and guard against a category of extraordinary financial calamities forming an intrinsic and perennial feature of economic reality.

The real trouble with finance is twofold. To appreciate the nature of these two sources of trouble and the relation between them is to acquire part of the intellectual equipment that we need to better address, without superstition, the problems of the slump.

The first trouble with finance is that it operates in an institutional setting not of its own making, from which there arise destabilizing forces that it cannot control. In fact, financiers can only partly understand these forces, much less manage them, from the vantage point of their activity. Each of these sources of instability represents at least a partial cause of one of those varieties of danger that, according to the now fashionable discourse, generate unquantifiable uncertainty rather than unquantifiable risk.

That finance operates in an institutional context not of its own making is simply a special case of a more general truth: that the market economy cannot produce its own institutional framework. The institutions of the market are not created in the market. They are fashioned in politics as well as in thought and are embodied in law. The idea that the market in general and the financial market in particular generate their own institutional form becomes plausible only in the light of another idea, the practical influence of which in the affairs of modern societies can hardly be overestimated. This is the idea that a market economy has a single necessary and natural form, expressed above all in a particular system of rules and rights of contract and property.

This idea underlies much of the contemporary discussion of finance and regulation. One of its implications is that the proper task of regulation—of finance or of any other branch of market activity—is to remedy particular market defects, of imperfect competition or asymmetrical information. What this idea disregards may be the most important need in the work of regulation and reform: to reshape the arrangements that define the market economy in every area, including finance. If, as is in fact the case, the market economy has radically different institutional forms, expressed in law, with distinct consequences for the path of economic growth as well as for the distribution of wealth, power, and income, a discourse about localized market flaws and remedies for such flaws is incomplete. The issue is always also: Which market economy do we want, and what way of solving today's problems will help us move toward it?

Consider an open, partial list of attributes of the institutional setting in which finance operates and from which there may arise destabilizing forces that overwhelm the financiers' calculations and expectations.

A first attribute of this setting is at once negative and fundamental: the institutional context within which finance operates at any given time is a relatively ramshackle construction. It is not the unavoidable expression in legal detail of the necessary organization of a market economy. It is the surprising and contingent outcome of practical and visionary contests, stretching back in time. It is susceptible at any moment to piecemeal revision, no less decisive in its influence for being fragmentary.

Consider, as an example, the institutional context of American finance at the time of the outbreak of the recent crisis. A simple way to describe it is to say that it was the product of a prior partial hollowing out of the regulatory framework of finance established at the time of the New Deal. The uneven hollowing out took place under the prodding of that loose combination of practical and intellectual influences that is responsible for much of institutional change in history: the economic power gained by high finance, translated into political influence, and the intellectual influence of theoretical and practical ideas that came to prominence in that period. Among the theoretical ideas were doctrines such as "rational expectations theory" and "real business-cycle theory" that discounted the efficacy of governmental action in a range of economic affairs. Among the practical ideas was the view that the untying of investment banks from some of the restraints imposed in the New Deal period represented a requirement of competition among large-scale financial firms in the global economy; the New Deal restraints came to be disparaged as burdensome remnants of a bygone era.

Such a haphazard institutional compromise can be hard to change on account of all the powerful interests and prejudices that shield it. Yet once that shield is punctured in any direction by opposing ideas and interests, the compromise can change. Even a partial change can decisively alter the situation and the evolution of finance.

A second attribute of the institutional setting in which finance operates is to be subject to the effects of technological innovation or revolution on economic life. These effects are never direct and determinate; they are always mediated by institutional arrangements. The role of institutions in mediating them only increases the uncertainty of their impact.

A third attribute of the institutional context of finance is the variable divergence between two forces that operate upon it: on the one hand popular support, wielding the suffrage, and on the other economic power, manifest in the granting or the denial of confidence. In all contemporary democracies, these two forces regularly diverge. A force that loses in the course of electoral politics and public policy can hope to strike back through disinvestment and capital flight. A line of action that claims to conform to the dictates of financial confidence can be defied and defeated in politics. The relation between these two sets of outcomes conforms to no higher logic; it is open to the consequences of the next step in economic or political action.

A fourth attribute of the institutional framework in which financial activity now takes place has to do with the intractable limits to the replacement of a progressive redistribution of wealth and income by the popularization of consumer, credit-card, and mortgage credit. Within a narrow range of experience, the broadening of access to credit can produce some of the same effects of a progressive redistribution of wealth and income, whether such redistribution occurs through an enlargement of economic and educational opportunity or through the retrospective means of taxation and social spending. That a democratization of credit cannot match the work of redistribution, however, even in the narrow task of sustaining a market in mass-consumption goods and services, the genealogy of the recent crisis has once again shown. The consequences of this failure in the functional equivalence between greater access to credit and greater sharing of wealth and income can at any moment generate destabilizing forces.

A fifth attribute of the institutional context in which finance operates is its susceptibility to the effect of the intellectual fashions influencing the conduct of monetary policy by central banks. What will be the contrasting attitudes to the evils of inflation and deflation? Or the relative weight placed on the goals of monetary stability and full employment? Or the trust placed in policy regimes such as inflation targeting and its rivals? The answers to these questions lack a secure basis in any economic analysis with a rightful claim to the authority of science. Yet they nevertheless may exert powerful effects, generating other destabilizing forces.

A sixth attribute of the institutional ground on which finance operates is international anarchy. There is not now a commonly accepted monetary basis for the world economy. The periods in which such a basis was widely accepted—the heyday of the gold standard until its collapse in the 1920s and the rule of the original Bretton Woods system from its conception in the aftermath of the Second World War to its collapse in August 1971— have been followed by periods of relative national autarchy and international disorder. The precarious and contested role of the dollar as the international reserve currency merely masks this disorder and attenuates its consequences.

An expression of this disorder is that in choosing which two aims marked out by the so-called trilemma of fixed exchange rates, monetary sovereignty, and free capital flows are to be preferred (given that all three of them at once cannot be had), the major national and regional economies of the world have made divergent and contradictory choices. China has chosen the first and the second elements of this trilemma; the United States, the second and the third.

The present anarchy in the monetary arrangements of the world has helped make possible the vast imbalances between countries (beginning with China) that run huge surpluses of trade and saving, on the one hand, and countries (the United States first among them) that import and consume much more than they produce and live off borrowed money, on the other.

The international anarchy and its expression in these imbalances represents yet another source of tremendous destabilizing mechanisms in the setting of finance, even for the capital that continues to stay at home, as most capital does.

This enumeration of attributes of the context of finance amounts to an open list of forces that both separately and conjointly can at any moment wreak havoc on financial calculation. The identity of the particular sources and phenomena is constantly changing: what it is now is not what it was a generation ago, and a generation hence it will not be what it is now.

The forms of destabilization that arise from these sources cannot in principle be avoided by any financial innovation. In fact, even the first source of instability—the fateful but haphazard, contingent, and therefore revisable character of the institutional setting within which finances operates—cannot be easily understood, much less controlled, from the vantage point of the financiers. For them, the sole sufficient antidote is a prudence so guarded that it contradicts the requirements of risk taking and entrepreneurship.

From the perspective of government and society, however, there is a possible response to the problem presented by the first trouble with finance. The generic character of the response is what we call "financial deepening" in contrast to "financial hypertrophy." By "hypertrophy of finance," we understand increase in the size of the financial sector, of its share in profit, talent, and influence, regardless of the service that it renders to the real economy. By "financial deepening," we mean the intimacy of the relation between finance and the real economy: not only consumption but also and above all production and innovation. The more broadly based the engagement of finance in the whole cycle of production and exchange and the greater the number of independent sources as well as consumers of finance, the less likely it is that there be a specifically financial crisis that is not simply the expression in finance of a crisis in the real economy. Financial deepening thus understood is the development of which financial hypertrophy represents the perversion.

Regulation as conventionally understood—the correction of localized market deficiencies, such as inequalities of bargaining power and asymmetries of information—cannot ensure financial deepening the better to avoid financial hypertrophy. Regulation cannot do so unless it is practiced as the first step toward innovations in the arrangements governing the relation of finance to the real economy that put the former more effectively at the service of the latter.

The first trouble with finance, then, is its perennial vulnerability to the destabilizing forces that arise from an institutional setting beyond its control or even beyond its field of vision. The second trouble with finance is that, regardless of the interests and intentions of individual bankers, entrepreneurs, and consumers, it may not be able to perform its supposed goal of channeling the saving of society into productive investment. Its ability to serve this goal is hostage to the institutional arrangements governing the relation of finance to the real economy and to the possibilities of production. Those arrangements may either tighten or loosen this relation.

The standard identity of aggregate saving with aggregate investment makes it difficult even to formulate the problem. It becomes even harder to do so because the categorical language of national accounts, established after the Second World War under the influence of Keynes and his followers, turns this identity into a terminological tautology.

In this way, this identity reinforces the tilt of dominant thinking about the economy and the role of finance within it. The market will route saving into its most efficient uses, the available language of national accounts as well as the predominant doctrines in economics prompt us to believe. To the extent that it fails to do so, the failure must be due to a localized market failure—imperfect competition, unequal power, asymmetrical information—which it is the proper aim of regulatory rule and policy to redress or to counterbalance. Such is the approach that has continued, despite all evidence to the contrary, to shape almost all contemporary thinking about the regulation of finance.

FINANCE: TURNING THE BAD MASTER INTO A GOOD SERVANT

The familiar categories and the prevailing ideas may make it difficult to study how different institutional arrangements may either tighten or loosen the link between finance and the real economy. They may make the very statement of such a problem seem nonsensical. It is nevertheless a real problem in a real world. It will not vanish simply because our preferred ways of talking and thinking fail to accommodate it.

That institutional arrangements, expressed in law, decisively modify the extent to which saving is channeled into production and productive investment can be shown by homely examples. All agents of finance, including all manner of banks, are themselves legal constructions, subject to a long, variable, and often surprising institutional evolution. The pension regimes of the present—a major way in which saving has come to be held and deployed—are relatively recent creations. The way in which pension saving becomes available for productive investment is entirely determined by the rules under which these regimes operate. A particular form of financial activity such as venture capital that seems very directly to exemplify the putative major role of finance is an innovation with an uncertain future: What, for example, can and should be the respective roles of private and public venture capital?

Under the institutional arrangements of present-day market economies production is largely self-financed on the basis of the retained and reinvested earnings of private firms. The extent to which it is self-financed, although always overwhelming, is nevertheless variable. We have reason to suppose that the existing variations are only a subset of a much broader range of possible variation.

We have only to consider historical experience to appreciate how in the past institutional innovations have succeeded in making finance more useful to production. If they have made it more useful in the past, they can again make it more useful in the future. The early-nineteenth-century United States, for example, witnessed a struggle over the national banks. During the presidency of Andrew Jackson, this struggle culminated in the dissolution of the Second Bank of the United States and in the subsequent development of the most decentralized system of credit that had ever existed in a major country: a network of local banks, whose potential remains to this day far from being exhausted. This banking network placed finance more effectively at the service of both the local producer and the local consumer than it had previously been in the United States or elsewhere.

An advance of this kind can be achieved again, not by repeating the institutional formulas of an earlier epoch but by institutional innovations suited to the present circumstance. Such innovations would give practical content to the idea of financial deepening. Their working assumption must be that it is not enough to cut finance down to size—by requiring, for example, more stringent capital-leverage ratios or even by imposing absolute limits on the size of financial firms if we fail to establish arrangements that make finance more useful to production and innovation. We do not serve the deepening of finance—in the sense defined here—merely by combating its hypertrophy.

The relation between the two troubles with finance becomes clear in the course of the effort to deal with these troubles. In the spirit of a pragmatist experimentalism, the answer to the speculative question comes in practice.

To the susceptibility of finance to destabilizing forces that arise from the institutional setting in which it operates—forces beyond its reach and even beyond its view—there is no effective response other than financial deepening: the broadest possible grounding of finance in the whole work of the real economy, in every step of the cycle of production and exchange. Such a grounding does not advance spontaneously or automatically as a result of the sheer quantitative expansion of financial activity; it depends on the institutional arrangements governing finance and its relation to the real economy.

Such arrangements may so disfavor the connection that they help generate financial hypertrophy without financial deepening. This is a recurrent phenomenon in world economic history. We have seen an example of it in the events leading up to the recent worldwide financial and economic crisis.

This reasoning shows that the only way we can effectively deal with the first trouble is also the generic character of the response to the second trouble. The idea of financial deepening marks out the conceptual space in which to address, through institutional innovation detailed in law, the relation of finance to the real economy in general and to production in particular. Just as economic institutions can organize a market economy in different ways, with different consequences for the trajectory of growth as well as for the distribution of advantage, so the part of this institutional order that deals with the role of finance can either strengthen or weaken the service that finance renders to production and to the real economy as a whole.

It is this simple but vital fact that our established ideas and nomenclature prevent us from fully acknowledging or even describing. A discourse about regulation that identifies as its task the redressing of localized market failures further entrenches this way of thinking and talking. In every real dispute about regulation, the subtext has to do with alternative pathways for the reorganization of the area of social and economic practice in question. Regulation, properly understood, is still regarded as the first step toward institutional reconstruction.

Nothing in this view implies any reason to deny or to suppress the speculative element in finance. These ideas do not contradict the conventional view that speculative financial activity can be useful in generating information and organizing risk. It is an intrinsic feature of finance to make informed bets about future states of affairs. Some of these gambles may function (as in hedging devices) to limit rather than to extend risk. Others may have no such risk-containing use without thereby ceasing to be useful and legitimate.

One of the many dimensions in which one way of organizing a market economy in legal detail may be better than another is that it encourages greater diversity and experimentation in the forms of production and exchange. That means making use, in the organization of market economy, of the principle that market economies can take alternative legal-institutional forms.

The conventional idea of freedom to recombine factors of production within an institutional framework of production and exchange that is left unchallenged and unchanged can and should be broadened into an unconventional idea of greater freedom to experiment with the institutional forms of a market economy. Among such forms are the regimes of contract and property. A national economy should not be fastened to a single version of itself. Its institutional organization should radicalize the organized anarchy that is the genius of a market order.

One of the many terrains for such variation in the legal-institutional setting of a market economy concerns the room for speculative activity, which may properly be much greater in some economic sectors and contexts than in others. Instead of allowing only a modicum of speculation, it may be better to prohibit speculation altogether in some settings and to give it the freest rein in others. In that way, we refuse to entrench as institutional dogma what can and should be open to experiment and collective learning.

Whether, however, society gives greater or lesser space to speculative activity, it must still shape the relation of financial speculation to the agenda of production in the real economy. In this respect, neither what the government wants nor what the financiers seek is decisive. The crucial point lies in the institutional arrangements that make finance, including the most speculative forms of financial activity, either more or less useful to the expansion of output and to the enhancement of both total factor and labor productivity. The problem of speculative finance turns out to be just one more field in which to confront the distinction between the hypertrophy and the deepening of finance.

STIMULUS RECONSIDERED

These ideas provide a point of departure for the design of a response to the slump that is adapted to a wide range of circumstances. Underlying this response is a conception of the path to socially inclusive economic growth—which, together with national independence, is the most widely professed policy goal in the world today—and of the role that public as well as private finance can play in the achievement of that objective. If the central topic of this book is the road to recovery, its secondary subject is the intellectual practice that can free us from the superstitions that continue to block this road.

In the end, it is not enough to reorganize the economy; it is also necessary to reorient economics. A text like the present one can address this ulterior subject only by indirection and suggestion, but it must address the subject nevertheless. The problem is not simply that much of the world, especially its richest part, has chosen the wrong response to the slump under the influence of powerful interests that have already profited and stand to gain much more from this misdirection. The problem is that policy continues to be bent under the yoke of illusion—at the end of the day, illusion about the possible institutional arrangements of a market economy.

Let us begin by retaking the thread of the earlier argument about why a stimulus, deployed in the circumstances of a contemporary society, is always likely to be too limited in its magnitude as well as in its instruments to achieve its proposed objectives. Under the conditions of a slump preceded by a crisis of confidence in the debt burden weighing on both households and firms (a "balance-sheet recession"), expansionary monetary policy conducted by central banks is likely to be relatively ineffective. A minimal or even negative cost of money will not in and of itself induce firms and households to invest or to consume if their income or profits

have already collapsed and their debt exposure has come to seem dangerous or even unsustainable.

Under such conditions, fiscal policy is likely to be the sole relatively effective instrument, and indeed this fiscal policy will be more in the form
of governmental spending than in the form of tax reductions. The reason
for this fact is simple and well established: the money saved by a lower tax
obligation will tend to be used to pay debt down rather than to spend or to
invest. It is the circumstance to which the policy tools of vulgar Keynesianism are most directly suited.

When, however, a dynamic of exorbitant indebtedness does not form a
major part of the circumstances of the crisis and the slump, monetary
stimulus, together with fiscal stimulus in the form of lower taxes rather
than of higher public spending, may take the upper hand.

Whether the crisis and the slump are of the first nature or of the second, and whether therefore fiscal or monetary stimulus must perform the
leading role in addressing them, the same basic constraint will hold for the
reasons we have examined. Under peacetime conditions, the stimulus will
be too small to secure a decisive recovery. The proponents of more stimulus will protest, but to little avail, and their frustrated insistence will
form a predictable part of the situation. A half-hearted stimulus, appear-
ing (to its proponents) to be disproportionately small in relation to the severity of the slump, will be the only stimulus ever achieved.

If the crisis and the slump are significant—as they have been in many
countries in the course of these recent events—the stimulus will fail to
secure a vigorous and broad-based recovery. It will fail not only because it
is too small but also because it is unaccompanied by the institutional innovations that can favor socially inclusive economic growth. In both respects, the practice of the stimulus will be unlike the experience of the
war economy. That experience, we have argued, benefited from the combination of a much higher mobilization of physical, financial, and human
resources with bold experimentation in the arrangements of production
and exchange, coordination and competition.

None of this discussion provides a reason to forego stimulus, designed
according to the nature of the crisis and the slump. However, the stimulus
should be practiced and pressed with no illusion that it will be sufficient to
ensure strong and inclusive recovery. In the real conditions in which any
contemporary stimulus can be wielded, it plays two roles.

Its first role is to prevent the aggravation of the crisis or of the subsequent slump. In so doing, it gives time to develop the intellectual con-

tent and the political basis for a program of broad-based and inclusive growth.

Its second role is to serve, so far as feasible, as the first step in such a program, a down payment on its intentions. With ingenuity and luck, the stimulus can be so designed that it incorporates in fragmentary and anticipatory form some elements of the inclusive growth project while helping to create more favorable conditions for the adoption of other elements.

The crucial attribute that would enable a short-term program of recovery to perform this role is some limited combination of the two elements of the war economy: heightened demand for consumption and investment goods and a series of institutional innovations suggesting the proposed direction for advance. Consider each of these concerns in turn.

Both monetary and fiscal stimulus may strengthen demand for consumption and investment goods. However, expansionary monetary policy does so only indirectly. It can create a circumstance in which households and firms are not discouraged from going further into debt in the pursuit of entrepreneurial or consumption opportunities. In circumstances in which the household and the firm already find themselves bent under the yoke of debt and the anticipation of a benign economic future has already dissipated, such encouragement is likely to prove insufficient. That is precisely the circumstance of a balance-sheet recession.

And what if the cost of borrowing money is made negative? The government may in effect pay firms and households to borrow by any number of devices. The firms and households may still prefer to use the money simply to pay down their debts rather than to extend them. Or the central bank (were it free from the worship of sound money) might simply opt to debase the currency by any number of other devices, thus redistributing wealth from creditors to debtors. It would do so under cover of the bias of the law, which refuses to recognize in this redistribution a taking of property, which requires compensation.

The redistributive effect may weaken the unwillingness to risk and to invest but only at the cost of a planned inflation, with all the sequel of social consequences and political reactions that such an event has regularly produced. The remedy may be universally regarded as worse than the evil that it was designed to correct.

Even if monetary policy could be effective in the circumstance of a slump subsequent to a debt overhang, it cannot by its very nature serve as the means with which to prefigure a project of inclusive growth. Monetary stimulus may perform the first role of the stimulus—to avoid the worsening of the crisis or of its aftereffects and to buy time. It may do so either because the economic downturn is not contaminated by excess debt or because, even if it is, cheap money may help. It is, however, incapable of performing the second role of a stimulus: to foreshadow a different economic future.

For that role, only fiscal stimulus suffices. In fact, only one species of fiscal stimulus can do the job: the species that involves public spending as opposed to tax abatement. In the performance of the foreshadowing role, the diminishment of taxation is likely to suffer limitations similar to those faced by monetary policy. At least, it will suffer such limitations unless the grant of the tax favors is subject to the requirement that taxpayers invest the money foregone by the government in certain ways and to specific ends. The imposition of such a requirement, however, turns the tax favors into the equivalent of a public-spending program.

A fiscal stimulus, understood in this restricted sense, should emphasize each of the components of the growth strategy we later outline. Its chief concern should not be further to divert public resources to failing big financial organizations or to inefficient mass-production industries. It should prefer those uses of governmental resources that strengthen the supply as well as the demand side of the economy. It should also give priority to the commitment of public resources that combines such two-sided stimulus with an opening to the institutional innovations useful to broad-based and inclusive economic growth. In this way, the stimulus mimics features of the war economy.

Imagine three large directions for such a project. We later discuss each of them in greater detail.

One direction has to do with tightening the link between saving and production: diminishing the extent to which the production system is required to finance itself, as it does in all contemporary market economies, while much of the productive potential of saving gets squandered in a financial casino. This direction implies investing in the organizations that most directly connect saving to productive investment: the country's network of local banks. It also suggests use of independent public entities—administered independently and professionally and subject to the discipline of market competition—to imitate the work of private capital.

A second direction is the enhancement of the productive apparatus through governmental action and investment. The most important addressees of such action are the many small and medium businesses responsible for generating the vast majority of jobs and output in every contemporary economy. The most promising method of such enhancement is the propagation of successful local practice and the opening of access to credit, technology, knowledge, and knowledge-based capabilities. The favorable institutional setting is one that organizes a form of coordination between government and firms that is decentralized, pluralistic, participatory, and experimental.

The radicalization of the experimental impulse so important to innovation and thus to growth ought to count for more than any dogmatic preference for a particular sector of the economy. To this principle, however, there are two important exceptions.

The first exception is the most traditional object of any program of public expenditure: public works undertaken to improve the physical infrastructure of productive activity. Here the reason for the exception is the contribution of such investment to the feasibility and productivity of first-order productive activity.

The second exception is public investment or public incentives to private investment in the technologies, products, and services of a low-carbon economy. The ground of this exception is the need to prepare a growth strategy that is not self-defeating.

The third direction of priority public investment in a fiscal stimulus foreshadowing another future is the development of human capabilities through the generalization of a form of education that marshals information selectively as a tool for strengthening our powers of analysis, prefers cooperation to the combination of individualism and authoritarianism in learning, and approaches every subject dialectically through contrasting points of view. Generic and flexible conceptual and practical capabilities rather than task-specific skills and freedom from the mental constraints of the immediate circumstance are the overriding concerns of this form of education.

We shall soon have occasion further to elaborate the content of such of an alternative. What matters for the moment is to appreciate the role that a stimulus can perform in anticipating it. Each of the three directions we have just described combines a target for investment with a principle of reorganization.

Fiscal and monetary stimulus cannot be the core of a program of vigorous and inclusive economic recovery. If properly understood and designed, however, it can represent the first step of such a program. The mistaken view of its potential, professed by the vulgar Keynesians, gets in the way.

THE FALSE ALTERNATIVE PRESENTED BY THE EXAMPLE OF THE EMERGING ECONOMIES

The large emerging economies, especially three of those that have came to be known under the abbreviation BRIC—Brazil, Russia, India, and China (later BRICSA, with the addition of South Africa)—have been relatively successful in dealing with the consequences of the recent crisis. This relative success has sometimes supported the belief that these three countries—Brazil, India, and China—have already discovered the secret of an alternative. To some, it has seemed that we need only to bring into the light of theory and then to implement as policy the path that they have already opened up. Before addressing the program of recovery, to be foreshadowed by the design of the stimulus, we should pause to consider to what extent their experience offers a road map, indeed a shortcut, to a recovery plan. For this purpose, we take Brazil as the chief focus: free of some of the complications that attend the experience of its much larger BRIC equivalents, its experience enables us directly to grasp something unexpected.

The relative success of the large emerging economies (at least insofar as we can take Brazil as the example) in mitigating the consequences of the crisis and in averting a slump fails to provide a model worthy of imitation. The issue is not so much that the relative success has depended on conditions that are too peculiar to be readily reproduced throughout the world. It is rather that this success is bought at too high price with regard to the task of the future. Their success illuminates certain vital aspects of the workings of contemporary economies but without marking a path to vigorous, broad-based, and socially inclusive recovery. It has helped avoid a greater evil without ensuring access to a yet greater good. It deserves to be understood as a revelation rather than to be followed as an example.

A first factor explaining the relative success of these emerging economies is the use of governmentally controlled banks to ensure the continuation of credit flows. It is a great advantage to count such banks among the instruments of public policy. However, it is not as great an advantage as genuine financial deepening would be: a tightening of the link between finance and production, enhanced by a broadening of access to credit, especially credit for producers, by enterprises in all sectors and of every scale. Better to decentralize and democratize the whole of finance than to use banks controlled by the state to make up for the deficiencies of an unreconstructed banking system.

There is no reason in principle why governmentally controlled banks cannot be used to help fund small and medium businesses, start-ups included, and to mimic the work of private venture capital. In this way, they would work—and in fact they have sometimes worked—as a front line in the deepening and democratization of finance. However, in a very divided and unequal society, as the large developing countries generally are, the distribution of subsidized credit has more often favored a relatively small number of big enterprises with sweetheart deals by the state. In Brazil, for instance, the major part of these resources has been used to benefit a small group of big private business under the pretext of helping to turn them into "world champions." In China, it has served largely to maintain the funding for governmental-owned enterprises.

Dualism in the credit market—two different markets for credit, organized by different rules and with unequal prices for money—has been characteristic of these economies. Such dualism has repeatedly created the means with which to favor a few and disfavor the many.

Sometimes the dualism takes the form (as it does now in Brazil and China) of a contrast between an administered market in subsidized credit and a relatively freer market in nonsubsidized credit. At other times, it takes the form (as it has in economies marked by financial repression) of credit rationing: someone in the government gets to decide who has access to scarce credit. One way or another, the expansion of credit under the conditions of credit dualism, although motivated by the effort to prevent a slump, magnifies the impact of the preexisting inequalities.

A second factor is relative autarky: the degree to which a national economy is independent of the world economy. Despite the vast changes in recent decades that have brought the large emerging economies into the global economy, it is only recently that these economies have ceased to be relatively autarchic. In 1960, foreign trade represented 14 percent of Brazil's GDP and 9 percent of China's.

A paced and limited integration into the world economy, subordinated to the requirements of a national development strategy, is better than an unconditional integration. By "unconditional integration," we mean one that accepts the present allocation of comparative advantage among national economies as the basis for a place in the world economy and then goes on to subordinate the national strategy to the constraints imposed by this global niche.

However, the best movement is one that enhances integration but seeks to shape it in the service of a project designed to create new comparative advantages. The most effective way to create them is not dogmatically to choose sectors that are supposedly bearers of the future (as if the future did not have to make its own choices). It is to empower experimentalism: by establishing arrangements that broaden economic and educational opportunity; by giving small and medium businesses access to forms of credit, technology, marketing, and knowledge normally reserved to big businesses; by propagating successful local practice; and, above all, by creating the means and the conditions for pluralism and experimentation in the institutional forms of the market economy—that is to say, in the ways of organizing production and exchange.

Every path of globalization and toward globalization must then be judged by the standard of whether it serves such a program. By this standard, the conditional integration of the large emerging economies into the global economy cannot be judged a success; such integration is simply the avoidance of a lesser evil rather than the attainment of a greater good. Success would have required more integration achieved under the aegis of a systemic project friendlier to experimentalism and pluralism than the form of globalization that has thus far prevailed.

Such a project would put free trade in its place as a means rather than as an end. It would take as its goal not the maximization of free trade but the construction of an open world economy in forms allowing for the coexistence of alternative national development strategies and alternative experiences of civilization. It would reject the institutional maximalism that now characterizes the trajectory of globalization—the requirement that trading countries accept, as the condition of engagement in an open world economy, a particular version of the market economy: the version suiting the interests and the prejudices of the dominant powers. In place of this institutional maximalism, this project would establish an institutional minimalism: a maximum of economic openness with a minimum of restraint on institutional diversity and innovation. It would attenuate the contrast between the freedom granted to things—and then to money—to cross natural frontiers and the denial of any such equivalent prerogative to workers. And it would require such respect for rights and labor standards as can assure that free labor, as the human basis of the world economy, be really free, not servile subordination under the disguise of the employment contract.

In no area is the contrast between the lesser evil and the greater good more striking than with regard to finance itself. A simple reason why many of the large emerging economies—the BRIC economies in particular—did relatively better in the crisis than the advanced economies is that they refused to open their capital accounts fully. In this way, they limited their vulnerability to the national effects of international financial turmoil.

Consider, again, the case of Brazil. Brazil had generally followed the major Latin American economies in accepting what was in effect a proxy for the nineteenth-century and early-twentieth-century gold standard. Of the gold standard it has been rightly said that its guiding purpose was to make the level of economic activity depend on the state of business confidence—confidence, that is to say, in government policy. Most of the Latin American republics had accepted in the closing decades of the twentieth century a constellation of policies and ideas yielding a similar effect: acquiescence to a low level of domestic saving, consequent dependence on foreign capital, and openness to foreign capital, whether loan capital or portfolio capital, including greater freedom for capital to enter and leave. The practical result was to make the national government relatively more dependent on international financial confidence. However, rather than being seen as a problem, this dependence was embraced as a solution: it tied the hands of national governments, inhibiting, or so it was supposed, the pursuit of economic adventurism in the double form of populist handouts and trade protectionism.

There was, however, an exception to this surrender to the functional equivalent of the gold standard: continuing limits to the openness of the capital account. These limits proved important in explaining the relative success of these emerging economies in resisting the effects of the crisis of the early twentieth century.

Nevertheless, in accord with the spirit of our argument, closure to world finance is not as desirable as openness to it on the basis of financial deepening, a mobilization of national resources (in which a war economy without a war is the limiting case), and an institutional broadening of economic and educational opportunity. Such a basis provides elements of a strong national project. The dangers of financial openness do not grow simply, as the conventional discourse assumes, in proportion to the absence of regulatory precautions. They also and above all grow in proportion to the avoidance of conditions that bring the national economy to its knees by making it dependent on foreign finance and financial confidence.

A third factor accounting for the relative success of some of the large emerging economies but not others was the boom in commodity prices. It is a factor that, among the BRIC countries, was wholly pertinent only to Brazil. Russia's extraction of rents from nature in the form of oil and gas was narrowly focused and made the Russian economy susceptible to volatility in the price of those natural resources. Brazil's established comparative advantage was already secure over a wide spectrum of primary products, from foodstuffs to minerals and fuels, and Brazil found in China a market of almost boundless appetite. China in turn was able to use the export of manufactured goods as an alternative to the deepening of its internal market.

The significance of an extended boom in commodity prices was and is relative to what came next. Would the wealth generated from the production and export of primary products be used to help finance a qualitative change oriented to total higher labor and total factor productivity and to the generalization of advanced, experimentalist practices of production? Or would it turn into the opposite, an easy escape from the need to undertake any such transformation? The bounty of nature was again not the best, only a second best and a temptation, until converted into a resource for reconstruction.

We cannot find in the recent and relative success of the large emerging economies the lineaments of a program of recovery and reconstruction of enduring and general interest to humanity. What we can find is a record of fragmentary insight and luck in the avoidance of disaster: a series of distant second bests rather than the demarcation of a reliable path.

RECOVERY: A DIRECTION

A crisis of the size that the global economy has undergone is an opportunity to remake the market through institutional innovations designed to serve two commanding aims: to place finance more fully at the service of the real economy and to organize a national and global growth strategy based on a broadening of economic and educational opportunity. Such a project is distinct from both vulgar Keynesianism and market fundamentalism. It differs as well from an equally traditional emphasis on public works to rebuild infrastructure, whether associated with the cause of a "green" recovery or not. And it is likely to face the same limits that constrain expansionary fiscal and monetary policy.

The alternative we need is one shaped by two overriding and connected goals. The first goal is to prevent the productive potential of saving from being wasted in a financial casino by placing finance more effectively at the service of production than it is under the established institutional arrangements. The second goal is to keep the constructive potential of the labor from being squandered or diminished by the denial of economic and educational opportunity to the majority of working men and women. The key to the fulfillment of these aims is a trajectory of innovations in the institutional arrangements of the market economy.

We do not need a crisis such as the one from which we are only now emerging to embrace and advance a program marked by commitment to these twin goals. However, a crisis supplies a fast track to its advancement. It does so by weakening the obstacles of interest and of prejudice that such a program must face as well as by making more visible the links between the innovations it proposes and the concerns of ordinary men and women. At the same time, it represents an experiment, offered by history, in causal connections that are normally hidden from view.

In the design and implementation of such a program, there is today a preliminary requirement to fulfill. That requirement is decisively to cast aside the division between a densely regulated sector and a thinly regulated sector of finance. This regulatory dualism has been for more than half a century the dominant regulatory approach to finance. It has been justified in the name of the idea that the high-net-worth individual and financial professionals who operate in the sector be subject to diminished monitoring of close supervision.

The consequence of regulatory dualism has been to make it possible to repackage and implement in the thinly regulated sector everything that is prohibited in the densely regulated one. Regulatory dualism set the stage for massive evasion of regulatory strictures. The most important form of this evasion was the growth, alongside the banking system, of "shadow banking"—financial organizations that act as banks but are not classified as banks and not made subject to the regulatory requirements that recognized banks have to meet. The result was to help turn part of finance into

a self-regarding free-for-all, with the concerns of the real economy de-
moted from subject to pretext.

Regulation should be inclusive and apply to the world of high-net-
worth individuals and financial professionals as much as to the general
public. It should also be designed to foreshadow, insofar as possible, the
structural recovery program we now outline.

Such a program would advance along three lines of reciprocally reinforcing initiatives.

The first line consists of measures intended to make finance serve the
real economy rather than serve itself. We have remarked that under the
present arrangements of market economies the production system is
largely self-financed on the basis of the retained and reinvested earnings
of private firms. Theoretically, the role of banks and stock markets is to
finance production as well as consumption. The increase in financial
activity in the past few decades has had little to do with the funding of
long-term investment in productive capacity and in the improvement of
productivity. It has had increasingly more to do with asset trading and
position taking by highly leveraged financial institutions.

Under these established arrangements, the real economy risks becoming the alibi rather than the concern of finance. Each successive layer of
ingenuity in the design of new financial products and services, composed
out of derivatives of the underlying, unified property right, takes the previous layer as its subject, and the transactions of the real economy recede
to an ever more distant and irrelevant horizon. Wealth, influence, and talent, debased and wasted, accrue to a form of economic activity that has lost
any close and real connection to the imperatives and the opportunities of
production. In this direction, finance does relatively little good to the
real economy in good times and threatens to do immense harm to it in bad
times.

We can do better. We can innovate in the arrangements governing the
relation of finance to the real economy and make the accumulated saving
of society better serve the economy's productive potential. For example,
we can establish rules and taxes that discourage credit in operations unrelated to expansion of GDP. In the United States, we can tap the country's
remarkable, unappreciated, and underutilized network of local banks,
helping them better to combine decentralization with sophistication.

Such an effort is not mere regulation as conventionally understood. It
is regulation as a first step to reorganization.

The second direction of this program of broad-based and socially inclusive economic growth is the reinvention of industrial policy. Its chief target should be the small and medium-size businesses that in every major economy in the world represent the chief sources of jobs and output. Its method should be the expansion of access to credit, to technology, to advanced knowledge and practice, to facilities for the organization of networks of cooperation that combine the benefits of flexibility and of scale. Its characteristic concern should be to propagate successful organizational and technological innovations wherever they may arise. Its temper should be that of a patient and fearless experimentalism.

The major developed and developing economies have moved beyond the form of industrial organization that emerged in the late nineteenth century and that came to prevail in the first half of the twentieth: the mass production of standardized goods and services, with rigid machines and production processes, dependence on semiskilled or narrowly skilled labor, stark contrasts between jobs involving supervision and jobs involving execution as well as among specialized tasks of execution, and clear-cut separations of areas of activity considered appropriate either to cooperation or to competition. However, no contemporary national economy has gone beyond such mass production in all its activity, only in particular sectors.

The rich and emerging economies alike boast advanced sectors characterized by the relatively decentralized and flexible production of nonstandardized goods and services, by knowledge-intensive labor, by the softening of contrasts between supervision and execution as well as among rigid specialties at the factory or office floor, by a more thoroughgoing mixture of cooperation and competition, and, above all, by a practice of permanent innovation. Under the aegis of this form of production, the best firms come more closely to resemble the best schools. The thrust of this shift is toward an economy in which the relation between labor and machines is so arranged that labor time is increasingly devoted to those operations that we have not yet learned to repeat and consequently cannot yet express formulaically and embody in machines.

However, even in the richest and most egalitarian contemporary societies (some of the European social democracies), such vanguard practices remain confined to relatively isolated parts of the economy, from which the majority of the workforce continues to be excluded. The power of the state can and should be used to open the economic and educational gateways of access to this productive experimentalism. To this end, we need a form of association between governments and firms that is neither the American model of arm's-length regulation of business by government nor the Northeast Asian model of formulation of unitary trade and industrial policy, imposed top down by a governmental bureaucracy: we need a form of strategic coordination between governments and firms that is pluralistic, participatory, and experimental. Its aim would be to help make the conditions and instruments of advanced production available to larger parts of the economy and the society.

The third axis of this structural program is the educational counterpart to the second. Such an alternative requires an enhancement of the capabilities of ordinary men and women and consequently a significant advance in the quality of education. In the United States today, there are in fact two separate educational systems. One system, restricted to the best private schools and to the top tier of public schools, takes as its priority the mastery of the analytic skills and the discursive practices needed for the performance of high-level tasks in today's society. The other system, predominating in much of the public-school system, remains focused on shallow encyclopedic coverage of information and on the effort to impose a modicum of discipline on bored and restless young people. The first of these two pedagogic paradigms must be made the universal one while becoming far more rigorous and ambitious in its application. The second must be repudiated.

In a country, like the United States, that is very large, very unequal and federal in its organization, a premise of such an advance is the development of practices that reconcile the local management of the public schools with national standards of investment and quality. Redistribution of funding and teachers from richer places to poorer places is not enough; it is also necessary to implement procedures for corrective intervention in failing schools and school systems.

Every aspect of this three-part program requires institutional innovations, not just commitment of resources. A premise of such innovations is that it is not enough to regulate the market economy or to compensate for its inequalities by means of retrospective redistribution through the familiar tools of redistributive taxation and social spending. It is necessary to change how we organize our societies and economies to better achieve a decisive broadening of economic and educational opportunity.

Such an approach contradicts what has been the dominant model of ideological controversy over the past few centuries throughout much of the world. According to this hydraulic model, the central question is always "Market or government?"—more market and less government or more government and less market. A thesis of our argument is more market *and* more government. Democratize the market, do not just regulate it, and use the response to the financial and economic crisis and its aftermath as an occasion to undertake this democratizing work. Without such a project of socially inclusive economic growth, we cannot act effectively on the implicit link between redistribution and recovery.

An alternative like this one costs money. However, it need not cost anything like the countless billions that have already been largely wasted throughout the world on propping up financial institutions and financiers whose contribution to the real economy was modest or negative or who had concentrated in their own hands a share of profit and talent that no account of the requirements and interests of production can justify.

More than money, however, such an alternative requires ideas. Economics as it is now practiced has largely failed to generate the ideas we need. The psychological and anti-institutional bent of its dominant tradition has rendered it poorly equipped for the work at hand. The method that economics embraced at the time of the Marginalist revolution in the late nineteenth century and then perfected through the general-equilibrium analysis of the twentieth century has turned it into a sham counterpart to natural science, with the crucial empirical and normative assumptions that give life and direction to economic analysis relegated to the role of factitious stipulations. Its newfound empirical interests—for example, in behavioral finance—so completely disconnect behavioral tendencies from their contingent and revisable institutional presuppositions that they generate little insight and almost no usable guidance for those who address real-world problems, including recovery from the slump.

In this vacuum of no ideas, the ghosts of the intellectual alternatives of nearly a hundred years ago—a shrunken Keynesianism and a fossilized market orthodoxy—have been called up out of sheer desperation if not out of conviction. They have been invoked by men and women who claim to speak with the authority of an economic science but who for the most part have never visited a factory or even mastered the history of their own discipline.

Use the crisis to remake the market economy. Remake the market economy by undertaking the institutional innovations that can give more access to more markets for more people in more ways. Take the stimulus as the holding operation that is all it can be, and keep your eyes focused on the prize: the growth project, designed to include and to empower as well as to enrich.

Insist on doing what progressives in the United States and elsewhere have largely failed to accomplish: come up with a proposal that responds to the interests and aspirations of the country's broad working-class majority. In so doing, such a program would also provide a sequel to Roosevelt's New Deal and to the social-democratic settlement in mid-twentieth-century Europe. Now, however, the emphasis would no longer fall narrowly on safeguards against economic insecurity or on high-level redistributive social entitlements. It would fall on what matters most: the institutional innovations needed to give ordinary men and women a better chance to live larger lives.

NOTE: KEYNES, VULGAR KEYNESIANISM, AND THE ROAD BEYOND THEM

The crisis of 2007–2009 was preceded, as we have remarked, by a partial hollowing out of many of the rules, regulations, and arrangements, especially for the discipline of finance, that in the United States were associated with Roosevelt's New Deal and in Europe with the social-democratic settlement of the mid–twentieth century.

The institutional compromise of the mid–twentieth century, in both its American and its European versions, was predicated on the abandonment by the forces that had mounted a challenge to the established institutional order of the North Atlantic societies of any more consequential attempt to reorganize the worlds of power and production in the interest of the common man and woman. In exchange for this renunciation, however, national governments were allowed to increase their power to counteract economic insecurity (through unemployment insurance and pension schemes) and to diminish inequality through the retrospective redistribution of wealth and income by the mechanisms of tax and transfer.

The United States soon abandoned the attempts, characteristic of the early New Deal, to innovate in the institutional arrangements of the market economy and of the relations between government and firms. The focus of policy fell first on the containment of economic insecurity and then on the popularization of opportunities to consume and the consolidation of a market in mass-consumption goods. The European social democracies advanced, through different paths and in different variations, toward a political economy and a social policy devoted to the maintenance of a high level of universal (and therefore redistributive) social entitlements, paradoxically funded through the regressive taxation of consumption. Humanity sought to drown its sorrows in consumption and called this solace justice.

It was not by these means, however, that the world overcame the slump of the 1930s. It was—as we have already recalled—the war that did it. The war economy combined massive mobilization of physical, capital, and human resources with innovations in the institutional arrangements governing the relations among firms as well as between firms and governments. Such innovations, rather than serving as points of departure for postwar developments, remained quarantined: they were dismissed as pertinent only to the peculiar circumstances of a war economy.

Teachings, like those of Keynes and his Swedish contemporary Wicksell, that advocated a governmentally induced rise of "aggregate demand" through public spending had only a modest effect on the economic conditions. The war did much better on account of both the magnitude of the resource and human mobilization it produced and the breakthrough effects of the attending institutional innovations.

Vulgar Keynesianism is the doctrine summarized in the IS-LM graphs of the standard economic textbooks written by Keynes's American followers in the last decades of the twentieth century. They rendered Keynes intellectually and politically palatable by leaving out the more dangerous and enigmatic parts of his ideas. They recast his doctrine as a theory of some of the tools needed to mitigate business cycles and to reconcile monetary stability with full employment in the established regulated market economy.

A practical concern and the strategy for addressing it were foremost in the evolution of vulgar Keynesianism: sustaining aggregate demand, especially a mix of fiscal and monetary policies, to wring the most employment from the economy without arousing (too much) the demons of inflation.

Insofar as vulgar Keynesianism was a theory, it was and is the theory of the use of these specific tools in this distinctive historical context. It required no break with general-equilibrium analysis, only recognition of multiple possible equilibriums in an economy, some of them compatible with massive underutilization of resources, especially labor. It took the whole institutional structure of the state and the economy for granted. Its intention was to normalize, not to subvert, reconstruct, or reimagine.

The association of the practical toolbox of macroeconomic theory with the recognition of multiple equilibria, some more desirable than others, accounted for almost the entirety of vulgar Keynesianism, whether dressed up in pseudomathematical representations or not.

Vulgar Keynesianism found its principal intellectual adversary in a range of connected theories that articulated what its opponents took to be the futile and counterproductive character of the governmental initiatives on which the vulgar Keynesians prided themselves. Some of these alternative theories (e.g., the quantitative theory of money) emphasized the importance of money and its management by government in determining the prospects for the combination of economic stability with economic growth. They prized constant and reliable rules about the money supply.

Other theories (e.g., real-business-cycle theory) exposed the powerlessness of governmental initiative. In particular, they argued for the powerlessness of fiscal policy to bring about economic recovery by raising aggregate demand above the level compatible with the economy's supposedly predetermined potential to grow.

Yet other views (e.g., rational expectations theory) suggested that the policy instruments favored by the vulgar Keynesians would be robbed of much of their efficacy by the protective measures taken by economic agents. If the agents expect higher taxes to lie in wait for the future, they would, for example, spend less and save more now.

These allied and convergent theories had as their central idea the beliefs that the market order has a determinate logic and determinate implications, that attempts to tamper with it are likely to prove either ineffective or costly, and that impersonality, universality, and constancy in the applications of the same rules of that order are to be preferred to the fine-tuning of would-be know-it-alls.

These doctrines claimed the authority of the mainstream of economic theorizing and profited from the unconvincing record of vulgar Keynesianism as a guide to policy. Keynes's ideas had (contrary to legend) exerted little influence on the early forms of the social-democratic compromise, preceding the Second World War. However, the right-wing attack on the prescriptions of vulgar Keynesianism and the reaffirmation of the orthodoxies of the 1920s in thinking about the management of the economy helped undermine the economic argument for social democracy.

It is impossible to understand the structure of practical economic debate in much of the world today without appreciating that it has been shaped very largely by a contest between the believers in a determinate logic of the market economy and the vulgar Keynesians, but against a background of widespread consensus between both groups about both the fundamentals of economic theory and the established institutional arrangements of a market economy. At no moment, for example, was the part of those arrangements governing the relation of finance to production brought into question.

When the crisis of 2007–2009 broke out and later produced the sequel of a "jobless recovery," the progressives' and social democrats' chief intellectual response, especially in the United States and Europe, was to resort once again to the vulgar Keynesian toolbox.

They allowed for only such adaptations of the toolbox as seemed required by the distinctive conditions of a balance-sheet recession, in which firms and households alike were concerned to rebuild their balance sheets and deflation often seemed a more immediate peril than inflation. Chief among these adaptations was the aggressive use of monetary policy (in the form of "quantitative easing") to combat the deflationary danger and to reinforce the uncertain effects of a fiscal stimulus that never seemed large enough. In the ensuing debate, the progressives were reputed or reputed themselves to be those who demanded more stimulus and called for a postponement of the inevitable fiscal reckoning. Such was the putatively progressive message propagated in the newspapers and recognized in the public conversation as the touchstone of opposition to the moneyed interests.

What is the salvageable theoretical core of Keynes's theory beyond the limits of vulgar Keynesianism as well as beyond the boundaries of the kind of slump that aroused his imagination and directed his will? It may seem strange to ask such a question so late in the day, given the immense influence of Keynes's ideas. It is nevertheless useful to ask it and to attempt to answer it: the answer suggests both the value and the inadequacy of the approach we find in Keynes's work. Something vital to insight into a crisis and a slump such as those the world has recently faced are missing there. The missing element must be produced and then combined with the indispensable insights that we can find in Keynes and in some of his intellectual allies.

The whole of Keynes's theoretical system, as expounded in the *General Theory* and in writings that preceded and prepared it, can be reduced in a few propositions stated in a language in many respects alien to Keynes's own.

In stating these propositions, it is useful to represent the view laid out in *General Theory* as the account of a special case of depressed economic activity. It is not a special case merely in the sense that it takes as its inspiration a crisis and a slump in which a dynamic of exorbitant indebtedness plays no major part in the unfolding of events, in contrast to what happens in balance-sheet recessions. It is also a special case in the sense that it offers the theoretical elaboration of grounds for a particular response to the slump: one in which a governmentally induced rise of aggregate demand performs a central role. The primacy accorded to this special case gives the vulgar Keynesians reason to claim for their views and proposals the authority of the master.

Keynes's own occasional and popular writings of the 1920s and 1930s explore a much broader range of possible responses to the Depression, including responses that would use governmental power to shape the course of the investment (as the large emerging economies have done today). Keynes, however, feared that such proposals would place him in the company of the socialists and compromise his influence. He wanted to shine and to influence in his own time, not just to bet on posterity. He was unwilling to embrace truth at the cost of marginality—truth for which the world, his world, was unprepared. For this reason, his occasional and popular writings are often more philosophical than the theoretical protosystem worked out in *General Theory*. Insofar as Keynes has something more than a theory of the special case to offer, it is to be found in those popular writings more than in his most comprehensive work.

The view that emerges from a comparison of *General Theory* with these richer and shadowy antecedents can be summarized by the following nine propositions.

1. *A money economy is different from a barter economy.* Money matters. It is not a transparent veil. The relative and changing desire to hold liquid balances rather than to invest or to spend may be a powerful influence on the level of economic activity.
2. *Quantifiable risk differs from unquantifiable uncertainty.* Both are at issue in economic life. The inscrutability of the future and its power to defy our attempts to predict and to contain it are fundamental features of our circumstance. One of the special

and important forms of this inscrutability concerns how other people will respond to the unexpected. At any given time, our attitude to money carries the imprint of our apprehensions or hopes about the uncertain future. More specifically, finance, although indispensable to the economy, is by its very nature a hotbed of trouble and illusion, embroidered by greed and shadowed by fear.

3. *Economic life cannot be adequately understood on the model of instrumental rationality: the selective and comparative marshalling of limited means toward the fulfillment of predetermined ends.* Economic life is a field of aspirations—fear, hope, and greed—and illusions, especially illusions about what the future holds in store for us.

4. *Say's law is false.* Supply does not ensure its own demand. It is true that the price for the unwanted good or service may fall until it is wanted, but only until an advantage has turned into a disaster for someone who took a risk.

5. *More generally, supply and demand may adjust in any given economy at different levels of economic activity and employment.* Among the multiple possible equilibriums, some may support high or full employment of resources; others may be compatible with large-scale idling of labor.

6. *Not only are there multiple equilibria consistent with different levels of employment, but there is also a persistent tendency to disequilibrium.* Equilibrium, in the sense described by the Marginalist economics of the late nineteenth century and developed by the general-equilibrium theories of the twentieth century, is the limiting case rather than the normal state of affairs. Disequilibrium typically takes the form of descending to a lower-level equilibrium or ascending to a higher-level one, when lower and higher are defined with respect to the level of employment. Through a chain of cumulative effects, a localized event in an economy, whether it is the result of decisions taken by firms or households or the result of exogenous shocks, can produce results that seem disproportionately greater than their triggers.

7. *The danger of falling into lower-level equilibriums increases because of the rigidity of many prices in a modern economy.* The most important instance of such rigidity is rigidity in the price of labor: it

can rise more easily than it can fall. (The significance of this thesis in Keynes's protosystem is often exaggerated. It is, in any event,
an insight to be found in Marshall and in Marshall's disciple,
Pigou.)

8. *The state can and should act to wrench an economy out of a lower-
level equilibrium.* It can do so by making up for the dearth of
private spending and investment.

9. *The beneficial effect of such a governmental intervention may
be greatly enhanced by the reverse and positive side of the vicious
downward cycle of economic depression:* one inducement to invest
and to spend leads to another in a virtuous circle of confidence
and enterprise.

A great virtue of the way of thinking summarized in these nine propositions is to be relatively free of the analytic emptiness into which, on
the pretext of rigor, the Marginalist turn tempted economics. Ever since
the latter move, the purest forms of economic analysis, the ones that set the
most exacting standards for the discipline, have been the ones that make
no causal-empirical or normative claims. They provide a pure apparatus of
analysis, which operates to explain the world or to guide policy on the
basis of empirical or normative stipulations provided to it from the outside.
It is a strategy of invulnerability through immunity to controversy. It
imposes, as such a strategy always does, the denial of the opportunity for
self-subversion and progression in thought. It turns the mathematical representation of economic ideas into an expression of hypothetical reasoning
rather than an instrument of contestable causal inquiry.

It is a merit of Keynes's protosystem that it is relatively free of this defect. It makes a host of causal claims about how economies work. Moreover, it shows no embarrassment in avowing its devotions and revulsions.

It nevertheless suffers from two connected defects, characteristic of the
dominant tradition of economics throughout its history, before and after
the Marginalism of the late nineteenth century. These defects compromise the value of Keynes's insights for understanding and overcoming of
the slump. The ideas and methods capable of remedying them do not
simply fill a gap in our knowledge; they modify the significance of what
we have already discovered.

The first such defect is the psychological and anti-institutional bias
that runs through the entire history of English political economy after

Adam Smith. (Smith was free of this defect, as was his sole intellectual counterpart in the history of economics, Karl Marx.) This tradition is the chief source of the economic ideas now dominant in the world. The theoretical centerpiece of this bias is the assumption that, despite minor national variations, a market economy has a single natural and necessary institutional form.

In speaking of a market economy, we make, according to this view, implicit reference to a detailed system of private-law rules, beginning with the regimes of property and contract. The diversity of legal traditions in the world, such as the distinct doctrinal taxonomies of the civil-law and common-law worlds, does not diminish and cannot disguise the functional convergence. According to this view, this convergence, rather than being the outcome of a history whose constraints it should be our purpose to overcome, is the progressive revelation of a truth.

It is remarkable that this idea of the inner legal logic of the market economy has maintained its ascendancy in the face of its deconstruction by 150 years of legal analysis. No theme is more constant in the legal thought of this historical period than the step-by-step and often involuntary discovery of the multiplicity of alternative institutional forms, defined in legal detail, that a market economy can take, each form with different consequences for the distribution of advantage as well as for the organization of production and exchange.

Keynes's view presents a striking example of the theoretical and practical assumptions of this approach. The entire discourse concerns the transmutations of large-scale economic aggregates within an institutional order that is left not only unchallenged but also (save for in particular organizations, such as the stock market) unnoticed. A corollary of this view is the failure to consider the implications of alternative sets of institutional arrangements to govern the relation of finance to the real economy with respect to the level and course of economic activity. This failure of vision is all the more striking in an economic theory that takes as its point of departure the observation that a money economy and a barter economy work in radically different ways. For what is finance but the enactment of the power of money to go its own way and, in going its own way, to serve the real economy for better or worse?

All of the central categories in Keynes's *General Theory*—the propensity to consume, the preference for liquidity, and the state of long-term expectations—are psychological. In the spirit of the tradition that formed

Keynes and against which he staged his incomplete insurrection, he represents these categories as psychological forces unqualified by particular contingent and revisable institutional settings.

A central idea of this book has been that the crisis, the slump, and the recovery cannot be adequately understood and confronted without taking into account the institutional indeterminacy of the market economy and therefore also the relation of finance to the real economy. The same principle applies to the arrangements governing the relations between governments and firms. It must ultimately apply as well to the basic rules of property and contract. It is the point of Marx's criticism of English political economy all over again, only expunged of the taint of functionalist necessitarianism running through his social theory: the economists have represented as laws of the economy what are only the laws of a particular type of economy—that is to say, of a certain way of organizing production and exchange.

The second major flaw that Keynes's mature theory shares with the tradition against which he rebelled is its lack of an account of the diversity of the stuff on which the mechanisms of competitive selection established by a market economy operate. The results of competitive selection of products, of forms of production and exchange, and of alternative dispositions of resources and of time must depend on the range of the alternatives from which the comparative exercise may choose.

The more we come to think of innovation and experimentation in the forms as well as in the objects of production and exchange as central to economic growth, the more significant this problem becomes. A theory that takes the supply of the diverse stuff to which competition applies for granted can supply no proper account of innovation or experimentation and therefore no adequate view of growth. It must accept as given what it should explain and show how to change.

It is true that much of the economic theorizing of recent decades has focused on innovation and that among these theories some have sought to provide an account of technological innovation consistent with the established body of economic theory (e.g., endogenous-growth theory). However, these developments have remained confined largely to technological innovation as distinguished from institutional innovation.

They have nothing to say, for example, about the significance of the existence of different sovereign states in the world as an opportunity to radicalize experimental divergence in the forms of economic life or about the ways in which the effect of technological innovation is always shaped by the institutional setting in which it takes place or about the prospects for giving the genius of the market—as a system for the experimental discovery of new possibilities of production—a more general and more radical expression. When technological innovation is separated from these other forms of experimentalism, it appears to be innovation about things, but all economic innovation, even when it appears to be about things, is at bottom innovation in the ways we cooperate. Its true object is society rather than nature.

Think of the issue this way. It is as if the established economic theory has half of the contemporary Darwinian synthesis in the life sciences, the half that is about competitive selection, but is bereft of the half that is about the diversification of the genetic material on which natural selection works. The result is a truncated theory, powerless to grasp what innovation is and can become and therefore unreliable as a guide to recovery and prosperity.

Nothing in Keynes's doctrines or in the vulgar Keynesians' ideas and little in their adversaries' teachings suggest a way to redress this truncation of insight. Any vigorous response to the slump must see the recovery as an occasion not to get back to business as usual once the shadow has passed but to create an economic order in which many-sided innovation assumes a more central role.

This theoretical deficiency gains practical significance today in the light of circumstances to which the argument of this book has drawn attention. A new form of practical organization has emerged in the world. It cannot adequately be described as simply high-technology, knowledge-intensive production. Its methods and practices translate practical experimentation into a way of working together. It does more than destandardize products and services and replace many forms of centralized production with decentralized contractual networks. It also attenuates the contrast between jobs of supervision and jobs of execution. It attenuates rigid contrasts among specialized jobs. It gives a practical and collective form to the process of analytical decomposition and synthetic recombination. It breaks down the contrasts between cooperation and competition, traditionally associated with distinct realms of activity. It increases our chances of creating an economic system in which people will use machines to do whatever they have learned how to repeat and reserve their time for that which does not yet lend itself to formula and mechanical repetition. There is better reason to hope that in the future no person will need to work as if he were a machine, in denial of his nature and in forgetfulness of his power. To move in this direction is to strike a decisive blow in favor of economic growth and individual empowerment.

In the world today, however, the advanced productive practices of the knowledge economy remain largely confined to insular vanguards. The vast majority of the economically active population remains locked out of these parts of the economy, and the revolutionary methods in which they pioneer continue to be largely denied to the rest of the production system.

The response to the crisis and the slump would provide an opportunity to extend the reach of this experimental form of production. This outcome, however, can be achieved only by that combination of heightened resource mobilization and institutional innovation that characterized the war economy. Moreover, because the ambitions of this agenda are more general and far reaching than those of any war effort, it would require as well a vast advance in the intellectual equipment of the ordinary working population.

The institutional arrangements would at the outset be those that innovate in the relations between governments and firms beyond the limits of the American model of arm's-length regulation of business by government and beyond the Northeast Asian model of centralized, bureaucratic formulation of a single-minded trade and industrial policy. They would also be those that favor practices of cooperative competition among firms and among teams united in contractual networks. The educational empowerment would be designed to afford ever larger numbers of workers and citizens mastery of practical and conceptual capabilities that are both generic and flexible.

We must solve these problems in ways that also reshape the relation of production to nature. We must seek the development of a less-predatory approach to the natural base and setting of production so that our commitment to preserve the natural setting of human life is less a pretext to abandon large conflicts and controversies over alternative forms of social and economic organization (as if nature were a great garden in which we seek refuge from the disappointments of history) than an occasion to reinvent such contests in more telling form.

Vulgar Keynesianism has nothing to contribute to the pursuit of these concerns. Much the same can be said of Keynes's economics. It is a theory of the inducements and inhibitions to spend and to invest within an institutional setting of production and exchange that the theory takes for granted. Like the theoretical tradition against which it staged an incomplete rebellion, it lacks a view of production other than as a shadowy extension of the system of exchange. It leaves unexplained and even unremarked the diversity of the material from which a mechanism of competitive selection selects. Most fundamentally, its view of causation in economics is almost wholly psychological; it exaggerates the psychologism of English political economy, which Marginalism tried to escape at the cost of causal emptiness. It is, for all its heterodoxy, an insider's view. Its ideas no longer suffice to make sense of our circumstance and our possibilities. It is powerless to guide us in making use of the opportunity for insight and transformation that crisis and its aftermath have given us.

Notes

INTRODUCTION

1. Two canonical presentations of this literature are Peter Hall and David Soskice, "An Introduction to Varieties of Capitalism," in *Varieties of Capitalism: the Institutional Foundations of Comparative Advantage* (Peter Hall and David Soskice, eds., 2001), and Peter Hall and Kathleen Thelen, "Institutional Change in Varieties of Capitalism," in *Debating Varieties of Capitalism* (Bob Hancké ed., 2009).

2. See Barrington Moore Jr., *Social Origins of Dictatorship and Democracy: Lord and Peasant in the Making of the Modern World* (1966), esp. at 413–432, and John Rawls, *Justice as Fairness: A Restatement* (1999), at 136, and preface to the revised edition of *A Theory of Justice* (1999).

3. The term *financial deepening* is commonly used in contemporary economics. See, for example, Edward S. Shaw, *Financial Deepening in Economic Development* (1973), at 3–16. I use this term in a sense that is related to this conventional usage but more specific. I define it cumulatively by theoretical discussion and historical example.

4. See Stewart C. Myers and Nicholas S. Majluf, "Corporate Financing and Investment Decisions When Firms Have Information That Investors Do Not Have," 13 *Journal of Financial Economics* 187 (1984), and Stewart C. Myers, "The Capital Structure Puzzle," 39 *Journal of Finance* 575 (1984).

5. See Franco Modigliani and Merton Miller, "The Cost of Capital, Corporation Finance, and the Theory of Investment," 48 *American Economic Review* 261 (1958).

6. The concept of financial hypertrophy as I use it and develop it in this book is in turn loosely related to the commonly used concept of financialization; I often employ the terms *financial hypertrophy* and *financialization* as synonyms. The reader will recognize, however, that both terms take on a special

meaning in the context of the ideas of this book: central concepts are theory dependent. For a historically informed discussion of the idea of financialization as used in the contemporary literature, see Greta R. Kripner, *Capitalizing on Crisis: The Political Origins of the Rise of Finance* (2011), at 27–57.

1. THE PAST AND FUTURE OF AMERICAN FINANCE SEEN THROUGH THE LENS OF CRISIS

1. For a brief history and description of the Washington Consensus, see John Williamson, *What Should the World Bank Think About the Washington Consensus?* Peterson Institute for International Economics (July 1999), and Javed Burki and Guillermo E. Perry, *Beyond the Washington Consensus: Institutions Matter*, World Bank (1998).

2. See the essays collected in Narcis Serra and Joseph E. Stiglitz (eds.), *The Washington Consensus Reconsidered: Towards a New Global Governance* (2008).

3. See Joseph E. Stiglitz, "Is there a Post–Washington Consensus Consensus?" and Dani Rodrik, "A Practical Approach to Formulating Growth Strategies," in *Washington Consensus Reconsidered* (Serra and Stiglitz eds.), at 309 and 356. See also Justin Yifu Lin and Celestin Monga, *Growth Identification and Facilitation: The Role of the State in the Dynamics of Structural Change*, World Bank Policy Research Working Paper no. 5313 (May 2010).

4. See Simon Johnson and James Kwak, *13 Bankers: The Wall Street Takeover and the Next Financial Meltdown* (2010), at 18–22; Robert V. Remini, *Andrew Jackson and the Bank War* (1976); and Peter Temin, *The Jacksonian Economy* (1969).

5. See David M. Kennedy, *Freedom from Fear: The American People in Depression and War, 1929–1945* (1999); Eric Rauchway, *The Great Depression and the New Deal* (2008); and Ellen D. Russell, *New Deal Banking Reforms and Keynesian State Capitalism* (2008).

6. For an overview of the New Deal financial reforms, see Jane D'Arista, *The Evolution of U.S. Finance*, vol. 2: *Restructuring Institutions and Markets* (1994), at 65–72; Rauchway, supra; and Russell, supra.

7. See Robert Shiller, *The Subprime Solution: How Today's Financial Crisis Happened and What to Do About It* (2008); Richard K. Green and Susan M. Wachter, *The Housing Finance Revolution* (2007); and David C. Wheelock, *The Federal Response to Home Mortgage Distress: Lessons from the Great Depression*, Federal Reserve Bank of St. Louis (2008).

8. For a discussion of the ideas underpinning the New Deal reforms, see Kennedy, supra; Rauchway, supra; and Mark Blyth, *Great Transformations: Economic Ideas and Institutional Change in the Twentieth Century* (2002).

9. See D'Arista, *Evolution*, at 2:65–73, and *FDIC: The First Fifty Years—a History of the FDIC, 1933–1983* (1983).

10. On the nature and significance of the financial orthodoxy of the time, see Blyth, supra.

11. See Shiller, supra; Green and Wachter, supra; and Wheelock, supra.

12. See D'Arista, *Evolution*, at 2:65–68, and Ben. S. Bernanke, "Nonmonetary Effects of the Financial Crisis in the Propagation of the Great Depression," in *Essays on the Great Depression* (2000).

13. See Shiller, supra, and Russell, supra.

14. It is widely acknowledged that these national developments interacted with the arrangements for dealing with current-account deficits and the enormous imbalances between major economies that arose in the decades following the collapse of the Bretton Woods regime in August 1971.

15. See Richard Duncan, *The Corruption of Capitalism* (2009), and Arthur E. Wilmarth Jr., "The Transformation of the U.S. Financial Services Industry, 1975–2000: Competition, Consolidation, and Increased Risks," 2002 *University of Illinois Law Review* 215 (2002). See also Randall Dodd, "Subprime: Tentacles of Finance," 44 *Finance and Development* 15 (2007).

16. See Jane D'Arista and Tom Schlesinger, *The Parallel Banking System*, Economic Policy Institute Briefing Paper (1993), and Hyman P. Minsky, "The Emergence of Financial Instability in the Postwar Period," in *Stabilizing an Unstable Economy* (1986).

17. See Charles W. Calomiris, "The Regulatory Record of the Greenspan Fed," 96 *American Economic Review* 170 (2006); Daniel K. Tarullo, "Financial Regulation in the Wake of the Crisis," speech at the Peterson Institute for International Economics, Washington, D.C. (June 8, 2009); and Ben S. Bernanke, "Housing, Housing Finance, and Monetary Policy," speech at the Federal Reserve Bank of Kansas City's Economic Symposium, Jackson Hole, Wyoming (August 31, 2007).

18. See Peter R. Fisher, "What Happened to Risk Dispersion?" 11 *Financial Stability Review* 29 (2008); Markus K. Brunnermeir, "Deciphering the 2007–2008 Liquidity and Credit Crunch," 23 *Journal of Economic Perspectives* 77 (Winter 2009); and D'Arista, *Evolution* (discussing the role of regulatory arbitrage in the move from banking to markets from the 1970s on).

19. See Gary B. Gorton, "Slapped in the Face by the Invisible Hand: Banking and the Panic of 2007," paper presented at the Federal Reserve Bank of Atlanta's Financial Markets Conference: Financial Innovation and Crisis, Atlanta (May 2009), and Timothy F. Geithner, "Reducing Systemic Risk in a Dynamic Financial System," remarks at the Economic Club of New York (June 2008). See more recently Gary B. Gorton, "Some Reflections on the Recent Financial Crisis," in *The Maze of Banking: History, Theory, and Crisis* (2015).

20. See Blyth, supra.

21. See Jeffrey N. Gordon, "Letter to the SEC on Money Market Fund Reform," submitted in response to the Security and Exchange Commission's request for comments on its proposed Money Market Reform Rule announced in Release no. IC-28807 (September 2009) (referring to the collaboration between the commission and market participants in the development of money-market mutual funds in the 1970s as an alternative to bank deposits). See also Minsky, supra (discussing the government's role in the development of many different financial products during the decade of the 1970s).

22. See Gordon, supra; D'Arista and Schlesinger, supra; and Geithner, "Reducing Systemic Risk."

23. See Minsky, supra, and D'Arista and Schlesinger, supra.

24. See Ben S. Bernanke, "The Future of Mortgage Finance in the United States," presentation at Symposium: The Mortgage Meltdown, the Economy, and Public Policy, Berkeley, Calif., October 31, 2008, and Green and Wachter, supra.

25. See Bernanke, "Future of Mortgage Finance," and Green and Wachter, supra.

26. See Tobias Adrian and Hyun Song Shin, *The Shadow Banking System: Implications for Financial Regulation*, Federal Reserve Bank of New York Staff Report no. 382 (2009), and Tobias Adrian and Hyun Song Shin, *Financial Intermediation, Financial Instability, and Monetary Policy*, Federal Reserve Bank of New York Staff Report no. 346 (2008).

27. See Bernanke, "Future of Mortgage Finance," and Dodd, supra.

28. See D'Arista, *Evolution*, and Edward M. Gramlich, *Subprime Mortgages: America's Latest Boom and Bust* (2007).

29. See Bernanke, "Future of Mortgage Finance"; *The Turner Review: A Regulatory Response to the Global Banking Crisis*, Financial Services Authority (2009); Jane D'Arista, "Systemic Regulation, Prudential Matters, Resolution Authority, and Securitization," statement before the Committee on Financial Service, U.S. House of Representatives, 111th Cong., 2nd sess. (October 29, 2009).

30. See Bernanke, "Future of Mortgage Finance," and Green and Wachter, supra.

31. See Fisher, supra; Geithner, "Reducing Systemic Risk"; Paul Krugman, *The Return of Depression Economics and the Crisis of 2008* (2009).

32. See D'Arista, *Evolution*; Wilmarth, supra; and Franklin R. Edwards and Frederic S. Mishkin, "The Decline of Traditional Banking: Implications for Financial Stability and Regulatory Policy," *Federal Reserve Bank of New York Policy Review*, July 1995.

33. See Adrian and Shin, *Shadow Banking System*; Adrian and Shin, *Financial Intermediation*.

34. This has been the prevailing view among academic finance theorists, at least until the present crisis. See, for example, *Turner Review*, supra; Bernanke, "Housing"; Raghuram G. Rajan, "Has Financial Development Made the World Riskier?" *Proceedings, Federal Reserve Bank of Kansas City*, August 2005.

35. See D'Arista, "Systemic Regulation"; Jane D'Arista, *U.S. Debt and Global Imbalances*, Political Economy Research Institute Working Paper Series no. 136 (May 2007); *Turner Review*, supra; and United Nations Conference on Trade and Development (UNCTAD), *The Global Economic Crisis: Systemic Failures and Multilateral Remedies* (2009).

36. See Gorton, supra; Brunnermeir, supra; and Geithner, "Reducing Systemic Risk."

37. See *Turner Review*, supra, and D'Arista, "Systemic Regulation."

38. The shadow-banking sector relied both explicitly and implicitly on the provision of credit and liquidity support from commercial banking institutions. See D'Arista and Schlesinger, supra, and Minsky, supra.

39. See Daniel K. Tarullo, "Towards an Effective Resolution Regime for Large Financial Institutions," remarks given at the Symposium on Building the Financial System of the 21st Century: An Agenda for Europe and the United States (March 18, 2010); Daniel K. Tarullo, "Confronting Too Big to Fail," remarks at the Exchequer Club, Washington, D.C. (October 21, 2009); Johnson and Kwak, supra; and Wilmarth, supra.

40. This view has been the prevailing one among U.S. policy makers since the start of the financial crisis. See, for example, Laurence H. Summers, "Financial Stability: Retrospect and Prospect," remarks at the Stanford Institute for Economic Policy Research, Stanford, Calif. (March 12, 2010), and Timothy F. Geithner, "Causes of the Financial Crisis and the Case for Reform," testimony before the Financial Crisis Inquiry Commission (May 6, 2010).

41. For examples of this idea in the U.S. setting, see Edmund S. Phelps and Leo M. Tilman, "Wanted: A First National Bank of Innovation," *Harvard Business Review*, January–February 2010; Shiller, supra; and Stiglitz, supra. The view is much more common outside the United States. See, for example, Turner, supra; Lin and Monga, supra; and UNCTAD, supra.

42. See Congressional Oversight Panel, *July Oversight Report: Small Banks in the Capital Purchase Program* (July 14, 2010), and Congressional Oversight Panel, *December Oversight Report: Taking Stock: What Has the Troubled Asset Relief Program Achieved?* (December 9, 2009). For a detailed discussion of the government's policy response to the crisis, including a description of the content, character, and magnitude of the different components of the Troubled Asset Relief Program (TARP) and other programs, see *SIGTARP: Initial Report to Congress* (February 6, 2009) and the more recent report *SIGTARP: Quarterly Report to Congress* (July 21, 2010).

43. See *SIGTARP: Initial Report; SIGTARP: Quarterly Report;* and Congressional Oversight Panel, *December Oversight Report,* at 59.

44. For a review of the government's foreclosure mitigation efforts, see Congressional Oversight Panel, *An Assessment of Foreclosure Mitigation Efforts After Six Months* (October 9, 2009).

45. Fannie and Freddie have proven their worth in the context of the financial crisis by providing both a counterweight to the collapse of private label securitization and an instrument in the government's effort to prevent foreclosure by restructuring and refinancing outstanding mortgage obligations. This fact has not gone unnoticed. See, for example, Bernanke, "Future of Mortgage Finance," and Secretary Timothy Geithner, written testimony provided to the Committee on Financial Services, U.S. House of Representatives, 111th Cong., 2nd sess. (March 23, 2010). See also Federal Housing Finance Agency, *Conservator's Report on the Enterprises' Financial Performance* (August 26, 2010).

46. This point is widely shared, even by critics of the current administration. For a discussion of the Fed's unconventional use of monetary policy during the crisis, see Ben S. Bernanke, "Federal Reserve Policies in the Financial Crisis," speech delivered at Greater Austin Chamber of Commerce (December 1, 2008), and Ben S. Bernanke, Stamp Lecture, London School of Economics (January 13, 2009).

47. See Congressional Oversight Panel, *May Oversight Report: The Small Business Credit Crunch and the Impact of the TARP* (May 12, 2010), and Congressional Oversight Panel, *December Oversight Report.*

48. For a discussion of this theme in an emerging-market context, see essays in Stiglitz, *Post–Washington Consensus Consensus.* See also many of the case studies included in Dani Rodrik (ed.), *In Search of Prosperity: Analytic Narratives on Economic Growth* (2003).

49. See Phelps and Tilman, supra. For a more extended discussion of the frailty of venture capital even in the United States, see Josh Lerner, *Boulevard of Broken Dreams: Why Public Efforts to Boost Entrepreneurship and Venture Capital Have Failed—and What to Do About It* (2009).

50. President Barack Obama signed into law the Wall Street Reform and Consumer Protection Act, Pub. L. 111-203, H.R. 4173, or Dodd–Frank Act, on July 21, 2010.

51. Several recent studies track the continuing decline in loan balances across the industry as a whole, especially in the areas of small and medium business. See, for example, the recently released FDIC Quarterly Banking Profile (second quarter, 2010), indicating a continuing decline in loan balances for the fifth time in the past six quarters.

52. See John C. Coffee Jr., *Bail-Ins Versus Bail-Outs: Using Contingent Capital to Mitigate Systemic Risk,* Columbia Center for Law and Economic Studies Working Paper no. 380 (September 10, 2010).

53. See Peter L. Rousseau and Richard Sylla, *Emerging Financial Markets and Early U.S. Growth*, National Bureau of Economic Research Working Paper no. 7448 (December 1999). See also Johnson and Kwak, supra, at 14–37.

54. There is little evidence to support the alleged efficiency gains of large-scale conglomerate banking. For a summary of the debate and the evidence, see Johnson and Kwak, supra, at 211–213. For an opposing view, see Charles W. Calomiris, "The Costs of Rejecting Universal Banking," in *U.S. Bank Deregulation in Historical Perspective* (2000).

55. See Rousseau and Sylla, supra, and Richard Sylla, "U.S. Securities Markets and the Banking System, 1790–1840," *Federal Reserve Bank of St. Louis Review*, May–June 1998.

56. See John R. Walter, "Not Your Father's Credit Union," 92 *Federal Reserve Bank of Richmond Economic Quarterly* 353 (Fall 2006).

57. See Rousseau and Sylla, supra, and Sylla, supra.

58. See Johnson and Kwak, supra, at 23–28, and Russell, supra, at 65–82.

59. Several recent Obama administration initiatives echo this theme, including the proposed $30 billion Small Business Lending Fund, the Community Development Capital Initiative, and the Bank for Infrastructure. These and other initiatives are discussed in Congressional Oversight Panel, *July Oversight Report*, and on the Department of Treasury's website at http://www.financialstability.gov.

60. See Chairman Gary Gensler, testimony before the Financial Crisis Inquiry Commission (July 1, 2010), and Duncan, supra, at 148–159.

61. See Fisher, supra, and D'Arista, *Evolution*.

62. For a general overview and defense of the basic position, see Daniel K. Tarullo, "Financial Regulatory Reform," speech at the U.S. Monetary Policy Forum (February 26, 2010).

2. THE PAST AND FUTURE OF FINANCIAL REFORM: FROM REGULATION TO REORGANIZATION

1. For a parallel presentation of the argument of this chapter and further exploration of the ideas informing my approach, see Tamara Lothian, *Rethinking Finance Through Law: A Theoretical Perspective*, Columbia Law and Economics Working Paper no. 412 (November 21, 2011), http://ssrn.com/abstract=1962843, and Tamara Lothian, "Beyond Macroprudential Regulation: Three Ways of Thinking About Financial Crisis, Regulation, and Reform," 3 *Global Policy* 410 (2012). For the wider context of these views in ideas about the alternative futures of the market economy, see Tamara

Lothian, "What's Law Got to Do with It? Crisis Growth, Growth, Inequality, and the Alternative Futures of Legal Thought," 18 *Theoretical Inquiries in Law* (forthcoming).

2. This claim is universally accepted. In theory, the idea that finance—or savings—is important to the production of wealth has been a mainstay of economic theory since classical political economy (whether in Adam Smith's or Karl Marx's formulation). The idea is equally present in modern growth theory, even though the precise nature of the causal nexus remains controversial. Recent empirical studies and policy discussions take the premise as given. See, for example, *The Turner Review: A Regulatory Response to the Global Banking Crisis*, Financial Services Authority (March 2009). A third source is provided by recent studies of financial liberalization, especially in developing countries and global markets.

3. See John Maynard Keynes, *The General Theory of Employment, Interest, and Money* (1936), and Hyman P. Minsky, *Stabilizing an Unstable Economy* (1986).

4. In the U.S. setting, these ideas have been most clearly and forcefully articulated by Lawrence Summers and Timothy Geithner.

5. Under established economic and political arrangements, there has always been a tension between finance and the real economy, given both the structure of financial markets and the organization of production. Yet this tension has deepened in recent years in response to many different factors. The next section in this chapter identifies a series of policies, ideas, and arrangements that may have contributed to this situation.

6. This comparison is developed, for example, in the work of post-Keynesians, including Gerald A. Epstein (ed.), *Financialization and the World Economy* (2005), and Greta R. Krippner, *Capitalizing on Crisis: The Political Origins of the Rise of Finance* (2011). See also Adair Turner, "Reforming Finance: Are We Being Radical Enough?" Clare Distinguished Lecture in Economics and Public Policy, Cambridge, U.K. (2011); Adair Turner, "The Financial Crisis and the Future of Financial Regulation," speech delivered at The Economist's Inaugural City Lecture, Cambridge, U.K. (January 21, 2009); Adair Turner, "What Do Banks Do? What Should They Do?" in *The Future of Finance: The LSE Report*, London School of Economics Report (Adair Turner et al. eds., 2010); and Jane W. D'Arista, *The Evolution of U.S. Finance*, vol. 2: *Restructuring Institutions and Markets* (1994).

7. Adair Turner has most eloquently and insistently emphasized this point in his many jeremiads against policy makers' and regulators' reliance on prevailing economic orthodoxy of the time. See also Paul Krugman, *The Return of Depression Economics and the Crisis of 2008* (2009), echoing Keynes; Perry Mehrling, *The New Lombard Street: How the Fed Became the Dealer of Last*

Resort (2011); and Ross Levine, "An Autopsy of the US Financial System," 2 *Journal of Financial Economic Policy* 196 (2010).

8. The main focus of my argument is on the second level—that is, the arrangements linking finance to the real economy. But I remark in passing on each of the other levels as well.

9. Ben S. Bernanke, "Housing, Housing Finance, and Monetary Policy," speech at the Federal Reserve Bank of Kansas City's Economic Symposium, Jackson Hole, Wyoming (August 31, 2007); Randall Dodd, "Subprime: Tentacles of a Crisis," 44 *Finance & Development* 15 (2007).

10. See Dodd, supra; D'Arista, supra; and Edward M. Gramlich, *Subprime Mortgages: America's Latest Boom and Bust* (2007).

11. See Charles W. Calomiris, "The Regulatory Record of the Greenspan Fed," 96 *American Economic Review* 170 (2006); Daniel K. Tarullo, "Financial Regulation in the Wake of the Crisis," speech at the Peterson Institute for International Economics, Washington, D.C. (June 8, 2009); and Bernanke, "Housing."

12. For a similar point developed in a different setting, see Michael Pettis, *The Volatility Machine: Emerging Markets and the Threat of Financial Collapse* (2001). Both my book and Pettis's illustrate the contribution of direct experience of financial markets to the theoretical exploration of the content, character, and consequences of historically specific financial policies and arrangements.

13. The first three institutional tendencies have as their main theme the emergence and expansion of increasing financial hypertrophy in the U.S. and global economies.

14. For a recent expression of this view, see Kenneth Rogoff, "Is Modern Capitalism Sustainable?" Project Syndicate (December 2, 2011), https://www.project-syndicate.org/commentary/is-modern-capitalism-sustainable?barrier=accessreg. It continues to be the prevailing view even though the metaphors change from time to time. "Throwing the baby out with the bath water" used to be the standard expression employed to describe the (assumed) narrowness of realistic alternatives. A new expression has recently emerged: "A plan beats no plan."

15. Note the distinguishing character of the approach taken here. A common form of criticism begins by accepting a given set of widely shared understandings and then attacking the reforms enacted as imperfect realizations of these understandings. My argument is different. My point is to understand and evaluate the new Dodd–Frank reforms from the standpoint of a different conception. From this perspective, the problem is not the fragmentary character of the financial reforms—reforms will always be fragmentary—but the inadequacy of the ideas and idea world informing the reforms. For a summary

of the ideas informing my approach, see Lothian, *Rethinking Finance Through Law.*

16. This part proposes an alternative approach to the interpretation and development of the Dodd–Frank reforms. The enactment of the Dodd–Frank Act in July 2010 did not end the debate over the meaning and development of many of its most controversial provisions. As many have noted, the passage of the legislation simply made more urgent the task of agreeing upon and developing the detailed rules and regulations to be used in implementing the reform agenda. In each major area of legislation, legal and institutional understanding as well as imagination would be crucial.

3. THE DEMOCRATIZED MARKET ECONOMY

1. See, for example, Samuel P. Huntington, *Political Order in Changing Societies* (1968), at 20–22.

4. THE DEMOCRATIZED MARKET ECONOMY IN LATIN AMERICA (AND ELSEWHERE)

An earlier version of this chapter was published as Tamara Lothian, "The Democratized Market Economy in Latin America and Elsewhere: An Exercise in Institutional Thinking Within Law and Political Economy," 28 *Cornell International Law Journal* 169 (1995).

1. For two classic articulations and defenses of this growth strategy by two of its most influential theoreticians and practical exponents, see Celso Furtado, *Desenvolvimento e subdesenvolvimento* (1963), and Raúl Prebisch, *Transformación y desarrollo: La gran tarefa de América Latina* (1970). For an understanding of this political economy as a genuinely political invention underdetermined by economic constraints, see Carlos H. Waisman, *Reversal of Development in Argentina: Postwar Counterrevolutionary Policies and Their Structural Consequences* (1987), at 164–205.

2. For a discussion of the development of ideas about the import-substitution aspect of this growth strategy, see Werner Baer, "Import Substitution and Industrialization in Latin America: Experiences and Interpretations," 7 *Latin American Research Review* 95 (1972).

3. For a study of the forms and consequences of economic dualism in a particular Latin American economy, see Edmar L. Bacha, *Os mitos de uma decada*, Colecao Estudos Brasileiros, vol. 9 (2d ed. 1978).

4. See Paul R. Krugman, *Rethinking International Trade* (1990).

5. Macroeconomists interested in Latin America have produced a constant stream of denunciations of populist economic policies, rejecting them as self-defeating while failing to understand them from a broader social and political perspective. See Rudiger Dornbusch and Sebastian Edwards, "Macroeconomic Populism," 32 *Journal of Developmental Economics* 247 (1990). For an instructive set of national studies, see Rudiger Dornbusch and Sebastian Edwards (eds.), *The Macroeconomics of Populism in Latin America* (1991).

6. I recognize that there is also a plausible case for interpreting original Keynesianism as marked by a minimalist technocratic view of state capacity, which would bring it closer to pseudo-Keynesianism. See Donald Winch, "Keynes, Keynesianism, and State Intervention," in *The Political Power of Economic Ideas: Keynesianism Across Nations* (Peter Hall ed., 1989), at 107, 110–113.

7. For a discussion invoking unresolved social conflict as the decisive influence upon populist distributivism, see Jeffrey D. Sachs, "Social Conflict and Populist Policies in Latin America," in *Labor Relations and Economic Performance* (Renato Brunetta and Carlo Dell'Aringa eds., 1990), at 137.

8. These restraints are severe enough in many developing countries to make urgently needed agrarian reform practically impossible.

9. For a progress report on how the neoliberal project was performing in particular Latin American countries as of 1990, see John Williamson, *The Progress of Policy Reform in Latin America* (1990).

10. For a systematic statement of the stabilization component of the Washington Consensus that demonstrates how mainstream ideas can be broadened to incorporate some of the "heterodox" appeal to social compacts and wage–price freezes as methods of dealing with inertial and expectations-based elements of high and chronic inflation, see Rudiger Dornbusch et al., "Extreme Inflation: Dynamics and Stabilization," in *Brookings Papers on Economic Activity 2* (William C. Brainard and George L. Perry eds., 1990).

11. For a discussion of the theory and practice of liberalization and of its links to other elements of the Washington Consensus, see Nora Lustig, *Mexico: The Remaking of an Economy* (1992), at 114. Lustig's book serves more generally as a case study of the implementation of the neoliberal project in a particular country, as viewed by its defenders.

12. Discussion of the reorganization of the public sector is tainted by a failure to appreciate the diversity of legal-institutional forms that the public enterprises might assume. For a characteristic statement of the neoliberal view, see Felipe Larrain and Marcelo Selowsky, "Comparative Analysis, Lesson, and Policy Conclusions," in *The Public Sector and Latin American Crisis* (Felipe Larrain and Marcelo Selowsky eds., 1991), at 283, 315–318.

13. The dominant approach among influential international economists interested in problems of practical policy in Latin America continues to be

characterized by a combination of unjustified faith in spontaneity (markets will do the job once stabilization and structural adjustment take place) and undisguised disappointment at the slowness or indifference that such market forces often continue to exhibit long after the prescribed stabilization and adjustment have been imposed. See Rudiger Dornbusch, "Policies to Move from Stabilization to Growth," in *Proceedings of the World Bank Annual Conference on Development Economics* (1990), at 19, reprinted in Rudiger Dornbusch, *Stabilization, Debt, and Reform: Policy Analysis for Developing Countries* (1993), at 32.

14. See Vincent A. Mahler, "Income Distribution Within Nations: Problems of CrossNational Comparison," 22 *Comparative Political Studies* 3 (1989), at 3, 18–21. The Gini coefficient provides one statistical measure of income inequality within nations. For an alternative approach, see United Nations Development Program (UNDP), *Human Development Report 1994* (1994), at 164. This method compares income inequality within countries in terms of the ratio between the highest and lowest fifth of the population. During the period 1980–1991, the ratio for Brazil was 32.1, and the ratio for Mexico was 13.6. Ratios for China, Indonesia, and Ethiopia were 6.5, 4.9, and 4.8, respectively.

15. For a discussion emphasizing the path-dependent effects of a singular history, see Ezra F. Vogel, *The Four Little Dragons: The Spread of Industrialization in East Asia* (1991).

16. For a comparative analysis underlining the relation between economic strategies and political capabilities, see David Felix, "Import Substitution and Late Industrialization: Latin America and Asia Compared," 17 *World Development* 1455 (1989).

17. See Peter Evans, "Class, State, and Dependence in East Asia: Lessons for Latin Americanists," in *The Political Economy of the New Asian Industrialism* (Frederic C. Deyo ed., 1987), at 203, 215–217.

18. See Denis Fred Simon, "Taiwan's Emerging Technological Trajectory: Creating New Forms of Competitive Advantage," in *Taiwan: Beyond the Economic Miracle* (Denis Fred Simon and Michael Y. M. Kau eds., 1992), at 123, 138–143.

19. See Alice H. Amsden, "Asia's Industrial Revolution," *Dissent*, Summer 1993, at 328.

20. For an early study drawing attention to this point, see Bela Balassa, "Industrial Policies in Taiwan and Korea," 106 *Weltwirtschaftliches Archiv* 55 (1971).

21. For a discussion of the content, conditions, and consequences of educational investment, see Alice H. Amsden, *Asia's Next Giant: South Korea and Late Industrialization* (1989), at 215–239.

22. My understanding of the variations and instruments of the government–business partnership owes a heavy debt to Robert Wade, *Governing the*

Market: Economic Theory and the Role of Government in East Asian Industrialization (1990), at 73–112, 297–381. It is the great merit of Wade's analysis that he presents a detailed and unsentimental view of the collusive strategies binding political and economic elites together.

23. Yet even in the Taiwanese variant, scholars have identified an alliance between government and big business that overshadows the help given to smaller firms. See Dan Fred Simon, "External Incorporation and Internal Reform," in *Contending Approaches to the Political Economy of Taiwan* (Edwin A. Winckler and Susan Greenhalgh eds., 1988), at 144–146.

24. See Paul R. Krugman (ed.), *Strategic Trade Policy and the New International Economics* (1992).

25. In recent years, political and intellectual elites in several Latin American countries, including Brazil, Argentina, and Paraguay, have made a concerted effort to replace American-style presidential regimes with parliamentary government. Brought to a plebiscite in Brazil on November 15, 1992, with the support of the great majority of the politicians and the media, voters overwhelmingly rejected the parliamentary proposal, correctly understanding it as an effort to confiscate popular sovereignty. A small group of academics associated with Yale University professor Juan Linz have been influential in the advocacy of parliamentary ideas. Their proposals provide a case study of the infirmities associated with thinking about government institutions deficient in both social-structural insight and constructive institutional imagination. See Juan J. Linz, "The Perils of Presidentialism," in *Parliamentary Versus Presidential Government* (Arend Lijphart ed., 1992), at 118.

26. I owe my view of these problems to Roberto Mangabeira Unger, "A forma de governo que convém ao Brasil," in *A alternativa transformadora: Como democratizar o Brasil* (1990).

27. See Tamara Lothian, "The Political Consequences of Labor Law Regimes: The Contractualist and Corporatist Models Compared," 7 *Cardozo Law Review* 1001 (1985–1986). Such a hybrid labor-law regime was subsequently prefigured in the Brazilian Constitution of 1988 and is now a topic of debate in other Latin American countries.

28. See Heidi Kroll, *Reform and Monopoly in the Soviet Economy*, Center for Foreign Policy Development Briefing Paper no. 4, Brown University (1990), at 3–10, 22–23.

29. For a discussion of the gap between what the neoliberal project prescribes for the formerly Communist economies and the minimal requirements for economic growth, see Jan Kregel and Egon Matzner, *The Market Shock: An Agenda for Socioeconomic Reconstruction of Central and Eastern Europe* (1992).

30. I developed these views in the course of a series of business trips to Russia. Particularly illuminating were conversations in June and September 1992

with industrial managers who were holdovers from the Soviet regime and were associated with the League of Industrialists, chaired by Arkady Volsky.

31. Valery Zorkin, chairman of the Russian Constitutional Court, interviewed by the author, Moscow (January 1992).

32. For studies of different possible and actual combinations of widespread share distribution with their pooling in government-established investment funds, see David Lipton and Jeffrey Sachs, "Privatization in Eastern Europe: The Case of Poland," in *Brookings Papers on Economic Activity 2*, at 293, 313–32; Roman Frydman and Andrzej Rapaczinski, *Privatization in Eastern Europe: Is the State Withering Away?* (1994), at 46–74. On the extension of these concerns and proposals to Russia, see Maxim Boycko and Andrei Schleifer, "The Voucher Program for Russia," in *Changing the Economic System in Russia* (Anders Aslund and Richard Layard eds., 1993), at 100–111.

33. On organizations between government and industry, see the section "Democratizing the Hard State," "2. The Intermediate Organizations," earlier in this chapter.

34. See, for example, Charles F. Sabel, *Work and Politics: The Division of Labor in Industry* (1986), at 194–231; see also Michael J. Piore and Charles F. Sabel, *The Second Industrial Divide: Possibilities for Prosperity* (1984).

35. For a general exploration of post-Fordist production that emphasizes the weakening of the contrast between task setting and execution in production, see Piore and Sabel, supra. For a view exploring the development of regimes of cooperative competition both among networks of small firms and within large firms, see Michael H. Best, *The New Competition: Institutions of Industrial Restructuring* (1990), at 17–19, 236–250. My view of cooperative competition draws heavily on Best's work.

36. Students of post-Fordist industrial organization have explored the significance of the northern Italian experience. See Sabel, supra, at 145–167, and Best, supra, at 203–226.

37. See Charles Sabel and Jonathan Zeitlin, "Historical Alternatives to Mass Production: Politics, Markets, and Technology in Nineteenth-Century Industrialization," *Past & Present*, August 1985, at 133.

38. See the section "Democratizing the Hard State 2. The Intermediate Organizations," earlier in this chapter.

39. On the Kaldor-style expenditure tax, see Nicholas Kaldor, *An Expenditure Tax* (1955).

40. See Alexander Gerschenkron, *Economic Backwardness in Historical Perspective* (1962), at 11–16.

41. See Josef Esser, "Bank Power in West Germany Revised," 13 *West European Politics* 17 (1990); Charles F. Sabel et al., "Making Money Talk: Towards a New Creditor–Debtor Relation in German Banking," in *Rela-*

tional Investing, ed. John C. Coffee, Ronald J. Gilson, and Louis Lowenstein (1993).

42. On John Dewey's characteristically American formulation of this idea, see Robert B. Westbrook, *John Dewey and American Democracy* (1991), at 433.

43. See Bruce Ackerman, *We the People: Foundations* (1991), at 6–7; compare Emile Durkheim, *The Elementary Forms of Religious Life* (J. W. Swain trans., 1969), at 240–242, contrasting the ecstatic and the routinized moments of collective consciousness, as exemplified by the experience of religion.

44. See Tamara Lothian, "The Criticism of the Third-World Debt and the Revision of Legal Doctrine," 13 *Wisconsin International Law Journal* 421 (Spring 1995).

45. American legal thought has explored legal pluralism through the lens of legal-process insight while resisting or ignoring its pertinence to substantive law. See Lon L. Fuller, "The Forms and Limits of Adjudication," in *The Principles of Social Order* (Kenneth J. Winston ed., 1981).

46. See Wesley Hohfeld, "Some Fundamental Legal Conceptions as Applied in Judicial Reasoning," 23 *Yale Law Journal* 16 (1913).

5. ECONOMIC PROGRESS AND STRUCTURAL VISION

1. For the canonical early statement of the thesis of secular stagnation, see Irving Fisher, *The Debt–Deflation Theory of Great Depressions* (1933).

2. See Douglass C. North, *Institutions, Institutional Change, and Economic Performance* (1990), and Oliver E. Williamson, *The Economic Institutions of Capitalism* (1985). An earlier tradition of American institutional economics was better able to grasp the specific problems posed by the explanation of institutional evolution and to resist the impulse to see it from the perspective of the assumptions of post-Marginalist economics. See John R. Commons, *Legal Foundations of Capitalism* (1924). The French "regulation school" has made a similar effort within the limits of the necessitarian assumptions that it has inherited from Marxism. See Michael Aglietta, *A Theory of Capitalist Regulation: The US Experience* (David Fernbach trans., 1979).

3. For a late example of comparative law as doctrinal taxonomy, see René David and John E. C. Brierly, *Major Legal Systems in the World Today: An Introduction to the Comparative Study of Law* (1968), based on René David, *Les Grands Systèmes du Droit Contemporain* (1964).

4. For an early example of the functionalist approach in comparative law, see Arthur von Mehren, *The Civil Law System* (1957).

5. See Tamara Lothian, "The Political Consequences of Labor Law Regimes: The Contractualist and Corporatist Models Compared," 7 *Cardozo Law Review* 1001 (1985–1986).

6. The few notes in the remaining sections of this chapter are meant to guide the reader to texts that explore the historical events addressed here. My purpose in these sections is not to present a revisionist view of the events that I discuss, based on research into primary sources. It is to show how ideas advanced in this book may prompt us to reinterpret the significance of these events. Their reinterpretation has practical importance: it allows us to approach historical experience as a field of possibilities and discoveries wider and richer than those countenanced by the conceptions now prevailing in economics and legal thought. The purpose of the notes is to point the reader to work presenting a fuller view of the developments to which I allude.

7. For general accounts of the economic history of the United States, see Jonathan Hughes and Louis P. Cain, *American Economic History* (2003); Michael Lind, *Land of Promise: An Economic History of the United States* (2012); Douglas C. North, *The Economic Growth of the United States 1790–1860* (1961); David A. Hounshell, *From the American System to Mass Production 1800–1932* (1984); and Robert Whaples and Dianne C. Betts (eds.), *Historical Perspectives on the American Economy* (1995). For texts that help elucidate the events and ideas in early American economic and financial history discussed here, see Thomas K. McCraw, *The Founders and Finance* (2012); Jane W. D'Arista, *The Evolution of U.S. Finance*, vol. 2: *Restructuring Institutions and Markets* (1994); Larry Neal and Lance Davis, "Why Did Finance Capitalism and the Second Industrial Revolution Arise in the 1890s?" in *Financing Innovation in the United States 1870 to the Present* (Naomi R. Lamoreaux and Kenneth L. Sokoloff eds., 2007); and Howard Bodenhorn, *A History of Banking in Antebellum America: Financial Markets and Economic Development in an Era of Nation-Building* (2000), at 84–118. On the relation of finance to the corporate form, see William C. Roy, *Socializing Capital: The Rise of the Large Corporation in America* (1997), esp. at 41–77, 115–143, and 247–254, and Martin J. Sklar, *The Corporate Reconstruction of American Capitalism, 1890–1916: The Market, the Law, and Politics* (1988).

8. See Bray Hammond, *Banks and Politics in America from the Revolution to the Civil War* (1957), at 405–450. On the struggle over the Second Bank of the United States, see Robert V. Remini, *Andrew Jackson and the Bank War* (1967); Peter Temin, *The Jacksonian Economy* (1969); Paul Kahan, *The Bank War: Andrew Jackson, Nicholas Biddle, and the Fight for American Finance* (2015); and the documents collected in George Rogers Taylor, *Jackson vs. Biddle's Bank: The Struggle Over the Second Bank of the United States* (1972).

9. Franklin D. Roosevelt, "Address at Oglethorpe University, May 22, 1932," in *Public Papers and Addresses of Franklin D. Roosevelt*, vol. 1: *1928–1932* (1938), at 639.

10. Hugh S. Johnson, *The Blue Eagle from Egg to Earth* (1935), at 169.

11. I am indebted to the writings of Brandeis and Douglas about finance and sympathize with their reconstructive intentions. I nevertheless believe that they failed to recognize and address this and other enigmas of contemporary finance and that their reform proposals remained deficient in institutional reach. See Louis Brandeis, *Other People's Money and How the Banks Use It* (1914), and William O. Douglas, *Democracy and Finance* (1914).

12. See Wolfgang Schivelbusch, *Three New Deals* (2006); R. J. Overy, *The Nazi Economic Recovery, 1932–1938* (1982), at 23–35; Dan P. Silverman, *Hitler's Economy: Nazi Work Creation Programs, 1933–1935* (1998), at 28–47, 147–174, 219–246; and David Schoenbaum, *Hitler's Social Revolution: Class and Status in Nazi Germany, 1933–1939* (1966), at 1–42, 73–112.

13. For a comparative discussion of the war economies of the Second World War, see Mark Harrison (ed.), *The Economics of World War II: Six Great Powers and in International Comparison* (1998), and Alan S. Milward, *War, Economy, and Society* (1977), esp. at 99–131. For the American experience of the war economy, see the discussion in David M. Kennedy, *Freedom from Fear: The American People in Depression and War, 1929–1945* (1999), at 615–668.

14. Quoted in Richard Polenberg, *War and Society: The United States, 1941–1945* (1980), at 220.

15. See, for example, Clayton M. Christensen and Michael E. Raynor, *The Innovator's Solution: Creating and Sustaining Successful Growth* at 32–51 (2003).

16. For a sympathetic but critical account of the main line of development economics in the second half of the twentieth century, see Dani Rodrik, "The Past, Present, and Future of Economic Growth," in *Towards a Better Global Economy: Policy Implications for Citizens Worldwide in the 21st Century* (Franklin Allen et al. eds., 2014).

17. For a canonical statement of the heterodox interpretation of East Asian development, see Robert Wade, *Governing the Market: Economic Theory and the Role of Government in East Asian Industrialization* (1990), at 73–112.

18. See Alexander Gerschenkron, *Economic Backwardness in Historical Perspective* (1962).

19. Here and throughout this book I draw on empirical studies of finance and its relation to the real economy. These studies have informed criticism of what is often described in the literature as "financialization." Although my explanatory and programmatic arguments diverge from many of the assumptions and recommendations in this literature, making broader claims and proposing more radical changes than it would countenance, I have relied heavily on its

discoveries. Each of the three enigmas of finance invoked in the introduction and discussed in this chapter find at least support in the empirically informed critique of financialization. For an overview, see Robin Greenwood and David Scharfstein, "The Growth of Finance," 27 *Journal of Economic Perspectives* 3 (2013). See also Robert W. Parenteau, "The Late 1990s US Bubble: Financialization in the Extreme," in *Financialization and the World Economy* (Gerald A. Epstein ed., 2005); Robert Boyer, "A Finance-Led Growth Regime," in *Financialization at Work* (Ismail Erturk et al. eds., 2008); Adair Turner, "What Do Banks Do? What Do Credit Booms and Busts Occur? What Can Public Policy Do About It ?" in *The Future of Finance and the Theory That Underpins It*, London School of Economics Report (Adair Turner et al. eds., 2010); and Andrew Haldane et al., "What Is the Contribution of the Financial Sector: Miracle or Mirage?" in *The Future of Finance*. For programmatic ideas motivated by the criticism of financialization, see Raghuram G. Rajan and Luigi Zingales, *Saving Capitalism from Capitalists: Unleashing the Power of Financial Markets to Create Wealth and Spread Opportunity* (2004), at 108–125, and Massimo Amato Luca Fantacci, *Saving the Market from Capitalism* (Graham Sells trans., 2014). These and other proposals motivated by the criticism of financialization recall, in the changed historical circumstances, arguments and proposals like those of Louis Brandeis and William O. Douglas. Like these earlier ideas, the contemporary response to financialization suffers from a deficit of institutional insight and imagination. Unlike them, it fails to connect the critique of finance with the critique of the established forms of democracy. Although sharper in economic analysis, it is often narrower and shallower in programmatic reach.

20. Joseph A. Schumpeter, *The Theory of Economic Development: An Inquiry Into Profits, Capital, Credit, Interest, and the Business Cycle* (Redvers Opie trans., 1934), at 74, originally published in 1912.

21. Turner, "What Do Banks Do?" at 6. See also Adair Turner, *Between Debt and the Devil: Money, Credit, and Fixing Global Finance* (2016). On similar lines, see Raghuram G. Rajan, *Has Financial Development Made the World Riskier?* National Bureau of Economic Research Working Paper no. 11728 (2005).

22. See Andrew Sheng and Ng Chow Soon, *Shadow Banking in China* (2016); Shen Wei, *Shadow Banking in China: Risk, Regulation, and Policy* (2016); and Andrew Collier, *Shadow Banking in China: The Rise of Capitalism in China* (2017).

23. See Ronald H. Coase, "The Economics of Broadcasting and Advertising," 56 *American Economic Review* 440 (1966).

24. That even lawyers and economists working within the mainstream of legal and economic thought could recognize and embrace some part of this conception of legal analysis as institutional imagination is shown by many in-

fluential writings of the twentieth century. See, for example, Adolf A. Berle and Gardner Means, *The Modern Corporation and Private Property* (1968), at 119–252, 293–313.

25. See Rudolf Hilferding, *Finance Capital: A Study of the Latest Phase of Capitalist Development* (Morris Watnick and Sam Girdon trans., 1981), originally published in 1923.

APPENDIX

1. See Richard Koo, *The Holy Grail of Macroeconomics: Lessons from Japan's Great Recession* (2009), at 39–84.

Index

academic culture, 328–30
Ackerman, Bruce, 191
active globalization, 214, 242, 278
advanced practices of production:
conditions for, 284; confinement
of to vanguard, 78, 80, 117, 122,
136, 230, 234, 290, 293, 296, 324,
330, 386; and economic growth,
294–301; in economic history,
123–24, 230, 283, 285; economy-wide
dissemination of, 17, 80, 97–98,
115–16, 122, 125, 136, 230, 243, 275,
283, 286, 291, 308, 310, 314, 323;
and efficiency, 122, 285; financing of,
285–86; government role in, 278,
287, 300; Marx and Adam Smith on,
284–85; and technology, 27, 278–79,
283, 294–96; in world of today,
385–86. *See also* knowledge economy
and production
agency, 117, 134–35; collective, 214,
246; and democracy, 121, 335;
enhancement of, 122–23; and labor
relations, 121–22
aggregate demand, 25, 80, 271;
Keynesianism on, 278, 377, 380
agrarian reform, 156, 399n8
agriculture, 6, 107–8, 223–24, 248,
252, 282

alternative-law movement, 189, 190–91
American exceptionalism, 33, 36
anarchy, international, 355–56
Argentina, 146, 149, 175, 177, 401n25
asset-backed commercial securities, 43,
87, 90
associational contracts, 164
autonomous finance. *See* external
finance

balance-of-payments crises, 145
Banco Nacional de Desenvolvimento
Econômico e Social (Brazil), 181
Bank for Infrastructure, 395n59
Bank of International Settlements, 53,
93, 311, 350
banks and banking: alleged efficiency
of large-scale, 57, 395n54; in Brazil,
300, 314–16; and capital markets,
46–47; in China, 318–20; and crisis
of 2007–2009, 55, 89; Dodd-Frank
Act on, 96–97; as financial
component, 203; financial
concentration by, 59, 249, 251; and
financing of production, 319, 372;
Glass-Steagall Act on, 89, 258;
government/central bank
relationship, 147, 182; history of,
179–80; local banks, 49, 52, 57, 58,